CONTINENT IN CRISIS

RECONSTRUCTING AMERICA
Andrew L. Slap, series editor

Continent in Crisis

The U.S. Civil War in North America

Brian Schoen,
Jewel L. Spangler, and
Frank Towers, Editors

FORDHAM UNIVERSITY PRESS
NEW YORK   2023

Copyright © 2023 Fordham University Press

All rights reserved. No part of this publication may be reproduced, stored in a retrieval system, or transmitted in any form or by any means—electronic, mechanical, photocopy, recording, or any other—except for brief quotations in printed reviews, without the prior permission of the publisher.

Fordham University Press has no responsibility for the persistence or accuracy of URLs for external or third-party Internet websites referred to in this publication and does not guarantee that any content on such websites is, or will remain, accurate or appropriate.

Fordham University Press also publishes its books in a variety of electronic formats. Some content that appears in print may not be available in electronic books.

Visit us online at www.fordhampress.com.

Library of Congress Cataloging-in-Publication Data available online at https://catalog.loc.gov.

Printed in the United States of America

25 24 23   5 4 3 2 1

First edition

Contents

Introduction: The United States Civil War Era and Sovereignty on the North American Continent
Brian Schoen and Frank Towers | 1

1 Fugitive Slaves, Free Soil, and the Contest over Sovereignty in the U.S.–Mexico Borderlands, 1821–1867
Alice L. Baumgartner | 19

2 Inveterate Imperialists: Contested Imperialisms, North American History, and the Coming of the U.S. Civil War
John Craig Hammond | 36

3 Walker to Riel: State Consolidation on the Margins of Empire
Amy S. Greenberg | 65

4 Reform Wars, Royal Visits, and U.S. Views of Popular Sovereignty in 1860
Brian Schoen | 85

5 "The Pirates and Their Abettors in This Province": Sovereignty, Violence, and Confederate Operations in Britain's Atlantic Colonies, 1863–1865
Beau Cleland | 119

6 "A Long-Cherished Plan": Detroit and the U.S. Annexation of Canada during the Nineteenth Century
John W. Quist | 152

| | 7 | From Memphis to Mexico: The U.S. Army's Assertion of Sovereignty during Reconstruction
Andrew L. Slap | 174 |
| | 8 | "Hold the Fort": Securing the Soldiers' State in Nineteenth-Century America
Susan-Mary Grant | 189 |
| | | Conclusion: Law and Order in Nineteenth-Century North America
Brian Schoen and Frank Towers | 221 |

Acknowledgments 229
List of Contributors 231
Index 233

CONTINENT IN CRISIS

Introduction

The United States Civil War Era and Sovereignty on the North American Continent

Brian Schoen and Frank Towers

Civil wars are, by definition, domestic affairs, but they are seldom only domestic affairs. International events can generate internal political strife or disintegration. Groups within a nation can see different, even contradictory, visions for what their relationship with the world might look like. Yet even if a civil war is mostly domestic in origin, it inevitably becomes an international event. Once a nation goes to war with itself, its sovereign power in the international state system falls into doubt, causing other powers to readjust their relationship with the divided state. Opposing sides in civil wars each claim sovereignty for themselves and make international recognition one test of their own claims to legitimacy in demanding the right to rule. Although protagonists in civil wars usually frame their cause in nationalist terms, their ideas, constituents, and resources for carrying on their struggle usually go beyond national boundaries. Furthermore, civil wars have the habit of being contagious within a given region of the globe. Disruptions in one state impinge on brewing conflicts in neighboring states, causing waves of change that have unpredictable outcomes, as evidenced by recent regional multistate conflicts in Eastern Europe, Central Africa, and the Middle East.[1]

In light of these observations, this volume explores the era of the Civil War in the United States through the interrelated geographic and political frameworks of the North American continent, the region most immediately affected by and connected to the upheaval in the United States, and through the concept of sovereignty, or the right to rule, a concept at the heart of the competing claims to power that ran through the Civil War and related conflicts. The essays in this volume began as conference papers for a meeting in Banff, Alberta, Canada, in 2015 focused on the theme "Remaking North American Sovereignty." Unlike other published scholarship from that conference that has looked at the impact of the crisis of the 1860s on politics beyond U.S. borders, this volume focuses squarely on the United States and its place in transnational histories.[2]

Rather than assuming that the borders of North America were set, our authors appreciate the fluidity and uncertainty that contemporaries themselves felt. This contingency was evident in the connections among the United States, Mexico, and British America in the Civil War era and extended from these continental groundings across the Atlantic and Caribbean. For North America the trajectories of Mexico, the United States, and Canada cannot be fully understood without an appreciation for the ways these polities reacted to, aggressed on, and collaborated with each other. The U.S.-Mexico War of 1846–1848 is the most obvious example. Treaties negotiated between Britain and the United States in the 1840s that set lasting boundaries are another, as are the numerous wars and treaty regimes that defined relations between these settler-colonial states and Indigenous nations in the interior West. In the 1850s Mexico experienced a civil war and then, in 1861, an invasion by France, which subsequently installed their client Emperor Maximilian as the head of state. Meanwhile, by the late 1860s, British North America had transformed itself into the self-governing Dominion of Canada. On the Great Plains the Comanche, Blackfoot, Sioux, and Apache vied against the encroachments of these settler-descended states, holding their own well into the next decade and beyond. The history of the U.S. Civil War was interrelated, or "entangled," with the histories of neighbors to the north, south, and west.[3] This volume shows some of the ways that those entanglements tangibly shaped the political processes and structures of power within the United States and North America more broadly.

As a wave of scholarship in the past decade or more has shown, the U.S. Civil War was not confined to the borders of the prewar republic. It spilled out into the world in unpredictable ways. This volume's focus is on the North American landmass. This focus is not intended to diminish other geographies of the international Civil War, and several chapters recognize the vast scholarship that has demonstrated how the conflict stretches across the Atlantic and Caribbean and into South America.[4] Yet this volume's focus is squarely on the continent.

In using the label "North America" for the territory that came under the rule of Canada, Mexico, and the United States after 1865, we do not pretend that North America was universally understood to designate those three countries in the mid-nineteenth century. It is true that some nineteenth-century geographers described North America as Mexico, the United States, and Britain's northern colonies,[5] but it is also the case that "North America" was a term used by others to designate the United States and the British colonies to their north, excluding

Mexico. Not to mention that the word "continent" as a designation for various land formations is itself problematic.[6] Thus, we use "North America" to indicate the states and people that existed within the present-day boundaries of Canada, Mexico, and the United States. In this respect we follow the work of Alan Taylor and others who have studied the continental history of the Early Republic in similar ways.[7]

Intrinsic to the effort to see how the U.S. Civil War reverberated worldwide is the question of sovereignty, a term that should be understood as a claim to the right to rule as well as the practical exercise of that power. Rebels, revanchists, and republicans all shared the aim of asserting sovereignty over a given territory and people, and they shed blood in the name of that abstract goal. As recent scholarship has shown, the actual exercise of the power to rule was never unitary and always contested. Would-be nation makers claimed the goal of sovereignty not only as a practical aim of interstate relations, but also as a rallying cry for their own version of nationalism, another ideological tremor shaking the foundations of the nineteenth-century interstate system.[8]

In the wake of eighteenth-century revolutions against imperial monarchies, the right to self-rule grew as an objective for a myriad of struggles between peoples. By the mid-nineteenth century, the exigencies of a growing interconnected world placed heightened demands on European states and their western derivatives to control their territory, police their borders and inhabitants—especially nonwhites—and to consider how best to regulate trade. The American Civil War took place at the pivot toward what Charles Maier has called Leviathan 2.0.[9] As the essays in this volume demonstrate, seeking sovereignty inevitably brought the question of using other sovereigns and interstate relations as means to fulfilling that ambition. At multiple levels of the conflict, protagonists in the Civil War advanced competing sovereign claims. Those claims went beyond whether or not the United States would prevail over the Confederacy to encompass questions such as federalism's divided powers, citizenship and its rights, Indigenous-settler relations in the West, and international diplomacy. In each case, an outcome in one arena—for example, successes or failures in conquering Native peoples—said something about the extent of the nation-state's sovereign claims overall. Battles in one of these areas could reframe developments elsewhere. When viewed in its North American context, the Civil War's many battles over sovereignty can be understood not as intrinsically American issues but rather as part of regional and global negotiation of the right to rule.[10]

The foregoing claims about the transnational dimensions of the U.S. Civil War may seem odd to Americans used to thinking about that conflict as a fundamentally national story focused on the internal character of the United States. Within that framework, the Civil War is a key plot point in America's national development. In that narrative, an imperfect founding left the nation half slave and half free, a contradiction in the national character that had to be resolved one way or another. Its resolution in a bloody war that purged the nation of the sin of slavery fits into a redemptive story of sacrifice in the name of progress. That view shaped public memory and found more muted expression in professional scholarship for much of the twentieth century. In the tumult of the twenty-first century, the "war for freedom" narrative continues to capture public memory in the push to overthrow the legacy of the enslavers and their Confederate project even as the Lost Cause defense of the Confederacy finds expression in white supremacist claims for the Confederacy as part of an appeal to an ethnonationalist version of the American story.

Without necessarily endorsing these perspectives in full, generations of historians have delved deeply into the national, regional, and local dimensions of mid-nineteenth-century American life to pull out the many ways that the war emanated from and reflected back on the question of national identity. That inward focus on the U.S. Civil War as a distinctly American story—an American tragedy, patriotic gore, a second founding, an unfinished revolution—remains a powerful touchstone for historians, but in recent years it has been supplemented by scholars' curiosity about the international dimensions of the conflict. That interest has been sparked by changes inside and outside the academy, including everything from the end of the Cold War and the latest round of globalization to academic departments' recognition that even the standard courses on U.S. history would benefit from an appreciation for connection beyond national borders.[11]

As with everything in the history of ideas, there is no beginning point for an international history of national history. In the nineteenth century, Francis Parkman framed the development of the Thirteen Colonies as a continental story, and much of that era's emphasis on the internal dynamics of U.S. history was itself a reaction against the so-called "germ theory" of a European-inflected development in the offshoot colonies and postrevolutionary republic.[12] In the early twentieth century when the call to write national history drove the development of the discipline as an academic enterprise, diplomatic and immigration historians nonetheless looked at the United States as part of a global history. The historiography of the Civil War, has, therefore, always drawn to it scholars interested in its place in world history.[13]

In the Cold War era, Civil War historians often framed the conflict as part of a broader process of world-historical development commonly known as modernization. In that scheme the United States, western Europe and a few other settler-colonial offshoots of the British Empire had set off on a path to a more common global future of industrial economics, political democracies, and cosmopolitan cultures. In this version of the Civil War, the North, the site of free labor and industry, stood for the future, and the South, defending the institution of slavery, fought to hold onto the past. That international perspective on the conflict meshed with a widespread explanation, or master narrative, of global historical change that accompanied the rise of the West in the nineteenth century. By the 1960s the concept of Western modernity had become a debating point that rallied supporters who glorified the West's achievements and critics who called out the West's hypocrisy. Despite their differences, historians agreed that whether virtuous or vicious, the leading edge of change in the nineteenth century could be found in western Europe and the northeastern United States.[14]

For Civil War era historians working in the decades between 1960 and 1990, this larger perspective on the nineteenth century served as the background for more pressing research questions arising from the civil rights revolution and its implications for the 1860s. Innovative studies rescued the abolitionists from their consignment to the asylum, recognized the achievements of enslaved Americans in the fight for freedom, reassessed white Southerners' commitment to secession, and introduced gender as a category for studying the sectional conflict. Yet even as it innovated methodologically and expanded the range of historical subjects, this scholarship propelled onward the story of a clash of a modern North and a tradition-bound South, keeping the focus within the national borders.[15]

Since the 1990s the master narrative of modernity as an explanation for the Civil War has collapsed. Its demise was overdetermined. Certitude about the West's place at the forefront of history has always been challenged by historians concerned with and born into the communities on the losing end of Western imperialism. After the horrors of the Second World War, scholars in the West began questioning the progressive promise of technology, capitalism, and the nation-state. French poststructuralists, American anthropologists, and British neo-Marxists all contributed to a growing dissatisfaction with treating the West as the standard against which the past should be judged.[16]

In Civil War studies, this broad current of intellectual change manifested as doubt. Historians lost certainty about the differences between the sections, the inevitability of war, and the incompatibility of slavery with industrial capitalism.

In the next decades, breakthrough studies of slavery's centrality to antebellum capitalism, the contingency of the Civil War's outbreak, and cultural similarities between the sections undermined scholars' confidence in the clash of civilizations narrative.[17] Skepticism about older frameworks has resulted in a welcome pluralism. In the past decade the field has been characterized by its diversity more than anything else. Memory, medicine, environment, death and dying, refugees, political friendships, and the weirdness of the war have flourished alongside continued interest in the enduring questions of what caused the war, how it was fought, and what the peace meant.[18] The growth of transnational approaches to the conflict has occurred amid this greater scholarly pluralism.[19]

The new international history of the Civil War differs from what came before in several ways. In the last twenty years historians have adopted insights from the burgeoning field of transnational studies to look at the international dimensions of the Civil War as part of large-scale changes happening above and beyond the borders of any particular government. Rather than look at the larger world for what it can say about an intrinsically national history, the more recent works on the Civil War and the world look for the ways that histories crossed borders and in that way trace the elusive transnational connections of a period best known for the surge of nationalism and the push to establish nation-states.[20] Put differently, new scholarship presses against domestically bounded narratives—whether triumphalist or defeatist—by reminding us that secession and civil war were emerging features of modern political life, and hence the dynamics illustrated by the U.S. Civil War were not as unique as Americans have typically assumed.

This volume departs somewhat from other trends in international histories of the American Civil War. Some of the best work on the transnational history of the Civil War has looked at its politics through the lens of ideas. Historians have shown that Civil War debates over nationalism and slavery looked abroad and drew in foreign actors. They have also compared state building, war-making, and postwar reconstruction. This volume and its earlier companion (*Remaking North American Sovereignty: State Transformation in the 1860s*) zero in on the problem of sovereignty as a public conflict over who should rule and how. That focus directs transnational history to the connections between ordinary North Americans and their relationship to state power.

Geographically, this volume's emphasis on the continent of North America seeks to bring together what are often competing eastern and western fields of vision in the Civil War's international dimensions. Its spatial orientation is north, south, and west, but only glancingly east. The Atlantic and the Great Powers of Europe have been the main subject of interest in the recent drive to internationalize the history of the Civil War, and for good reason. Great Britain was the world's superpower of the mid-1800s, its colonies bordered the United States, it was America's dominant trading partner, and the countries shared culture and language. All of this makes Anglo-American aspects of the conflict leap out. Next to Britain stood France, an imperial state with ambitions to reestablish their empire in the Americas, and Spain, which used the disruption in the United States to firm up control over its colony in Cuba and reassert its sovereignty over the eastern half of Hispaniola. Beyond these powerful states, the close ties between immigrants from Ireland and Germany and their home countries have made the connections between Civil War America and western Europe a starting point for exploring the international aspects of the era.[21]

Simultaneous with the growth of transatlantic histories of the Civil War, scholars researching Indigenous Americans and the U.S. West have upended long-held narratives about the inevitability of U.S. conquest. Indigenous states dominated the political economy of the West well into the 1870s, and disrupted the sovereign ambitions of settler-colonial projects in Mexico, the United States, and British North America. Taking note of these insights, historians of the Civil War era are paying more attention to the role of the West in the conflict.[22]

Broadening the chronological and geographic lens for thinking about the Civil War and shifting the center of the story to the continent provide insights into what Elliot West once referred to as the United States' "Greater Reconstruction," which took place from the 1840s to the 1870s.[23] The empire-building project often called "westward expansion" forced a racial crisis that not only helps explain why there was a Civil War but also what one of its longer effects would be: the consolidation of a continental nation through the postwar effort to monopolize violence in the west. A detailed map from 1830 would provide little assurance that the United States would dominate western North America. In the 1830s and early 1840s, political parties in the United States fought over questions of law and sovereignty and especially over how to remove Indians and to subject slaves in the east. Texas Annexation and the U.S.-Mexico War not only pushed those tendencies farther west, they also transformed them entirely by making them thoroughly transnational in nature.[24]

Resolving the United States' problems from the 1840s onward required war and treaty-making with Mexican and Indian rivals as well as attention to British North America. Those dynamics deepened partisan and sectional rifts within the Union, but they also placed new demands on the tools of sovereignty that Americans had become accustomed to wielding. De facto controlling a vast continent, especially one inhabited by diverse peoples intent on rejecting the state, proved much harder than negotiating the de jure borders meant to define the state. Yet white Americans, like British Canadians and especially like Mexican political elites, proved determined to exert control even though, and perhaps even because, they were not a homogenous group. Indeed, Americans' imperial ambitions and the federal apparatus that had facilitated them had proven powerful enough to fight over. And so in 1861 many soldiers and officers who had cut their military teeth in western territories fighting Indians and patrolling a tenuous border with Mexico or a more secure one with Canada, headed east, literally bringing war home. The violent Civil War created one of the larger war zones in modern history fought by some of the largest armies of the nineteenth century.

Even as the critical mass of war-making moved east, armed conflict in the West continued. Simultaneous with the war to end slavery Lincoln and his Republican successors fought to extinguish Indigenous sovereignty west of the Mississippi. Those projects came together under the name of the sovereign nation-state that exerted equal powers over its territory and brooked no rivals to its powers within its borders. In the West the drive for national sovereignty led to ethnic cleansing, massacres, and the subjugation of peoples who wanted no part of American nationality. In the East the same armies, led by the same commanders, delivered millions of African Americans from bondage and put down a rebellion by a cadre of white supremacists who wanted to extend the system of racial slavery to the Pacific and beyond. As Steven Hahn has argued, looking across these geographies for common threads opens up new perspectives on every side of the Civil War Era.[25]

The essays that follow explore the themes of sovereignty and transnationalism in Civil War history from the prewar eras to the postwar reconstruction. Alice Baumgartner starts us on what was a fast-evolving situation on the Mexican-American border, showing us the transnational awareness of the most pragmatic of abolitionists. Black fugitive slaves along the Southern border challenged sovereign claims, which in turn generated major problems at the centers of U.S. and Mexican power. Like other chapters in this volume, hers reveals that dynamics on the often-overlooked periphery both illuminate the nature of nineteenth-century sovereignty and sometimes determined its course. She shows that Mexican and U.S. populations and officials reacted "in distinct ways to common stimulus" concerning fugitive slaves and territorial sovereignty. As Anglos entered their northern provinces, Mexicans welcomed them as part of a social contract and flexibly applied federalist principles and comity to accept Texas slaveholding into a polity that had otherwise prohibited it. Yet talk of U.S. annexation soon followed Texas Independence. That prospect led Mexican officials to reverse course and constitutionally outlaw domestic slavery "without exception" in 1837, even as fugitive slaves were provided limited legal haven. The contested loss of Texas led Mexican officials away from a definition of sovereignty based on volitional agreement to a social contract and toward one of firmer territorial control of sovereign claims. In 1849, this new emphasis and fears of further American imperialism led the Mexican Congress to declare any slave free simply by setting foot on Mexican soil. Reformers in Mexico subsequently translated this into a claim that the state had a natural right to not only declare personal freedom and territorial sovereignty but to expropriate church lands and Indigenous *ejidos*, or communal land.

In the United States, the fallout from the U.S.-Mexico War increased slaveholders' support for the radical view that the "Constitution protected enslaved property everywhere in the United States, even in states and territories where slavery was abolished." This theory shifted the legal terrain over the return of fugitive slaves, which politicians and courts had often struggled to define. Baumgartner demonstrates that slaveholders pushed past comity or national federal sovereignty to instead apply the principle of "legal portability," whereby slaves carried the status of their resident locale with them anywhere they went. The notorious *Dred Scott* decision elevated that doctrine as supreme even over comity or federal sovereignty. As Mexicans were moving toward a stronger central standard for determining the intersection between freedom and territory, the United States Supreme Court was creating a variegated legal structure that blurred those lines. Texans were quick to seek to apply this idea of legal portability in their demands on Mexican neighbors.

John Craig Hammond's chapter argues that these arguments took place amid a "third great imperial struggle in the Americas." Hammond joins other scholars who argue that the United States might best be seen not as a nation-state or an unfinished nation, but as an empire.[26] Antebellum citizens of the United States and their representatives assumed the nation should and would expand its borders. Yet unlike seventeenth- and eighteenth-century precursors, this struggle for continental supremacy unfolded as part of a battle over the future of slavery. The nearby presence of British and Mexican free-soil empires appeared as threats to Southern slaveholders, and hence became motivating factors within American domestic politics. Yet not just Southerners and Douglas Democrats but also "Republicans increasingly understood sectional conflicts over Kansas, California, and the trans-Mississippi West as inseparable from impending conflicts over Mexico, Cuba, the Caribbean, and Central America." Like

Baumgartner, Hammond's imperial lens draws our attention toward the West and reminds us that the dynamics that led to civil war cannot be stripped from a world of Spanish, French, and British empires which continued to vie for influence and territory.

Amy Greenberg's comparative study of William Walker and Louis Riel and their similar fates demonstrates "just how contingent the process of state consolidation actually was." The white supremacist Walker and the Métis leader Riel might seem an odd pairing, but Greenberg skillfully shows how both men repeatedly found themselves asserting sovereign claims that butted up against institutions and forces purporting to serve national and imperial authorities. Those could come in the form of official power and courts, and from private actors who could exert more power on-the-ground than distant governments. Of paramount importance in determining Walker's fate was shipping magnate Cornelius Vanderbilt's withdrawal of support, while Riel found his peoples' fate, and eventually his own, tied to the maneuverings of the Pacific Railroad Company.

Ironies abound, suggesting that nation-making was often an indirect process. Walker's failure in Nicaragua generated a backlash at home that likely thwarted, or at least postponed, American imperialism while accelerating the nation-making of the Latin American countries he threatened. Riel, who after a long exile in the United States, was shot for treason in 1885 after launching another separatist rebellion, nonetheless helped to bring Manitoba into the Canadian Confederation, thus furthering ambitions to convert Britain's North American possessions into a single, self-governing dominion.

Greenberg's engaging retelling implicitly reminds us that national consolidation, be it in the United States, Canada, or Costa Rica, did not happen as part of some natural or inevitable process but as the result of conscious actions taken by political actors with access to the modern technologies of control—capital, transportation, legal processes, and most especially military power. Thus, the case of Riel and Walker presents modern American readers with a quandary. Knowing Walker's purpose was taken on behalf of a slave empire, it is easy to cheer on the combination of international and national forces that brought his filibustering and attempted nation-building to an end. Yet one has to also grapple with the reality that those same apparatuses targeted and ultimately destroyed Riel, a far more sympathetic individual. In both cases, Greenberg notes, "Few acts serve to highlight the power of the state more than putting a man to death."

Brian Schoen's chapter examining the continental context for the election of 1860 and secession suggests some of the ways that events typically seen only domestically were filtered through the types of imperial contests and comparisons that Hammond discusses. Mexico's Reform War between Liberals and Conservatives highlighted the long shadow cast by Mexican defeat in 1848. Continued instability not only forecasted elements of the United States' own civil war, it encouraged opportunistic Democrats within and outside the Buchanan administration to hungrily eye additional land cessions and access to extraterritorial transit and mining rights. Heightening border violence provided further incentive for establishing a military protectorate, even as the Buchanan administration hoped to extract favorable terms from Juárez's Liberal government based in Veracruz. Yet even when the McLane-Ocampo Treaty offered several of those, united opposition from northern Republicans and a dividing Democratic party thwarted passage, leaving attentive viewers to wonder if sectional and partisan extremism was sapping the nation's ability to protect its interests abroad, thus opening up the prospect of European meddling.

The situation on and over the northern border with the provinces of British North America contrasted sharply with that of Mexico but would, as Schoen and pieces by John Quist and Beau Cleland demonstrate, continue to weigh heavily on American minds. For Schoen the young Prince of Wales's much-covered visit to British Canada and then to the United States provided Americans a mirror that allowed them to see themselves in a new way. American, and some foreign, newspapers fixated on the raucous nature of American crowds and fretted that the sharp electioneering and hotly contested election reflected poorly on the nation. The burst of Anglophilia established some goodwill, but it was isolated and short-lived.

International aspects of Civil War hostilities rather quickly drove a wedge into the prewar détente between the United States and Great Britain. As Mexicans had previously learned, keeping friendly neighbors during a time of civil war was difficult business. Now it was the Union's turn to watch in horror as their northern neighbors defined a type of neutrality that looked rather unequal. Those challenges take center stage in Beau Cleland's examination of how Confederate operatives and their British sympathizers in the Maritime colonies took advantage of British neutrality, relative provincial autonomy, and divided sovereignty to support the Confederate war effort. Studies of European neutrality typically focus on the centers of empire—Paris, London, Madrid, Vienna. Cleland, however, shows that much of the important action took place in locales far removed.

Halifax merchants seized on the American Civil War to lift their flagging economic fortunes. Informal, which is to say uncommissioned, Confederate diplomats found them and the largely Roman Catholic population of the region fertile ground for both moral and material support. In late 1863, a group of British subjects led by a Nova Scotian went well beyond the typical blockade running and conspired to capture a Union vessel, the *Chesapeake*, "in the name of the Southern Confederacy." The attempt failed but only after a Union ship violated British "neutral" waters to retake the vessel. The largely forgotten incident sparked a complex sequence of legal problems for British and American officials, which tested the meaning and parameters of neutrality. Cleland's fascinating account reveals that official British neutrality could echo faintly in colonial courts, even those in close proximity to the North Atlantic base for the Royal Navy. It also reminds us, as other chapters in this volume do, that non-state actors or individuals acting on behalf of other states could meaningfully shape the course of events and shows how government claims to wield unquestioned sovereign power clashed with the messy reality of power's exercise at the edges of empire. Indeed, Davis's government in Richmond increasingly saw such unconventional naval warfare and unofficial raids from Canada, despite their illegality under international law, as a necessary means to securing Confederate national independence. Not completely unlike the cross-border activity that haunted whites' understanding of the porous southern border discussed by Baumgartner, Hammond, and Schoen, naval privateering threatened to destabilize the previously pacified maritime borderland between the United States and Canada.

Detroit, the location on that border where the prince had crossed into the United States, offers John Quist an ideal backdrop from which to assess Americans' continued fascination with the prospect of Canadian Annexation. Not to be outdone by their Southern Democratic adversaries in their territorial ambition, northern Whigs and Republicans saw the British provinces as a ripening fruit that the United States could soon pluck. Traditionally, however, scholarship has tended to see the Civil War as a breaking point, a moment when fears of American-style dysfunction paved the way for Canadian Confederation and an end to American annexationist dreams. Looking closely at Detroit's partisan newspapers and Michigan's powerful U.S. senator, Zachariah Chandler, Quist uncovers quite a different story, one whereby Republicans and Democrats continued to see Canada first as compensation for the *Alabama* claims and sometimes simply as part of America's manifest destiny. Indeed, into the 1870s Michigan Republican leaders, freed from concerns of slavery's expansion, offered full-throated arguments for American expansion throughout North America. The Grant administration and his more cautious Secretary of State Hamilton Fish, however, saw things differently. They focused instead on national consolidation rather than expansion.

Official fighting between organized Confederate and Union armies might have ended in 1865, but disputes over who exerted sovereign control remained.

INTRODUCTION: THE UNITED STATES CIVIL WAR ERA AND SOVEREIGNTY   13

As Andrew Slap demonstrates, war mobilization led the U.S. Army to exert unprecedented power and greater independence from civilian control. That power continued well after the war, in both domestic contexts like Reconstruction-era Memphis and across the Mexican border. While Congress and the Johnson administration became famously bitter rivals over who controlled Reconstruction, U.S. Army officials on the ground took matters into their own hands. Confronting the Memphis Riots in May 1866, General George Stoneman, albeit belatedly, insisted that the army take control in defiance of Johnson's order to return such matters to civilian authority. While generals stationed in the former Confederacy fought to maintain a precarious peace, others, including Generals Ulysses Grant and Philip Sheridan, flirted with foreign war. Against the backdrop of Archduke Ferdinand Maximilian's French puppet regime in Mexico, both men undermined Secretary of State William Seward's official policy of neutrality by patrolling and occasionally crossing the border and by funneling weapons to Mexican Liberals. Sheridan's wartime experience led him, Slap implies, to lose patience with civilian efforts at diplomacy in Mexico, in keeping order during a Chicago fire, and ultimately and perhaps most devastatingly in the Far West, where the presence of Native peoples continued to challenge the reality of American sovereignty. Slap's chapter reminds us that the U.S. Army acted not only as an instrument for civilian American policy, but also that it appropriated, for good and ill, its own claims for sovereign control.

Closing out the volume, Susan-Mary Grant takes a long view of Northerners' conceptions of nationalism, manhood, and sovereignty from the Civil War to the end of the nineteenth century. In an exploration of the military's many engagements between 1861 and 1900, Grant identifies the cultural ideal of martial manhood "as the link between the spatial and the spiritual dimensions of state sovereignty." Looking beyond the legal structure of sovereignty, Grant argues for nationalism as the binding force that defined the legitimacy of the right to rule in the U.S. imperial project. As she points out, supporters of the Union often expressed contradictory ideas about the relationship of Americans to the federal government. What they agreed on was the centrality of American men carrying arms to fulfill national destiny. The flurry of change wrought by the Civil War and its aftermath overwhelmed bureaucratic attempts to define and exert sovereignty. In their place, Grant argues, America's postwar leaders "located the heart of the body politic and the spark that animated its existence as a state, in the soldier."

By starting with the problem of slavery and ending with the status of veterans, this volume follows a familiar trajectory of the Civil War era, but at every step its authors push at unknown and under-appreciated aspects of the period by paying attention to claims about sovereignty that entangled the U.S. Civil War in the affairs of North America and the world. Collectively, these chapters illustrate some of the rich scholarship that is situating the causes, course, and consequences of the Civil War within a broader continental context. They suggest that there is much to be learned about the nature of America's sovereignty crisis by appreciating the international dynamics surrounding it. In no way do these chapters attempt a comprehensive history of sovereignty in mid-nineteenth-century America. Instead, gathered in one place they aim to spark readers' curiosity, reframe older debates, and invite new questions and new paths for studying the transnational history of the Civil War Era.

Notes

1. Gregory P. Downs, *The Second American Revolution: The Civil-War Era Struggle over Cuba and the Rebirth of the American Republic* (Chapel Hill: University of North Carolina Press, 2019), 6–8. Aaron Sheehan-Dean, *Reckoning with Rebellion: War and Sovereignty in the Nineteenth Century* (Gainesville: University Press of Florida, 2020), chap. 2; David Armitage, *Civil Wars: A History in Ideas* (New York: Alfred A. Knopf, 2017); Jay Benson, Joshua Lambert, and Erik Keels, *Reassessing Rebellion: Exploring Recent Trends in Civil War Dynamics*, One Earth Future, March 2019, http://dx.doi.org/10.18289/OEF.2019.035; James D. Fearon, "Civil War and the Current International System," *Dædalus: The Journal of the American Academy of Arts & Sciences* 146 (Fall 2017): 18–32; Jeffrey T. Checkel, ed., *Transnational Dynamics of Civil War* (Cambridge, UK: Cambridge University Press, 2013); Don H. Doyle, ed., *Secession as an International Phenomenon: From America's Civil War to Contemporary Separatist Movements* (Athens: University of Georgia Press, 2010).

2. In addition to this volume, essays from the Banff conference appear in revised form in William A. Blair, ed., "Crises of Sovereignty in the 1860s: A Special Issue," *Journal of the Civil War Era* 7, no. 4 (2017), and Jewel L. Spangler and Frank Towers, eds., *Remaking North American Sovereignty: State Transformation in the 1860s* (New York: Fordham University Press, 2020).

3. For entangled history see Michael Werner and Benedicte Zimmermann, "Beyond Comparison: *Histoire croisée* and the Challenge of Reflexivity," *History and Theory* 45, no. 1 (2006): 30–50; Eliga H. Gould, "Entangled Histories, Entangled Worlds: The English-Speaking Atlantic as a Spanish Periphery," *American Historical Review* 112, no. 3 (2007): 764–786; Melissa Macauley, "Entangled States: The Translocal Repercussions of Rural Pacification in China, 1869–1873," *American Historical Review* 121, no. 3 (2016): 775–779.

4. For the Caribbean see Downs, *The Second American Revolution*; Thomas Schoonover, "Napoleon Is Coming! Maximilian Is Coming? The International History of the Civil War in the Caribbean Basin," in *The Union, the Confederacy, and the Atlantic Rim*, ed. Robert E. May (Gainesville: University Press of Florida, 2013), 115–144; Wayne H.

Bowen, *Spain and the American Civil War* (Columbia: University of Missouri Press, 2011); Edward B. Rugemer, *The Problem of Emancipation: The Caribbean Roots of the American Civil War* (Baton Rouge: Louisiana State University Press, 2009); Matthew Pratt Guterl, *American Mediterranean: Southern Slaveholders in the Age of Emancipation* (Cambridge, MA: Harvard University Press, 2008).

For examples of the Civil War's transatlantic and South American connections see Neils Eichorn, *Liberty and Slavery: European Separatists, Southern Secession, and the American Civil War* (Baton Rouge: Louisiana State University Press, 2019); Don H. Doyle, ed., *American Civil Wars: The United States, Latin America, Europe and the Crisis of the 1860s* (Chapel Hill: University of North Carolina Press, 2017); Don H. Doyle, *The Cause of All Nations: An International History of the American Civil War* (New York: Basic Books, 2015); Vitor Izecksohn, *Slavery and War in the Americas: Race, Citizenship, and State Building in the United States and Brazil, 1861–1870* (Charlottesville: University of Virginia Press, 2014); Andre M. Fleche, *The Revolution of 1861: The American Civil War in the Age of Nationalist Conflict* (Chapel Hill: University of North Carolina Press, 2012); Howard Jones, *Blue and Gray Diplomacy: A History of Union and Confederate Foreign Relations* (Chapel Hill: University of North Carolina Press, 2010).

5. For examples see Henry Tudor, *Narrative of a Tour in North America: Comprising Mexico, the Mines of Real del Norte, the United States, and the British Colonies* (London: J. Duncan, 1834); James Bentley Gordon, *An Historical and Geographical Memoir of the North-American Continent; Its Nations and Tribes* (Dublin: J. Jones, 1820).

6. Martin W. Lewis and Karen E. Wigen, *The Myth of Continents: A Critique of Metageography* (Berkeley: University of California Press, 1997).

7. Alan Taylor, *American Revolutions: A Continental History, 1750–1804* (New York: W. W. Norton, 2016) and *American Republics: A Continental History of the United States, 1783–1850* (New York: W. W. Norton, 2021). Also see Paul Mapp, *The Elusive West and the Contest for Empire, 1713–1763* (Chapel Hill: University of North Carolina Press, 2011); Caitlin Fitz, *Our Sister Republics: The United States in an Age of American Revolutions* (New York: W. W. Norton, 2016); Thomas Richards Jr., *Breakaway Americas: The Unmanifest Future of the Jacksonian United States* (Baltimore: Johns Hopkins University Press, 2020).

8. James Pickett, "Written into Submission: Reassessing Sovereignty through a Forgotten Eurasian Dynasty," *American Historical Review* 123, no. 3 (2018): 817–845; Zvi Ben-Dor Benite, Stefanos Geroulanos, and Nicole Jerr, eds., *The Scaffolding of Sovereignty: Global and Aesthetic Perspectives on the History of a Concept* (New York: Columbia University Press, 2017); Terry Nardin, "The Diffusion of Sovereignty," *History of European Ideas* 41, no. 1 (2015): 89–102; Hent Kalmo and Quentin Skinner, eds., *Sovereignty in Fragments: The Past, Present and Future of a Contested Concept* (Cambridge, UK: Cambridge University Press, 2010); James J. Sheehan, "The Problem of Sovereignty in European History," *American Historical Review* 111, no. 1 (2006): 1–15.

9. Charles S. Maier, *Leviathan 2.0: Inventing Modern Statehood* (Cambridge, MA: Harvard University Press, 2012).

10. For a recent exploration of this pattern see Sheehan-Dean, *Reckoning with Rebellion*, chap. 3.

11. Informative accounts of this shift are Ian Tyrrell, "Reflections on the Transnational Turn in United States History: Theory and Practice," *Journal of Global History* 4, no. 3 (2009): 453–474, and Lynn Hunt, *Writing History in the Global Era* (New York: W. W. Norton, 2014).

12. Francis Parkman, *France and England in North America*, 7 vols. (1865–1896); Karen R. Jones and John Wills, *The American West: Competing Visions* (Edinburgh: Edinburgh University Press, 2009), 41.

13. Ella Lonn, *Foreigners in the Confederacy* (Chapel Hill: University of North Carolina Press, 1940); Milledge L. Bonham, *The British Consuls in the Confederacy* (New York: Columbia University, 1911); Ephraim D. Adams, *Great Britain and the American Civil War*, 2 vols. (New York: Longmans, Green, 1925); Frank Lawrence Owsley, *King Cotton Diplomacy* (Chicago: University of Chicago Press, 1931). There was another burst of scholarship in the 1960s and 1970s. See, for example, D. P. Crook, *The North, the South, and the Powers, 1861–1865* (New York: Wiley, 1974); Harold Melvin Hyman and H. C. Allen, *Heard Round the World: The Impact Abroad of the Civil War* (New York: Knopf, 1969). For a summary of the diplomatic literature see Jay Sexton, "Civil War Diplomacy," in *A Companion to the U.S. Civil War*, ed. Aaron Sheehan-Dean (Hoboken, NJ: John Wiley & Sons, 2014), 741–762.

14. Perhaps the most influential example of this approach to the Civil War is James M. McPherson, *Battle Cry of Freedom: The Civil War Era* (New York: Oxford University Press, 1988). Another influential example is Eugene D. Genovese, *The Political Economy of Slavery: Studies in the Economy and Society of the Slave South* (New York: Pantheon, 1965).

15. Frank Towers, "Partisans, New History, and Modernization: The Historiography of the Civil War's Causes, 1861–2011," *Journal of the Civil War Era* 1, no. 2 (2011): 237–264.

16. For a recent account of this era in historiography see Sara Maza, *Thinking about History* (Chicago: University of Chicago Press, 2017).

17. Walter Johnson, *Soul by Soul: Life Inside the Antebellum Slave Market* (Cambridge, MA: Harvard University Press, 1999); James L. Huston, *Calculating the Value of the Union: Slavery, Property Rights, and the Economic Origins of the Civil War* (Chapel Hill: University of North Carolina Press, 2003); Edward L. Ayers, *In the Presence of Mine Enemies: War in the Heart of America, 1859–1863* (New York: W. W. Norton, 2003); Jonathan D. Wells, *The Origins of the Southern Middle Class, 1800–1861* (Chapel Hill: University of North Carolina Press, 2004).

18. For a comprehensive survey of these developments see Aaron Sheehan-Dean, ed., *The Cambridge History of the American Civil War*, 3 vols. (New York: Cambridge University Press, 2019).

19. Georg G. Iggers, Q. Edward Wang, and Supriya Mukherjee, *A Global History of Modern Historiography*, 2nd ed. (London: Routledge, 2017), 310–340.

20. In addition to the sources cited in note 4, see David T. Gleeson and Simon Lewis, eds., *The Civil War as Global Conflict: Transnational Meanings of the American Civil War* (Columbia: University of South Carolina Press, 2014); Jörg Nagler, Don H. Doyle, and Marcus Gräser, eds., *The Transnational Significance of the American Civil War* (New York: Palgrave Macmillan, 2016); David Prior, ed., *Reconstruction in a Globalizing World*

(New York: Fordham University Press, 2018); David Prior, *Between Freedom and Progress: The Lost World of Reconstruction Politics* (Baton Rouge: Louisiana State University Press, 2019); Sheehan-Dean, *Reckoning with Rebellion*. For a recent review of this scholarship see Enrico Dal Lago, "Writing the U.S. Civil War into Nineteenth-Century World History," *Journal of the Civil War Era* 11, no. 2 (2021): 255–271.

21. Doyle, *The Cause of All Nations*. In the *Cambridge History of the American Civil War*, vol. 2, see Andre Fleche, "The Civil War in the Americas," 319–341, and Brian Schoen, "The Civil War in Europe," 342–365.

22. For an overview see Stacey L. Smith, "Beyond North and South: Putting the West in the Civil War and Reconstruction," *Journal of the Civil War Era* 6, no. 4 (2016): 566–591. Also see Adam Arenson and Andrew R. Graybill, eds., *Civil War Wests: Testing the Limits of the United States* (Oakland: University of California Press, 2015); Virginia Scharff, ed., *Empire and Liberty: The Civil War and the West* (Oakland: University of California Press, 2015); Steven Hahn, *A Nation without Borders: The United States and the World in an Age of Civil Wars, 1830–1910* (New York: Penguin Random House, 2016), 270–316; Jay Sexton, "Steam Transport, Sovereignty, and Empire in North America, 1850–1885," *Journal of the Civil War Era* 7, no. 4 (2017): 620–647; Alice Baumgartner, *South to Freedom: Runaway Slaves to Mexico and the Road to the Civil War* (New York: Basic Books, 2020); Megan Kate Nelson, *The Three-Cornered War: The Union, the Confederacy, and Native Peoples in the Fight for the West* (New York: Simon and Schuster, 2020); Kevin Waite, *West of Slavery: The Southern Dream of a Transcontinental Empire* (Chapel Hill: University of North Carolina Press, 2021).

23. Elliot West, "Reconstructing Race," *Western Historical Quarterly* 34, no. 1 (2003): 6–26.

24. Richards Jr., *Breakaway Americas*.

25. Steven Hahn, "Slave Emancipation, Indian Peoples, and the Projects of a New American Nation-State," *Journal of the Civil War Era* 3, no. 3 (2013): 307–330; Steven Hahn, "The United States from the Inside out and the Southside North," in *Remaking North American Sovereignty*, 36–60.

26. Paul A. Kramer, "Power and Connection: Imperial Histories of the United States in the World," *American Historical Review* 116, no. 5 (2011): 1348–1391; Eliga H. Gould, *Among the Powers of the Earth: The American Revolution and the Making of a New World Empire* (Cambridge, MA: Harvard University Press, 2012); Peter S. Onuf, *Jefferson's Empire: The Language of American Nationhood* (Charlottesville: University Press of Virginia, 2000).

1

Fugitive Slaves, Free Soil, and the Contest over Sovereignty in the U.S.-Mexico Borderlands, 1821–1867

Alice L. Baumgartner

The story of the Underground Railroad—the slave catchers and their hounds, the candle in the window of a safe house, the North Star rising at dusk—is a familiar one.[1] But not every track ran north. From the ranch lands and plantations of the South Central United States, enslaved people took a different route, escaping by the thousands to Mexico.[2]

These freedom seekers have been the occasional subjects of scholarly interest. Ethnohistorians have studied formerly enslaved people who joined the Seminole community in northern Mexico in order to understand the relationship between Blacks and Indians.[3] Political historians have asked why the Mexican government protected free Blacks, runaway slaves, and Black Seminoles from the United States, concluding that a liberal policy "discouraged further American incursion."[4] A more recent round of scholarship moved the focus from the center to the periphery, from state politics to local realities. Influenced by James C. Scott's theories of state formation and popular resistance, these studies examine how the policies of both nations came up short. To some historians, a combination of physical insecurity and bureaucratic intransigence prevented freedom seekers from joining Mexico's political community. Mexico's emancipatory rhetoric was just that—rhetoric.[5]

These historians have made important contributions to our understanding of freedom seekers in Mexico, but the study of fugitive slaves also reveals much about how political authority was conceived. Enslaved people who escaped to Mexico occupied an uncertain legal status—an uncertainty that imbued them with symbolic importance. Who could claim jurisdiction over these fugitives? Their enslavers (because the runaways owed them service)? The U.S. government (because they escaped *from* American soil)? The Mexican government (because they escaped *to* Mexican soil)? How these questions were answered is a little window into a big story about conceptions of political authority in nineteenth-century North America.

Placing the same communities that interested earlier historians under a new lens—sovereignty—raises two very different questions. First, what does this history tell us about changing notions of sovereignty in Mexico and the United States in the nineteenth century? And, second, why did these developments give rise to what Gregory Downs calls "a hemispheric age of republican crisis" in the 1850s and 1860s?[6] To answer these questions, we have to follow legal and political developments at various levels of government in both Mexico and the United States. This makes for a complicated story, so some signposting is in order.

After securing its independence from Spain in 1821, Mexico's leaders did not establish a clear policy with respect to fugitive slaves, forcing local officials to make their own calculations about whether to protect or return freedom seekers. During the Texas Revolution, Mexico's president, Antonio López de Santa Anna promised freedom to enslaved people who escaped to Mexican lines, justifying this policy on the grounds that the Texas rebels had broken the social contract and forfeited the constitutional protections of their "property" rights. In 1837, Mexico's Congress abolished slavery across the nation. Less than a decade later, as the United States Congress debated a joint resolution annexing the Republic of Texas, Mexican leaders proposed a radical free-soil policy, which promised freedom to *all* enslaved people who set foot in Mexico, not just those whose enslavers had broken the social contract. The loss of half of Mexico's territory gave rise to a conception of sovereignty in which territory accorded rights, rather than race.[7]

In the United States, the conquest and incorporation of Mexican territory led to a different understanding of sovereignty. The Treaty of Guadalupe Hidalgo, which ended the Mexican-American War, marked the first time that the United States had acquired territory where slavery was abolished by law. The threat that Mexican abolition posed to the balance of power between the slaveholding and nonslaveholding states led Southern politicians to adopt what had once been a radical view that the Constitution protected enslaved property everywhere in the United States, even in states and territories where slavery was abolished. Reaching a nonslaveholding jurisdiction did not grant rights to freedom seekers, as in Mexico. From this perspective, slavery was no longer a legal condition, from which enslaved people could escape, but a permanent status, defined by race.

By examining Mexico's and the United States' evolving policies with respect to fugitive slaves, this chapter builds on important scholarship that explores freedom seeking in North America. In the process, it seeks to correct a trend in transnational scholarship of looking primarily to Europe for ideas that influenced the United States, rather than to Latin America—or, for that matter, Asia and Africa. The few studies that have examined Latin America's influence on the United States have focused on the negative example of political instability and racial equality that the region provided.[8] This is an important part of the story, but it is only a part. By exploring how understandings of freedom in Mexico shaped the extension of slavery in the United States, this chapter makes the case that Mexico did more than provide a negative example: It, in fact, shaped conceptions of sovereignty in ways that would contribute to the outbreak of civil war in the United States.

Mexico's war of independence against Spain forged a link in the popular imagination between personal emancipation and national independence that led state and national leaders to make inroads against slavery. In 1821, Agustín de Iturbide, the general who secured Mexico's independence, abolished all distinctions of race and caste. Three years later, Mexico's Congress prohibited the importation of enslaved people from abroad, promising freedom to illegally imported slaves from the moment they set foot on Mexican soil. Meanwhile, between 1824 and 1827, nine of Mexico's nineteen states prohibited the slave trade or decreed that "no one is born a slave." Seven states also abolished slavery altogether.[9] But what did this antislavery legislation mean for freedom seekers? Although Mexico's Congress had not established a clear policy on fugitive slaves, freedom seekers repeatedly made the case that its antislavery laws applied not just to enslaved people within Mexico but to all enslaved people who reached its soil—an argument that Mexico's leaders came to accept on the eve of war with the United States.

Almost as soon as Mexico secured its independence from Spain, enslaved people fled from the United States to secure their freedom under its laws. Nearly a hundred enslaved people escaped from Louisiana in 1822.[10] All of them seemed to be heading towards the Sabine River, on the other side of which, they would, according to the *Courrier de la Louisiane*, enjoy "an unrestrained equality of human rights, without regard to birth, or condition, title, name, descent, or color."[11] Seven years later, in 1829, a Black man named José Francisco Laviña petitioned the mayor of Allende, Coahuila, to free his wife, an enslaved woman in San Antonio de Béxar.[12] That same year, two men and a woman from the De León Colony of Téjas arrived in Guerrero, Coahuila, just south of the Rio Grande, and asked "to know if they were free."[13]

The flight of enslaved people to Mexico concerned slaveholders in the United States. In 1831, U.S. Minister to Mexico Anthony Butler tried to secure an extradition treaty that included the return of freedom seekers. But Mexico's Congress was divided about the article that provided for their extradition. Some of the representatives were in favor of returning fugitive slaves. Refusing to do so, they argued, would provide a pretext for slaveholders from the United States to invade Mexico.[14] But others countered that the Mexican government did not have the resources to maintain a large and costly army on its three-thousand-mile frontier to "hunt for negroes."[15] Those who opposed the extradition of freedom seekers also argued against the treaty on moral grounds, articulating "beautiful reasons" and "philanthropic doctrines" against slavery.[16] As the impasse threatened to derail ratification of the entire treaty, the U.S. minister to Mexico agreed to withdraw the article relating to fugitive slaves. On December 18, 1831, Mexico's Congress ratified the treaty, without the controversial article.[17] The extradition of enslaved people who escaped to Mexico would be "a matter for discussion in the future."[18]

In the absence of an official policy, local officials made their own decisions when fugitive slaves petitioned for their freedom. Some enslaved people found a measure of protection in Mexico. In 1832, when three freedom seekers from Louisiana petitioned for "protection under the Mexican flag" at Anahuac, Texas, Juan Davis Bradburn sent them to work on the fort, while asking his superiors for guidance. Bradburn had not received any instructions from Mexico City when several weeks later, a planter named William H. Logan claimed the freedom seekers as his property. Refusing to return them, Bradburn explained, "Military commanders are not posted to the frontier to determine national questions."[19]

But pressure from the United States often forced Mexican officials to return enslaved people, as the three enslaved people who escaped to Anahuac in 1832 learned. After Bradburn refused to return them to Louisiana, thirty armed colonists from Brazoria put Anahuac under siege. To avoid an uprising, Colonel José de las Piedras, the Mexican commander at Nacogdoches, negotiated with the colonists, agreeing to return the freedom seekers and to relieve Juan Davis Bradburn of his duties.[20] The fate of these three enslaved people was not unusual. In 1831, the commander of the Port of Veracruz returned two enslaved people who had escaped from New Orleans by concealing themselves on board a ship.[21] Four years later, the mayor of Campeche returned a freedom seeker named Jean Antoine who had escaped by sea from Louisiana in the hold of a brig called the *General Santa Anna*.[22]

During the Texas Revolution, when an unwieldy coalition of Mexicans and Anglo-Americans revolted against the centralist government under President Antonio López de Santa Anna, Mexico's leaders started to promise freedom to fugitive slaves under certain circumstances. To defend their uprising, the Texas revolutionaries used John Locke's theory of the social contract, claiming that they seceded only after the Mexican government tried to centralize power—an attempt at centralization that violated the social contract, forged between state and citizen when Mexico still operated under a federal system. This was the same language that Mexico had used to justify its independence from Spain.[23] The Texas revolutionaries claimed only to be exercising the rights that Mexico had asserted fifteen years earlier. As Benjamin Green, the United States chargé d'affaires in Mexico, explained, to call Texas a "rebellious colony," was to call into question "the right of Mexico to rid itself of its dependence on Spain."[24]

To make the case that Mexican independence was justified but the Texas Revolution was not, the government in Mexico City argued that although citizens might have the right to revolt, the social contract did not apply to the revolutionaries in Texas. The Anglo adventurers had broken Mexico's colonization laws both by importing enslaved people and failing to convert to Catholicism. "The lack of compliance has destroyed the pact," wrote President Antonio López de Santa Anna in March of 1836.[25] Having broken the social contract, the Texans were no longer entitled to its protections. As a result, Santa Anna directed his generals to "give protection to all those unhappy slaves who groan beneath the whip of some colonists who, in contradiction of the laws of this country, keep them in their service."[26] Enslaved people must have learned about the order quickly, because a month later, on April 3, 1836, fourteen enslaved people and their families arrived at the Mexican lines near the Navidad River in Texas. General José Urrea sent them "in freedom" to Victoria, Tamaulipas. More soon followed.[27]

The order to free enslaved people who escaped to Mexican lines was not a principled defense of liberty but a calculated attempt to undermine the war effort in Texas. After the Texas Army routed Mexican forces at the Battle of San Jacinto on April 21, 1836, Mexican leaders continued to view antislavery as a means of returning Texas to the national fold. In 1837, as a part of that effort, Mexico's Congress abolished slavery "without exception."[28] Defending liberty allowed Mexico to assume the mantle of righteousness. Texans, for all their talk of "liberty" and "rights of man," were destroying the "true liberty" of enslaved people.[29] Abolishing slavery also galvanized public support for Mexico around the world. From Scotland to New York, antislavery societies condemned Texas as a "loathsome republic" that had exercised its political liberty in defense of slavery.[30] In addition, the abolition of slavery threatened to destabilize the Republic of Texas by encouraging enslaved people to revolt or escape.[31] By "condemn[ing]" slavery, Mexico's "laws and customs" might encourage the "two million slaves" in the U.S. South to "take up arms," according to the Mexico City newspaper El Imparcial.[32]

Abolition in Mexico did not stop the United States Congress from debating, and eventually signing, a joint resolution to annex the Republic of Texas. As war with the United States loomed, Mexican authorities adopted an even more radical policy with respect to freedom seekers. In 1844, the minister of foreign relations ordered no more runaways to be returned to the United States, "or else we will not be able to count on the slaves of the Southern states in case of a war with that country. We risk losing their sympathies at the moment that we most need them to conquer Texas."[33] That same year, Mexico's Congress passed a law that fugitive slaves be given passports "wheresoever they may land" to permit them to remain in the country.[34] "*Libre sois!*" Mexican newspapers announced to the people of color in Louisiana, Texas, and Florida.[35] Freedom seekers had argued for years that Mexico's antislavery laws should apply not only to enslaved people within Mexico, but to all enslaved people who reached its soil. Now, at long last, Mexican leaders accepted their arguments.

These measures conveyed to the United States that a war with Mexico would also be a "war with the blacks and with the Indians."[36] Indeed, during the Mexican-American War, African Americans enlisted in the army and received instruction in the "handling of firearms" as members of the National Guard.[37] A report circulated that 600 freedom seekers ("well drilled in flying artillery tactics") had joined the Mexican army.[38] These numbers must have been exaggerated, but the runaways who did enlist impressed their commanders. General Mariano Arista boasted that these men would defend "with determination" the country "in which they found liberty."[39] As "natural enemies" of the United States, the commanding general of the state of Tamaulipas reported that African Americans "had always been quick to lend their services to the Mexican Republic."[40]

If enslaved people resisted their masters using what scholars call "weapons of the weak"—malingering, feigning ignorance, working slowly—governments could, too.[41] Mexico's radical antislavery policy was a powerful weapon in the hands of a weak government. This policy was not overtly belligerent—France and England had articulated similar freedom principles—but it did provide Mexico with ideological support, as well as military allies. And it would have profound consequences for the future of slavery in the United States.[42]

The loss of half of its territory committed the Mexican government to antislavery—and to a conception of sovereignty in which rights inhered in territory rather than in lineage. For the United States, the conquest of Alta California and Nuevo México was also significant, because it marked the first time that the U.S. congressmen had to organize territories where slavery was abolished by law.

Northern politicians favored prohibiting slavery in the conquered territories, but their proslavery colleagues recognized that such a result would destroy the balance of power between North and South. To protect their sectional interests, some Southern politicians adopted what had once been a fringe position: that the Constitution protected enslaved property everywhere in the United States, and as a result, that Southern laws could be applied even to states or territories that had abolished slavery. As this theory gained acceptance, it shaped debates not only over the expansion of slavery, but over the return of freedom seekers from Mexico.

On August 6, 1846, several months after war broke out with Mexico, David Wilmot, a Democrat from Pennsylvania, proposed prohibiting slavery and involuntary servitude in any territories conquered from Mexico. Wilmot argued that Mexico's 1837 abolition of slavery meant that any land ceded to the United States after the Mexican-American War would enter the Union as free territories. Though duty-bound to protect slavery where it existed, Wilmot was opposed to the extension of such a "great moral, social, and political evil" where it had already been abolished.[43]

Some congressmen raised the question of whether the abolition of slavery in Mexico made the Wilmot Proviso redundant. If slavery could not exist in the conquered Mexican territories, then, they argued, the "peculiar institution" could not legally extend to the Mexican cession, proviso or no proviso.[44] "If the territory will be free when it is annexed, and Congress has no power to make it slave, where is the necessity for the adoption of the amendment?" wondered Richard Brodhead of Pennsylvania in 1847.[45] That same year, Isaac Parrish of Ohio credited the "advocates of this proviso" with showing that "slavery cannot exist in any territory that may be acquired of Mexico, until those who would establish it there . . . ask and obtain its sanction by the action of this Government, and needs no negative expression to prohibit it."[46] To Senator James W. Bradbury of Maine, the proviso was "an unnecessary enactment," for slavery had already been as prohibited by Mexican laws as by any act of Congress. "These laws remain in force; and the proviso is now there, prohibiting slavery throughout their entire extent."[47]

Southern politicians recognized that any prohibition on slavery in the conquered Mexican territories would imperil the political balance between the slaveholding and nonslaveholding states. If the territories seized from Mexico joined the Union as free states, then all of the remaining Western territories would be closed to slavery. On February 19, 1847, four days after the House of Representatives passed the Wilmot Proviso, Senator John C. Calhoun of South Carolina presented a set of resolutions before the Senate that would protect enslaved property in the Mexican Cession. Calhoun argued that any restriction on slavery "despoiled" slaveholders of their property and deprived them of their "constitutional rights" under the Fifth Amendment. If the territories were the common property of all citizens, slaveholders could not, in good faith, be excluded from them. The "peculiar institution" would exist wherever the flag was planted. From this perspective, the Missouri Compromise line, which had prohibited slavery north of 36°30′ in the Louisiana Purchase since 1820, was unconstitutional. Previously, Calhoun had been "willing to acquiesce in a continuance of the Missouri Compromise, in order to preserve, under the present trying circumstances, the peace of the Union." But, now, Calhoun argued against federal interference with slavery under any circumstances. "Let us be done with compromises," Calhoun urged. "Let us go back and stand upon the Constitution!"[48]

In 1850, Senator Henry Clay of Kentucky sought to resolve the controversy over the Mexican Cession by proposing a compromise that, among other things, provided for the organization of the territories of Utah and New Mexico. Although the measure did not prohibit slavery—a concession to the South—Clay made clear that the institution was unlikely to be reestablished. "That as slavery does not exist by law, and is not likely to be introduced into any of the territory acquired," he explained, "it is inexpedient for Congress to provide by law, either for its introduction into or exclusion from any part of the said territory."[49] Mexico's laws abolishing slavery would remain in effect in its ceded territories, until the "people" voted to alter or to uphold those laws.

Forbidding slavery from the former Mexican territories, whether by Mexican law or the Wilmot Proviso, was unacceptable to John C. Calhoun. On March 4, 1850, Calhoun argued that Clay's compromise excluded slaveholders from the former Mexican territories by "an indirect course," in order to avoid the "united and determined resistance of the South." If Congress could not legislate on slavery in the territories, then Mexico's laws against slavery remained in effect. "The necessary consequence," Calhoun objected, "is to exclude the South from that territory just as effectually as would the Wilmot Proviso." Clay's compromise would therefore put the South at a permanent disadvantage. The balance of power "effectually and irretrievably" would cease to exist. The proslavery society shaped by Southern planters would have no means to protect itself against "encroachment and oppression," by which Calhoun meant enforced, unilateral emancipation.[50]

Convinced by Calhoun's arguments, a growing number of Southern politicians demanded an explicit guarantee that the federal government would respect their constituents' property in the territories, in accordance with the Fifth Amendment. On May 15, 1850, Jefferson Davis of Mississippi, the future president of the Confederacy, decided "to test the sense of the Senate on the single question, whether the right to the service of man—whether the right of property in slaves, as it exists in the slaveholding States of the Union, shall receive the same protection which other property shall receive in the territories of the United States." He proposed an amendment to prevent the territorial legislatures of Utah and New Mexico "from legislating against the rights of property growing out of the institution of slavery."[51]

Congress was at an impasse. Did Mexico's laws abolishing slavery apply to the conquered territories until the "people" decided to overturn them? Or did the Constitution protect enslaved "property" in the Mexican cession? Unable to agree on answers, the representatives decided to organize the Utah and New Mexico Territories without prohibiting or permitting slavery, leaving it to the Supreme Court to decide the nature and limits of congressional authority over slavery in the territories. As potential test cases wound their way through the judicial system, Congress continued to argue over these issues. In 1854, Congress voted to overturn the Missouri Compromise, which had—in supposed violation of constitutional protections of property rights—prohibited slavery north of 36°30' in the Louisiana Purchase. Not long thereafter, pro- and antislavery settlers came to blows over the status of slavery in the newly organized Kansas Territory.

On March 6, 1857, the Supreme Court issued a decision in *Dred Scott v. Sanford* that sought to resolve the growing controversy over whether the Constitution protected enslaved "property" even in jurisdictions that had abolished slavery. The plaintiff, an enslaved man named Dred Scott, had sued for his freedom in Missouri because he had resided with his enslaver John Sanford (misspelled Sandford in court papers) in the Wisconsin territory, where Congress forbade slavery under the Missouri Compromise, as well as the free state of Illinois. The question before the Supreme Court was whether the laws of Illinois or Wisconsin could emancipate Scott, given his residence in those places. Chief Justice Roger Taney decided in the negative. "As Scott was a slave when taken into the State of Illinois by his owner, and was there held as such, and brought back in that character, his *status*, as free or slave, depended on the laws of Missouri, and not of Illinois," Taney wrote.[52] The Constitution protected property, and Taney argued that the laws of the state from which Dred Scott came would determine whether or not he counted as person or property.[53]

According to this interpretation, enslaved people could not secure their freedom by reaching a jurisdiction that prohibited slavery. In Mexico, however, a different vision of sovereignty had emerged, one in which reaching free territory could emancipate enslaved people. In 1857, the same year that the United States Supreme Court ruled that enslaved people would be held in bondage, anywhere they went, Mexico's Congress adopted a new constitution that promised freedom to enslaved people from the moment they set foot on the national soil.[54] The difference between the Mexican Constitution and the *Dred Scott* holding, rendered so close in time, did not pass without notice. The *New York Tribune* noted in 1857 that the Mexican Constitution "wholy [sic] repudiated the Taney interpretation of the rights of man."[55] That repudiation was an embarrassment to Americans who saw their republic as the standard-bearer of liberty in the Americas, but it also was a significant threat to slavery in the South Central United States. Slaveholders were convinced that their very lives were in danger. Residents of Washington-on-the-Brazos feared that runaways were "lurking" in the canebrakes.[56] Five hundred Texans signed a petition criticizing Mexico's Constitution as a "great grievance" and an insult to "the institutions and national honor, dignity and interests of the whole confederation."[57]

The Texas legislature decided to take matters into its own hands. On December 10, 1857, Representative Thomas Freeman McKinney rose to speak in the Texas House of Representatives. In his hand was the draft of an act that would encourage the capture of slaves escaping "beyond the limits of the U. States" by granting one-third of the runaway's value to the man who returned him to the Travis County sheriff.[58] Just as Dred Scott's status was determined by the laws of Missouri, McKinney argued that enslaved people who escaped across the Rio Grande remained in bondage by virtue of the laws of Texas: They were not, in other words, subject to Mexico's laws promising freedom to all enslaved people who set foot on the national soil. After McKinney finished reading his bill aloud, the representatives, mostly Democrats, burst into applause. Although the Constitution prohibited the states from drafting their own foreign policy and the Neutrality Act of 1794 forbade armed incursions into nations with which the United States was at peace, the "Act to Encourage the Reclamation of Slaves, Escaping beyond the Limits of the United States" did not provoke debate. The bill passed in the Texas House of Representatives on January 25, 1858, with 63 yeas and 9 nays.[59]

The conquest of Mexican territories convinced a growing number of Southern politicians that the U.S. Constitution protected their enslaved "property" even in states and territories whose legal systems did not recognize slavery. No jurisdiction could free enslaved people, because their status was defined by the laws of the state from which they came. According to this view, slavery enjoyed legal protections, not just in the jurisdictions that recognized it, but everywhere. This argument had profound consequences for slavery and sectional controversy in the United States: It contributed to the overturning of the Missouri Compromise, the outbreak of violence in Kansas, the Supreme Court's decision in the Dred Scott case, and, ultimately, the birth of a new political coalition, the Republican Party, whose success in the election of 1860 led to the outbreak of the U.S. Civil War.

Mexico does not often figure in the global history of abolition. In *Abolition*, Seymour Drescher dismisses the Mexican case in a single sentence.[60] David Brion Davis's magisterial *The Problem of Slavery in the Age of Revolutions* dedicates two paragraphs to Mexico.[61] But Mexico contributed in important ways to global debates about slavery and freedom. Fugitive slaves had escaped for years to Mexico, claiming their freedom on the grounds that its antislavery laws applied not just to enslaved people within Mexico, but to all enslaved people who touched its soil. On the eve of war with the United States, Mexico's leaders, at last, adopted policies that reflected the principles that fugitive slaves had repeatedly articulated on claiming their freedom.

Mexico's policies had profound consequences for slavery in the United States. Not only did the promise of freedom encourage enslaved people to escape to Mexico, but the conquest of Alta California and Nuevo México in 1848 also forced Congress to grapple with the question of what the status of slavery would be in territories where the "peculiar institution" had been abolished by law. Northern politicians argued that Congress could not reestablish slavery where it did not exist, while proslavery politicians threatened to secede if slavery were excluded from the former Mexican territories. To avoid a civil war, congressmen agreed not to legislate on slavery in the ceded territories, instead allowing "the people" to decide for themselves. But a growing cadre of proslavery politicians accepted the previously radical position that the Constitution protected slavery everywhere. From this perspective, slavery was not a condition, recognized only in jurisdictions that permitted human bondage, but a permanent status, determined by race.

For all that abolition in Mexico did to provoke sectional controversy in the United States, Mexico's contribution to broader debates about freedom has been overlooked. Even after David Wilmot proposed his famous proviso to prohibit slavery in the conquered Mexican territories, congressmen struggled to believe that Mexico had adopted such radical antislavery policies.[62] During the debates over the Wilmot Proviso, Senator John Berrien of Georgia argued that "the power over this subject of slavery belonged to the separate States of the Mexican Republic."[63] Edward D. Hannegan of Indiana contended that slavery could not have been abolished because peonage continued in Mexico, under the terms of which the creditor could sell his debtor "as a slave for all time."[64] Even if the Mexican government had abolished slavery, Senator Joseph Underwood of Kentucky denied that those laws operated in a territory as unpeopled as the northwestern reaches of Mexico.[65]

Historians have also been skeptical of Mexico's antislavery laws. They have rightly pointed out that Indigenous bondage continued in Mexico, long after chattel slavery was abolished. And they have explored how coercive labor practices like debt peonage and indentured servitude retained many of the hallmarks of slavery. These caveats are important. The lives that freedom seekers forged for themselves in Mexico were not free from coercion or racism. But it is also important to acknowledge that every post-emancipation society in the Americas grappled with similar inconsistencies. The difficulties of enforcement do not invalidate the significance of emancipation in the Northern states, Canada, or Haiti. Nor should they in Mexico.

Recognizing the significance of Mexico's antislavery policies helps shift the common account of U.S. expansion in the mid-nineteenth century—an account in which the United States government could impose its will upon its Latin American neighbors without consequence. The prevailing view of Mexico remains of a country so unstable that the presidency changed hands forty-nine times between 1824 and 1857 and so poor that soap cakes sometimes took the place of coins.[66] This view, though it has elements of truth, is incomplete. Economic success or brute force often moves the levers of history. But, as this chapter has argued, power can take on other, subtler forms: the promise of freedom, or the rumor of enslaved people taking up arms against their enslavers.

Notes

1. Wilbur H. Siebert published the first scholarly study of the Underground Railroad, a romantic account of an organized network of abolitionists that spanned the northern United States. See Siebert, *The Underground Railroad from Slavery to Freedom: A Comprehensive History* (New York: Macmillan, 1898). Larry Gara's *The Liberty Line* consigns most of the stories that Siebert collected about the Underground Railroad to folklore. See Gara, *The Liberty Line: The Legend of the Underground Railroad* (Lexington: University of Kentucky Press, 1961). More recently, Eric Foner uses the journal of the newspaper editor Sydney Howard Gay to argue that a secret network did, in fact, exist. See Foner, *Gateway to Freedom: The Hidden History of the Underground Railroad* (New York: W. W. Norton, 2014).

2. Estimates are varied and imprecise. A fugitive slave told Frederick Law Olmsted that forty runaways had arrived in Piedras Negras in a mere three months. See Frederick Law Olmsted, *A Journey through Texas* (New York: Mason Brothers, 1859), 323–327. John "Rip" Ford estimated in 1851 that 3,000 slaves had escaped to Mexico. See Randolph B. Campbell, *An Empire for Slavery: The Peculiar Institution in Texas, 1821–1865* (Baton Rouge: Louisiana State University Press, 1989), 63. Historian Ronnie C. Tyler puts the number, vaguely, in the "thousands." See Tyler, "Fugitive Slaves in Mexico," *Journal of Negro History* 57, no. 1 (1972): 12. Quintard Taylor estimates that 4,000 fugitive slaves escaped to Mexico. See Taylor, *In Search of the Racial Frontier: African Americans in the American West, 1528–1990* (New York: W.W. Norton, 1998), 60.

3. Kenneth W. Porter, "Relations between Negroes and Indians within the Present Limits of the United States," *Journal of Negro History* 17, no. 3 (1932): 349. Kevin Mulroy, *Freedom on the Border: The Seminole Maroons in Florida, the Indian Territory, Coahuila, and Texas* (Lubbock : Texas Tech University Press, 1993), and Kevin Mulroy, *The Seminole Freedmen: A History* (Norman: University of Oklahoma Press, 2007). Juan Manuel de la Serna, "Rumbo al Sur. Rebelión y fuga de los esclavos de Texas entre 1822 y 1860," *Anuario de Estudios Latinoamericanos* 30 (1998): 133–160.

4. Taylor, *In Search of the Racial Frontier*, 60. For a similar argument, see Campbell, *An Empire for Slavery*, 62, and Rosalie Schwartz, *Across the Rio to Freedom: U.S. Negroes in Mexico* (El Paso: Texas Western Press, 1975), 2.

5. Sarah Cornell, "Citizens of Nowhere: Fugitive Slaves and Free African Americans in Mexico, 1833–1857," *Journal of American History* 100, no. 2 (2013): 351–374. For studies of how fugitive slaves reveal the lack of state control over the border and its meaning, see James David Nichols, "The Line of Liberty: Runaway Slaves and Fugitive Peons in the Texas–Mexico Borderlands," *Western Historical Quarterly* 44, no. 4 (2013): 413–433, and Sean Kelley, "'Mexico in His Head': Slavery and the Texas–Mexico Border, 1810–1860," *Journal of Social History* 37, no. 3 (2004): 709.

6. Gregory P. Downs, "The Mexicanization of American Politics: The United States' Transnational Path from Civil War to Stabilization," *American Historical Review* 117, no. 2 (2012): 392.

7. For important studies on antislavery in early national Mexico, see Jaime Olveda Legaspi, "La abolición de la esclavitud en Mexico, 1810–1917," *Signos Historicos* 29 (January–June 2013): 8–34; Jorge Delgadillo Núñez, "La esclavitud, la abolición y los afrodescendientes: Memoria histórica y construcción de identidades en la prensa mexicana, 1840–1860," *Historia Mexicana* 274 (October–December 2019): 743–788; Celso Thomas Castilho, "La cabaña del Tío Tom (Uncle Tom's Cabin), la esclavitud atlántica y la racialización de la esfera pública en la ciudad de México de mediados del siglo XIX," *Historia Mexicana* 274 (October–December 2019): 789–835; Gerardo Gurza-Lavalle, "Against Slave Power? Slavery and Runaway Slaves in Mexico–United States Relations, 1821–1857," *Mexican Studies/Estudios Mexicanos* 35, no. 2 (2019): 143–170.

8. Downs, "The Mexicanization of American Politics."

9. Ayuntamiento de Santa Rita de Morelos to Honorable Congress, March 25, 1825, fondo Comisiones, Segundo Congreso Constitucional, Primer Periodo Ordinario, Archivo del Congreso del Estado de Coahuila (ACEC). The nine states were Chihuahua,

Coahuila y Téjas, Estado de México, Michoacan, Nuevo León, Oaxaca, Puebla, Veracruz, and Yucatán. The constitutional congresses of Jalisco, Durango, and Estado de Occidente (Sinaloa/Sonora) abolished slavery with the promise of indemnification. In Chihuahua, Querétaro, and Chiapas, the representatives declared the end of slavery but instructed the legislature to establish a process by which slaves would be freed. The constitution of both Tabasco and San Luis Potosi promised freedom and citizenship. For an excellent summary of this legislation, see Jaime Olveda Legaspi, "La abolicion de la esclavitud en Mexico," 8–34.

10. Unsigned extract, St. Martinsville, July 9, 1822, box 1, Slavery Collection, Louisiana State University Special Collections, Baton Rouge, Louisiana (hereinafter cited as LSU).

11. "Mexico, an Empire," *Courrier de la Louisiana*, July 29, 1822, 1.

12. Laviña was originally from New Orleans and had been living in Allende for eight months. It is unclear whether he had escaped from slavery in Téjas, or whether he was free. His wife's name was Maria Regina Rodríguez. José Maria Felán, Juzgado de la Villa de Allende, to Gov. Constitucional del Estado de Coahuila y Téjas, October 16, 1829, exp. 15, folder 1, caja 11, Fondo Siglo XIX (FSXIX), Archivo General del Estado de Coahuila (AGEC).

13. The men were reported to be from Guinea. Judge of Guerrero to J. M. Viescas, October 18, 1829, folder 63, box 6, Múzquiz Collection, Beinecke Rare Books and Manuscript Library (BRBML). Luis Lombraña to Governor of Coahuila y Texas, December 19, 1829, exp. 11, folder 8, caja 12, FSXIX, AGEC.

14. Notes of Consejo De Gobierno (Castillo, Bustamante, Echeverria), October 21, 1831, folder 5, file 23, AEMEUA, SRE.

15. Senate Committee on Foreign Relations, December 7, 1831, f. 24, folder 5, file 23, AEMEUA, SRE.

16. Ibid. For more on the debate in Mexico's congress, see David Lee Child, *The Texan Revolution* (Washington, DC: J. & G. S. Gideon, 1843), 33.

17. Committee on Foreign Relations, December 18, 1831, f. 18, folder 5, file 23, AEMEUA, SRE. Schwartz, *Across the Rio to Freedom*, 13.

18. Francisco Pizarro Martínez al Encargado de Negocios, April 7, 1832, folder 9, file 20, AEMEUA, SRE.

19. Report to Comandante General, Estados Internos de Oriente, 1832, folder 91, box 3, Wagner, BRBML.

20. Alcalde of Nacogdoches to the Political Chief of Texas, June 29, 1832, Nacogdoches Archives, Texas State Archives.

21. Consejo de Gobierno to Senate, October 21, 1831, f. 15, folder 5, file 23, AEMEUA, SRE and Consejo de Gobierno to Senate, December 2, 1831, f. 24, folder 5, file 23, AEMEUA, SRE.

22. Libro que registra las entradas de embarcaciones mexicanas al Puerto de Nueva Orleáns, 1831–40, fs. 1–22, folder 1, box 32, Relaciones Exteriores, Archivo General de la Nación (AGN).

23. Nettie Lee Benson, *The Provincial Deputation in Mexico: Harbinger of Provincial Autonomy, Independence, and Federalism* (Austin: University of Texas Press, 1992); Jose-

fina Zoraida Vázquez, *El Primer Liberalismo Mexicano: 1808–1855* (Mexico City: Museo Nacional de Historia, 1995); Jordana Dym, "'Our Pueblos, Fractions with No Central Unity': Municipal Sovereignty in Central America, 1808–1821," *Hispanic American Historical Review* 86, no. 3 (2006): 437–438.

24. Benjamin E. Green to José María de Bocanegra, July 4, 1844, *Siglo XIX*, 3.

25. "La ley de colonización ya no existe porque la rebelión de los colonos y la falta de cumplimiento a lo pactado la ha dejado destruida." Santa Anna to José Urrea, March 23, 1836, vol. 1, *Documentos para la historia de la guerra de Texas*, New York Public Library.

26. Antonio López de Santa Anna to Joaquin Ramirez y Lesma, March 8, 1836, vol. 1, *Documentos para la historia de la guerra de Texas*, New York Public Library.

27. José Urrea, *Diario de las operaciones militares de la división que al mando del general José Urrea hizo la campaña de Téjas* (Victoria de Durango: Manuel Gonzales, 1838), 24.

28. For more on abolition in Mexico see Manuel Ferrer Muñoz, *La cuestión de la esclavitud en el México decimonónico: Sus repercusiones en las etnias indigenas* (Bogota: Instituto de Estudios Constitucionales, 1998), 24; Alice L. Baumgartner, *South to Freedom: Runaway Slaves to Mexico and the Road to the Civil War* (New York: Basic Books, 2020), 99–122.

29. J. M. de Castillo y Lanzas to John Forsyth, March 8, 1837, roll 2, vol. 4, Notes from the Mexican Legation in the United States to the Department of State, RG59, M54. This document can be found in Spanish in vol. 4, *Documentos para la historia de la guerra de Texas*, New York Public Library.

30. "Westchester County Anti-Slavery Society," *Emancipator* [New York, New York] January 12, 1837: 146, *19th Century U.S. Newspapers*, Web. 30 Oct. 2016. For other examples of resolutions, see "War in Texas," *Edinburgh Scotsman*, in Benjamin Lundy, *The War in Texas* (Philadelphia: Merrihew and Gunn, 1837), 55.

31. Consejo de Gobierno to Senate, October 21, 1831, f. 15, folder 5, file 23, AEMEUA, SRE and Consejo de Gobierno to Senate, December 2, 1831, f. 24, ibid.

32. "Cuestión de Tejas," (copied from *El Imparcial*, 1837) *Siglo XIX* (June 27, 1842), 1–4. For another example of this rhetoric, see "Batalla de los libres en Tejas," *El Mosquito Mexicano* (September 6, 1836), 1–2. See also Delgadillo, "La esclavitud, la abolición y los afrodescendientes," 743–788.

33. Mexican Legation in U.S.A. to Secretary of Foreign Relations, September 22, 1844, no. 1265, f. 64, folder 1, file 29, AEMEUA, SRE; Buenaventura Vivó to Minister of Foreign Relations, "Muy reservada," April 23, 1854, folder 5, file 44, AEMEUA, SRE.

34. Bocanegra, "Decree relating to passports," *Diario del Gobierno* (July 27, 1844), encl. Green to Calhoun, July 30, 1844, vol. 12, reel 13, Despatches from U.S. Ministers to Mexico.

35. "Revista de Periódicos," *El Siglo Diez y Nueve* (January 2, 1844), 3.

36. "Interesantísimo Historia de Tejas," *El Monitor Constitucional* (March 25, 1845), 3. ("Manifesto muy claramente que una Guerra con los mexicanos lo seria tambien con los negros y con los indios.")

37. José Ignacio Guerrero to Foreign Minister, Ciudad Victoria, January 25, 1844, f. 75, vol. 37, Cartas de Seguridad, AGN. For more on African Americans joining the Mexican

army, see *Eco del Norte de Tamaulipas*, October 15, 1845. Robert H. Ferrell, *Monterrey Is Ours! The Mexican War Letters of Lieutenant Dana, 1845–1847* (Lexington: University of Kentucky Press, 1990), 45. "Mexico," *Democratic Telegraph and Texas Register* 11, no. 27 (July 8, 1846), 2. Paul Foos, *A Short, Offhand, Killing Affair: Soldiers and Social Conflict during the Mexican–American War* (Chapel Hill: University of North Carolina Press, 2003), 98. A volunteer from Arkansas insisted that the Black man serving as an interpreter for a mayor in northern Mexico was a runaway "once belonging to a gentleman in the State of Tennessee, and who had absconded about ten years since." Foos, *Short, Offhand, Killing Affair*, 145.

38. "We find," *Telegraph and Texas Register* 10, no. 26 (May 25, 1845), 2.

39. Arista to de la Vega, Comandante General de Tamaulipas, Tampico, August 29, 1849, f. 81–83, exp. 3072, Archivo Histórico de la Secretaría de Defensa Nacional (AHSDN).

40. De la Vega to Arista, Tampico, August 18, 1849, fs. 43–45, vol. 3072, AHSDN.

41. Keila Grinberg has found Uruguay using antislavery to the same effect against Brazil. See Keila Grinberg, "Emancipación y guerra en el Río de la Plata, 1840–1865: Hacia una historia social de las relaciones internacionales," *Historia Mexicana* 69, no. 2 (2019): 693–743.

42. For more on the freedom principle, see Sue Peabody, *"There Are No Slaves in France": The Political Culture of Race and Slavery in the Ancient Regime* (Oxford: Oxford University Press, 1996); Cristina Nogueira Da Silva and Keila Grinberg, "Soil Free from Slaves: Slave Law in Late Eighteenth- and Early Nineteenth-Century Portugal," *Slavery and Abolition* 32, no. 3 (2011): 432; Sue Peabody and Keila Grinberg, "Free Soil: The Generation and Circulation of an Atlantic Legal Principle," *Slavery and Abolition* 32, no. 3 (2011): 331–339; Ada Ferrer, "Haiti, Free Soil, and Antislavery in the Revolutionary Atlantic," *American Historical Review* 117, no. 1 (2012): 50.

43. August 8, 1846, *Congressional Globe* (*CG*) (29th Congress, 1st session), 1214.

44. February 27, 1850, *CG* (31 Cong., 1 Sess.), 401.

45. February 9, 1847, *Congressional Globe Appendix* (*CGA*), (29 Cong., 2 Sess.), 331.

46. February 10, 1847, *CG* (29 Cong., 2 Sess.), 380.

47. April 11, 1850, *CGA* (30 Cong., 1 Sess.), 516.

48. February 19, 1847, *CG* (29 Cong., 2 Sess.), 454–455.

49. January 28, 1850, *CG* (31 Cong., 1 Sess.), 395.

50. March 4, 1850, *CG* (31 Cong., 1 Sess.), 411.

51. May 15, 1850, *CG* (31 Cong., 1 Sess.), 1003.

52. *Dred Scott v. Sandford*, 60 U.S. 393 (1856), 452.

53. *Dred Scott v. Sandford*, 60 U.S. 393 (1856), 449–450.

54. "Noticias: Congreso Constituyente, Julio 18 de 1856," *Diario Oficial* (July 19, 1856), 3. Mexican Constitution of 1857, Article II, X, and XV. For the Constitution of 1857 in general, see Erica Pani, "Entre transformar y gobernar: La Constitución de 1857," *Historia y política: Ideas, procesos, y movimientos sociales* 11 (2004): 65–86. For the antislavery provisions of the Constitution of 1857, see Karl Jacoby, *The Strange Career of William Ellis: The Texas Slave Who Became a Mexican Millionaire* (New York: W. W. Norton, 2016), 17–18; Schwartz, *Across the Rio to Freedom*, 51.

55. "No Slave-Catching in Mexico," *Liberator*, May 15, 1857.
56. "If Something Is Not Done," *Washington American* 2, no. 22 (April 14, 1857), 2.
57. A petition of 500 "Texian Subscribers" to the House and Senate of the United States, March 24, 1858, printed in H. M'Bride Pridgen, *Address to the People of Texas on the Protection of Slave Property* (Austin, 1859), 15–16.
58. Bills and Resolutions, December 10, 1857, Records of the Seventh Legislature, Texas State Archives.
59. "A bill for the reclamation of fugitive slaves," January 25, 1858, *Appendix to the Official Journal of the House of Representatives of the Seventh Legislature of the State of Texas* (Austin: John Marshall & Co., 1858), 671.
60. Seymour Drescher, *Abolition: A History of Slavery and Antislavery* (Cambridge: Cambridge University Press, 2009), 45.
61. David Brion Davis, *The Problem of Slavery in the Age of Revolution, 1770-1823* (Ithaca, NY: Cornell University Press, 1975), 80, 90.
62. "General Intelligence," *Vermont Chronicle* (Bellows Falls, Vermont), December 4, 1829, p. 193.
63. February 11, 1850, *CGA* (31 Cong., 1 Sess.), 208.
64. July 24, 1848, *CG* (29 Cong., 2 Sess.), 229.
65. February 26, 1849, *CG* (30 Cong., 1 Sess.), 323.
66. Mark Wasserman, *Everyday Life and Politics in Nineteenth-Century Mexico: Men, Women, and War* (Albuquerque: University of New Mexico Press, 2000), 46. "The Journal of a Volunteer Officer in the Mexican War," by W. W. H. Davis, Captain and Aide-de-Camp of Brigadier General Cushing, 1846–1848, Doylestown, Pennsylvania, draft, typescript, f. 259, folder 85, box 7, W. W. H. Davis Papers, BRBML.

2

Inveterate Imperialists

Contested Imperialisms, North American History, and the Coming of the U.S. Civil War

John Craig Hammond

In the months preceding the election of 1860, newspapers were ablaze with stories that the Knights of the Golden Circle—a quasi-secret society of proslavery expansionists—sought to establish a proslavery protectorate in northern Mexico. Like many Southern papers, the *Daily Louisville Democrat* advocated for the colonization of northern Mexico through processes deemed "Americanization" and "Southernization." By 1860, "Americanization" and "Southernization" had become euphemisms for imperialist processes by which Anglo-Americans moved into a territory and established plantation slavery while the "Spaniard mongrel" population was forced to "retreat or perish." In the process, republican government replaced anarchy and despotism while a biracial social order consisting of superior Anglo-Americans governing inferior African American slaves supplanted the "mongrel" population of Native Americans, Spaniards, and Africans. The *Daily Louisville Democrat* agreed on the necessity of Southernization in Mexico, but it denounced the Knights. A Stephen Douglas organ, the *Daily Democrat* charged that the Knights had broken up the Charleston convention and divided the Democratic Party as part of its larger scheme to sever the Union and bring Mexico into a Southern empire for slavery outside of the Union. The *Daily Democrat* did not object to the immorality of the conquest of Mexico, the forced expulsion of its population, and the establishment of racial, plantation slavery. Like the Knights, Douglas Democrats advocated conquest and empire. Unlike the Knights, they insisted that it be done by, within, and for the existing Union.[1]

Such disputes were common on the eve of the Civil War, as proslavery newspapers, politicians, and pundits celebrated their preferred scheme for Southernizing California, Mexico, Central America, the Caribbean, and even Brazil. Proslavery expansionists differed over exactly what regions to the south and west would be Southernized in the immediate future. They disagreed on the means by which these regions would be Southernized, just as they differed over whether a particular place would become a territory, a state, a protectorate, or a colony. By 1860, they increasingly split over whether these places would be added to the present Union or to a separate Southern confederacy. Regardless of their differences, and even when they dismissed the Knights themselves, influential Southern and Democratic politicians endorsed the "Southernization" of "the tropics" and perhaps even "South America." And Southernization had to come sooner rather than later; Republicans allegedly stood ready to annex "Cuba, Mexico, and Central America" so that *Free Soil* States may be erected South of us." Reflecting the urgency of empire but indifferent as to means, a Memphis paper cared little whether it was "the United States, Sam Houston, or the Knights of the Golden Circle" who would "take all Mexico"; it simply wanted it done.[2]

The Knights of the Golden Circle might have been a chimera, the brainchild of a deluded con man, but the imperial hopes and fears they inspired were real to Americans on the verge of disunion. Northern newspapers frequently reprinted reports of Knights' activities. Some were prosaic, simply repeating that "the object is declared to be the Americanizing and Southernizing Mexico, and looking to the establishment of a southern confederacy." Some Republicans ridiculed the Knights, who had become the farcical embodiment of intemperate proslavery imperialism. "The principal object" of Southern slaveholders had become "to invade Mexico, carrying the Bible, the pocket-pistol, negro slavery and the other blessings of civilization in their train," deadpanned one lampoon. "Give me Mexico, or give me death!" ended a parody speech allegedly delivered by Knights founder "Major General" George Bickley. Another published a scathing mockery of Southern imperialists as nineteenth-century Don Quixotes, titled "Modern Chivalry—A Manifesto."[3]

While some Republicans ridiculed Southern imperialists, others countered with their own visions of empire. In September of 1860, William Seward spoke of annexing "New Brunswick, Nova Scotia and Canada," reflecting standard Republican assumptions that Canada would sooner or later join the free labor states of the North, whether peacefully or by force. But Seward would also add "what remains of Mexico, all the West Indies and Central America" when they could be acquired with assurances that slavery would not be introduced there. Seward was not alone in envisioning some kind of hemispheric union of free labor and republican governments. William Rounseville Alger was the kind of Boston Unitarian minister who migrated easily from the Whigs to the Republicans in the 1850s. In his July 4, 1857, oration, he laid out competing imperial visions for the Americas. That the United States would dominate Mexico and the Caribbean Rim stood beyond dispute. The question facing the United States was whether it would impose slavery and aristocracy there, or foster the development of free labor and republicanism. In one vision, "a great Slave Empire covering the southern half of the continent" would emerge unless the United States halted slavery's expansion. So long as the United States permitted slavery's expansion, aristocratic slaveholders would seek new territory in Mexico, Central America, and the Caribbean. The peoples of those regions would resist closer union with the United States as it would lead inevitably to conquest, slavery, and slaveholder aristocracy. But if the United States passed laws forever prohibiting slavery's expansion, the racially diverse peoples of the Caribbean Rim would invite the United States to assist them in establishing their own free labor and republican governments with racially homogenous populations. Those tropical, free labor republics would also provide a destination for emancipated slaves from the United States, facilitating the movement of various peoples to the latitudes that Providence had set aside for their particular race. Ultimately, these racialized republics would join some kind of hemispheric, free labor union, under the protection and tutelage of the United States.[4]

When Democrats and Republicans, Northerners and Southerners, Unionists and disunionists, thought about sectional conflict, they rarely kept their musings within the boundaries of the United States or the free and slave states. Instead, sectional conflict frequently took place in overlapping continental, hemispheric, Atlantic, and international contexts. Within these broader geographies, they used empire to construct a hemispheric, Manichean struggle pitting free labor against slave labor, democracy against aristocracy and monarchy, and popular sovereignty against slaveholder sovereignty and the Slave Power. Beginning in the 1840s, and deepening in the 1850s, Southern whites forged an imperial ideology that called for the creation of a vast empire for slavery in the Americas. Responding directly to the rise of Southern proslavery imperialism, Northern whites created an imperial ideology based on democratic-republican forms of government and free labor. Although imperialist enslavers and their Northern allies found an institutional home in the Democratic Party, the North's free labor imperialism found its place in the Republican Party. By the late 1850s, Democratic and Republican imperialists advocated the imposition of their particular forms of sovereignty, race, labor, and republican government onto their sectional rivals as well as onto borderland regions in the trans-Mississippi West, Mexico, the Caribbean, and Central America. In the 1850s the United States became an empire increasingly divided by antagonistic imperial visions for the broader Americas; by 1860, Democrats and Republicans had become de facto imperial rivals.

Historians have traditionally treated conflicts between free labor and slave labor as battles over labor systems and sectional cultures, or in terms such as agrarianism versus industrialism, and premodern versus modern civilizations. But as their most ardent advocates understood matters, free labor and slave labor—along with the particular notions of capitalism and republican government associated with them—were imperial ideals that stood at the vanguard of American, Atlantic, and even global political economy and civilization. Republicans and Democrats, Northerners and Southerners, believed that the unique attributes of their section made them worthy of imposition on the broader Americas.[5] Empire was more than an oft-used term in the years preceding the Civil War. It was an organizing ideal, an ideological construct, by which many Democrats and Republicans understood the events surrounding the election of 1860, along with the United States' ongoing and future relationship with Europe and the Americas. More broadly, free labor and slave labor provided competing visions for how political systems, economics, and race would unfold across the Americas with proper support from the federal government or an independent Southern confederacy.[6]

Writing an imperial history of mid-nineteenth-century North America is obviously beyond the scope of this chapter. Instead, the following pages situate antebellum and Civil War historiography in the broader literature on imperial North America in a long nineteenth century, and seek to integrate antebellum U.S. political history into a larger North American history. This chapter also identifies the contours of rival imperial ideologies centering on slave labor versus free labor, and competing notions of race and government. Its analysis is meant to be suggestive rather than definitive, but nonetheless requires a few important preliminaries. As historian Jay Sexton notes, mid-century empire came in "multiple configurations" and was "pluralistic and protean." Republicans and Democrats differed among themselves nearly as much as they disagreed with each other about their preferred imperial ambitions. Second, though recognizing the plurality of mid-century imperialism, this chapter follows historian Paul A. Kramer in defining "the imperial" as "a dimension of power in which asymmetries in the scale of political action, regimes of spatial ordering, and modes of exceptionalizing difference enable and produce relations of hierarchy, discipline, dispossession, extraction, and exploitation."[7] Civil War–era imperialism involved desires to impose hierarchical systems of government, labor, and race on peoples defined—in various terms—as inferior, and living both within and outside of the areas where the United States exercised effective sovereignty. Empire became a feature—not an aberration—of late antebellum politics. Would-be imperialists conceived of the peoples of the Americas in racial terms and obsessed over racial differences; they devised racial theories about the fitness of certain races for self-government; they mused on what climates and regions Providence had designated for different races, and forged plans to realize them; they identified their partisan and sectional rivals as rival imperialists, and thought of struggles for the Americas as a looming imperial conflict. In the election of 1860, would-be imperialists sought control of the federal government. They expected to use state power to impose their preferred systems of race, labor, and republican government on the various peoples and regions of the trans-Mississippi West, the Caribbean, Mexico, Central America, and South America while denying the same to their de facto imperial foe.

The literature on empire and the United States is vast, rich, and sophisticated.[8] It is also underutilized by historians of the mid-nineteenth century and the Civil War era, despite the transnational and global turns in United States history. Holding to a paradigm where imperial ambitions emerged in the United States only in the later decades of the nineteenth century, mid-nineteenth-century historiography has mostly eschewed treating the United States as an imperial power or analyzing the conquest, acquisition, and settlement of the trans-Mississippi West and northern Mexico as the machinations of an aggressively expansionist empire. The unwillingness to see empire in the Civil War era has also been influenced by post–World War II political science convictions that the natural progression of modern politics moves from empires to nation-states, that empire is the antithesis of freedom, and that liberal democracy resides in nation-states rather than in empires. Furthermore, nineteenth-century historiography's tight chronological divisions, along with Civil War–era historiography's narrow focus on the East, makes it difficult to situate the Civil War era in a broader history of imperial North America that took place over the course of a long nineteenth century. Until very recently, the Mountain and Pacific West, the U.S.-Mexico Borderlands, Central America, and the Caribbean were treated as either subspecialties in Civil War–era history or as the places where only the most deluded of Southern slaveholders projected their expansion fantasies. When acknowledged, Civil War–era imperialism was turned into an aberration, cast onto some of the most reprehensible characters in American history or reduced to the passion of a few individuals. In other cases, clear manifestations of empire are analyzed with nineteenth-century euphemisms for imperialism, "filibustering" and "manifest destiny." Historical terms that should be subjected to analysis instead become analytical categories themselves. In other cases, conquests are normalized as neutral, natural processes of "expansion." In reducing "conquest" to "expansion," historians turn a verb and a series of contingent, contested processes into a noun and an inevitability.[9]

Antebellum and Civil War historians understandably resist framing a conflict between slavery and freedom, or a war to restore a nation-state, as a broader conflict pitting would-be imperialists against one another. Even in the best literature on expansion, historians are reluctant to use empire to analyze what antebellum Americans themselves understood to be imperialism. Thus, a recent article replaces the "manifest destiny" and "filibustering" of previous generations of historians with "the expansionist project of the U.S. government."[10] In another recent article on the Civil War and empire, the clear imperial intentions of antebellum Democrats and Republicans are overlooked in favor of a paradigm that pushes off the emergence of "an imperial nation-state" until Reconstruction.[11] A lack of conceptual clarity on the importance of empire is also evident in a recent, groundbreaking synthesis on slavery and capitalism that frequently invokes "empire" and "imperial" as adjectives, but leaves these terms' contested meanings, implications, and significance unpursued.[12] Thus, while the transnational turn in United States history has produced more continental analyses of North America during the Civil War period, these works tend to treat the imperial ambitions and actions of the U.S. nation-state as something other than imperialism, to naturalize them as "expansion," to push them off to the postwar period, or to simply assume them as natural and inevitable.

Outside of Civil War historiography, empire as a category of analysis provides historians with a valuable conceptual framework for writing transnational, continental, Atlantic, and global histories of the United States. Historians who take a long view of United States history have demonstrated that in inheriting the core of Britain's eighteenth-century North American empire, the United States acted as an aspiring imperial state from its inception. Indeed, in these readings, the U.S. War for Independence seems as much an internal civil war over the direction of the British Empire in North America as it was a colonial independence movement. Historians of the early American republic, in particular, have effectively treated the United States as one of several nation-states, confederacies, and imperial powers competing for sovereignty and supremacy over the peoples and places of North America—the imperial issues that animated the political conflicts of the 1850s, the processes of disunion, and then the Civil War and Reconstruction. Just as historians of the early republic have moved from east to west and from the late eighteenth century into the mid-nineteenth century, Western historians have moved from west to east, and from the early twentieth century to the mid-nineteenth century. In doing so, Western historians have demonstrated that state power stood at the center of conflicts over the division of territory, control of land and labor, the meanings and practices of race and ethnicity, voluntary and involuntary migrations, autonomy and sovereignty, conquest and subjugation—again, imperial issues that stood at the center of the Civil War. Moving backward from U.S. Western history and forward from the early American republic, what was once the history of the expansion of the United States has converged as the distinct field of North American history. At its best, North American history examines how various states, peoples, and groups understood and sought autonomy, sovereignty, and mastery for themselves and over others—the same issues that animated late antebellum and Civil War politics.[13]

Since 2000 historians have increasingly extended North American history into the middle third of the nineteenth century. A recognition that the United States operated as an imperial power on the North American continent across a long nineteenth century emerges from these works. Their analyses offer Civil War–era historians an important opportunity to use empire to rethink the history of the mid-nineteenth-century United States in continental, Atlantic, and hemispheric contexts. Extending empire to the Southwest borderlands, Pekka Hämäläinen and Brian Delay show how the Comanche created an empire in a contested borderland, and how Indian-Mexican violence and the depopulation of large swaths of northern Mexico provided racial and ideological justifications for U.S. conquest and the imposition in Texas of racial, chattel slavery. Turning from North American history to world history, Jane Burbank and Frederick Cooper's grand account of empires in world history treats the nineteenth-century United States as a great landed empire whose experiences in conquering large swaths of the North American continent involved important parallels with the Russian Empire. A composite union of diverse parts with often conflicting interests, the United States sought to address internal conflicts through near-constant conquest and expansion. Employing his own notions of empire and the imperial, Max Edling counters interpretations which normalize the United States' conquest of the core of the North American continent by deeming it "expansion." Edling instead argues that the United States operated as the last of the great, imperial European states. As Edling demonstrates, the establishment of a European-style, fiscal-military state enabled the United States to claim and establish sovereignty over an enormous swath of the North American continent. The United States became North America's most successful imperial power in the nineteenth century because it adopted the fiscal policies of North America's great eighteenth-century imperial power, Great Britain. These fiscal policies financed political institutions and economic developments that allowed the United States to deploy the accoutrements of state power—especially war and state-sanctioned violence—more extensively than any polity or group of people claiming sovereignty in contested regions. Collectively, these works demonstrate the value of analyzing mid-nineteenth-century United States history through the lens of empire, and as part of a larger series of struggles for sovereignty, supremacy, and mastery over the peoples and places of North America and its attendant regions, Central America and the Caribbean.[14]

Analyzing the Civil War era through empire involves more than the imposition of a historian's theoretical construct onto the past. Late antebellum politicians and voters understood themselves to be engaged in a third great imperial struggle in the Americas. In the seventeenth and eighteenth centuries, white colonists in British North America imagined themselves as part of an eschatological, imperial conflict that pitted Protestant liberty against Catholic despotism. American independence shifted popular and official understandings of these imperial struggles in important ways. By the early 1800s, United States citizens and policy-makers conceived of a series of imperial struggles that pitted virtuous white republicans of the New World against British monarchists and their alleged Black and Native American allies. In this new cosmological configuration, the monarchical British sought to undermine the incipient republics of the Americas by using as proxies people of African descent who were deemed incapable of self-government, and Native Americans who were allegedly unfit for civilization. Operating from this ideology, from the 1770s through the 1850s the federal government worked with state and local authorities to execute a near-ceaseless series of borderland skirmishes and conquests with Native Americans, non-Anglos, and runaway and free Blacks, all of whom were allegedly backed by British agents. Between independence and the last Seminole War, which did not end until 1858, the United States forced over three hundred peace and cession treaties on Native Americans, state or federal authorities engaged in numerous military actions against maroon settlements, both grand and petit, while diplomats forged treaties with a host of European powers with claims on the North American continent. In the eight decades separating independence and the Civil War, the United States used state-sanctioned war, violence by nonstate actors, and diplomacy to forge what became competing free labor and slave empires in an ever-expanding series of borderlands that, by the 1850s, extended to Mexico and Cuba, California and Kansas. In the years immediately preceding the Civil War, Northern and Southern whites had every intention of using state power to acquire more territory in the very near future, even if their aspirations were thrown into disarray by the Civil War.[15]

In taking a long view of the politics of slavery in the United States, it becomes clear that domestic political struggles over slavery were often entangled with larger imperial conflicts centering on questions of slavery and sovereignty in the many contested borderlands of North America. The weakness of state power in these contested regions invited challenges to slaveholder mastery and sovereignty from a variety of actors who had their own reasons for opposing the expansion of slavery, the United States, or both. In response, slaveholders demanded that state power be used to prop up their authority and to protect slave states from potential invasions and combined Native American and slave rebellions. These demands led to both political conflict in Washington and state intervention wherever slaveholder sovereignty seemed threatened. The resulting actions frequently resulted in conquest and expulsion, along with the expansion and consolidation of both state power and slaveholder mastery on the once-contested fringes of state power. For various reasons, from the 1790s until the 1840s, politicians managed to address borderland threats to slavery and mastery without irreconcilable sectional conflict at home.[16]

Having conquered and claimed sovereignty over the core of the North American continent at mid-century, antebellum Americans confidently expected their territorial expansion to continue into the future and across the Western Hemisphere. As one Southern writer boasted in 1850, the United States had become a "vast empire" and could look to continued territorial acquisitions in the future.[17] But as sectional conflict intensified in the 1850s, Northern and Southern expansionists devised imperialist ideologies justifying their particular notions of race, labor, and government. At the same time, Southern whites and Democrats in the North increasingly projected onto the Republican Party the imperial and racial proclivities they once reserved for the British: Republicans allegedly incited slave rebellion, favored emancipation in borderland areas, and sought the settlement of free Blacks in the Caribbean in order to undermine slavery. Likewise, Republicans increasingly replaced the British with Southern whites and Northern Democrats as antagonists who favored aristocracy and pauper labor over free labor and democratic self-government in the broader Americas. They also increasingly used terms once reserved for Native Americans—savagery and barbarity—to describe their Southern foes. As a result, contemporaries frequently framed the sectional crises of the 1850s—disunion, and then civil war—as part of a broader imperial conflict that pitted free labor imperialists against proslavery imperialists. The language, ideologies, and practices of imperialism were ever-present in Civil War–era politics and culture, and many Americans were proud imperialists, including Northerners and Southerners, free Blacks and whites, Democrats and Republicans, Unionists and Confederates. For many contemporaries, the election of 1860 centered on geopolitical matters and the course of empire as much as domestic issues, while domestic issues concerning slavery were always informed by larger imperial and geopolitical considerations.

Southern proslavery imperialism arose, in part, as a response to growing hemispheric and transatlantic antislavery movements, and to the proliferation of active, free-soil borderlands in the regions surrounding the slave South. In 1842, Virginian Henry Wise called for the annexation of Texas and the conquest of Mexico to prevent slave flight and foreign invasion. With the conquest of northern Mexico, Wise expected that "the extension of slavery would not stop short of the Western Ocean," and that Southern slavery would be secured from the Atlantic to the Pacific. Wise's hopes for security went unrealized. Despite Texas annexation and victory in the U.S.-Mexico War, Southern slaveholders sensed that they were on the verge of becoming surrounded by potentially hostile powers, peoples, and free-soil borderlands. Slaveholders feared that these borderlands invited slave flight, foreign invasion (led by free Black soldiers, whether from the Caribbean or the North), slave rebellion, abolition, race war, and the subjugation of Southern whites. By the late 1850s, slaveholder expansionists responded to these threats by forging an aggressive, proslavery imperialism that sought "perfect security for slavery" through the establishment of slaveholder sovereignty in free-soil borderlands, whether through coerced annexation, by conquest, or by using state power to force slave state sovereignty onto border regions, including the free states of the North.[18]

The locations of the free-soil borderlands that threatened Southern slavery shifted and grew over the course of the 1850s, as did calls for further conquest. As part of the Compromise of 1850, the federal government created a separate New Mexico Territory out of Texas's western claims. Texas slaveholders objected to the creation of a free-soil borderland that invited foreign invasion, not just of Texas, but of the entire Mississippi Valley plantation complex. The paying off of Texas's debt was not worth the "security afforded by the extension of the South western frontier and with the greater security from approach by a foreign enemy of our great Southern Empire, and the ten millions of inhabitants now reposing in security on the broad valleys of the Mississippi."[19] The U.S.-Mexico War had been launched to impose slavery on Santa Fe and northern Mexico, not to give the region over to free soil and the problems that created for slaveholders from Texas to the Mississippi Valley.

To protect slavery in the Mississippi Valley plantation complex, slavery had to be secured in all of the United States' southern and western borderlands. A decade later, Texans' long-term fears of foreign invasion were replaced by short-term concerns about slave flight. In 1859, members of the Texas Democratic State Convention proposed "the occupation of Mexico by the United States in case of refusal to enter into a treaty of extradition of runaway slaves." Mexico must recognize and uphold U.S. and Texas law on slave flight, or the U.S. was obligated to occupy Mexico. As the election of 1860 neared, the acquisition of Mexico gained new urgency for Southern expansionists. The Knights of the Golden Circle justified their intended Southernization of northern Mexico by pointing to fears that a Republican-controlled federal government would instead acquire the region. "Since the North will only accept national domain as 'free territory,' ... the South should, by all means, prevent the acquisition of any territory in the South by the federal government." Mexico had to be acquired lest the Republicans do so first. The Knights proposed immediately establishing an independent state in northern Mexico. Once "Southernized," the region would then be added to the United States by treaty (as was the case with Texas), or it would become a constituent part of a separate Southern confederacy.[20]

In the 1850s the Caribbean also again became a dangerous borderland that had to be incorporated into a growing Southern empire for slavery. Proslavery imperialists favored Cuban annexation in part because of its lucrative plantation operations and large enslaved population. But fears of a foreign invasion being launched from an abolitionized Cuba also structured Southern imperialists' calls for annexation. The abolition of French slavery in the late 1840s created worries that Britain and France were pressuring Spain to do the same in Cuba. By the early 1850s, Southern defenders of slavery feared that Cuba would be abolitionized, followed by a British-sponsored organization of a "free negro empire" centered on Cuba, Jamaica, and Haiti. In response to filibustering expeditions and U.S. demands that Spain cede Cuba, the governor of Cuba allegedly threatened to "Africanize" the island: freeing and arming slaves to repel a U.S. invasion. Fears of "Africanization" made demands for Cuban annexation more pressing, as Southern whites feared that an expansive "Black empire" would lead to a European-sponsored invasion led by free Black Caribbean soldiers. When Spain appointed a new governor to Cuba, the urgency of annexing Cuba subsided, but the necessity of doing so did not. By 1855, Democrats sympathetic to Southern demands for Cuba warned once again that European powers would create a "confederated free negro empire" led by Haiti, Jamaica, and Cuba. As the election of 1860 neared, fears of French and Spanish interference waned but were replaced by concerns that a Republican-dominated government would work with Britain's "free negro empire" to abolitionize the Caribbean with an eye toward destroying slavery in the United States. Looming free labor and free Negro empires had to be outflanked by the establishment of a vast empire for slavery across the tropics.[21]

The proslavery Democratic imperialism that came into its own in the 1850s differed in its details from individual to individual, and various calculations entered into an individual's particular preferences regarding the shape, course, and creation of empire. Some foresaw a future where American slaveholders reigned over plantations in the Amazon basin. Others rested content with an empire consisting of a "Golden Circle": Mexico and the territories lining the Gulf of Mexico and the Caribbean. Some advocated for the immediate conquest of Cuba and portions of Mexico; others wanted Cuba now, northern Mexico later. Others still sought Central America, both for its cash crop-producing potential and for its key transportation routes between the Atlantic and the Pacific, Europe and East Asia. Irish and Southern nationalist John Mitchel exemplified the differences within proslavery imperialism. Mitchel joked that he was a "moderate." All he wished for was "a Dissolution of the Union—Revival of the African Trade-Mexico and the West India Islands—and establishment of a potent Southern Confederacy, based on slavery; that's all." He identified as a moderate, however, because "as for the conquest of the Northern States, I would defer that." Proslavery imperialists might have dickered over the details of empire, but they were largely in agreement that the North, the British, and free Blacks formed rival, hostile imperial powers in competition for supremacy in the Americas. They were equally confident that slaveholders would meet that challenge by creating a vast empire for slavery, whether by and within the Union, or through a separate Southern confederacy. The South's particular form of society, economy, and government, which placed whites in the role of governing Blacks, was superior and destined—by race, fortune, and Providence—to overtake the regions of America fit for cash crops and slave labor. Slaveholders might have been losing power and influence within the Union, but by their own measure they were growing stronger and more influential—indeed, indispensable—in the global economy and in the progressive march of Western civilization. Whether they would realize their imperial destiny within or outside of the Union made little difference to them by 1860.[22]

Southern imperialists accordingly framed the aftermath of the election of 1860 as part of a fundamental imperial struggle. The calendar had not yet turned to December before a Georgia newspaper predicted that "the wide boundaries of Southern Empire" would be expanded in the "next glorious war" that the new Southern confederacy would use to expand its borders. During the secession winter, newspapers took to referring to the United States as an "Abolition Empire," an epithet once reserved for the British in the Caribbean. Robert Toombs warned the Georgia legislature that Lincoln's election placed their state and their property in slaves under "the ban of the empire," necessitating disunion and the creation of a new "empire of the Western Continent" that would stand for centuries. Southern papers framed Confederate independence as either a struggle between competing empires, or as the first step toward "the rise of a great Southern Empire out of the ashes of a dissolved Union." The always belligerent *Charleston Mercury* compared the Confederacy to the Roman Empire and deemed the Gulf of Mexico and the Caribbean "the American Mediterranean," then promised the Confederacy would "extend their dominions far and wide" before fighting had even broken out. When disunion turned to war, a Virginia paper referred to "the present struggle for empire on this continent between thirty millions of people." A Georgia newspaper reporting on a battle in Virginia, wrote that "the God of Battles smiles upon the new republican Empire of the South!" while a Memphis paper deemed the Union "the LINCOLN empire." The purpose of independence was not simply to preserve slavery at home. Only an independent Southern confederacy could defend the South against aggressive Republican imperialists while projecting the South's superior systems of government, economics, and social organization abroad. The new Southern confederacy would obtain its independence soon enough; when it did, a glorious future awaited them in the "wide boundaries of Southern Empire."[23]

Northerners—Black and white—proved equally ardent imperialists. As early as 1854, Republicans contended that the immediate future promised an immense struggle between a Northern-based free-soil empire and the South's aspirations to create a "great slave empire" that included the states of the North.[24] Over the next six years, Republicans increasingly understood sectional conflicts over Kansas, California, and the trans-Mississippi West as inseparable from impending conflicts over Mexico, Cuba, the Caribbean, and Central America. For Republicans, sectional conflict centered on slaveholder efforts to establish a single sovereignty regarding race, slavery, and property rights in the present borders of the United States, in preparation for expected territorial conquests in Mexico, the Caribbean, and Central America. In the empire allegedly sought by slaveholders, the federal government would protect slaveholders' rights wherever and when-

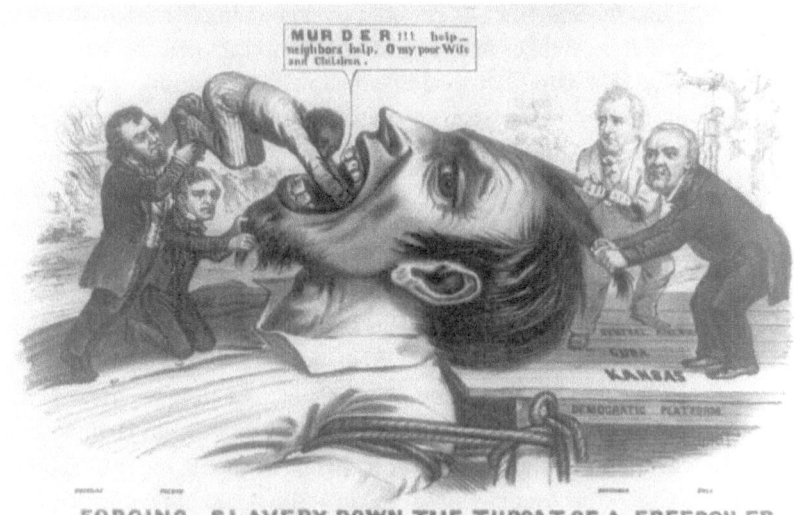

Figure 1. John L. Magee, "Forcing Slavery Down the Throat of a Freesoiler," Philadelphia, 1856. This widely reprinted lithograph from 1856 illustrates how Democrats and Republicans had tied domestic issues such as slavery in Kansas to larger imperial designs on Cuba and Central America.

ever they sought to exercise them, whether in Mexico or Massachusetts, Kansas or Cuba, California or Curaçao.[25]

Republicans joined contemporaneous fights over a territorial slave code and the rights of slaveholders in free states to a larger conflict over a looming empire for slavery. By the late 1850s, slaveholders claimed that the federal government was obligated to protect their property rights in the free states, in the western territories, and in territories to be acquired in the future. Enslavers held that slave state sovereignty followed both slaves and enslavers into free states and the territories. As Jefferson Davis remarked, "We will never have obtained all of our rights until the legislation of congress shall amply protect slave as it does all other property." Republicans feared that these novel notions would become constitutional law should the Democrats prevail in the election of 1860. Lincoln's warning that "we shall lie down pleasantly dreaming that the people of Missouri are on the verge of making their State free; and we shall awake to the reality, instead, that the Supreme Court has made Illinois a slave State" was more than hyperbole to contemporaries. Georgia Senator Robert Toombs's apocryphal post–*Dred*

Scott promise that the Supreme Court would soon grant him "the right to call the roll of his slaves from Bunker Hill" stoked Northern fears that the Slave Power was on the verge of making slavery a fully nationalized institution. Just as had happened with the *Dred Scott* case, Republicans and Southern Democrats alike expected the Supreme Court to issue a ruling favorable to slaveholders in the case of *Lemmon vs. the People of New York* if the Democrats won the 1860 elections. Both groups anticipated that the Slave Power–dominated Supreme Court would rule that slaveholders possessed a constitutionally protected natural right to exercise their property rights in slaves wherever the Constitution stood supreme.[26]

Debates over slaveholder property rights in the free states were not just about slavery in Illinois or New York; they were also pregnant with implications about slavery's future in the trans-Mississippi West, Mexico, Central America, the Caribbean, and even Brazil. Soon-to-be Republicans advanced this claim as early as 1854. In what became his standard speech while stumping for anti-Nebraska candidates across Pennsylvania in 1854, David Wilmot laid out a stark vision of a "vast slave empire" overtaking the Americas. Wilmot warned that the Kansas-Nebraska Act was part of a larger scheme by the "Slave Aristocracy" to "obtain another slice of Mexico, annex Cuba, revive the African Slave trade, restore slavery in St. Domingo, enter into an alliance with Brazil, and finally to abolish the Missouri Compromise and extend slavery into all of the territory of the nation." Similarly, while stumping for Republicans in New Hampshire in 1856, minister Eden Burroughs Foster warned that slaveholders sought to create a "universal empire to Slavery; to extend this iron rule from Northern lake to Southern gulf; from the hoarse roar of the Atlantic to the milder dashings of the Pacific." Two years later, the *New York Times* drew a direct link from the *Dred Scott* decision to Buchanan administration overtures for an alliance with Brazil based on "a great domestic institution, common to both countries, fixed and deeply rooted in their soil." At the 1860 Chicago Convention, David Wilmot once again warned that slaveholders sought the "nationalization of slavery" as the first step toward establishing "a great slave empire" across the Americas. By 1860 it had become received wisdom among Republicans that the future of slavery in places such as "New Mexico" was inseparable from Southern efforts at "making a slave empire to encroach on free territory, and swallow the Gulf and tropics." The sanctity of slaveholder property rights in places such as New York and New Mexico would determine slavery's status in the trans-Mississippi West; it would also determine the future of slavery and republican government in the Southern states, Mexico, the Caribbean, and South America. Republicans feared—and Democrats allegedly gloated—that slaveholders aimed to nationalize slavery within the existing United States while forging an empire for slavery abroad.[27]

Fears of a "vast empire for slavery" informed Republican positions during the secession winter of 1860–1861. A provision in the Crittenden Amendments required that the federal government recognize and protect slavery in all territories south of the 36°30′ line, including all territory "hereafter acquired." The amendment would have placed a territorial slave code in the Constitution, a Southern demand since the *Dred Scott* ruling. It would also open much of the trans-Mississippi West to slavery, while justifying Southern demands that a slave state be carved out of southern California. Republicans thus contended that the "Crittenden resolutions" stood as a blatant attempt "to constitutionalize the extension doctrine" so that slaveholders could create "an empire for slavery greater than that which already exists." Equally important, Democrats and Republicans agreed that this provision stood as an open invitation to acquire—by whatever means necessary—territory outside the boundaries of the United States. As Southern imperialist Robert Toombs acknowledged, the Crittenden amendments would give over all of the Americas, from 36°30′ "to the south pole," to Southern slaveholders. Recognizing Republican aspirations to empire, Toombs pointed out that the North was welcome to "the whole continent to the North pole." Republicans countered that if accepted, the amendment would "lay a broad and deep foundation of a slave empire, embracing the *whole* territory, present and prospective, of the United States." Republicans objected not to empire, but to slave empire.[28]

A looming "empire for slavery" informed Republican insistence on a complete prohibition on slavery's expansion, both within the present union and in any future territorial acquisitions. Abraham Lincoln warned fellow Illinois Republican Elihu Washburne that any compromise on expansion would lead "immediately" to "filibustering and extending slavery" outside the borders of the Union. He warned Pennsylvania congressman James Hale that if the Republicans yielded on the 36°30′ line, slaveholders would demand the conquest of new territory, "*ad libitum*. A year will not pass, till we shall have to take Cuba as a condition upon which they will stay in the Union." Writing to William Seward, Lincoln again tied compromise on expansion to "slave empire." "I am inflexible" on slavery's expansion, insisted Lincoln. To allow expansion absent a complete prohibition on slavery would simply "put us again on the high-road to a slave empire." New York Republican Roscoe Conkling best expressed Republican rationale tying a complete prohibition on slavery expansion to efforts to defeat southern aspirations to a hemispheric empire for slavery. Conkling warned that federal guarantees for slavery south of the 36°30' line "would amount to a perpetual covenant of war against every people, tribe, and State owning a foot of land between here and T[i]erra del Fuego" at the southern tip of South America. Conkling warned that the federal government would become "the armed missionary of slavery" should Republicans assent to Southern demands. Conkling recounted how slaveholders had used borderland quarrels to forge an empire for slavery on the core of the North American continent over the previous seventy years, and he warned that these would continue into the future. Guaranteed federal protections for slavery south of 36°30' promised that "eternal quarrels would be pecked across the frontier lines" of contested borderlands. Slaveholders would then cry "the Government must protect its citizens and demand indemnity for hostilities; and thus, for purposes of land-stealing and slave-planting, we should be launched upon a shoreless and starless sea of war and filibustering." Like other Republicans, Conkling foresaw a future of ceaseless "land-stealing and slave-planting" on the road to a hemispheric empire for slavery.[29]

The language, concerns, and outlook of Wilmot, Lincoln, and Conkling involved something more than what historians euphemistically name "the expansionist project of the U.S. government." This was the language and practice of empire, and Republicans imagined themselves to be engaged in an epic, imperial struggle with slaveholders for the future of republican government in the Americas. Republicans responded to Southern and Democratic imperialism by forging their own free-soil ideology that was rife with imperial overtones, as is evident in William Seward's speech on Kansas. "Free labor has at last apprehended its rights, its interests, its power, and its destiny," announced Seward. Free labor was both "organizing itself to assume the government of the Republic" and preparing for an "invasion." Seward envisioned a hemisphere-wide battle between free labor Republicans and slaveholding aristocrats in the borderlands where these groups found themselves in conflict. Seward promised his rivals that the North's free labor insurgency "will henceforth meet you boldly and resolutely here [in Washington]; it will meet you everywhere, in the Territories and out of them, wherever you may go to extend slavery. It has driven you back in California and in Kansas, it will invade you soon in Delaware, Maryland, Virginia, Missouri, and Texas. It will meet you in Arizona, in Central America, and even in Cuba." Seward's "expansion of the empire of free white men" would be realized through federal "intervention in favor of free labor and free States," whether in border states, or in external areas such as Mexico, Central America, and the Caribbean. For Republicans such as Seward, the political battles surrounding 1860 were both a struggle for control of the federal government and a conflict for the fate of slavery and freedom in the Americas. Whoever won control of the federal government would use state power to remake the United States and the Americas on the basis of free labor and republican government or slave labor and aristocracy.[30]

Republican visions of a free-soil, trans-Mississippi West were intimately bound up with notions of empire. Lincoln envisioned "a race of empire across" the continent to "the Pacific," pitting free society against slave society. Wisconsin Senator James Doolittle praised homesteaders colonizing the trans-Mississippi West using federally financed railroads as "more majestic and powerful than the grand army of Napoleon." Notions of a free labor empire manifested themselves in political songs. "That freedom which our fathers won, Their sons will ever dare maintain, Our empire 'neath the setting [i.e., western] sun," would "not be cursed with Slavery's chain," held one popular song from the 1860 Republican campaign. Another contended that while "WESTWARD the star of empire's way, And formeth Freedom's brightest ray; Slave-dealers do the light deplore, For *they* man's dearest rights ignore." Conversely, the North's "hardy sons, inured to toil," would "consecrate" the West's "virgin soil, To Freedom, and the rights of man, Slave-owners, only, hate the plan." Protected from slavery's expansion, a free labor empire would flourish in the trans-Mississippi West. "No unrequited lab'rer's toil, Shall curse our teeming virgin soil, But freemen shall homesteads subdue, And labor thus shall have its due." State power would pacify or remove Native Americans. State power would facilitate settlement and integration of the trans-Mississippi West into the Union with homestead acts and federally supported railroads. State power would "boldly and resolutely" forge a free labor empire from "Arizona" to "California and in Kansas."[31]

A free-soil West would also facilitate free labor's peaceful but inevitable conquest of the slave states. The promise of homesteads, railroads, and respect for white labor would draw non-slaveholding whites from the South to the West. Once in the free-soil West, Southern white emigrants would become evangelicals for the glories of free labor. In turn, they would serve as advocates of emancipation in the South, hastening abolition there while securing the sanctity of free labor in the West. Republicans differed over the details of emancipation in the South, but many agreed on a broad outline by which the federal government could constitutionally bring the present limits of the United States under the dominion of free white labor. Once in control of the federal government, Republicans would facilitate the abolition of slavery in the border states through a program of federally financed emancipation and colonization. As slavery fell in the border states, its demise would follow elsewhere. Republicans anticipated that non-slaveholding Southern whites, particularly in the border states, would support emancipation tied to colonization while becoming eager free labor advocates in the process. The abolition of slavery and the forced colonization of Southern Blacks would also open the former slave states to free white labor from Europe and capital from the North. Virginia would become like New York as free white labor and capital would pour into the Southern states. As William Seward promised, free labor "will invade you soon in Delaware, Maryland, Virginia, Missouri, and Texas."[32]

Republicans tied the peaceful, free labor conquest of the slave states to the creation of a racialized, free labor empire in the Caribbean and Central America. Federally financed emancipation and colonization would facilitate Republican desires to foster the growth of racially distinct, free labor republics in the climates that nature or Providence had created for particular races. Republicans accepted that non-Anglo-Americans possessed a natural right to the fruits of their labor and republican government. But at the same time, they held that republican self-government and free labor could be exercised equitably only in racially homogenous republics, located in the regions and climates set aside by Providence for particular races. Republicans also held that whites and Blacks could never live together as equals in a self-governing democracy; whether that was due to incorrigible white racism or inherent Black inferiority made no difference to Republicans. Finally, Republicans argued that nature and Providence had designated the "temperate zones"—in which Republicans included most of the American South—for whites, and that Black labor alone was suitable for the production of cash crops in the tropics. Frequently writing in providential terms, Republican colonizationists held that it was moral, progressive, providential, and an advancement of civilization to colonize freed Blacks in the tropics while reserving the present United States for whites. Historians have long treated colonization with contempt for eminently understandable reasons. Furthermore, historians remain wary of engaging with colonization because it almost always becomes entangled with questions regarding Abraham Lincoln's proclivities on race. Regardless of colonization's practicality, and despite widespread opposition from white and Black abolitionists, Republicans pointed to colonization whenever they spoke of emancipation, and they almost always framed both in terms of establishing Black republics in the tropics that would fall under the tutelage of the United States. Lincoln and other Republicans understood colonization as an imperial project.[33]

Emancipation and colonization were central to Republican visions of race and republicanism, free labor and empire in the Americas. Most Republicans deemed African Americans either unfit or unwelcome for citizenship in the United

States. Republicans nonetheless contended that emancipated slaves could serve as foot soldiers for a free labor republicanism that would colonize freedmen and women in the Caribbean and Central America. Free from the racial prejudices that marked everyday life in the United States, Blacks would prosper and thrive while demonstrating the superiority of free labor in producing cash crops. Freedmen and women would also strengthen republican government in the nascent republics of Central America while transforming Caribbean colonies into free labor republics. Republicans differed over where free labor, Black republics would be established, how numerous they would be, and to what extent they would be affiliated with the United States. One newspaper believed that former slaves would create a "great central negro empire in Hayti" that would then spread free labor and republican government to the Caribbean. Some included all or only parts of the Caribbean; some included Mexico, others Central America. Some included all of these places. Francis Blair Jr., for example, expected emancipation and colonization to produce "a dependency peopled by our 4,000,000 of freed blacks, whose superior intelligence would dominate all the races of the tropics, and bring them under our influence." Despite these differences, mainstream Republicans almost universally subscribed to colonization, and they understood colonization in terms of imperial competition in the broader Americas.[34]

Republicans added a definitive imperial element to their plans for emancipation and colonization; these free labor, Black republics would fall under the protection and influence of the United States. They would also serve as a counter to British designs in the Americas, and secure to the United States coveted transit routes across Central America and the Isthmus to the Pacific. Equally important, colonization would further surround the South with a "cordon of freedom," outflanking Southern efforts to establish or reestablish slavery in the Caribbean, Mexico, and Central America. The maritime free-soil borderlands secured in the Caribbean would place further pressure on Southern slaveholders to begin the process of emancipation. At the same time, the establishment of free labor Black republics in the Caribbean and Central America would end Southern imperialism and filibustering. Finally, Mexico would be free of meddling from Southern slaveholders, allowing it to stabilize as a free labor republic suitable for Spanish and Indian races.[35]

Republican concerns about empire were bound up with larger questions concerning economics and government. As Republicans understood matters, unfree labor—whether slavery, serfdom, or pauper labor—was natural to aristocratic regimes, as were massive, state-imposed systems of inequality. Whether in England's fields and factories, Russia's wheat steppes, or the South's cotton plantations, aristocrats relied on unfree labor and used state power to maintain their privileged places in society. As slaveholders undertook the process of disunion over the secession winter of 1860–1861, Republicans increasingly shared the conviction that slaveholders "longed for monarchy" and aimed for "a negro and cotton empire, with slavery for its basis." Indeed, it became something like conventional wisdom among Republicans that the "Military Adventurers of the new Confederacy" went for secession so that they could create a *"great Slave Empire"* that would "take in Mexico, Central America, and the West India Islands." Conversely, in a democratic, constitutional republic, free labor was the ideal if not always the norm. The people used government to enact policies fostering a rough equality of condition while favoring labor and the small-scale ownership of productive property over land engrossment and unfree labor. Republicans understood the Civil War in no small part as a conflict over what form of production would predominate in the Americas. Slaveholders stood for land and capital engrossment by the few, and slave and pauper labor for the many; unchecked, they would establish a "negro oligarchy extending all the way to Central America." Free labor Republicans, in contrast, sought an equitable distribution of land and capital, worked by free labor, with families striving for property ownership, competency, and independence. The "slaveocracy" went for disunion out of an "anxious desire to disintegrate and ruin the north." Aristocratic slaveholders had done so because they recognized that "the free states were advancing so fast in the march of improvement that they must necessarily dwarf and overthrow the slave empire" with a free labor empire of their own.[36]

Fears of an empire for slavery influenced Republican determination to prevent the establishment of an independent Southern confederacy through war. Republicans expected an independent confederacy to assemble a "southern army of conquest." That army would create a "vast slave empire in the southern portion of this continent," running from the Potomac, the Ohio, and the 36°30′ line in the West, all the way to South America. The "cardinal law of the slave empire" would result in "an hereditary Senate and Executive," "armed despotism" for the peoples of the Americas, and slavery for whites and Blacks alike. Secession and disunion had to be stopped to preserve free labor and republican government within the existing union and in the broader Americas.[37]

Many voters and politicians understood the sectional conflicts that culminated in civil war as part of a larger contest centering on what kind of nation the United States would be, and what kind of empire it would forge in the Americas. Many Republicans and Democrats, Northerners and Southerners, framed the political battles surrounding 1860 as a struggle for control of the federal government, the outcome of which would determine the fate of slavery, free labor, and republican government in the Americas. The United States had spent the seven decades between independence and the 1850s forging an empire on the core of the North American continent. In the years immediately preceding the Civil War, Americans—white and Black, Northerners and Southerners, Democrats and Republicans—had every intention of extending that empire in the very near future, even if their aspirations were thrown into disarray by the Civil War. Nonetheless, the would-be imperialists who went to war in 1861 understood well their nation's place in the larger imperial history of nineteenth-century North America, just as they hoped to determine its imperial future.

When situated in a continental and hemispheric context, the United States Civil War emerges as another chapter—albeit one of singular significance—in a larger saga of autonomy, sovereignty, and supremacy that involved various groups, states, and would-be imperial powers. Alan Taylor has demonstrated that the American Revolution was part of a larger rupture in the imperial history of North America and the Caribbean. In the same vein, recent works on geopolitical conflicts and empire in nineteenth-century North America suggest that the geopolitics of competing empires in North America ended or shifted dramatically, not in 1804 or 1815, but during the extended North American crisis of 1861 through 1876. Disunion and Civil War, then, were not only defining moments for the United States as a nation-state; they were also defining moments in a larger North American history defined by imperial conflicts involving a myriad of peoples seeking to gain or maintain sovereignty for themselves and dominion over others.[38]

Notes

1. "The Citizens of the Southern States," *Daily Louisville Democrat*, September 2, 1860; "Revival of the Slave Trade, No. IX," *Edgefield* (SC) *Advertiser*, March 23, 1859. Southern Whig anti-expansionists had largely accepted the inevitability of expansion by the 1850s. See, for example, *Cong. Globe*, 35th Cong., 2nd sess., 1344–1355. For the borderland conflicts stemming from the flight of enslaved men and women from the United States to Mexico that drove calls for conquest, see Alice L. Baumgartner's contribution to this volume and her book *South to Freedom: Runaway Slaves to Mexico and the Road to the Civil War* (New York: Basic Books, 2020).

2. "Knights of the Golden Circle! A Southern Confederacy! Mexico to Be Added!" *Daily Louisville Democrat*, September 2, 1860; *Memphis Daily Avalanche*, April 2, 1860; "The Knights of the Golden Circle . . . ," *New York Herald*, April 5, 1860.

3. Lowell (MA) *Daily Citizen and News*, July 18, 1860; *Cincinnati Daily Commercial*, March 30, 1860; April 6, 1860; "Modern Chivalry—A Manifesto," *New York Daily Tribune*, July 26, 1860.

4. *The National Divergence and Return: Speech of William H. Seward, at Detroit, September 4, 1860* (Albany: Weed, Parsons, 1860), 4; William Rounseville Alger, *The Genius and Posture of America: An Oration Delivered Before the Citizens of Boston, July 4, 1857* (Boston: Daily Bee, 1857), 33. For older, Northern expectations of a hemispheric, free labor union that included Mexico and Canada, see, for example, "Texas; Sea Empire," *Newburyport* (MA) *Herald*, August 5, 1836.

5. For Southern white understandings of their section as modern, cosmopolitan, at the forefront of government and economics, and therefore most worthy of expansion, see Matthew Karp, *This Vast Southern Empire: Slaveholders at the Helm of American Foreign Policy* (Cambridge, MA: Harvard University Press, 2016); Edward E. Baptist, *The Half Has Never Been Told: Slavery and the Making of American Capitalism* (New York: Basic Books, 2014); Brian Schoen, *The Fragile Fabric of Union: Cotton, Federal Politics, and the Global Origins of the Civil War* (Baltimore: Johns Hopkins University Press, 2009); Walter Johnson, *River of Dark Dreams: Slavery and Empire in the Cotton Kingdom* (Cambridge, MA: Harvard University Press, 2013); L. Diane Barnes, Brian Schoen, and Frank Towers, eds., *The Old South's Modern Worlds: Slavery, Region, and Nation in the Age of Progress* (New York: Oxford University Press, 2011). For Republican beliefs that free-labor republicanism represented the pinnacle of republican society see James L. Huston, *The British Gentry, the Southern Planter, and the Northern Family Farmer: Agriculture and Sectional Antagonism in North America* (Baton Rouge: Louisiana State University Press, 2015); Marc Egnal, *Clash of Extremes: The Economic Origins of the Civil War* (New York: Hill and Wang, 2009). For Republican and international understandings of the Civil War as a conflict between democratic-republicanism and monarchy, slave labor and free labor, popular and hereditary sovereignty, see Don H. Doyle, *The Cause of All Nations: An International History of the American Civil War* (New York: Basic Books, 2015); Gregory P. Downs, *The Second American Revolution: The Civil War–Era Struggle over Cuba and the Rebirth of the American Republic* (Chapel Hill: University of North Carolina Press, 2019).

6. For three recent works that analyze the late antebellum period as part of a larger imperial conflict, see Karp, *Vast Southern Empire*; Kevin Waite, "Jefferson Davis and Proslavery Visions of Empire in the Far West," *Journal of the Civil War Era* 6, no. 4 (2016): 536–565; Robert E. May, "The Irony of Confederate Diplomacy: Visions of Empire, the Monroe Doctrine, and the Quest for Nationhood," *Journal of Southern History* 83, no. 1 (2017): 69–106. Though all three works are valuable in understanding the Civil War as a larger imperial conflict, Karp too neatly separates domestic and foreign issues for U.S. slaveholders while May and Waite overlook the rival, dialectic imperialism that pitted Republicans against Democrats.

7. Jay Sexton, "Steam Transport, Sovereignty, and Empire in North America, circa 1850–1885," *Journal of the Civil War Era* 7, no. 4 (2017): 622; Paul A. Kramer, "Power and Connection: Imperial Histories of the United States in the World," *American Historical Review* 116, no. 5 (2011): 1349.

8. Kramer, "Power and Connection."

9. For transnational works that employ empire to varying degrees, see Amy S. Greenberg, *Manifest Manhood and the Antebellum American Empire* (New York: Cam-

bridge University Press, 2005); Heather Cox Richardson, *West from Appomattox: The Reconstruction of America after the Civil War* (New Haven, CT: Yale University Press, 2007); Daniel Walker Howe, *What Hath God Wrought: The Transformation of America, 1815–1848* (New York: Oxford University Press, 2007), especially 701–705; Matthew Pratt Guterl, *American Mediterranean: Southern Slaveholders in the Age of Emancipation* (Cambridge, MA: Harvard University Press, 2008); Edward B. Rugemer, *The Problem of Emancipation: The Caribbean Roots of the American Civil War* (Baton Rouge: Louisiana State University Press, 2008); Patrick J. Kelly, "The North American Crisis of the 1860s," *Journal of the Civil War Era* 2, no. 3 (2012): 337–368; Gale L. Kenny, "Manliness and Manifest Racial Destiny: Jamaica and African American Emigration in the 1850s," *Journal of the Civil War Era* 2, no. 2 (2012): 151–178; Steven Hahn, "Slave Emancipation, Indian Peoples, and the Projects of a New American Nation-State," *Journal of the Civil War Era* 3, no. 3 (2013): 307–330; Robert E. May, *Slavery, Race, and Conquest in the Tropics: Lincoln, Douglas, and the Future of Latin America* (New York: Cambridge University Press, 2013); Adam Arenson and Andrew R. Graybill, eds., *Civil War Wests: Testing the Limits of the United States* (Oakland: University of California Press, 2015); Rachel St. John, "The Unpredictable America of William Gwin: Expansion, Secession, and the Unstable Borders of Nineteenth-Century North America," *Journal of the Civil War Era* 6, no. 2 (2016): 56–84; Johnson, *River of Dark Dreams*. Robert E. May's seminal *The Southern Dream of a Caribbean Empire, 1854–1861* (Baton Rouge: Louisiana State University Press, 1973) was long neglected by Civil War–era historians, his subjects and arguments treated as curiosities and footnotes.

10. St. John, "The Unpredictable America of William Gwin," 57.

11. Hahn, "Projects of a New American Nation-State," 309.

12. Baptist, *The Half Has Never Been Told*.

13. Jeremy Adelman and Stephen Aron, "From Borderlands to Borders: Empires, Nation-States, and the Peoples in Between in North American History," *American Historical Review* 104, no. 3 (1999): 814–841; Kathleen DuVal, *The Native Ground: Indians and Colonists in the Heart of the Continent* (Philadelphia: University of Pennsylvania Press, 2006); François Furstenberg, "The Significance of the Trans-Appalachian Frontier in Atlantic History," *American Historical Review* 113, no. 3 (2008): 647–677; John Craig Hammond, "Slavery, Settlement, and Empire: The Expansion and Growth of Slavery in the Interior of the North American Continent, 1770–1820," *Journal of the Early Republic* 32, no. 2 (2012): 175–206; John Craig Hammond, "Slavery, Sovereignty, and Empires: North American Borderlands and the American Civil War, 1660–1860," *Journal of the Civil War Era* 4, no. 2 (2014): 264–298; Alan Taylor, *American Revolutions: A Continental History, 1750–1804* (New York: Norton, 2016); Baumgartner, *South to Freedom*; Arenson and Graybill, eds., *Civil War Wests*; Hahn, "Projects of a New American Nation-State."

14. Pekka Hämäläinen, *The Comanche Empire* (New Haven, CT: Yale University Press, 2008); Brian DeLay, *War of a Thousand Deserts: Indian Raids and the U.S.-Mexican War* (New Haven, CT: Yale University Press, 2008); Jane Burbank and Frederick Cooper, *Empires in World History: Power and the Politics of Difference* (Princeton, NJ: Princeton University Press, 2010); Max M. Edling, *A Hercules in the Cradle: War, Money, and the American State, 1783–1867* (Chicago: University of Chicago Press, 2014). See also William

Earl Weeks, *New Cambridge History of American Foreign Relations*, vol. 1: *Dimensions of the Early American Empire, 1754–1865* (New York: Cambridge University Press, 2013), 210–272; Jay Sexton, *The Monroe Doctrine: Empire and Nation in Nineteenth-Century America* (New York: Hill and Wang, 2011); Pekka Hämäläinen, "Reconstructing the Great Plains: The Long Struggle for Sovereignty and Dominance in the Heart of the Continent," *Journal of the Civil War Era* 6, no. 4 (2016): 481–509; Maria Angela Diaz, "To Conquer the Coast: Pensacola, the Gulf of Mexico, and the Construction of American Imperialism, 1820–1848," *Florida Historical Quarterly* 95, no. 1 (2016): 1–25.

15. Matthew J. Clavin, *The Battle of Negro Fort: The Rise and Fall of a Fugitive Slave Community* (New York: New York University Press, 2019); Paul D. Naish, *Slavery and Silence: Latin America and the U.S. Slave Debate* (Philadelphia: University of Pennsylvania Press, 2017); Caitlin Fitz, *Our Sister Republics: The United States in an Age of American Revolutions* (New York: Norton, 2016); Robert G. Parkinson, *The Common Cause: Creating Race and Nation in the American Revolution* (Chapel Hill: University of North Carolina Press, 2016); Sam W. Haynes, *Unfinished Revolution: The Early American Republic in a British World* (Charlottesville: University of Virginia Press, 2010); Taylor, *American Revolutions*; Karp, *Vast Southern Empire*; Edling, *A Hercules in the Cradle*; Hammond, "Slavery, Sovereignty, and Empires."

16. Clavin, *Battle of Negro Fort*; Karp, *Vast Southern Empire*; Baumgartner, *South to Freedom*; Hammond, "Slavery, Sovereignty, and Empires."

17. "Our Foreign Policy," *Southern Literary Messenger*, January 1, 1850, 1.

18. *National Intelligencer*, April 14, 1842; John Randolph Tucker, "The Great Issue: Our Relations to it," *Southern Literary Messenger*, March 1861, 168. Historians long maintained that expansion sprang from the internal contradictions of slavery's political economy. In its classic form, see Eugene Genovese, *The Political Economy of Slavery: Studies in the Economy and Society of the Slave South* (New York: Random House, 1965). More recently, Johnson, *River of Dark Dreams* and Baptist, *The Half Has Never Been Told* argue that slave-labor capitalism created contradictions and crisis that slaveholders sought to address through expansion. While I grant these points, Southern mania for empire sprung from fears that they were becoming surrounded by an array of abolitionists, backed by state power. For Southern fears of being surrounded by a "cordon of freedom" to the North and West that would force the South to abolish slavery or face invasion and rebellion, see James Oakes, *The Scorpion's Sting: Antislavery and the Coming of the Civil War* (New York: Norton, 2014). For fears of being surrounded by maritime free labor borderlands that invited flight to, and invasion by, a British-organized force of free Blacks from the Caribbean see Karp, *Vast Southern Empire*. For the ways that hostile borderlands drove the violent expansion of slave societies in the Americas since the 1660s, see Hammond, "Slavery, Sovereignty, and Empires."

19. "Santa Fe Meeting," *Democratic Telegraph and Texas Register* (Houston), July 18, 1850.

20. "Sketch of the Proceedings of the Democratic State Convention," *State Gazette* (Austin), May 14, 1859; "Knights of the Golden Circle," *New York Herald*, April 5, 1860; "Knights of the Golden Circle!" *Daily Louisville Democrat*, September 2, 1860. For conflicts along the Texas-Mexican border, see Baumgartner, *South to Freedom*.

21. "General Quitman's Letter," *Woodville* (MS) *Republican*, May 13, 1851; "St. Domingo and Cuba," *Daily Picayune* (New Orleans), November 14, 1852; "London Times and the Cuban Slave Trade," *New York Herald*, September 7, 1853; "Message of Gov. Hebert," *Mississippi Free Trader* (Natchez), January 31, 1854; "Cuba: Its Africanization," *New York Herald*, April 3, 1855; "Division of California," *Semi-Weekly Mississippian*, May 23, 1859. For additional examples of fears that an abolitionized Cuba threatened the South with invasion, see, for example, *New Orleans Courier*, November 26, 1854, and *Richmond Enquirer*, May 9, 1854, and May 16, 1854. For Southern claims that the North formed a free labor empire similar to the British empire, see, for example, Edward B. Bryan, *Letters to the Southern People Concerning . . . the African Slave Trade* (Charleston, SC, 1858), 58, 61. For long-standing Southern claims that Britain was forming an essentially emancipationist empire, see Karp, *Vast Southern Empire*. For desires to conquer Cuba and its relationship to Mexican annexation, see Downs, *Second American Revolution*, especially 55–93.

22. "All Sorts of Items," *Weekly Telegraph* (Houston), May 12, 1858. For Southern white and Democratic claims to an expansive empire for slavery, along with differences over the precise location of a Southern empire, the purposes it would serve, and how it would be obtained, see, for example, "Destiny of the Slave States," *DeBow's Review*, September 1854, 280; "A Journey in Central America, By a Virginian," *Alexandria* (VA) *Gazette*, March 28, 1856; "Southern Thought Again," *DeBow's Review*, November 1857, 450; Albert Gallatin Brown, "Speech Delivered at Hazelhurst . . . Sept. 11, 1858," in *Speeches, Messages and Other Writings of the Hon. Albert G. Brown . . .* (Philadelphia: James B. Smith, 1859), 594; Jefferson Davis, "Speech at State Fair at Augusta, Me," *Speeches, Summer of 1858 . . .* (Baltimore: John Murphy and Co., 1859), 28; "Revival of the Slave Trade, No. IX," *Edgefield* (SC) *Advertiser*, March 23, 1859; "Division of California," *Semi-Weekly Mississippian*, May 23, 1859; Edward A. Pollard, *Black Diamonds Gathered in the Darkey Homes of the South* (New York, 1859), 107–112; "Popular Fallacies Corrected," *San Antonio Ledger and Texan*, April 28, 1860; "The Citizens of the Southern States," *Daily Louisville Democrat*, September 2, 1860; *Proceedings of the Conventions at Charleston and Baltimore* (Washington, 1860), 49, 104; "Virginia—Past, Present, and Future," (Augusta, GA) *Daily Constitutionalist*, March 9, 1861; John Randolph Tucker, "The Great Issue: Our Relations to It," *Southern Literary Messenger*, March, 1861, 161–188; *Address of Hon. John S. Preston, Commissioner from South Carolina, To the Convention of Virginia, February 19, 1861* (Columbia, SC, 1861). For Southern fears of invasion from white Northerners, see Jon Grinspan, "'Young Men for War': The Wide Awakes and Lincoln's 1860 Presidential Campaign," *Journal of American History* 96, no. 2 (2009): 357–378. For the essential unity of Southern elites on the need for an aggressive proslavery imperialism, see Karp, *Vast Southern Empire*.

23. "The Three Ideas," *Daily Constitutionalist* (Augusta, GA), November 24, 1860; "Our Washington Correspondence," *Charleston Mercury*, February 4, 1861, and February 14, 1861; "Our Richmond Correspondence," *Charleston Mercury*, April 26, 1861; *Speech of Hon. Robert Toombs: On the Crisis . . .* (Washington, DC: Lemuel Towers, 1860), 13, 15; "Our Domestic and Foreign Relations," *DeBow's Review*, 6 (September 1861), 287; "Grand Military Review," *Standard Saturday* (Clarksville, TX), February 23, 1861; "Our Washington Correspondence," *Charleston Mercury*, February 26, 1861; *Daily*

Express (Petersburg, VA), August 19, 1861; *Savannah Daily Morning News*, July 31, 1861; "No Time for Red-Tape and Diplomacy," *Memphis Daily Appeal*, September 13, 1861.

24. John Hale, Hiram Barney, and John Jay, *Free Democratic Address to the People of the State of New York* (New York, 1854); James A. Hamilton, *Fremont: The Conservative Candidate* . . . (n.p., 1856); "Cuba Annexation—Southern Plans of Empire," *New York Daily Times*, May 19, 1854.

25. "Address of the Republican Convention at Pittsburgh . . .," *New York Daily Times*, March 1, 1856; Speech of William H. Seward, *Congressional Globe,* 35th Cong., 1st sess., 945; "Speech of Horace Greeley at Auburn, California, August 6," *New York Daily Tribune*, September 4, 1859; "Inaugural Address of William Dennison," *Ashtabula Weekly Telegraph* (Ohio), January 14, 1860; "'The Plan of Mr. Jefferson Davis' From the Spectator," (Boston) *Littel's Living Age* 3rd ser., vol. 13 (April 1861), 241–243; Cassius M. Clay to Abraham Lincoln, February 6, 1861, Abraham Lincoln Papers, Library of Congress, Washington, DC (hereinafter cited as ALP); "The Progress of the War," *Douglass' Monthly*, September 1861.

26. "Speech at Jackson, May 29, 1857," in *The Papers of Jefferson Davis*, 15 vols., ed. Lynda Lasswell Crist and Mary Seaton Dix (Baton Rouge: Louisiana State University Press, 1971–2015), 6:120; "Speech at Springfield, Illinois," June 16, 1858, in *The Collected Works of Abraham Lincoln*, 8 vols., ed. Roy Prentice Basler (New Brunswick, NJ: Rutgers University Press, 1953) (hereafter *CWAL*), 2:463; "A Solemn Thing," *Chicago Tribune*, February 9, 1861. See also "The Political Campaign Opened," *Daily Cleveland Herald*, August 20, 1859; "The Lemmon Slave Case," *Semi-Weekly Mississippian* (Jackson), May 4, 1860; "The Lemmon Case—Proposed Remedy," *Charleston Mercury*, March 26, 1859; "The Lemmon Slave Case," *Daily Exchange* (Baltimore), January 30, 1860; "The Lemmon Case," *Lowell* (MA) *Daily Citizen*, January 27, 1860; "The Lemmon Slave Case—Its Final Adjudication in This State," *New York Herald*, January 26, 1860; "New York at Bar," *New York Daily Tribune*, December 24, 1860; Sarah L. H. Gronningsater, "'On Behalf of His Race and the Lemmon Slaves': Louis Napoleon, Northern Black Legal Culture, and the Politics of Sectional Crisis," *Journal of the Civil War Era* 7, no. 2 (2017): 206–241.

27. "Northern Pennsylvania—David Wilmot," *Pittsburgh Gazette*, July 13, 1854; "Hon. David Wilmot's Letter . . .," *Agitator* (Wellsboro, PA), August 17, 1854; Eden Burroughs Foster, *A North-side View of Slavery: A Sermon on the Crime against Freedom, in Kansas and Washington* . . . (Concord, NH: Jones & Cogswell, 1856), 37; "The Dred Scott Decision in Brazil," *New York Times*, February 16, 1858; "The Chicago Convention," *Cincinnati Daily Commercial*, May 17, 1860; "The Ruin of the Democratic Party," *Daily Missouri Democrat* (St. Louis), August 29, 1860; Speech of Senator Wigfall, *Cong. Globe,* 36th Cong., 2nd sess., 669.

28. "A Solemn Thing," *Chicago Tribune*, February 9, 1861; *Congressional Globe*, 36th Cong., 2nd sess., 335; "The Missouri Commissioners," *National Republican* (Washington, DC), February 8, 1861.

29. Lincoln to Elihu B. Washburne, December 13, 1860, *CWAL*, 4:151; Lincoln to James T. Hale, January 11, 1861, ALP; Lincoln to Seward, February 1, 1861, *CWAL*, 4:183; *Congressional Globe*, 36th Cong., 2nd sess., 651.

30. William H. Seward, *Freedom in Kansas . . . March 3, 1858* (Washington, DC, 1858), 13–14. For similar themes, see "God in History," *Chicago Tribune*, November 13, 1860. For growing militarism within the Republican Party, see Grinspan, "Young Men for War."

31. "Speech at Edwardsville, September 11, 1858," *CWAL*, 4:92; *Congressional Globe*, 36th Cong., 1st sess., 1631; "The Chicago Convention," *The Campaign of 1860: Republican Songs for the People . . .* (Boston: Thayer & Eldredge, 1860), 37; "The Gallant Sun of the West," and "The National Hurrah," in *Wide-Awake Vocalist; Or, Rail Splitters' Song Book* (New York: E. A. Dagget, 1860), 8–9; Seward, *Freedom in Kansas*, 14. For the importance of railroads as tools of asserting sovereignty over contested territory, see Hämäläinen, "Reconstructing the Great Plains"; Sexton, "Steam Transport, Sovereignty, and Empire."

32. Seward, *Freedom in Kansas*, 14. The most detailed and widely read plans for emancipation and removal are found in Hinton Rowan Helper, *The Impending Crisis of the South: How to Meet it* (New York: Burdick Brothers, 1857); Francis Blair Jr., *The Destiny of the Races of This Continent: An Address Delivered before the Mercantile Library Association of Boston . . .* (Washington, DC, 1859); Blair, *Colonization and Commerce: An Address before the Young Men's Mercantile Library Association of Cincinnati . . .* (n.p., 1859); Speech of Wisconsin Senator James Rood Doolittle, *Congressional Globe*, 36th Cong., 1st sess., 1631–1635; James Redpath, *A Guide to Hayti* (Boston, 1861). For Republican plans to force emancipation and colonization on the border states, see James Oakes, *Freedom National: The Destruction of Slavery in the United States, 1861–1865* (New York: Norton, 2013); Oakes, *Scorpion's Sting*.

33. Blair, *Destiny of the Races*; Blair, *Colonization and Commerce*; Redpath, *Guide to Hayti*; Helper, *Impending Crisis*; Seward, *Freedom in Kansas*; *Congressional Globe*, 36th Cong., 1st sess., 1631–1635. For Black and white support for various Republican colonization schemes, see Kate Masur, "The African American Delegation to Abraham Lincoln: A Reappraisal," *Civil War History* 56, no. 2 (2010): 117–144; Michael J. Douma, "The Lincoln Administration's Negotiations to Colonize African Americans in Dutch Suriname," *Civil War History* 61, no. 2 (2015): 111–137. As these works demonstrate, the Lincoln administration and Congressional Republicans aggressively sought agreements to colonize contrabands and emancipated slaves. For Civil War colonization efforts, see *Report on Colonization and Emigration, made to the Secretary of the Interior* (Washington, DC: Government Printing Office, 1862). For two recent attempts to address rather than dismiss Lincoln's and Republicans' fascination with colonization in the tropics, see Oakes, *Freedom National*, 272–282, 305–315; May, *Slavery, Race, and Conquest in the Tropics*, 230–276.

34. "Domestic," *The Independent*, June 6, 1861; Blair, *Destiny of the Races*, 24. For the various places expected to become part of an expanding U.S. empire peopled by emancipated slaves, see also John Sherman, *The Republican Party—its history and policy: speech . . . at the Cooper Institute, . . . New York, April 13, 1860* (n.p., 1860), 7; Blair, *Colonization and Commerce*; Redpath, *Guide to Hayti*; Helper, *Impending Crisis*; Seward, *Freedom in Kansas*.

35. For the metaphor of a "cordon of freedom," see Oakes, *Scorpion's Sting*. For uses of the "cordon" metaphor, see, for example, Blair, *Destiny of the Races*, 11; Speech of

Wisconsin Senator James Rood Doolittle, *Congressional Globe*, 36th Cong., 1st sess., 1631–1635; "Inaugural Address of William Dennison," *Ashtabula Weekly Telegraph*, January 14, 1860; Samuel T. Glover to Abraham Lincoln, September 29, 1861, ALP; "New Mexico and Old Mexico," *Chicago Tribune*, March 22, 1861. For Republican designs on the "tropics," see May, *Slavery, Race, and Conquest in the Tropics*.

36. Worthington G. Snethen to Abraham Lincoln, December 21, 1860, ALP; "The Aims of Secession," *New York Times*, February 7, 1861; "Pre-Ordained Disunion," *Chicago Tribune*, November 21, 1860; "New Mexico and Old Mexico," *Chicago Tribune*, March 22, 1861; "Why the Nation Refuses to Die," *North American and United States Gazette* (Philadelphia), October 4, 1862; Huston, *British Gentry, the Southern Planter*.

37. "Setting a Watch on the Filibusters," *New York Evening Post*, March 29, 1861; E. W. Reynolds, *The True story of the Barons of the South; or, The rationale of the American Conflict* (Boston: Walker, Wise and Company, 1862), 179. For understandings of the election of 1860, disunion, and war as a contest between the aristocratic advocates of a "great slave empire" and popular republican government, based on free labor, see, for example, Henry Jarvis Raymond to William Yowndes Yancey, December 10, 1860, in Henry Jarvis Raymond, *Disunion and Slavery. A Series of Letters to Hon. W. L. Yancey, of Alabama* (New York, 1861), 20–22; "Strong Language for the Union," *New York Evening Post*, January 10, 1861; "The Great Conspiracy," *New York Times*, February 5, 1861; "The Aims of Secession," *New York Times*, February 7, 1861; "For the Farmers," *Vermont Journal* (Windsor), June 1, 1861; "What is Peaceable Disunion?," *New York Times*, July 4, 1861; "What Would Peace Cost Us," *New York Evening Post*, September 25, 1861; Henry O'Reilly, *The Great Questions of the Times, . . . the Slaveholders' Rebellion Against Democratic Institutions . . .* (New York: C. S. Westcott, 1862), 16–22.

38. Patrick Rael, *Eighty-Eight Years: The Long Death of Slavery in the United States, 1777–1865* (Athens: University of Georgia Press, 2015); Taylor, *American Revolutions*; Edling, *A Hercules in the Cradle*; Kelly, "The North American Crisis of the 1860s"; Hammond, "Slavery, Sovereignty, and Empires."

3

Walker to Riel

State Consolidation on the Margins of Empire

Amy S. Greenberg

William Walker and Louis Riel were strikingly different figures: one an American adventurer, the other a Francophone Métis freedom fighter. They met their deaths twenty-five years and over two-thousand miles apart, both engaged in futile struggles to negotiate the shifting map of North American national sovereignty. Walker, a Tennessee-born San Francisco newspaper editor, renounced his U.S. citizenship after conquering Nicaragua in 1856. Deposed from power in 1857, he returned to a hero's welcome in the United States during a fund-raising tour, as he planned a return to the country he now considered his home. In 1860 he met his death in front of a Honduran firing squad after being captured by British authorities. Although he professed himself a Nicaraguan, American supporters assumed his ultimate goal was to annex Nicaragua to the United States.[1]

Louis Riel was born into a First Nations and Métis community in the Red River area of what was then known as Rupert's Land, a territory administered by the Hudson's Bay Company. After studying for both the priesthood and the law in Montreal, Riel returned to his homeland and led a resistance movement against the Canadian government as it attempted to assert sovereignty over Rupert's Land and its Métis inhabitants. Appointed president of the provisional government of Assiniboia during the final month of 1869, Riel helped negotiate the entrance of Manitoba into the Canadian Confederation, but was banned from Canada and forced into exile in the Dakota Territory. Repeatedly elected to the Canadian House of Commons while living with a Métis community in American territory, Riel was unable to assume office. Through a series of religious visions he became convinced he was the divinely chosen leader of the Métis people. He renounced his Canadian citizenship and became a U.S. citizen in 1883, but returned to Manitoba to fight for the rights of Métis and First Nations peoples. He led a second rebellion against the Canadian government in the Northwest Territories in 1885. Tried and convicted of treason, he was executed that same year.[2]

The twinned figures of Walker and Riel highlight the contours of empire and nation building in nineteenth-century North America. Shadowy figures just outside the normal chronological and narratival margins of the U.S. Civil War, Riel and Walker could be viewed as racial opposites, one fighting for white sovereignty in the Isthmus, the other for First Nation autonomy within a white confederacy he helped create. The "Gray-eyed Man of Destiny" was represented in the U.S. press as a frontier race hero: proof to those who desperately desired evidence of the superiority of American Anglo-Saxonism. As the *New York Herald* proclaimed at the time of Walker's conquest of Nicaragua, "There will be no lack of Anglo-Saxon volunteers for Walker as long as, with a few hundred such men, he can vanquish by thousands his deteriorated mixed Spanish and Indian enemies."[3]

The Métis Riel, in contrast, became the key figure in the emergence of a multiethnic Canadian identity, "the emblem of 'in-between-ness' who expresses a most basic fact of the Canadian experience: that of cultural hybridity."[4] In appearance and action he troubled racial categories rather than reified them. "An Indian speaking with the solemn gravity of his race looks right manful enough, as with moose-clad leg his mocassined [sic] feet rest on prairie grass or frozen snow-drift," argued the *Times* of London, "but this picture of the black-coated Metis playing the part of Europe's great soldier in the garb of a priest and the shoes of a savage, looked simply absurd."[5]

Walker's death, at the hands of British soldiers in Honduras in 1860, marked the end of antebellum filibustering. Riel's death, according to Jennifer Reid, solidified ethnic divisions in Canada into "explicit and permanent structures of opposition."[6] Riel is celebrated as a hero in parts of Canada, but forgotten in his adopted country. Walker is remembered with hatred in his adopted country of Nicaragua, and forgotten in the United States.[7]

But the similarities between the two men might be more revealing than their differences. Both trained for professions they never practiced, and both reinvented themselves on the frontier after failed marriage engagements. They each viewed the press as key to maintaining sovereignty, and edited newspapers while president. Both executed political opponents, and were in turn executed under questionable legal circumstances. Both manifested symptoms of megalomania, and earned the right to be called president, but were dismissed as "little Napoleons" by their opponents.[8] And both, significantly, were felled by coalescing empires able to harness the resources of emerging transportation systems: Cornelius Vanderbilt's steamboat lines proved crucial to Walker's undoing when a spurned Vanderbilt withheld needed supplies from Nicaragua, while the partially completed Canadian Pacific Railway facilitated the quick and decisive suppression of Louis Riel's second uprising in 1885.

Each of these similarities bears consideration by scholars of empire, since on the surface the imperial histories of Canada and the United States vary as dramatically as do their representative charismatic individuals, divided by era, space, language, and memory. It's worth wondering, for example, whether two distant executions shed new light on the place of state-sanctioned murder in nineteenth-century North American national consolidation.[9] Walker's 1860 execution was overshadowed by sectional tensions on the eve of the Civil War, but Riel's in 1885 drew widespread condemnation, precisely because of the precedent of amnesty set by the United States. "The world has outgrown the barbarous spirit which could look on and applaud the taking of the life of a political convict," wrote the St. Louis *Globe* in 1885. "It now demands that the fullest sense of mercy, consistent with political safety, should be accorded. That is what happened in the United States when the captured leaders of the rebellion fell within the just danger of the law." The *Cherokee Advocate* noted that "there was widespread disapproval of the hanging of Riel throughout Canada. . . . The course pursued by the Dominion of Canada in executing Riel under the charge of high treason is exactly opposite to the manner in which the United States treated leaders of the Great Rebellion."[10] Once one gets past the irony of the United States critiquing Canada for its "barbarity," it's difficult not to wonder if there was a moment when the use and meaning of the death penalty in North America might have been redefined, a moment lost with Louis Riel's execution.[11]

It's also worth considering the extent to which actions in Nicaragua and Manitoba conform to the model of the imperial press that Julie Codell has named "cohistories" of empire, virtual spaces where "joint histories, simultaneous, ideal, and 'real,' intervene in one another's texts in a dialogue between" metropolis and colony.[12] Both Walker and Riel used the press to appeal to the United States, and to ideals of American liberty, to gain support for their revolutionary actions outside the territorial boundaries of the state. It's no coincidence that Walker, who edited a San Francisco newspaper before embarking on his career as a filibuster, maintained a bilingual newspaper during his tenure in Nicaragua.[13] He repeatedly linked what he deemed the "struggle for liberty" in Nicaragua to American precedent, particularly in print statements.[14]

Riel, in turn, repeatedly spoke from prison to "his friends in the United States, where he declared most of them were."[15] The Wisconsin *State Register* reported on Riel's prison "manifesto," which appealed directly to U.S. readers. "The Canadian Government is trying to crush us with tyrannical acts. . . . Has the spirit of 1776, with splendid memories of courage and struggles, departed from the American people; has liberty no further triumph to achieve that the American heart has grown callous to the whisperings of justice?"[16] Clearly the virtual space created by and about these authors crossed national boundaries and intervened in the process of state formation.

The experiences of Walker and Riel also offer insight into the role of individual expatriation (or the right to freely exchange citizenship in one country for another) in the consolidation of states. Eric Schlereth has argued for a cosmopolitan understanding of the right to voluntarily change citizenship in the early nineteenth century based on immigration to Texas in the 1820s, but the fact that Walker's and Riel's attempts to change citizenship were almost universally ignored raises questions about the larger applicability of this thesis. As the Atchison *Daily* noted on September 5, 1885, the U.S. government "recognized the principle that every country has the right to determine for itself what constitutes treason, and is not disposed to question the right of Canada to have tried Riel for treason, even if he were an American citizen."[17]

The comparison of Walker and Riel suggests further grounds for consideration, including the relative importance of steamship and railroad in Walker's and Riel's histories, the role of personal reinvention in the creation of nationalism, and the manner in which Riel's spotty romantic career might be integrated into a larger narrative about the construction of gender and nineteenth-century adventuring.[18] Each of these similarities might highlight an imperial trajectory, or key transformation in national sovereignty and empire in North America.

But this essay focuses on perhaps the most intriguing connection between Walker and Riel: the role these two individuals played in the consolidation of North American federal power and national boundaries. A key theme in standard historical treatments of the American Civil War has been the centralizing and consolidating tendencies of the conflict. Not only did the war itself fix America's national boundaries, but the war effort helped centralize the U.S. economy and led to a vast increase in the power and reach of the federal government.[19] As a recent textbook puts it:

> Over the course of the long war, Republicans in Congress transformed a small, weak, central government into a major force in the nation's economic life. Part of the transformation lay in the war effort itself, which required mobilizing, supplying, and coordinating an enormous fighting force. But Congress also broadened the federal government's reach in other ways that had lasting impact beyond the war. With southern Democrats out of the picture,

Republicans were able to pass laws that created new revenue sources to finance the war, established welfare programs for veterans and their families, and stimulated economic growth through policies that favored business and encouraged western expansion.[20]

Whether or not there was a deliberate push by Republicans at the outset to use war as a means to promote capitalism and centralize the U.S. economy, in most narratives of the U.S. Civil War, such as the one just quoted, the consolidation of national power proceeds in a methodical, almost natural manner, along a clear trajectory tied to Union success in the war.

The "natural" and seemingly inevitable process of state consolidation through the war effort reflects economic ideas about capitalist development. But it also, interestingly, echoes the way nineteenth-century Americans conceptualized the reigning ideology of Manifest Destiny. Through the early decades of the nineteenth century, most Americans believed that expansionism would spread progress and enlightenment to all of mankind, and through the power of influence and persuasion America's Manifest Destiny would be revealed. Americans also believed, well into the nineteenth century, that America's territorial destiny would unfold in a peaceful and natural process, expressed through a feminized metaphor. In the expansionist vision of the 1830s, new territories would come to America, like "fruit dropping from a tree." In the 1840s and into the 1850s, the rhetoric of Manifest Destiny grew more heated, and more martial in tone, but that America's continental destiny was manifest never seems to have been in doubt for most Americans.[21]

Yet the experiences of William Walker and Louis Riel suggest just how contingent the process of state consolidation actually was in the nineteenth century. These two men were twins, above all else, in the unintended consequences of their failure. Exceptions that proved the rule, Walker and Riel played unexpected and entirely unintentional roles in the larger history of state consolidation in the Americas. This essay follows a chronological and northern trajectory, beginning in the 1850s in the Central American Isthmus and concluding in the 1880s in western Canada, revealing experiences that resist easy incorporation in narratives of methodical state consolidation, and suggest how problematic such narratives are.

William Walker first rose to national attention in the fall and winter of 1853 in an aborted attempt to capture land in Sonora and Baja California with a troop of rowdy Forty-Niners. Tried and acquitted (after eight minutes of jury deliberation) for violating neutrality laws, Walker was hailed as a hero by men in

San Francisco and further afield. Sonora was rich in silver, and after the easy victories of the U.S.-Mexico War, seemed a likely target for further territorial expansionism.[22]

But he found his true fame in Central America, where Britain, France, and the United States were in competition to control the shortest route from the Atlantic to the Pacific Ocean. A canal through Panama or Nicaragua promised to cut travel time from New York to the goldfields of California by weeks, and the tropical climate of the region offered agricultural possibilities that investors were anxious to capitalize on.[23]

However, the 1850 Clayton-Bulwer Treaty, which established the joint right of Britain and the United States to construct and control a canal through some portion of the Isthmus, appeared to stand in the way of U.S. expansionism. It became a "matter of abuse" in the United States, where expansionists chafed at any limits to their authority in the Americas. This was particularly true after Britain declared a portion of present-day Honduras their "Colony of the Bay Islands" in 1852.[24] A Central American canal was no minor issue during the Gold Rush. U.S. investment in transit across the Isthmus dwarfed all other foreign investments prior to the U.S. Civil War.[25]

Civil war in Nicaragua gave William Walker the opening he needed. He signed a contract with Liberal forces to bring American troops to the country, and left San Francisco in May of 1855 with fifty-seven armed men. With the financial support of Cornelius Vanderbilt, who hoped to capitalize on transit opportunities in a peaceful and U.S.-friendly isthmus, Walker and the Liberals defeated the conservative "Legitimist" government within six months of arriving in the country. Walker proclaimed himself commander-in-chief of the Nicaraguan Army and recruited American colonists, 10,000 of whom settled in the country.

Walker initially collaborated with Costa Rican president Juan Rafael Mora, but Mora and his supporters were understandably wary of the filibustering Yankee, and suspected, rightfully, that Walker's goal was to establish a Central American empire under U.S. control. The seeming unwillingness of the U.S. government to curtail Walker's actions, and the massive outpouring of support Walker was receiving in the U.S. press, caused increasing friction with both Nicaraguans and Costa Ricans.

In March of 1856, Mora mobilized Costa Rican troops for the first time in the nation's history, and with the support of the British (who feared U.S. hegemony in the region almost as much as did Costa Rican citizens), attacked Walker's army. In June of 1856 Walker named himself president of Nicaragua in a rigged election, staffed courts with English-speaking judges, began appropriating the property of his opponents (with the explicit goal of placing "a large portion of the land in the hands of the white race," he wrote), and perhaps most shockingly, revoked the 1824 edict that made slavery in Nicaragua illegal and reinstituted African slavery as part of the "Americanization" (really Southernization) of the country.[26] The Southern slaveholding American minister in Nicaragua, John H. Wheeler, officially recognized Walker's presidency, characterizing Walker as "an agent of a superior race that [will] replace the allegedly syphilis-infected, feeble races of Central America."[27]

Walker's actions were threatening enough to unite previously warring factions in Nicaragua. In an attempt to gain favor with economic backers in the United States, Walker revoked Vanderbilt's transit contract. Vanderbilt, in revenge, closed down all transit to Nicaragua on his ships, and began supplying Mora's forces with guns and money. In 1857, after two years of a war Walker understood in explicitly racial terms (it was only through the "employment of force" he wrote in his narrative of the war in Nicaragua, that there could be "fixed relations between the pure white American race . . . and the mixed Hispano-Indian race"), he was pushed out of power by a multinational army led by the Costa Ricans.[28]

Walker's invasion reverberated throughout South America. Nicaraguans condemned the "mob of foreign ingrates, race of vipers" who laid waste to their country.[29] A year after Walker was vanquished, Minister Mirabeau Buonaparte Lamar sensed "a deep seated terror" in Nicaragua, "that, when the Americans are admitted into it, the natives will be thrust aside—their nationality lost—their religion destroyed—and the common classes be converted into hewers and drawers of water."[30] Across South America the Chilean intellectual Francisco Bilbau proclaimed, "Walker is the invasion, Walker is the conquest, Walker is the United States. . . . The prophetic voice of a filibustering crusade which promises to its adventurers the regions of the South and the death of the South American initiative."[31]

To this day, there are few more potent symbols of American imperialism in Nicaragua than William Walker. When Sandinista leader Daniel Ortega protested U.S. intervention in Nicaragua under President Ronald Reagan in a 1983 address to the United Nations, he claimed that the Sandinista rise to power was the result of a "long struggle against U.S. domination" that began with William Walker in 1855. Former Nicaraguan President Violeta Barrios de Chamorro recounted in her 1996 autobiography that her parents visited her in boarding school to celebrate "the *Fiestas Patrias*, the holiday in which we commemorate our independence and the defeat of the American invader William Walker." Nicaraguan schoolbooks today highlight Nicaraguan valor in driving Walker from power.³² Critics of U.S. imperialism throughout Latin America point to Walker for historical precedent. As Cuban writer Eduardo Galeano argues, "Invasions, interventions, bombardments, forced loans, and gun point treaties followed one after the other."³³

Yet, as Michel Gobat has explored, the American invasion led upper-class Nicaraguans to embrace U.S. political, economic, and cultural forms in the creation of an Americanized and "highly cosmopolitan nationality." Rather than increasing anti-Americanism, "the Walker fiasco only strengthened the will of elite Nicaraguans to replicate the U.S. road to modernity." Upper-class Nicaraguans traveled to the United States in growing numbers and began "emulating the United States" in a variety of ways, including the institution of an independent press and civic associations.³⁴

Walker also played a key role in the reconfiguration of Central American power relations and national borders. Walker's invasion fostered Nicaraguan nationalism by providing a common foe for the first time. A once fractured country came together as virtually all races and classes joined together to fight Walker.³⁵

Scholars have also suggested that Walker's brief dictatorship, and Costa Rica's role in driving him from power, became a foundation myth of Costa Rican history. Mora's 9,000-man army returned home from Nicaragua with cholera, which quickly spread among the Costa Rican populace, killing over 10,000 civilians. But they also brought back the body of a martyred hero, Juan Santamaría, who, after having been shot in the arm, set Walker's encampment on fire in April 1856. He eventually lost his life in the conflict. Santamaría's sacrifice was celebrated as "an image of national unity," and his death became a national holiday. His legacy is almost impossible to avoid in modern Costa Rica, particularly for visitors who fly into the Juan Santamaría International Airport.³⁶

Putting aside the admittedly enormous matter of the thousands of Costa Rica fatalities due to cholera and war, Walker's long-term impact on Costa Rica was far from negative. Successful war against the filibuster led to national consolidation and increased nationalism. Walker provided Mora with the opportunity to expand Costa Rican power in the Guanacaste Region, and, as Luis Fernando Sibaja has argued, played a crucial role in defining the territorial boundary between Nicaragua and its southern neighbor. Scholars of El Salvador and Honduras, countries that joined Costa Rica in their war against Walker, also drew on the experience to consolidate their own national states.³⁷ The aftermath of Walker's Nicaraguan sojourn led Chile's leading newspaper, *El Mercurio*, to argue that "either it must imitate the United States by becoming a developed nation or suffer the same wretched fate as hapless Mexico," meaning dismemberment at the hands of avaricious Americans.[38]

Walker's impact on the United States was no less profound. The filibuster's tenure in Nicaragua was wildly celebrated by both Northern and Southern men as the ultimate expression of national might. His career appeared, in the mid-1850s, to offer the promise of both ever-expanding national borders, and an antidote to sectional discord. His "application" of force in Nicaragua in the name of the "white American race" offered a model of highly martial manhood and helped define masculine practices at home.[39]

But the long-term consequences of his actions were devastating. By promoting violence as the solution to problems, Walker and his supporters contributed to an agonal political culture that worsened sectional tensions and worked against forces of compromise on the eve of the Civil War. While some men in the United States believed that Walker's aggressive expansionism was immoral, others celebrated him and his filibuster followers for their fearlessness, skill in battle, and willingness to die for a virtuous cause. For these men, aggression became a virtue in itself.

As debates over the expansion of slavery led to increasingly acrimonious relations between the North and South, many men, ironically enough, looked south, to Latin America, for solutions. But victories for aggressive expansionism abroad could only reinforce the merit of martial virtues at home, further weakening the perception that the ability to compromise was, in fact, a virtue.

Bertram Wyatt-Brown has argued that for many Southerners, "the Civil War was reduced to a simple test of manhood."[40] But Walker's appeal cut across sectional divides, creating a climate in which both Northerners and Southerners naturally turned to violence as a solution to personal and national problems. Historians have long emphasized how debates over new territories enflamed sectional tensions by forcing the issue of slavery to the forefront of national debate.[41] But Walker's filibustering brought more than slavery to the public eye, it also lent support to an aggressive ideal of American manhood that was perhaps equally damaging to the hopes for peaceful sectional compromise.[42]

The implications of Walker's actions on U.S. state expansion were even more dramatic. President James Buchanan believed that Walker had "done more injury to the commercial & political interests of the United States" than "any man living." There is a great deal of proof that he was correct.[43] Robert E. May has argued persuasively that diplomatic efforts to annex new U.S. territories in the 1850s were critically undermined by filibustering. When James Gadsden negotiated with Mexico for a further territorial concession in the Southwest in 1853, he became convinced that Walker's invasion of Baja and Sonora hardened Mexican authorities against selling land in either state, and had it not been for Walker, he might have been able to purchase Baja California. Hawaii's prince Alexander Liholiho considered annexing Hawaii to the United States in the early 1850s, but the American minister there, David L. Gregg, believed that Walker's "recent operations in Lower California" turned the Hawaiian people against the United States. In 1856 Chile, Ecuador, and Peru went so far as to form a union to counter filibustering and invited all other Latin states to join.[44]

In his failures, then, William Walker thwarted both U.S. imperial expansion abroad and national unity at home, while conversely helping Central American countries, particularly Costa Rica, to consolidate their states and define their boundaries. Less than a year after he was captured by the British under questionable circumstances and put to death by firing squad in Honduras, the United States was torn apart by a Civil War Walker helped precipitate.

In terms of years and physical distance, the leap from Central America, to the U.S., to western Canada may seem precipitous. But the expansionist context that gave birth to Louis Riel as a political actor is in many ways similar to the American context that produced William Walker. The United States was busy building an empire in the 1840s and 1850s, while Canada in the 1860s and 1870s is perhaps best understood as an important outpost of the British Empire struggling with consolidation. Yet, as Doug Owram has explored, the idea of territorial expansionism into the Canadian Northwest was, in the 1870s and 1880s, vigorously supported by a coalition of Canadian politicians, businesspeople, railroad promoters, and journalists not dissimilar to promoters of Manifest Destiny in the United States in the 1840s and 1850s. As in the antebellum U.S., the Canadian expansionist movement of the 1870s and 1880s gained power precisely because it appeared to offer a solution to regional differences, and a means to align regional interests, during a period of high sectional dissension.[45]

Starting in the 1870s, Canada's west moved from being viewed as a wasteland to the key to Canada's future prosperity, and perhaps, even, as one London guide for emigrants to the region put it, "the future of this great Empire."[46] As the *Nor'Wester*, the only newspaper published in the Canadian Northwest, wrote in 1869,

> The NOW of this country finds a territory of immense extent occupied by about 14,000 civilized people; the THEN of ten years shall see a population of 500,000. Now we are almost isolated from the rest of the world; then we

shall have a large and energetic population upon our southern border, extending from Lake Superior to Puget Sound. . . . Now the eye wanders, without a resting place over our occupied plains, then it shall be arrested by the happy homes of thousands which dot the horizon."[47]

But first Canadians needed to attract immigrants, and for a variety of reasons Europe's immigrants seemed a great deal more attracted to the United States than to Canada. The solution, according to Canadian expansionists, was to compete with the United States utilizing tools that had proven remarkably effective south of the border: an aggressive policy of internal improvements and a booster literature that in its enthusiasm and exaggeration rivals any of the works written about the glories of Nicaragua and its potentials for a canal by U.S. boosters in the heyday of Walker's regime.[48]

The Reverend George M. Grant laid out the terms of the competition better than anyone in his 1872 book *Ocean to Ocean: Sanford Fleming's Expedition through Canada*. For Canada to successfully spread, ocean to ocean, it needed a railroad. Grant considered the construction of the transcontinental railroad one of the greatest accomplishments in U.S. history: "at this day as remarkable a monument to the energy of our neighbors as the triumphant conclusion of their Civil War."[49]

Canada needed an equal or better railroad, not simply because British Columbia joined the Canadian union in 1871 after being promised that a transcontinental railway would connect the province to Ontario within ten years, but because the future, indeed the very existence of the nation was at stake. "By uniting together, the British provinces had declared that their destiny was—not to ripen and drop, one by one, into the arms of the Republic—but to work out their own future as an integral and important part of the grandest Empire of the world."[50]

The Canadian Pacific Railway appeared to offer a solution to the problem of the West by opening up an exceptionally wonderful territory to settlement. "How does the country crossed by the Union and Central Pacific Railways compare with our own North-west?" Grant asked his readers. "The Pacific slope excepted, for there is nothing in British Columbia to compare with the fertile valleys of California, everything is so completely in our favour that there is no comparison. . . . California . . . is not a country to rear a healthy or hardy race."[51]

As for the rest of the western United States (Utah, Nevada, and Wyoming), "What a country to live in! Everywhere it has a uniform, dry, dusty, what an Australian writer would call 'God-forsaken' look!" Grant concluded that "the American desert is a reality. It is unfit for the growth of cereals, or in any way to support a farming population, because of its elevation, its lack of rain, and the miserable quality, or to speak more correctly, the absence of soil."[52]

All of this suggested the importance of vision, an arena in which the United States appeared vastly superior to Canada. Grant wrote:

> The enterprise that ran the pony express, that constructed telegraphs and a line of railway across such a country is wonderful; but not half as wonderful as the faith that sees in such a desert an earthly paradise, or the assurance that publishes its vision of what ought to be, for a picture of what is, or the courage that volunteers the sacrifice of any number of foreigners to prove the sincerity of its faith.[53]

Alex Rivington, British author of the 1872 tract *In the Track of Our Emigrants: The New Dominion as a Home for Englishmen*, agreed that western Canada was not only a fine place to settle, but with a proper railroad, could beat the United States at their own game. "The Americans are more enterprising than the Canadians in many ways; in the matter of emigration they are especially so," he admitted. But Canada's proposed railway would be the "pioneer of civilization" and "the most direct from Europe to Asia. It will thread its way over the Rocky Mountains, at a much lower level than its rival the Northern Pacific, and will not be so subject to a blockade by a snow-drift as the Central Pacific to San Francisco."[54]

But expansion into the Northwest had profound consequences on the Métis and Indigenous inhabitants of the region, who were already suffering in the 1870s due to dwindling herds of buffalo, a situation shared with Native inhabitants of the Great Plains. Herds were so diminished by the end of the 1870s that residents were close to starving on both sides of the U.S.-Canada border. And the Canadian response did nothing to reassure the Métis. "Incompetent and corrupt government officials, questions of land titles, surveys, and the advancement of an alien civilization itself" contributed to discontent in the Northwest expressed in increasingly vocal protests in the 1880s.[55]

Louis Riel had come to the salvation of the Métis once before, when he led an uprising that halted Canadian land surveys after the Hudson's Bay Company agreed to sell Rupert's Land and the Northwestern Territory to Canada. Under his leadership, the Métis National Committee organized to protect the rights of inhabitants of the region and was consolidated as a provisional government in 1869. The following year, after the Métis drew up a list of conditions necessary before they would join the Canadian Confederation, they formed a Provisional Government of Assiniboia, and in 1870, the Province of Manitoba entered the Canadian Confederation, with the federal government agreeing to reserve 1.4 million acres of land for Métis residents.

Riel, simultaneously elected to the House of Commons in Ottawa and banished from Canada for the part he played in the rebellion, lived in exile in the United States for the larger part of a decade starting in 1874, but in 1884 the Métis invited him back to help protect the rights of the Métis in Saskatchewan. Their complaints included the fact that their settlements were not serviced by the Canadian Pacific Railway.[56] Métis protests were met with armed force by the Canadian government. The Métis seized a parish church, formed a provisional government, and named Riel president. Two months of fighting resulted in the capture of Riel. The *Manitoba Free Press* sympathized with the rebels. "Wherever it is known that the half-breeds and Indians are in rebellion, it is known that they were first deceived and wronged, then neglected, finally allowed to prepare openly for an appeal to arms without a step being taken to hinder them."[57]

But most Canadians weren't as sympathetic. In July of 1885, Riel was charged with treason. He delivered an eloquent speech in his own support, but he was found guilty. The jury recommended clemency, but Riel received none. In November 1885, he was publicly executed to international condemnation.[58]

On the surface, Riel was the prototypical anti-colonial freedom fighter, protesting the expansion of the Canadian state at a key moment of imperial growth. The two uprisings he led in protest of the Canadian government's denial of Métis property established, according to two scholars, "his place in the pantheon of anti-colonial resistors [sic] in the late nineteenth century." There is a great deal of evidence that Riel's contemporaries, particularly journalists in Britain and Europe, understood his actions in an imperial rather than strictly Canadian context.[59] As one British paper remarked on the occasion of Riel's second uprising, "Our Canadian cousins, in proportion to their population and resources, seem to have got as tough a job on their hands on the Saskatchewan River as we have on the Nile."[60]

Since his death, scholars have closely tied Riel with regional disparities, arguing that he advocated regionalism over federalism. He has become, for many in Canada, a symbol of the federal government's neglect of the West.[61] It's easy to understand his life and death in these terms. The leading scholar of nineteenth-century Canadian expansion has argued that "the Riel rebellion was simply a crisis that dramatically illustrated a longer-run trend towards regionalism."[62]

But just as Walker's life and death had unintended consequences, so too did Louis Riel's. While his embrace as a hero of Canada's West, and in some sense a particularly regional figure, is far from surprising, it's worth considering the extent to which, in both life and death, Louis Riel helped consolidate the Canadian state.

First is the matter of the railroad. One reason why so much booster literature focused on the importance of the railroad in the 1870s and 1880s was because the Canadian Pacific was incomplete and in desperate need of funding. No better or more honestly managed than the U.S. railroads against which it was designed to compete, the Canadian Pacific found itself unable, on the eve of the 1885 rebellion, to marshal the political capital to compel continued expenditures by the government.[63]

Riel's war changed that equation dramatically. The Canadian Pacific offered to transport the 5,000 army recruits from Central and Eastern Canada to the end of the line in Winnipeg, whence soldiers marched over ice and were transported by sleigh to the front. Unrest on the South Saskatchewan provided a much-needed public image boost for the Canadian Pacific, and justified further federal investment in the struggling railroad.[64] The Canadian telegraph industry likewise used the rebellion as a means to increase financial backing, since an Eastern public was anxious for immediate news from the remote provinces.[65]

The state and railroad both benefited from Riel's actions, since ultimately the railroad made future uprisings unlikely, if not impossible. This fact was obvious enough in 1885 to the *Manchester Times*. Questioning the wisdom of Riel's execution, the British paper "thought that, under all the circumstances, a milder decision would have met the case. There is very little prospect of further rebellion. The rapid opening up of the Northwest, and especially the completion of the Pacific Railway, will go far to make these risings impossible."[66]

Riel also served to define and unify the state as an outlaw figure. Drawing on Georgio Agamben's writings on the *homo sacer*, a banned figure who is outside or beyond the law, Kevin Bruyneel has argued that Riel became proof and expression of Canadian sovereignty during his life. Banned from Canada after his first rebellion, Riel's political figure physically demarcated the boundaries of the nation. This was because, according to Agamben, "the relation of ban has constituted the essential structure of sovereign power" by tying together "the two poles of the sovereign exception; bare life and power, *homo sacer* and the sovereign. Because of this alone can the ban signify the insignia of sovereignty . . . and expulsion from the community."[67] Riel's ban thus served in the "production and signification" of Canadian sovereignty during his life.[68]

His jailing and execution also played significant and unexpected roles in Canadian state formation. Although Canadian reports of Riel's uprising and capture frequently pointed to the (imaginary) dangers of U.S. incursion into Canada on Riel's behalf, on the U.S. side of the border reports served to highlight the differences between the two countries.[69] When the Hudson's Bay Company ceded its territorial rights in North America in the spring of 1869, the *New York Commercial Advertiser* felt comfortable referring to the Northwest Territories as "undefined" and "at present a barren waste."[70]

That territory no longer seemed undefined in 1885. During Riel's first uprising, U.S. journalists marveled at "the universal attention thus drawn to the New Northwest."[71]

The ample press devoted to reports about Riel's two uprisings, his capture, and his execution offered U.S. readers the opportunity to explore the vast geography of Canada in quite a bit more detail. Riel was imprisoned in the settlement of Regina, described to Boston readers as "the capital of a vast territory, stretching north as far as Alaska, west to British Columbia, and known as the Northwest Territory." At the same time, security around his capture helped to strengthen the border between the U.S. and Canada, to "prevent any attempt at rescue which might be made by his countrymen in Canada or over the American border."[72]

As for the execution itself, few acts serve to highlight the power of the state more than putting a man to death. According to historian Desmond Morton, "Riel's death ended thoughts of rebellion. For Métis and Native peoples, the aftermath may have been tragic; for Canada it was tranquil. Canada's sovereignty was unchallenged from Kenora to Esquimalt."[73] The *Edmonton Bulletin* warned its readers at the close of 1884 that "the idea that the North-West is to eastern Canada as India is to Great Britain, is one that will, if not abandoned, lead to the rupture of confederation at no distant date."[74] But the Northwest was no India. These fears were clearly misplaced.

On the eve of his execution, Louis Riel wrote from his Regina jail cell that he would lose his "temporal life," on account of "having done all I could to better the condition of the people at large as an aboriginal, as an American, and as a prophet."[75] Walker, in the conclusion to the narrative he published just a month before his death, proclaimed that his army had written "a page of American history which it is impossible to forget or erase."[76] It is notable that the meaning of the word "American" is opaque in both texts. Scholars have cast both Riel and Walker as radicals on the periphery of state formation in North America, but peripheries are often more worthy of our attention than they first appear. In this case, both peripheries have earned the right to cast their struggles in an "American" context, while highlighting how contingent seemingly natural processes, from territorial expansion to state consolidation, actually are.

Notes

1. Valuable overviews of William Walker's career include Robert E. May, *Manifest Destiny's Underworld: Filibustering in Antebellum America* (Chapel Hill: University of North Carolina Press, 2002); Robert E. May, *The Southern Dream of a Caribbean Empire* (Gainesville: University Press of Florida, 2002); Amy S. Greenberg, *Manifest Manhood and the Antebellum American Empire* (Cambridge: Cambridge University Press, 2005); Frederick Rosengarten Jr., *Freebooters Must Die! The Life and Death of William Walker, the Most Notorious Filibuster of the Nineteenth Century* (Wayne, PA: Haverford House, 1976); Albert Z. Carr, *The World and William Walker* (New York: Harper and Row, 1963); Rafael Obregon Loria, *Costa Rica y la guerra del 56 (La campaña del tránsito) 1856–1857* (San José: Editorial Costa Rica, 1976); William O. Scroggs, *Filibusters and Financiers: The Story of William Walker and His Associates* (New York: Macmillan, 1916).

2. Good basic works on Louis Riel include Chester Brown, *Louis Riel: A Comic-Strip Biography* (Montreal: Drawn & Quarterly, 2013); Peter Charlebois, *The Life of Louis Riel* (Toronto: New Canada Publications, 1975); Thomas E. Flanagan, *Louis "David" Riel: Prophet of the New World*, rev. ed. (Toronto: University of Toronto Press, 1996), and Thomas E. Flanagan, *Riel and the Rebellion: 1885 Reconsidered* (Toronto: University of Toronto Press, 2000).

3. *New York Herald* quoted in Richard Slotkin, *The Fatal Environment: The Myth of the Frontier in the Age of Industrialization, 1800–1860* (New York: Atheneum, 1985), 252. On the Gray-Eyed Man of Destiny, see Amy S. Greenberg, "A Gray-Eyed Man: Character, Appearance, and Filibustering," *Journal of the Early Republic* 20, no. 4 (2000): 673–699.

4. Jennifer Reid, *Louis Riel and the Creation of Modern Canada: Mythic Discourse and the Postcolonial State* (Albuquerque: University of New Mexico Press, 2008): 71.

5. "The Half-Breed Insurrection," *Daily News* (London), April 4, 1885.

6. Reid, *Louis Riel and the Creation of Modern Canada*, 124.

7. Lauren L. Basson argues that the unwillingness of the U.S. press to accept Riel has reflected and contributed to changing understandings of what it meant to be a member of the U.S. nation and of civilization more broadly, suggesting the degree to which race, ethnicity, religion, and language were central aspects of U.S. national identity. "In the United States, by contrast, Riel is virtually unknown. His political activities in the United States and the controversies he provoked among senior members of the U.S. government have received almost no attention by U.S. historians or other scholars" (Basson, "Savage Half-Breed, French Canadian or White U.S. Citizen? Louis Riel and U.S. Perceptions of Nation and Civilization," *National Identities* 7, no. 4 [2005]: 370).

8. Walker was small in stature, and Riel's height a matter of dispute, but the latter's bulk and "massive" head, prevented viewers from characterizing him as "little." In both cases, the Napoleonic reference was likely to each figure's inflated sense of purpose. See Riel as "Little Napoleon" in "The Half-Breed Insurrection," *Daily News* (London), April 4, 1885.

9. William Blair has explored the significance of clemency to Confederates with regard to the consolidation of the U.S. state during reconstruction. William A. Blair, *With*

Malice toward Some: Treason and Loyalty in the Civil War Era (Chapel Hill: University of North Carolina Press, 2014).

10. *St. Louis Daily Globe-Democrat*, August 6, 1885; *Cherokee Advocate*, November 20, 1885. The *North American* (Philadelphia), expressed a similar view, August 3, 1885.

11. Kevin Bruyneel would suggest this is not coincidental, because Riel's death was understood as greater than, and perhaps essentially different from, state-sponsored execution. "In our time, Riel's execution is read as both less and more than a homicide. It is either the exceptional killing of a Métis rebel who stood in the way of Canadian expansion—and thus less than a homicide ... or the exceptional killing of a unique sovereign actor, a regicide if you will, who had to fall for a new province to be born and Canadian sovereignty to expand." Kevin Bruyneel, "Exiled, Executed, Exalted: Louis Riel, Homo Sacer and the Production of Canadian Sovereignty," *Canadian Journal of Political Science/Revue canadienne de science politique* 43, no. 3 (2010): 728.

12. Julie F. Codell, "Introduction: Imperial Co-Histories of the British and Colonial Press," in *Imperial Co-Histories: National Identities and the British and Colonial Press*, ed. Julie F. Codell (Madison, NJ: Fairleigh Dickinson University Press, 2003), 15.

13. Filibusters were, in Charles H. Brown's definition, "adventurers taking part in forays against friendly nations to foment revolution or capture the government." Charles H. Brown, *Agents of Manifest Destiny: The Lives and Times of the Filibusters* (Chapel Hill: University of North Carolina Press, 1980), 3.

14. William Walker, *The War in Nicaragua* (Mobile: S. H. Goetzel, 1860), 413. See also Walker's newspaper in Nicaragua, *La Nicaraguense*, 1855–1856 (http://www.latinamericanstudies.org/nicaragua/El_Nicaraguense-April-July-1856.pdf, http://www.latinamericanstudies.org/nicaragua/El_Nicaraguense-Aug-Nov-1856.pdf).

15. "Hanged for Treason," *Boston Daily Advertiser*, November 17, 1885, 1.

16. *Wisconsin State Register*, April 18, 1885.

17. "Louis Riel," *Atchison Daily Globe*, September 5, 1885, 1. On expatriation as "a transnational legal zone," see Eric R. Schlereth, "Privileges of Locomotion: Expatriation and the Politics of Southwestern Border Crossing," *Journal of American History* 100, no. 4 (2014): 995–1020. On the fact that Riel's American citizenship was "never" acknowledged, see Basson, "Savage Half-Breed," 369–388. The right to expatriation became federal law in the United States in the Expatriation Act of 1868.

18. See, for example, the *Galveston Daily News*, November 17, 1885, which concluded that Riel's execution was justified, in part, because "he was a failure as a military man, and earned the reputation of being an arrant [sic] coward." An "old schoolmate" of Riel's declared him "the man who had the hardihood, manhood, and courage to strike a blow for his race, and was about to expiate his loyalty to the half-breeds of the great Northwest upon the scaffold." "A Talk with Riel," in the *Rocky Mountain News* (Denver), November 17, 1885.

19. Vernon Burton, "Civil War and Reconstruction, 1861–1877," in *A Companion to 19th Century America*, ed. William L. Barney (New York: Wiley, 2001), 57–59; Sean Patrick Adams, "Wartime Political Economy," in *A Companion to the U.S. Civil War*, vol. 2, ed. Aaron Sheehan-Dean (New York: Wiley, 2014), 1073–1086; Heather Cox Richardson, *The Greatest Nation on Earth: Republican Economic Policies during the Civil War*

(Cambridge, MA: Harvard University Press, 1997); Richard Bensel, *Yankee Leviathan: The Origins of Central State Authority in America, 1859-1877* (Cambridge: Cambridge University Press, 1990); Mark Wilson, *The Business of Civil War: Military Mobilization and the State, 1861-1865* (Baltimore: Johns Hopkins University Press, 2006); Matthew J. Gallman, *Mastering Wartime: A Social History of Philadelphia during the Civil War* (Cambridge: Cambridge University Press, 1990), 292; Stanley Engerman, "The Economic Impact of the Civil War," *Explorations in Entrepreneurial History* 3 (1966): 176-199. Adams points out that the widespread "assumption" that the course of capitalism was "natural" is "flawed." Adams, "Wartime Political Economy," 1079.

20. David Henkin and Rebecca McLennan, *Becoming America: A History for the 21st Century* (New York: McGraw Hill, 2015), 406-407.

21. Amy S. Greenberg, *Manifest Destiny and American Territorial Expansionism: A Brief History with Documents* (Boston: St. Martin's Press, 2012), 1-38.

22. Basic information on Walker's career not otherwise cited in this and the following paragraphs is taken from Greenberg, *Manifest Manhood* and May, *Manifest Destiny's Underworld*.

23. See Greenberg, *Manifest Manhood*, 54-87.

24. May, *Southern Dream of a Caribbean Empire*, 88.

25. Mira Wilkins, *The Emergence of Multinational Enterprise: American Business Abroad from the Colonial Era to 1914* (Cambridge, MA: Harvard University Press, 1970), 28; Michael Gobat, *Confronting the American Dream: Nicaragua under U.S. Imperial Rule* (Durham, NC: Duke University Press, 2005), 23.

26. Walker, *The War in Nicaragua*, 253-254; David Whisnant, *Rascally Signs in Sacred Places: The Politics of Culture in Nicaragua* (Chapel Hill: University of North Carolina Press, 1995), 75-77.

27. Quoted in May, *Southern Dreams of a Caribbean Empire*, 97.

28. Walker, *The War in Nicaragua*, 430.

29. Quoted in Whisnant, *Rascally Signs in Sacred Places*, 78.

30. Quoted in May, *Manifest Destiny's Underworld*, 240.

31. Quoted in William F. Sater, *Chile and the United States: Empires in Conflict* (Athens: University of Georgia Press, 1990), 23.

32. Both quoted in May, *Manifest Destiny's Underworld*, 295.

33. Eduardo Galeano, *Open Veins of Latin America*, trans. Cedric Belfrage (New York: Monthly Review Press, 1973), 121; Rodrigo Lazo, *Writing to Cuba: Filibustering and Cuban Exiles in the United States* (Chapel Hill: University of North Carolina Press, 2005), 6.

34. Gobat, *Confronting the American Dream*, 6, 31, 41.

35. E. Bradford Burns, *Patriarch and Folk: The Emergence of Nicaragua, 1798-1858* (Cambridge, MA: Harvard University Press, 1991), 210-213.

36. Monica A. Rankin, *The History of Costa Rica* (Santa Barbara: ABC Clio, 2012), 56-61, quote on 60.

37. Luis Fernando Sibaja, "Filibusteros, financieros y cuestiones de limítrofes entre Costa Rica y Nicaragua," in *Filibusterismo y Destino Manifiesto en las Américas*, ed. Víctor Hugo Acuño Ortega (Alajuela, Costa Rica: Museo Histórico Cultural Juan Santamaría, 2010), 41-64. For the El Salvador and Honduran cases, see Carlos Gregorio López

Bernal, "Implicaciones political-sociales de la campaña contra los filibusteros en El Salvador: Las acciones de Gerardo Barrios," in *Filibusterismo y Destino Manifiesto en las Américas*, 183–202; Elizet Payne,"'Buscar lo cierto en lo ligorado': William Walker y la Guerra de 1856–1857 en la historiografia hondureña," in *Filibusterismo y Destino Manifiesto en las Américas*, 257–270.

38. Sater, *Chile and the United States*, 23.
39. Walker, *The War in Nicaragua*, 6.
40. Bertram Wyatt-Brown, *Honor and Violence in the Old South* (New York: Oxford University Press, 1986), 28; Nicholas W. Proctor, *Bathed in Blood: Hunting and Mastery in the Old South* (Charlottesville: University of Virginia Press, 2002), 72–73.
41. For two different views of the ill effects of Manifest Destiny on the Union, see David Potter, *The Impending Crisis, 1848–1861*, comp. and ed. Don E. Fehrenbacher (New York: Harper and Row, 1976); Michael Paul Rogin, *Subversive Genealogy: The Politics and Art of Herman Melville* (New York: Knopf, 1983), 106.
42. Greenberg, *Manifest Manhood*.
43. Buchanan quoted in T. J. Stiles, *The First Tycoon: The Epic Life of Cornelius Vanderbilt* (New York: Knopf, 2009), 307.
44. May, *Manifest Destiny's Underworld*, 240–241.
45. Doug Owram, *Promise of Eden: The Canadian Expansionist Movement and the Idea of the West, 1856–1900* (Toronto: University of Toronto Press, 1980). On expansionist ideology in the U.S. in the 1840s and 1850s, see Thomas R. Hietala, *Manifest Design: American Exceptionalism and Empire* (Ithaca, NY: Cornell University Press, 2002); Greenberg, *Manifest Manhood*.
46. Alex Rivington, *In the Track of Our Emigrants: The New Dominion as a Home for Englishmen* (London: Sampson Low, Marston, Low, & Searle, 1872), xii; Owram, *Promise of Eden*, 101–103.
47. *Nor'Wester*, September 21, 1869, quoted in Owram, *Promise of Eden*, 79.
48. On booster literature about Central America, see Greenberg, *Manifest Manhood*, 54–87.
49. Reverend George M. Grant, *Ocean to Ocean: Sanford Fleming's Expedition through Canada in 1872*, rev. ed. (London: Sampson Low, Marston, Searle and Rivington, 1877), 20.
50. Grant, *Ocean to Ocean*, 23.
51. Grant, *Ocean to Ocean*, 346.
52. Grant, *Ocean to Ocean*, 347–348.
53. Grant, *Ocean to Ocean*, 348.
54. Rivington, *In the Track of Our Emigrants*, xiv, ix.
55. Owram, *Promise of Eden*, 174.
56. George F. G. Stanley, "Louis Riel," http://www.thecanadianencyclopedia.ca/en/article/louis-riel/, accessed October 30, 2016.
57. *Free Press* (Manitoba), April 7, 1885. Quoted in Owram, *Promise of Eden*, 174.
58. Stanley, "Louis Riel."
59. Geoff Read and Todd Webb, "'The Catholic Mahdi of the North West': Louis Riel and the Metis Resistance in Transatlantic and Imperial Context," *Canadian Historical Review* 93, no. 2 (2012): 172.

60. "The Insurrection in Canada," *Reynolds's Newspaper* (London), May 3, 1885.

61. See, for example, Albert Braz, *The False Traitor: Louis Riel in Canadian Culture* (Toronto: University of Toronto Press, 2003), 89.

62. Owram, *Promise of Eden*, 177. There are also those who argue that Riel's uprisings changed almost nothing. For example, Bob Beal and Rod Macleod argue against the transformative power of 1885. See Beal and Macleod, *Prairie Fire: The 1885 North-West Rebellion* (Edmonton: Hurtig Publishers, 1984), 141–142.

63. John Lorne McDougall, *Canadian Pacific: A Brief History* (Montreal: McGill University Press, 1968); Richard White, *Railroaded: The Transcontinentals and the Making of Modern America* (New York: Norton, 2011), 207–208.

64. Reid, *Louis Riel*, 122–123; Brown, *Louis Riel*.

65. Reid, *Louis Riel*, 123; Alex Nalbach, "'The Software of Empire': Telegraphic News Agencies and Imperial Publicity, 1865–1914," in Codell, *Imperial Co-Histories*, 68–94.

66. *Manchester Times*, November 21, 1885.

67. Bruyneel, "Exiled, Executed, Exalted," 711–732; Georgio Agamben, *Homo Sacer: Sovereign Power and Bare Life*, trans. Daniel Heller-Roazan (Stanford, CA: Stanford University Press, 1998), 66.

68. Bruyneel, "Exiled, Executed, Exalted," 718.

69. Riel very briefly aligned himself with an annexation movement in the Midwest, but "the annexation movement never gained sufficient support from the U.S. federal administration to succeed." See Basson, "Savage Half-Breed," 372. For an example of Canadian fears of U.S. interference, see William McDougall's letter to Louis Riel, October 22, 1869, reprinted in the *New Nation*, April 15, 1885.

70. "The Hudson Bay Company Succumbs," *New York Commercial Advertiser*, quoted in the *Milwaukee Daily Sentinel*, April 15, 1869.

71. "The Manitoba Campaign," *Bangor Daily Whig and Courier*, June 17, 1870.

72. "Riel's Prison Life," *Boston Daily Advertiser*, November 17, 1885, 1. See also "Details of the Hanging," in the *Rocky Mountain News* (Denver), November 17, 1885.

73. Desmond Morton, "Images of Riel in 1998," *Canadian Speeches* 12, no. 2 (1998): 22, quoted in Bruyneel, "Exiled," 711.

74. *Edmonton Bulletin*, November 1, 1884.

75. "Riel's letters," *Boston Daily Advertiser*, November 17, 1885, 1.

76. Walker, *The War in Nicaragua*, 429.

4

Reform Wars, Royal Visits, and U.S. Views of Popular Sovereignty in 1860

Brian Schoen

The 1860 U.S. presidential election took place in the context of two events emblematic of the broader sovereignty questions defining North American geopolitics. In Mexico, the civil war or "Reforma War" between "Liberal" supporters of the 1857 constitution and "Conservative" opponents rallying around the military and the Catholic Church continued, accompanied by the specter of international intervention.[1] North of the border, Queen Victoria's North American subjects greeted the Prince of Wales in his much-anticipated fall 1860 tour, one intended to showcase the provinces' vitality and loyalty. That tour was extended to include the United States, bringing the heir to the British throne into the dividing republic in September and October of 1860, the height of electioneering.[2] When framed within the broader remaking of North American sovereignty, the timing of these events was more than coincidental. Canadians, Mexicans, and Americans were confronting, in their own ways, the broader geopolitical challenges of a world defined by globalizing forces, shifting and porous borders, and the continued strength and reach of European power into North America. These dynamics afforded the primary subjects of this essay, the citizens of the United States, with a multitude of reference points as they grappled with their own crises of order.

Both methodology and hindsight have prevented scholars from analyzing these events within the same frame. Deeply entrenched national histories have limited comparisons, something this volume joins other recent work to remedy. Sovereignty has typically been seen as something that emanates from central authority, rather than something that is experienced on the periphery in ways that rebound to the metropole. These events are also generally seen as sequels to bigger dramas. The presidential election appears chiefly as a prologue to Fort Sumter and the U.S. Civil War. Mexico's divisive conflict morphed into the French War of Intervention, a "foreign" conflict better suited for a postwar nationalist narrative that provided the much-celebrated Cinco de Mayo holiday. The first official royal visit to North America pales in significance to the move toward confederation in 1867.[3] At the time, though, participants had only fuzzy awareness of what might happen next.

Though born of particular circumstances, the visit of the Prince of Wales, the Reforma War, and the looming secession crisis reflected the interrelated challenge of governing in an interconnected global era characterized by a quest for national identity amid heightening violence. At mid-century, Mexicans, Americans, and Provincial British North Americans all grappled with the challenges of political cohesion following an Age of Revolutions, and amid the freer movement of diverse people, information, goods, and credit, as well as the accompanying debt. These and related changes enhanced by technologies like railroads and the telegraph brought about political volatility from below, threats from abroad, and debates about intercontinental and international free trade. These processes meant that American sovereignty was a concept defined as much on the edges of federal control as at its center.

Framing the U.S. sovereignty crisis of 1860 within a continental mental geography offers new understandings of how contemporaries viewed the federal union, while engaging multiple unfolding "North American Crises."[4] Both conceptually and practically, Mexicans' ongoing civil war and Canadians' embrace of British political culture, weighed heavily in U.S. observers' own political consciousness, especially as their own sectional crisis threatened assumptions of American exceptionalism, and devolved into secession.[5] These events were linked on the pages of newspapers, including the nation's largest—the *New York Herald*—and diplomatically, where U.S. policymakers sought to exert their influence amid debates demonstrating slavery's splintering political effect.

From a comparative perspective, developments on and across the U.S.'s legal border reminded Americans of their own nation's past (British provincial status) as well as an alarming possible future (institutional disintegration and anarchy). Looking north, Americans saw a conglomeration of British states struggling with ethnic and religious tensions, but also growing in economic potential and stabilizing their relationship with the British metropolis. Looking south, they perceived a chaotic space where republicanism and rule of law appeared to be failing. Mexican disorder, especially in light of failed republican movements in Europe and faltering republics elsewhere in Latin America, garnered significant attention. On the one hand, a broader continental perspective reinforced well-honed, if sectionalized, senses of U.S. exceptionalism. White Americans celebrated a civic culture that had avoided (despite the poor treatment of Catholics) serious religious strife and preserved individual white freedom while paying its own bills and avoiding anarchy. On the other hand, on the heels of Europe's mostly unsuccessful liberal revolutions in 1848, developments in Mexico highlighted how fragile popular government, including their own, could be.

Yet the Mexican civil war and the prince's visit were not merely symbolic reference points. The unstable nature of North American geopolitics blurred the lines between foreign and domestic policy in ways that contributed directly to the sectional conflict and ultimately secession. As John Craig Hammond and Robert May have shown, almost all Democrats and many Republicans still believed in American expansionism, and everyone was aware that divided republics or neglected provinces nearby could open or close opportunities for further territorial acquisitions.[6] If, as seemed apparent to many by 1860, British Canadians were tightening their bonds to Britain, U.S. expansion was more likely to head into Mexican lands, something that favored Southerners seeking to protect slavery's expansion.

Developments on and across national borders thus constantly pulled at partisan and sectional cords within the federal union, generating a polarizing mixture of desire and alarm that ultimately flowed into secession and Northerners' resistance to it. These dynamics highlighted the desirability of greater federal power, which in turn escalated concerns that partisan or sectional opponents might misuse that power at home and abroad. Selective memories led many white Southerners, especially in Texas, to excoriate the federal government for not doing enough to secure their southwestern border. Northern Republicans suspected that slaveholders and their supposed puppet, Buchanan, were stirring up trouble, hoping to make a bid for further acquisitions to be followed by slavery's expansion, this at a time when Canadians' evidenced loyalty to Britain militated against expanding the northern border. Civil War in the Mexican Republic and Canadian monarchism were intertwined with America's march toward secession, further elevating concerns that North America could again become a playground for European formal and informal imperialism. Americans' close tracking of these developments provided both symbolic references and practical challenges that informed their own descent into political chaos.

Intertwined Republics

Over his life former Texas president, United States senator, and then governor of Texas, Sam Houston, had come to appreciate that political independence was not an absolute. In his inaugural governor's message to Texans in December 1859, Houston insisted that "our own security must to a great extent, depend upon the conditions of things in Mexico."⁷ Throughout the long nineteenth century, U.S. politics were interlinked with the fortunes of the Mexican Republic opposite a shifting and porous border nearly 2,000 miles long. Scholars have long focused on the inflection points of the Texas Revolution, Mexican-American War, and the later Mexican Revolution. Attention has more recently suggested that the lives and stories in the world's two largest republics remained connected just before the American Civil War.⁸

The events that spiraled both nations into civil war in the late 1850s and early 1860s were propelled forward by the Mexican-American War's settlement. Defeat sent Mexico into an extended period of blaming and ultimately of dramatic reform. This, along with persistent national debt and concern about cross-border raids by U.S. citizens and Apache and Comanche Indians, furthered political instability. Mexican leaders from Santa Anna to Benito Juárez grappled with how to pay foreign creditors. They argued over whether American officials or investors could be seen as a trustworthy alternative. Needing funds to keep foreign creditors at bay, Santa Anna sold additional Mexican territory to the United States in the 1853 Treaty of Mesilla, known in the United States as the Gadsden Purchase. This cession became an oft-cited grievance of Ayutla revolutionaries, who pushed Santa Anna out of office in 1855 and sought to limit the power of the Catholic Church and the military.

Future leaders in that liberal movement, Benito Juárez, Melchor Ocampo, and José María Mata Reyes, forged plans while exiled in New Orleans, where they mingled with Cuban revolutionaries and sympathetic Americans. These liberals or "constitutionalists" looked to the United States as a model for the types of reforms they wished to make. The 1857 constitution they drafted included a clearer expression of individual rights and greater separation of church and state. It also prompted a conservative coup led by military and church leaders fearful of American-style democracy. The result was a civil war, or the Reform War, that forced U.S. policymakers and foreign governments into tough choices.⁹

Americans north of the border found that victory against Mexico also generated uncertainty. The Mexican War's repercussions coalesced into a sectional crisis over slavery's extension. In ways only recently appreciated, Mexico's antislavery actions impacted America's deepening divide over slavery. The 1846 Wilmot Proviso, which prohibited slavery in any future territories acquired from Mexico, gained political traction primarily because Northern Democrats and Whigs abhorred converting legally free Mexican soil into slaveholding U.S. territory. The 1848 Treaty of Guadalupe Hildago converted that metaphysical debate into a persistent wedge that eventually split the second party system in half. Adding to

Southern grievances, Mexico recognized no obligation to return fugitive slaves, a policy more vexing when, the following year, Mexican legislators passed the most aggressive antislavery measure on the continent: a law instantly emancipating any foreign slave who set foot on Mexican soil.[10]

The treaty and territorial transfer also made the United States legally responsible for controlling nearly 160,000 Lower Plains Indians, particularly the Apache and Comanche nations, who moved freely over boundaries they regarded as illegitimate. This proved costly as Americans moved 8,000 troops along the border to the tune of upwards of $12 million in New Mexico alone.[11] Finally, shifting boundaries brought over 100,000 residents of Mexican birth into the United States. Though treaty clauses called for fair treatment, local Anglos generated seeds of frustration that grew into an epidemic of borderland violence in 1859. In this and other ways, not just Texas's but the United States' security remained, as Houston noted, connected to conditions across and on the border.

Nineteenth-century geopolitics may have been moving toward creating "trans-border collusion among nation-states to curb the mobility and autonomy of borderlands."[12] It had not yet succeeded; borders remained permeable, contested, and for national leaders, problematic. In aggregate, these uncertain dynamics led to a central set of concerns: could republican governments preserve law and order on the periphery of their power? If so, how and at what expense and repercussions? One solution, favored by many Democrats, pointed toward exerting greater federal power into the borderlands.

Citizens of the United States liked to think they dictated continental politics. Regardless of party, most might have agreed with President James Buchanan's claim that "it is beyond question the destiny of our race to spread themselves over the continent of North America, and this at no distant day should events be permitted to take their natural course." Some Northerners might have disagreed with the general direction this course would take, as Buchanan predicted. "The tide of emigrants will flow to the south, and nothing can eventually arrest its progress. If permitted to go there peacefully, Central America will soon contain an American population which will confer blessings and benefits as well upon the natives as their respective Governments." The recent diplomat to Britain believed it could be done without conquest, "sanctioned by the laws of justice and honor." In his mind, Mexican disorder and desperation opened the door for further Gadsden-like deals giving the U.S. additional Mexican land.[13]

The president's faith in "natural courses" assumed a lot about both the wishes of "foreign" peoples and those he governed. Mexican liberals had little interest in ceding further lands, though they would offer Americans what had started to be termed the "right" of transit and to minerals. A growing number of Americans also questioned whether Mexican lands should be formally absorbed into the United States. Commercial interests, especially centered in New Orleans and New York, preferred to work with a stable Mexican government. Buchanan's own inherited minister to Mexico, John Forsyth, hit a common racist trope, and derided the idea of bringing so-called "mongrelized" Mexicans into the Union, stressing, "Should we not enjoy all the fruits of annexation" without "its responsibilities and evils? Could we not secure for our countrymen the enjoyment of the rich resources of the Mexican country, without the danger of introducing, into our social and political system the ignorant masses of the Mexican People?"[14] Forsyth joined others in believing that preserving Mexican solvency by making Mexico an economic protectorate would preserve order in both countries (and whiteness in the U.S.), further U.S. commercial interests, and keep European powers at bay. Even prior to 1860 Americans debated the merits of "dollars over dominion."[15]

That conversation took a new and more urgent turn in late 1857 when Forsyth saw "Mexican institutions ... crumbling to pieces" and European powers threatening intervention. In early 1858, a Conservative coup led by General Zuloaga and backed by many military and church leaders forced liberals from power. Led by Benito Juárez, supporters of the 1857 constitution reassembled and eventually formed a government at the port of Veracruz. Without clear guidance from Washington, Forsyth joined European officials in viewing control of the capital and military as justification to treat the Zuloaga government as the legitimate sovereign power. Forsyth also believed that Conservatives' reluctance to tax the Catholic Church might make them more likely to meet Buchanan's demand to sell additional territory. When they did not, however, Forsyth believed his and America's honor had been humiliated. That and rumors of Zuloaga negotiating with France and Spain for military support led him to resign his post, thus buying time for Buchanan and Secretary of State Lewis Cass to assess the embarrassing situation.

As Mexicans pushed deeper into an eventual three-year civil war, U.S. audiences read regular "advices from Mexico" exhibiting, as the *Detroit Advertiser* put it, a "country in a turbulent state of uproar and anarchy. Fighting was going in every direction, and pronunciamentos were as thick as black birds—highway robberies, assassinations and all kinds of outrage were the order of the day."[16] Throughout the U.S., analyses of institutional erosion, the coup, the rival governments, and resultant civil war struck a condescending, or at best a paternalistic, view of their Southern neighbors. Both a Massachusetts Republican and a Georgia Democrat referred to Mexico as "our India," an especially loaded comparison at the time when the British government was taking control from the East India Company.[17] South Carolinian William Boyce and Ohio Democrat Samuel Cox applied a different analogy, calling Mexico "our sick man," what "Turkey is to Europe."[18] These metaphors, particularly charged on the heels of the Sepoy Rebellion and Crimean War, revealed a shared American ethnocentrism, even racism, that subjected Mexico and its citizens to unequal status.

The deteriorating situation, accompanied by mounting tension along the Texas and Mexican border, generated urgency for U.S. action but not consensus about how to proceed. As early as February 1858 Texan Sam Houston asked his U.S. Senate colleagues to create a temporary military protectorate over Mexico's northern states, a move that would give some legal cover for deploying troops across the border. In the summer, several Democratic papers went a step further by reprinting a London *Times* editorial urging "the United States" to "consummate the work they have begun and annex the land of Montezuma and Cortez. Which even under the lash of the slave driver, will not regret the illusion of the liberty of the Mexican Republic."[19] President Buchanan may have agreed. The previous year, Congress had met Buchanan's $10,000 request for a naval squadron to protect American citizens in Paraguay. In December, he asked for congressional authority and funds to post soldiers in northern Mexico. Anglo-American power appeared to some Americans, and even some Britons, as the cure for persistent instability in "failed" Latin states.

The idea of a military protectorate was vague enough to offer multiple possible outcomes, thus garnering support on a variety of grounds. It ostensibly made sense to protect American commercial interests and prevent cross-border raiding until war had stopped. Others believed it encouraged long-term Mexican stability by possibly ending the war and preventing European intervention. When couched as part of an alliance, even Mexican liberals could envision the benefits of U.S. military assistance in an area their Conservative opponents had better control over. Buchanan and others may have also seen it as a way of acquiring leverage for future land purchases or commercial concessions via treaty. Most importantly, it forcefully responded to deteriorating circumstances on the ground and an uncertain diplomatic pathway forward.

Yet especially among Republicans, invasion across the border prompted concerns about violating international law and remembrances of the disruptive results of Americans' last armed venture onto Mexican soil. The contemplation of military force immediately raised questions about executive power, the prospect of a foreign war, the parameters of federalism, government economy, and slavery's potential future in the West. Locked in political battle over Kansas's proslavery Lecompton Constitution and mindful of a growing budget deficit due to the Panic of 1857 and the Utah War, Congress refused Buchanan's request. In April 1859, Buchanan could boast that his naval squadron had won what *Harper's Weekly* called the "War with Paraguay,"[20] but Mexico required more complicated domestic and foreign diplomacy.

Though willing to support whichever side offered the most, Buchanan increasingly saw Juárez's Liberal government as the better option. Drawing on prewar connections, Liberals played a better diplomatic game, gaining key access to Washington officials and important media outlets, including the *New York Herald*, which published several letters from Juárez's emissary to Washington, José María Mata. After receiving promising reports that the Liberal government would offer Americans favorable trade and transit rights and might even consider subsequently selling land, Buchanan's newly appointed emissary Marylander Robert McLane extended recognition on April 6, 1859.

This was an unusual step, one that subsequently provided Europeans considering Confederate recognition a precedent to rebut Unionist charges that doing so violated international law. At the time, it required justification to the American people, one offered in Buchanan's third annual message, a significant portion of which focused on Mexico. In his lengthy catalogue of Mexican atrocities against Americans, he described how the once-recognized "central government" of General Zuloaga had really been the "insurgent party" and "usurped authority." By contrast, the "constitutional" party, though not yet controlling the country, was "supported by a large majority of the people and the States," and hence should be legally recognized.[21] Support for the rule of constitutional law, as sanctioned by a perceived majority rule and popular sovereignty, thus justified Buchanan's flip-flop.

As a treaty that Buchanan delivered to the Senate the following winter was hammered out in negotiations, publicly covered events revealed the inability of any government to control the situation. News reports suggested that European powers were readying to intervene on behalf of the Conservative government. Then, in July 1859, Juan Cortina—a Mexican-born landowner residing near Brownsville—shot the town marshal in retaliation for a prior attack on one of Cortina's former employees. His actions should, as scholars familiar with Mexican sources have stressed, be viewed in the context of the repeated land dispossession and maltreatment of Mexican-born residents in Texas that violated the Treaty of Guadalupe. Tensions escalated, and on September 28 Cortina and his Mexican-born forces seized control of Brownsville. News of the seizure—though not the impetus for it—spread back east, joining conversations about how the U.S. should tackle their Mexican quagmire. Local militia and the Texas Rangers mobilized.[22]

With Congress out of session and political news light, American papers covered events in Mexico in some detail, reminding readers of the high stakes for constitutional republicanism, U.S. diplomacy, and North American independence from Europe. On October 18, 1859, the *New York Herald* (the largest subscribed paper in the nation), followed a thorough public airing of the situation with a strong endorsement of American intervention. Mata had already cultivated the paper's editors and its 84,000 subscribers to support recognition, but events on the Texas border and rumors of European intervention pushed the paper to embrace Buchanan's proposal for military action. Using a front-page map of Mexico, an extensive lead story, and articles from correspondents positioned in Texas and throughout Mexico, the paper contended that "constitutionalists" dominated the coasts and countryside and outnumbered the "church-party," "one to one and one-fifth." The same edition offered two accounts of the Cortina raid under the misleading heading: "MEXICAN BANDITTI CROSSING THE UNITED STATES BORDERS." One correspondent blamed the raid of a "band of robbers and assassins" on the "deplorable condition in which our government has left us," after the withdrawal of federal troops.[23] Neither mentioned that it had been Mexican Americans taking up arms to defend their rights.

In what was the most systematic public argument favoring intervention, the paper concluded that "nothing can save Mexico from utter annihilation as a republic but the powerful interference of our government, and we opine that it will be manifest to everyone" that the Juárez government should sell Sonora and Lower California "and apply the purchase money to bring the present strife to an end." "If the Mexican government cannot repress such outrages as these in the northern States lying on our border . . . we will be compelled in self defence to take these States and govern them ourselves."[24] The progress of events appeared headed toward the military protectorate that Buchanan had urged for the past year and would reiterate forcefully in his December annual message. Indeed, though the president repeatedly denounced "illegal" filibustering, his call for action inspired the secretive Knights of the Golden Circle, hoping to invade Mexico, to go on high alert. In the eyes of that organization's secretive members, mobilization answered a patriotic call.

In the interim, however, Americans crossing an internal border suggested that frontier violence had transferred into America's heartland. On the evening of October 16, John Brown led his party of twenty-two into Harpers Ferry, Virginia, hoping to spark a slave insurrection and create a free Black republic in the Appalachian Mountains. Fuzzy reports reached New York in time for the *Herald* to wedge a small headline "Startling News from Virginia and Maryland" between the multiple Mexican reports. Readers inaccurately learned that a "mob of negro insurrectionists, numbering several hundred and led on by white men, had seized" the federal arsenal.[25] As more accurate reports emerged, easterners learned that the borderland violence attached to Brown's name from killings in Kansas and Cortina's in the Southwest had migrated eastward. The discovery that Brown had plotted and recruited in Canada, shifted Southern eyes to the possibility that fluidity across the generally peaceful Northern international border might also represent a threat.[26] Yet Brown's subsequent sensational trial shoved updates about the Texas border and Mexico toward the back pages of newspapers and possibly halted momentum for intervention.

Collectively, though, Cortina's and Brown's "raids" further heightened white Americans' sense that the federal government needed to patrol borders, control persons of color, and manage the potential disorder created within a modern world. This was particularly true for Southern elites already on edge due to the July 1859 mass release of Hinton Helper's *Compendium of The Impending Crisis*, an abridged version of his revolutionary appeal to non-slaveholding Southerners. In some Texans' minds, Brown and Cortina became representative of a widespread abolitionist plot to terrorize white slaveholders.[27] Slavery's security and expansion and Mexican policy intersected in a meaningful way heading into the crucial election year of 1860.

The late 1850s has been seen as a crisis of "law and order" that prefigured the Civil War. International developments were key to that story, often becoming entangled with domestic politics.[28] The federal government, as well as its relationship to slavery, was most visible on the southwestern American border. White Southerners were full participants in the angst that emerged. To them chaos in Mexico and on the U.S.'s southern border evidenced the need for a stronger federal apparatus, which, as they saw it, didn't seem to be positively protecting slavery in states and territories. Such arguments, in turn, furthered Republicans' conviction that there was a Slave Power conspiracy.

Signs of institutional dysfunction came firmly into view in early 1860 as the House of Representatives proved incapable of selecting a Speaker, a standoff that highlighted the lasting political effects of Brown's raid and Helper's book. In the Senate, a series of different dramas unfolded, driven forward by Buchanan's annual message, the delivery of the McLane-Ocampo treaty terms, and demands from Texans, including their former colleague Sam Houston. In addition to justifying recognition of Juárez's government, Buchanan's December 1859 annual message again sought the power to "employ a sufficient military force to enter Mexico for the purpose of obtaining indemnity for the past and security for the future." "A government which is either unable or unwilling to redress such wrongs is derelict in its highest duty," he suggested.[29] Both his military and his diplomatic plans, however, floundered in an environment further toxified by inter- and intraparty warfare and sectional grievances.

Developments on the southern periphery again drove the national government into the spotlight. In his inaugural address as governor, Houston praised "the federal arm" for working with Texas Rangers to push Cortina's main force into Mexico. Still, he suggested, the dual threat of Indians and Mexican banditti kept the 2,000-mile border in chaos. The message Houston projected to Washington differed from that of other federal officials on the ground. Army officers ranging from Robert E. Lee to Sam Heintzelman, who commanded troops along the border, understood that Rangers were at least as culpable, having, in Heintzelman's words, been "burning all—friends and foes."[30] The reports sent to Commanding General of the Army Winfield Scott, who had just returned from calming a border dispute in the Pacific Northwest, suggested that the so-called "Rio Grande War" was purely an intrastate affair, "commenced by Texans, and carried on (vainly) by and between them."[31] Angry at the intimation, Houston, in letters to Buchanan, his cabinet officers, and Senate colleagues, declared that Mexico's disorder had spilled over into Texas. He demanded federal money and the mustering of 10,000 men, boasting that in thirty days he could "make reclamation upon Mexico for all her wrongs."[32] Buchanan's own special agent fretted that Houston might indeed take matters into his own hands.[33] Rumors that Cortina had a large following in Matamoros and concerns about extralegal actions by Mexicans, Texans, and Indians kept federal officials worried that the United States could be drawn into Mexico's civil war.

This fear pervaded Washington, DC, as the Senate debated a bill offering positive protection for slavery in the territories, argued over the funding of a special Texas Voluntary regiment, and privately discussed the McLane-Ocampo Treaty. In early March Texas's states' rights firebrand and Houston's intrastate nemesis, Louis Wigfall, proposed amending West Point's annual funding bill to include $1.1 million to create and pay a volunteer force of Texas Rangers. A South Carolinian by birth, Wigfall chastened the federal government for neglecting Texas, attributing it to the state's having only four electoral votes. His irregular request prompted a heated Senate and House debate over the boundaries of federal-state relations and the limits of executive leadership, all tinctured by partisan and sectional attitudes and framed in anticipation of upcoming party conventions.

Aspirants for the Democratic nomination, including Virginia Senator James Murray Mason, Jefferson Davis, and Stephen Douglas lined up to demonstrate themselves willing to protect the border. Aware of the complexity of the situation and concerned that it was "drifting" "into a war between the two countries," Davis believed more federal troops were required to fulfill "our duty of protection to Texas on the one side, and our obligations to Mexico on the other."[34] Like Douglas, he believed it necessary to place Texas troops "under the articles of war, where we can restrain and control them, and then let them defend the frontier."[35] Disorder within and outside of the Union were mutually reinforcing, leading many to urge stronger federal oversight.

As Democratic leaders positioned themselves as strong on defense, Republican leaders lambasted their ineptitude. Maine Senator William Fessenden demanded that "the Democratic party take the responsibility," even intimating it was censurable that the border had been intentionally left vulnerable to keep the issue alive and to justify Buchanan's plan for military intervention.[36] Senators from New Hampshire and Massachusetts questioned not only the need and expense for more troops but expressed fears that Buchanan or Houston would use them for territorial aggrandizement.[37] In April, similar debates in the House pitted advocates for additional federal aid, including Texas Representatives John Reagan, Andrew Jackson Hamilton, and the Mexican-born delegate from New Mexico, Mariano Otero, against northeastern Republicans who blamed Texans for the violence.[38]

Resistance to the Texas Volunteer Regiment bill likely furthered southwestern Democrats' (particularly the Texas delegation's) willingness to support William Yancey's Alabama Platform, which demanded a federal slave code for the territories.[39] In June after party conventions had concluded, senators (by a partisan vote of 23 to 18) amended the appropriation bill to include the proposal. The Treasury Department set aside $750,000 in its budget for the expense.[40] Yet the House, under a Republican-led coalition, defeated the Senate amendment.[41] Republican papers celebrated their side's "searching and unanswerable presentation of facts," which "utterly demolished the flimsy pretexts upon which this expenditure was proposed."[42] Deep South politicians decried what one Mississippi representative called the "cold-blooded spirit of sectional prejudice."[43] In the Conference Committee that met on June 19, the Senate rescinded its amendment, killing the Texas regiment bill, and handing Wigfall and other Texas fire-eaters what they may have wanted all along: propaganda for secession.

Congressional gridlock and partisanship also torpedoed Buchanan's broader diplomatic initiative with Mexico, the McLane-Ocampo treaty then being discussed in special secret executive session. Negotiated by special agent Marylander Robert McLane and Juárez's trusted minister, Melchor Ocampo, it reflected Liberals' desire not to cede territory but also the asymmetrical relationship between the two governments. It gave the U.S president the right to transport troops and military supplies along two approved routes through Mexican territory. It established commercial reciprocity but almost unilaterally placed the determination of duty-free items in the U.S. Congress's hands. A crucial passage obliged either government to "seek the aid of the other" for "safety and security" against foreign and domestic enemies. This clause's flexibility permitted Mexican liberals to pronounce it a valuable alliance (and a pathway to desperately needed funds) against European-backed conservatives. But the treaty did not commit the U.S. to respond. It could be interpreted as an open pass for limited U.S. military intervention to protect its expanded economic interests. McLane and the administration also saw it as a necessary weapon to keep foreign powers at bay. The price for Americans was merely $4 million, half of which would be kept to indemnify American citizens.

Pro-treaty forces across the U.S. political spectrum appreciated its strategic value and claimed the treaty would cut into British commercial dominance, secure transit to the Pacific, and possibly even lay the groundwork for future acquisitions.[44] Broadening U.S. support for Juárez's government and continued concern about European intervention generated bipartisan media endorsements for the treaty. One survey of newspapers suggests that twenty of thirty-four advocated ratification, including several important Republican papers such as the *Chicago Press and Tribune* and the *New York Times*.[45] The *New York Times* saw it as "the entering wedge by which this immense India of the West is to be opened to our citizens." After the terms were leaked, the *Times* predicted it would be ratified and declared it would accomplish the goal of "Americanizing Mexico."[46] Yet damning speeches on the eve of the Democratic convention in Charleston led Committee Chair Mason to temporarily pull back the treaty until after the party conventions.[47] Republicans highlighted fears of executive power and slave expansion; Wigfall and South Carolinian James Henry Hammond attacked the treaty for its potential for "the addition of that mongrel population."[48] After the conventions were over, Mexican diplomats and the Buchanan administration fought to save the treaty, but on May 31 the U.S. Senate handily rejected it: 27 to 18.[49]

The Senate's refusal to unseal the session records left newspaper editors, and subsequent historians, speculating about why the treaty failed. Pearl Ponce's examination suggests there was not one clear determinant. Republican opposition referred to concerns that trade reciprocity would harm American manufacturers; it also had to do with fears about Buchanan's "penchant for the war-making power" and that an "entangling alliance" with Juárez's forces would lead the nation into war rather than prevent it.[50] Regardless, afterward, sectional and partisan divisions were blamed for what many saw as a missed opportunity to stabilize Mexican liberal governance and expand U.S. market access and influence for the minimal cost of $4 million. Rejection befuddled McLane, Buchanan, and supporters, including a Boston contributor to the *Herald* who decried "shortsighted" Northern and Southern "extremists," who had shelved "the most advantageous [treaty] we have ever made with any nation."[51]

Historians disagree on what the treaty says about Mexican-American relations, but for our purposes here, the treaty's eventual postponement to the December session further suggested that dysfunction in Washington was costing the United States abroad.[52] Though Republican-leaning and usually a harsh critic of Buchanan, the *New York Times* blamed Republicans for choosing party over country, adding the failed ratification to its litany of why the Senate as a body had "greatly deteriorated in late years."[53] The *Times* rival, the *New York Herald,* concurred, lamenting the lack of statesmanship and arguing that the bipartisan rejection "furnishes striking evidence of the utter disintegration of all parties, and the miserable policy to which the country has been reduced by the agitation of the slavery question." Americans would be deprived of the "immense commerce of Mexico" due to "mere partisan politics and sectional squabbles."[54] Regardless of the reasons for the rejection, to the media and the public Congress had failed to implement a diplomatic or military strategy to resolve America's biggest foreign policy challenge.

That perception and failure to provide additional funds and troops could not have been more poorly timed for moderate Texans, as it merged with the central question of slavery's security within the Union. Just two weeks after the congressional session ended, a series of fires in central and north Texas generated fears of an abolitionist plot. Between July 8 and 12 dozens of fires burned large portions of Dallas and Denton. The apparent cause was high temperatures (between 106 and 110 degrees) that ignited highly unstable phosphorous "prairie matches" recently introduced into the area. Yet the actions of local slaves drew attention, and either real, forced, or falsified (it is hard to say which) slave confessions, congealed into regional and then national headlines that terror had struck Texas. Many local newspaper editors predicted that the plot was to culminate in a massive slave insurrection on August 6: the day for state elections.[55] Vigilance societies warned of more John Brown–like attacks. Immigrants, Northern merchants, and ministers came under particular scrutiny. The elections went off without any particularly heightened violence, but in the context of fear and frustration, Texans lined up behind militant state officials. It was an early indication of Southern Democratic candidate John Breckinridge's landslide victory in November, in which he won 75 percent of the votes over Houston's preferred Fusion ticket headed by John Bell.

Nationally, the collapse of the ratification of the Mexican treaty, as well as one with Nicaragua, appeared more damning because it expanded the vacuum into which European powers could step. News of French and British treaties with Nicaragua circulated. Spain had already informed U.S. officials that they were preparing for military action. In July the British Minister to Washington, Lord Lyons, asked Buchanan to work with Britain and France to mediate a truce. The Buchanan administration refused, citing its desire not "to discredit the Juárez Government or put it on the same level as its opponent."[56] In mid-August, the *New York Times* claimed "on the best authority" that France, England, Spain, and Prussia had signed a convention for the pacification of Mexico.[57] Political dysfunction had prevented Americans special access to Mexican markets and possibly lands, while offering European powers a likely entrance through the back door.

As threats of secession swirled during the fall presidential canvassing, Unionists feared that the United States might be poised to follow Mexico into the abyss. In mid-October, the *New Orleans Commercial Bulletin,* which supported John Bell's candidacy, warned of a land "drenched in civil and fraternal blood," declaring that "Mexico is but a faint picture of what our condition would be upon a gigantic scale."[58] A frustrated James Buchanan hoped that his countrymen would back away from that prospect and aimed his December message to Congress at halting secession and a final attempt to unite Americans behind a common Mexican policy. He at least took comfort in the fact that relations with Great Britain had significantly improved, as evidenced by the Prince of Wales' tour of the United States and visit to Washington, DC, in October 1860.

Princes and Provinces in the American Imagination

If events in Mexico provided an ominous portent of what the United States might become, developments in Canada reminded some Americans of where they had once been, and of improving relations with Great Britain. Though still marred by mutual suspicion, by 1860 a shared desire for profitable peace had fostered a "rapprochement" in British-U.S. relations.[59] Canada factored into this détente, as the Canadian annexation crisis of 1849 retreated from view and the reciprocity treaty of 1854 contributed to an uptick in cross-border trade, particularly with northern states.[60] Americans like William Seward continued to talk of Canada as "half annexed to the United States," though by the late 1850s most Canadians had moved beyond considering annexation desirable.[61] They took an especially dim view of America's highly partisan elections. The Toronto *Globe* decried that "questions of public policy, or enlarged statesmanship, are never discussed on the eve of an election." Instead political parties strive "to gain power by deceiving, coaxing, bribing, and betraying" the "ignorant unreasoning mass."[62] To Canadians, the U.S. political crisis evidenced not only slavery's bankruptcy but also the problem of excessive democracy unaided by the bonds of monarchy and religion. Those Americans following Canadian newspapers did not always see a pretty portrait of themselves.

When they thought of their place in the British Empire, Canadians worried more about neglect than oppression, leading to formal invitations that culminated in the eighteen-year-old prince's visit to lay the cornerstone of Ottawa's new Federal Parliament and to open the spectacular 9,144-foot Victoria Bridge spanning the St. Lawrence near Montreal. Westminster and (after some cajoling) the Queen welcomed the opportunity to demonstrate strength, not through a restrictive legalistic written constitution or armed military force, but through personal loyalty, inclusivity, and good governance.[63] Aiming to showcase the colonies' potential, Canada's diverse populations—French and English speakers, Protestants and Catholics, Black and white—sought royal attention by building arches and inviting the eighteen-year-old Edward and his entourage to visit their communities. Anglophiles in New York City extended their own invitation, and the foreign secretary Lord John Russell and Queen Victoria's husband Prince Albert convinced her that extending the trip to the United States would further thaw relations, just a few years removed from a Crimean War recruitment scandal and the dismissal of Britain's minister to the United States.

U.S. coverage of the Canadian tour was extensive, with major publications running daily or weekly updates. The *New York Herald* and *Frank Leslie's Illustrated News* hired correspondents to travel with the prince. American commentators noted, and at times mocked, the stoicism of the repeated ceremonial dedications. They could not, however, ignore the sincerity of patriotic feeling, something that tempered Northern expansionists' aspirations. Even the biggest controversy, the ultra-Protestant Orangemen's decision to build triumphalist arches, reflected excessive imperial pride, not its absence.[64] Religion may have been more politically disruptive in Canada (and Mexico) than in the U.S., but the visit to the United States heightened Americans' self-consciousness.

Americans' concern that the prince's visit would showcase American political dysfunction pervaded public coverage. The *Herald* anticipated that "Baron Renfrew," the name Albert took upon entering the United States, would find a favorable reception despite the "warm political contest going on, but there is no religious element in it."[65] The *New York Times* worried that the stay in New York would amount to "torture" and expose the prince to political "hacks" and "American rowdies": the "dirty Americans of no education and bad manners."[66] Fear that financing events would generate an embarrassing congressional debate, President Buchanan nearly torpedoed the DC visit but used discretionary funds and kept the affair more private.[67] The prince's arrival in Detroit on September 20 had an inauspicious start. As the prince disembarked, the estimated crowd of 30,000 well-wishers (two-thirds of Detroit's population) rushed the dock, nearly drowning the secretary to Canada's governor general under a paddleboat wheel. "Disorder reigned supreme," one Canadian correspondent wrote, suggesting that Americans "neglected to cultivate the love of order as ardently as they have cherished the love of liberty."[68] As the prince continued to St. Louis, Chicago, Cincinnati, and Pittsburgh, reporters continually commented on the crowd's diversity, zeal, and relative roughness.[69]

The visit dovetailed with the moment in U.S. urban history when, according to Mary Ryan, "social and cultural divisions of American cities moved beyond the theatrical stage to become violent struggles for power at the very center of the polity."[70] U.S. crowds and crowd control became part of a transatlantic dialogue about democracy's tendency toward disorder. Chicago was praised because "the police kept admirable order," while in Albany only "the hickory clubs of the policemen" kept the "vast crowds present" in good order.[71] Though Congress was out of session, the *New York Times* correspondent still lamented the "mobbish" scene at the White House levee: "No telegraphic statement can do justice to the inexcusable lack of prearrangement . . . not to speak of order. . . . The royal party have certainly seen Democracy unshackled for once."[72]

Concerns deepened as the entourage traveled to Richmond, Virginia, a stop added in response to criticism that the South had been neglected. Reports circulated that "ruffianly and depraved" lower-class whites shouted insults while the prince visited the city's statue of George Washington. Rumors that the prince would visit a Black church swirled, but a delegate went instead. Though the prince received an address from loyal subjects in Canada and the "Colored Citizens of Boston," generally speaking, Black efforts to draw attention to their plight were casualties of a celebrated Anglo-Saxon unity and pushed to the margins of the carefully orchestrated public spectacles. They were rarely mentioned in the papers.[73]

Of great concern to organizers was the trip's last leg through northeastern areas with denser Irish populations and during state elections likely to determine the presidency. It was an "unfortunate mistake," Boston and Philadelphia newspapers noted, that the prince would arrive in Philadelphia the evening of that state's crucial election. "Next to the election in New York in November, this is the last sight which we should wish the future ruler of Great Britain to witness," the *Boston Daily Advertiser* editorialized. "If the scenes then presented to his eyes do not give him an abiding hate for popular institutions, it will be because he can see much farther below the surface than most Englishmen," noted the newspaper edited by Nathan Hale, a powerful Boston Republican.[74] Careful planning and better crowd control prevented any disruption. In an episode dripping with historical irony, a Philadelphia opera audience serenaded the prince with "God Save the Queen."[75] The prince's entourage then traveled to New York, along with news of Republican victory in Pennsylvania. The centerpiece of that visit was a military parade that included the prince in martial uniform. Fortunately for organizers, the native Irish 69th militia refused to participate, making the largest single protest of the tour a silent one.

Local and pro-administration newspapers drew on this to push against the narrative of overly rowdy republicanism, spinning enthusiasm into a source of civic pride. Proud of the orderliness of the large New York crowd, which numbered at least 200,000 (some suggest as many as half a million) onlookers, the *Herald* declared that the tour was proof that in the United States "people enjoy the fullest amount of liberty without degenerating into license and anarchy."[76] "Penetrate the surface," Detroit's *Daily Advertiser* advised, and one would see "a great popular demonstration, unrestrained by the resources of a more artificial state of society."[77]

Yet the *Herald* spoke a bit too prematurely, and what transpired "on the surface" mattered, sometimes literally. The collapse of a New York hotel ballroom floor due to overcrowding and hasty construction, tarnished the New York stop. It typified, contributors to the *New York Times* wrote, "the salient trait of our wild, reckless, and brilliant civilization." Another speculated whether "it is absolutely impossible for us to do anything well?"[78] The New York *Evening Post* saw the collapsing floor as confirming "what John Bull terms, not without reason, our national vice, our recklessness of life, as exhibited in our hasty, imperfect, hand-to-mouth methods." With the eyes of the Anglophone world on New York, the result had proved "inconceivably humiliating."[79]

Other reports, including *Harper's Weekly*'s "The Prince and the Ladies," highlighted the large number of women in crowds, offering a gendered analysis intimating that events intended to evidence mutual national respect might be pushing toward unseemly and unpatriotic fawning. Drawing from American coverage, London's *Punch* magazine speculated that the eighteen-year-old prince passed the time looking for a partner among "one of Columbia's fascinating daughters." Buchanan's thirty-year-old single niece Harriet Lane became the source of some speculation, and allegedly Buchanan had her portrait removed from the prince's bedroom for fear of creating a scandal. According to Ian Radforth, most journalists "stuck with the story that the women of the United States, were smitten with the prince, so much so that they pushed at the very bounds of appropriate decorum."[80] The flirtatious coverage stressed real and future fealty between two countries, but also stirred angst that ladies of liberty had found the great-grandson of their former scourge so alluring.

In the final analysis, the tour succeeded in fostering goodwill between the two countries. Americans took special note of the prince's visit to Washington's tomb and his meeting with the last surviving veteran of the Battle of Bunker Hill. For some, including Buchanan and other DC insiders, the tour served as a distraction from the coming storm. As a focusing point in national and international political culture, however, the tour also revealed and amplified anxieties about the Union and its future. Did popular sovereignty create orderly societies and good governance or was it destined to devolve into cycles of political violence like those plaguing Latin America? Was the oft-supposed U.S. annexation of Canada really possible, or had the prince cemented a bond that the U.S. would never break? Should patriotic Americans be worried that republican men and women were so easily entrapped by the spectacle of monarchy, a charge that Irish American newspapers made and that many Northerners in turn leveled against slaveholding aristocrats who had pleaded in vain for more princely attention?

Speculation of the visit's effect continued. As Northerners elected Lincoln to the White House, the media looked for clues about how Britain perceived them as hosts. They came in reprints of English newspapers' coverage of the tour and through mostly favorable, long-form accounts written by correspondents traveling with the group. The British-born reporter for the *New-York Tribune* declared the trip a success, noting that the prince had "been enabled to glance, although hastily, at the moral and political phenomena of popular sovereignty which has earned for the United States the reputation of being the school of statesmen and the study of philosophers."[81] Yet on election day, November 6, the *New York Times*—which had endorsed Lincoln—reprinted a scathing London *Times* account of the prince's time in Richmond, where a "mob of four or five hundred slave-dealers, horse-dealers, small planters, liquor-store keepers and loungers, together with probably a large sprinkling of blackguardism from Ireland" had insulted the Queen's son. That article contrasted sharply with a London *News* piece the paper had reprinted ten days earlier praising the entourage's orderly reception in Lincoln's home state.[82] What Buchanan declared in his final annual message to be "a most auspicious event" that "cannot fail to increase the kindred and kindly feelings" between "the Government and people of both countries" could also be used to foster sectional overtones within the Union, suggesting that the slaveholding South represented the real threat to good order.[83]

Like a reflecting pool in motion, the prince's visit offered Americans a reminder of their own internal disputes and insecurities, including a rowdiness that didn't play well in Europe and which some feared might be imperiling the Union. It suggested that relations with a historical enemy had eased considerably, but also that an Anglophobia that had once united Americans might be dissipating at the time that sectionalism was dividing the country. Finally, it raised the prospect that Britain's presence in North America was likely more permanent than Americans had once thought.

Secession and the Reimagining of North American Sovereignty

Developments in Mexico and British North America thus offered important reference points for the secession drama that unfolded after Lincoln's election. Many disunionists argued—good evidence to the contrary—that federal foreign policy had stood in the way of greater direct trade with Britain, limited their access to Mexico, and failed to adequately protect their border. Unionists—north, south, and border—saw secessionists as perpetuating Mexican-style anarchy, while stressing that the positive relations between Northerners and Britons evidenced during the Prince of Wales's visit could prevent a cotton-based alliance with seceding states. The apparent rapprochement with *the* historical enemy, Britain, and public celebrations of a shared ethno-cultural Anglo-Americanism, however, weakened Anglophobia—traditionally a centripetal force that had held the Union together. Competing regionalized interpretations of this development undermined efforts, including Secretary of State William Seward's desperate spring 1861 attempt at promoting a foreign war to hold back a second secessionist wave.

Building upon pro-extension election arguments, leading immediate secessionists brushed aside anti-expansionist sentiment within their ranks, suggesting that freed from free-soil Republicans, an independent slaveholding South would somehow further international order. Some trumpeted a Southern Confederacy as a vehicle for a slave empire that would eventually encircle the Caribbean Rim and achieve direct trade with Britain. "Expansion seems to be the law and destiny of our institutions," Alabama state senator Lewis Maxwell Stone told his state's secession convention, concluding that "to remain healthful and prosperous within, and to make sure our development and power, it seems essential that we grow."[84] Union with a free-soil North no longer provided that vehicle. One New Orleans newspaper opined that Texans' recent frustration with the federal government would culminate in a revitalized Lone Star Republic or make the state an anchor for a Southern Confederacy: It "has every reason to expect from both England and France encouragement and support in the early annexation of Mexico, if not Central America."[85] The "manly" logic of slavery's post-independence expansion played well among groups aggrieved about their political and economic decline within the Union. Members of the mysterious Knights of the Golden Circle swiftly morphed from filibusterers into pro-secession militants, and from there into state-sanctioned soldiers.[86]

But secessionists didn't have to desire more territory to use the border as a shiv against the federal government. In those circles, disorder was projected, not as something Southerners had contributed to, but as a failure of U.S. power to protect white Southerners from non-white threats. Weeks before he resigned and joined the Texas secession convention, U.S. congressman and future Confederate postmaster general John Reagan argued that border instability justified secession: "We have a long Mexican boundary, and a long Indian frontier, infested by hostile savages throughout its whole extent; and yet this Government has refused for years to defend us against them." Should the president and General Scott (already maligned for insinuating that Texans had contributed to border instability) now act like Santa Anna had, Reagan intimated, Texans would not hesitate to again overthrow a "military despotism."[87] They didn't even wait to see.

Over the objections of Unionist Governor Houston, secessionists seized on an extralegal and probably illegal convention called by the chief justice of the Supreme Court. When Houston summoned the legislature in a desperate attempt to undercut that convention, state legislators who had been elected in August when frustration with failed Mexican diplomacy and fears about border instability and slave insurrection were at an inflection point refused. Instead, they retroactively validated the justice's action and handed over power to the secession convention. Referring to their state's unique entry into the Union and stressing their reliance on "the servitude of the African to the white race," Texans accused the federal authority of wavering between negligence and malevolence. "Partially under the control of these our unnatural and sectional enemies" it "has for years almost entirely failed to protect the lives and property of the people of Texas against the Indian savages on our border, and more recently against the murderous forays of banditti from the neighboring territory of Mexico."[88] Most Texans apparently assumed that the new Montgomery-based Confederacy, soon led by a man known for fighting Mexicans, would be more attentive to Texans' needs.

This selective narrative of federal neglect flowed naturally into one highlighting the escalating aggression of "non-slaveholding States" against the institution of slavery so central to Southern society. Referring to assumptions about the summer fires, Texas secessionists' "Declaration of Causes" accused Northerners of having invaded "Southern soil and murdered unoffending citizens," "sent seditious pamphlets," and "hired emissaries among us to burn our towns and distribute arms and poison to our slaves." Northerners, they claimed, "demand the abolition of negro slavery throughout the confederacy, the recognition of political equality between the white and negro races, and avow the determination to press on their crusade against us, so long as a negro slave remains in these States."[89] Very few white Northerners did, in fact, demand those things. Free blacks did. So too did many Mexicans.

And hence, to white Southerners like Reagan, Mexico became an illustration of the Union's future under "Black Republican" leadership. The United States would soon become like the governments of "Mexico and Central and South America," who "attempted to establish governments of mongrels, to enfranchise Indians and free negroes with all the rights of freemen, and invest them . . . with control of those governments. It was a failure there; it would be a failure here."[90] The virulent racism undergirding secession resonated especially deeply among white Southerners who believed they could indefinitely preserve a strict racial hierarchy.

Southern unionists also believed in white supremacy, and most believed in slavery. But they inverted the logic, suggesting that secession would amplify mistakes they believed Mexico had made. For them, a presumed slave empire would be disastrous for Anglo-Saxons accustomed to living as a racial majority. In that vein, the *Louisville Daily Journal* asked its readership to ponder: "Why should the enlightened people of these States assimilate themselves to the half-naked savages of Mexico and Central America, who change their governments with as much facility as they change their few and filthy garments?"[91] Assuming the Federal Union had no interest in acquiring more land inhabited by nonwhites, they assumed that economic ties and white nationalism dictated remaining in the Federal Union.

Other unionists drew direct political comparisons between secessionists and coup makers in Mexico's Conservative Party. Before Austin unionists, Governor Houston compared fire-eater William Yancey's so-called "Southern constitutional party" to the parties of Mexico: "They deem it patriotism now to overturn the Government" though constitutionally elected. "Let them succeed, and in that class of patriots they will be able to outrival Mexico."[92] Experience taught the old warrior that secession would lead to chaos and war, and despite his frustrations with Scott, Houston believed the Union a useful instrument for protecting Texans. Unlike governors elsewhere, he refused to seize federal property or call for a convention. To his critics, this brave position appeared timid, comparable to his early efforts to negotiate with, rather than destroy, Cortina. In the end, fear and frustration outweighed Houston's appeal for calm. On February 23, when secession was put to a public referendum, Texans voted for political rebellion, 46,188 to 15,149. Outside of North and Central Texas, areas with disproportionately large numbers of German immigrants, Southern independence ruled the day.

As secession came more fully into view, Northern minds also drew connections to Mexico's recent past. Secessionists, the *New-York Tribune* charged, were like "the people of South America and Mexico, who attempt to overturn the Government every time they are beaten in any election."[93] In October, around the time he welcomed the Prince of Wales to New York (as vice chair of that city's arrangements committee), Winfield Scott put to paper his "Views suggesting imminent danger." The speculative exercise, which he privately forwarded to leading "conservative" politicians and editors, and eventually to Lincoln, predicted that if the "glorious Union" was broken, "reuniting its fragments" would require "despotism of the swords. To effect such result, the intestine wars of our Mexican neighbors, would, in comparison with our struggles, sink into mere child's play."[94]

But Mexico also loomed as a cautionary tale against constitutional compromise, one that substantively and rhetorically stiffened Unionists' spines. Upon hearing that his inauguration might be held up until a constitutional convention could be called, Lincoln recalled pages from Mexico's history. The generally silent president-elect allowed a friend, probably Representative William Kellogg, to inform the *New York Herald* that he viewed any "concession in the face of menace, the destruction of the government itself," signifying "that our system shall be brought down to a level with the existing disorganized state of affairs in Mexico."[95] Lincoln's strategic comparison to Mexico immediately harkened to the constitutional bartering that had led to four changes in presidential leadership in 1855 and plunged Mexico into war. He insisted he would not "buy the privilege of taking possession of this government to which we have a constitutional right." With peace conventions and congressional petitions urging immediate constitutional or even extra-constitutional change, Lincoln's rare public statement quickly spread. Similarly, after the Confederate firing on Fort Sumter, his arch-political opponent, Stephen Douglas, told the Illinois state legislature that if secession were permitted to happen, "you will find the future history of the United States written in the history of Mexico."[96] In a matter of months, Americans had gone from discussing how to "Americanize Mexico" to fears that the United States was becoming Mexicanized, a concern that continued into the Reconstruction Era.[97]

Disunion opened a dizzying array of geopolitical possibilities, most of which have not been taken seriously by scholars. Yet the broader context presented here explains why contemporaries saw reorientation as not just possible, but likely. Newspaper reports and politicians' predictions reveal little consensus over how North American sovereignty would change, but few believed the geopolitical map would remain unaltered. The stereotypically level-headed Winfield Scott anticipated disunion would result in four "new confederacies," whose capitals would be Columbia, South Carolina; Albany, New York; Alton or Quincy, Illinois; and an unnamed capital for the Pacific States.[98] How separate confederacies might shake up international politics remained a subject of intense speculation.

As Jefferson Davis dispatched emissaries to Great Britain, France, Russia, Belgium, and to Juárez's government, Confederates highlighted their near monopoly on cotton and the economic potential of cutting out Northern middlemen and manufacturers. They also predicted that a long U.S.-Canadian border and an unresolved conflict over San Juan Island offered potential friction points that could spiral the remaining Union into war with Britain, thus increasing the likelihood of an Anglo-Confederate alliance.[99] Davis's ill-suited emissary to Mexico, John Pickett, was instructed to portray Southerners as the inheritors of the legacy of Henry Clay—one of the first Americans to advocate for Mexican recognition. He was even to inquire about an alliance with Juárez's government by highlighting the speed with which Confederates could dispatch troops to aid against "foreign invasion."[100] Pickett's condescension failed, and he was consistently outmaneuvered by Lincoln's minister, Thomas Corwin.

That outcome took months to determine, and many people north of the Mason-Dixon line continued to imagine the worst. Election arguments against a "Slave Power" flowed naturally into projections that a Confederate State would dominate Lower North America and the Caribbean Rim.[101] Cotton-fueled speculation of a Confederate-British alliance elevated anxiety that Northerners would be surrounded by hostile powers. Westerners feared that Confederate control of the Lower Mississippi Valley would limit their access to global grain markets. Southern dominance of Mexico and partnership with Europeans would curtail access to markets that had been offered in recent treaty negotiations. Nor did Juárez's military victory over Conservative forces in December assuage fears of Confederate expansion, especially after rumors of European encroachment gave way to the spring reality of Spain's seizure of San Domingo. That prompted the *Daily Boston Traveller* to believe that "there is nothing improbable of the idea of an alliance between Spain and Secessia for the partition of Mexico." The editors of that Republican newspaper angrily compared Confederates' disrespect for domestic and international law to those "same principles that prevailed in Barbary" a half-century earlier. These new Confederate "bucaniers" were, in short, lawless land pirates.[102]

Others picked up on British and Canadian news, highlighting that disunion generated embarrassing scenarios including the northern United States' reabsorption into British Canada. The Halifax *Morning Journal* and multiple Toronto papers proposed a "new territorial arrangement" that would welcome the northern Free States, whose population had showered affection onto the prince, into Canada.[103] A correspondent of the *Detroit Free Press* reported that a "scheme for the secession of the Upper Peninsula of this State and its annexation to Canada has been exposed in private circles." Reminiscent of U.S. efforts in northern Mexico, the project, allegedly underwritten by English capitalists interested in mining and railroad efforts, sought to seize on the "distracted state of the country."[104] U.S. coverage of these discussions drove home just how damaging disunion could prove.

As Unionists projected their disdain for anarcho-secessionists onto Confederates, some looked for signs that the Union remained the world's preferred partner and that advantageous conditions still existed. The *Herald* speculated that three million independent-minded Canadians were "ripe for admission into the free confederacy of the North." The report even speculated that Seward, the presumptive secretary of state, "flattering alike the Northwest and Canada, had fixed the capital of the new northern confederacy at or near St. Paul, Minnesota," a reference to a fall campaign speech.[105] Uniting this "northern confederacy of free states" on American terms, required selectively remembering the prince's tour, suggesting that "his Royal highness was received with greater *eclat*" in the United States and that "the disturbances in Canada during the Prince's visit were very considerable." Bennett's paper continued to urge the move, suggesting that the temporary absence of seceding states would allow the votes for annexation.[106]

In contrast to the *Daily Journal*'s speculations, northern newspapers supportive of the McLane-Ocampo treaty like the *New York Times* predicted that freed from the slave power, Mexican lands could now be absorbed into the Union. Referencing a speech by Ohio Senator Benjamin Wade, it lauded Republicans' willingness to embrace a protectorate, free trade, colonization, and eventually full annexation. "The majority of Mexicans," it predicted, would "welcome the Anglo-Saxon energy, intelligence and freedom" and "fly to the free Northern Confederacy."[107] This too was wishful thinking. The previous day Conservative forces conceded the capital to Juárez. The following month, Juárez's minister to the U.S., Matías Romero, traveled to Springfield, impressing on Lincoln his government's sympathy and his own country's desire to be left alone. Mexican military victory mingled with Lincoln's own concerns about further instability in the Southwest led the president-elect to rebuff annexationists within his own party. Instead, he appointed Thomas Corwin, an Ohioan who had opposed the Mexican-American War, and instructed him to work toward mutual stability.

The residue of the prince's visit in the North also initially blunted fears about an Anglo-Confederate alliance. Cotton interests couldn't be ignored, but by winter glowing accounts of the prince's travels through the northern states suggested that England held no "malevolence towards us in our present troubles."[108] As the *Daily Whig and Republican*, based in Quincy, Illinois, saw it, positive transatlantic coverage reflected a "magnanimity of feeling . . . which cannot fail to still further improve the relations bro't about by that occasion, and to promote national amenities in the future." Even before the year was out, an account of the tour tracing the New England portion of the journey suggested that "the reception of the Prince of Wales in the United States affords abundant proof of the depth and sincerity of the affection which is felt by our people for the mother country." Private dinners and side conversations between the prince's entourage and Northerners revealed "the most intimate character" and foretold "an era of still closer alliance between the people of New and of Old England."[109] *The Prince's Visit; A Humorous Description*, a broader and witty assessment written by the Jamaican-born New York émigré Raphael J. de Cordova, drove this point home further. His poetic and illustrated account appeared in April 1861 and ended with a speculative account of the Duke of Newcastle's summary comments to the future King as they pulled away from Portland, Maine:

There are reasons and right and judgements clear
In the Saxon blood that predominates there.
They *may* suffer trouble, and noise, and all that,
But 't will pass and be gone again, quicker 'an 's cat.
They are brethren of ours and brethren together;
They'll survive the storms of political weather.

. . .

They are England's best friends and her noblest pride.
"Adieu, then, my country!" the old DUKE cried;
"For an Englishman still finds his place at their side;
And on thy friendly shores—though on thine alone—
No difference finds he, no change from his own.
Mayest thou still be the favorite child of the Fates!
MAY GOD BLESS AND PRESERVE THEE, THOU UNION OF STATES!"[110]

As Skye Montgomery has shown, coverage stressed the blossoming of a special kinship, a shared sense of civilization, and a belief in a bond that transcended material interests.[111] During the visit, Americans had worried that the republic be perceived as a paragon of democratized law and order. Afterward, with the British press and royal family heaping private and public praise upon them, Northerners congratulated themselves on their success, and after Sumter, strengthened their resolve against Confederate anarchists.

The reality of political uncertainty generated widespread hopes and fears that themselves factored into the political process of disunion. Mexican weakness exacerbated existing tensions within the United States, ensuring that debates over slavery's status in the territories dovetailed with Americans' broader imperial concept. At the same time, American foreign policy failure in Mexico—evidenced militarily in the form of the Cortina or "Rio Grande" War and diplomatically in the failure of the McLane-Ocampo treaty—cast the American state (at least under Democratic leadership) as an appallingly weak one paralyzed by sectional and partisan tension. Secession-minded slaveholders convinced themselves of a better continental destiny outside the Union, one fueled by dreams of a commercially backed partnership with Britain. Republicans and Northern Democrats, by contrast, projected their anxiety about domestic and international order onto rebellious secessionists who had furthered instability in the Southwest and on the streets of Richmond.

In addition to telling us something about how the Civil War came about, triangulating the stories of British Canada, Mexico, and the United States also reminds us of several broader points concerning the North American crisis of the 1860s. Sovereignty is constructed in relational ways, as much on the conceptual boundaries of polities as within them. Border concerns, personal and state-sponsored diplomacy, and international relations crucially informed how people conceived of their own nation and others. Relatedly, understanding how North American sovereignty was remade in the mid-nineteenth century requires fixing an eye on the continued importance of Europe as both a cultural and a political reference point. That was as true for the dissolving United States as it was for British Canada and Mexico.

Notes

1. Erika Pani, "Law, Allegiance, and Sovereignty in Civil War Mexico, 1857–1867," *Journal of the Civil War Era* 7, no. 4 (2017): 570–596; Donathon C. Olliff, *Reforma Mexico and the United States: A Search for Alternatives to Annexation, 1854–1861* (University, AL: University of Alabama Press, 1981); Walter V. Scholes, *Mexican Politics during the Juárez Regime, 1855–72* (Columbia: University of Missouri Press, 1957).

2. Studies include William J. Baker, "Anglo-American Relations in Miniature: The Prince of Wales in Portland, Maine, 1860," *New England Quarterly* 45, no. 4 (1972): 559; Ian Walter Radforth, *Royal Spectacle: The 1860 Visit of the Prince of Wales to Canada and the United States* (Toronto: University of Toronto Press, 2004); Skye Montgomery, "Reannealing of the Heart Ties: The Rhetoric of Anglo-American Kinship and the Politics of Reconciliation in the Prince of Wales' 1860 Tour," *Journal of the Civil War Era* 6, no. 2 (2016): 193–219.

3. Several important recent books have thought globally, including Robert E. May, *Slavery, Race, and Conquest in the Tropics: Lincoln, Douglas, and the Future of Latin America* (Cambridge: Cambridge University Press, 2013); Don H. Doyle, *Secession as an International Phenomenon: From America's Civil War to Contemporary Separatist Movements* (Athens: University of Georgia Press, 2010); Andre M. Fleche, *The Revolution of 1861: The American Civil War in the Age of Nationalist Conflict* (Chapel Hill: University of North Carolina Press, 2012); Steven Hahn, *A Nation without Borders: The United States and Its World in an Age of Civil Wars, 1830–1910* (New York: Viking, 2016); Michael E. Woods, "What Twenty-First-Century Historians Have Said about the Causes of Disunion: A Civil War Sesquicentennial Review of the Recent Literature," *Journal of American History* 99, no. 2 (2012): 415–439. Still, recent accounts of secession scarcely mention Mexico or Canada. See Shearer Davis Bowman, *At the Precipice: Americans North and South during the Secession Crisis* (Chapel Hill: University of North Carolina Press, 2010); Harold Holzer, *Lincoln President-Elect: Abraham Lincoln and the Great Secession Winter 1860–1861*, reprint (New York: Simon & Schuster, 2009); Douglas R. Egerton, *Year of Meteors: Stephen Douglas, Abraham Lincoln, and the Election That Brought on the Civil War*, reprint (New York: Bloomsbury Press, 2013); Elizabeth R. Varon, *Disunion!: The Coming of the American Civil War, 1789–1859* (Chapel Hill: University of North Carolina Press, 2008), 1–15; Michael E. Woods, *Emotional and Sectional Conflict in the Antebellum*

United States (Cambridge: Cambridge University Press, 2014); Rachel A. Shelden, *Washington Brotherhood: Politics, Social Life, and the Coming of the Civil War* (Chapel Hill: University of North Carolina Press, 2013); A. James Fuller, *The Election of 1860 Reconsidered* (Kent, Ohio: Kent State University Press, 2013); Adam Goodheart, *1861: The Civil War Awakening* (New York: Alfred A. Knopf, 2011).

4. Patrick J. Kelly, "The North American Crisis of the 1860s," *Journal of the Civil War Era* 2, no. 3 (2012): 337–368.

5. For thoughtful expositions on American exceptionalism during the era see Andrew Lang, *A Contest of Civilizations: Exposing the Crisis of American Exceptionalism in the Civil War Era* (Chapel Hill: University of North Carolina Press, 2021); Timothy Roberts, *Distant Revolutions: 1848 and the Challenge to American Exceptionalism* (Charlottesville: University of Virginia Press, 2009).

6. See Hammond herein and May, *Slavery, Race and Conquest*.

7. "Inaugural Address," December 21, 1859, in *Writings of Sam Houston*, 8 vols., ed. Eugene Barker (Austin: University of Texas Press, 1938–1943), 7: 383.

8. Hahn, *A Nation without Borders*. For a good discussion of developments in American and Mexican relations see Marcela Terrazas y Basante, ed., *Las relaciones México-Estados Unidos, 1759–2010*, 2 vols. (México City, México: Instituto de Investigaciones Históricas-UNAM/ Secretaría de Relaciones Exteriores, 2012), esp. vol. 1; Ana Rosa Suárez Arguello and Marcela Terrazas Basante, eds., *Politica y Negocios: Ensayos sobre la Relación entre México y los Estados Unidos en el siglo XIX* (Ciudad Universitaria: Universidad Nacional Autónoma de México, 1997).

9. Olliff, *Reforma Mexico and the United States*; Scholes, *Mexican Politics during the Juárez Regime, 1855–72*; Omar S. Valerio-Jiménez, *River of Hope: Forging Identity and Nation in the Rio Grande Borderlands* (Durham, NC: Duke University Press, 2013).

10. Alice L. Baumgartner, *South to Freedom: Runaway Slaves to Mexico and the Road to the Civil War* (New York: Basic Books, 2020); May, *Slavery, Race, and Conquest in the Tropics*.

11. Richard Griswold del Castillo, *The Treaty of Guadalupe Hidalgo: A Legacy of Conflict*, 1st ed. (Norman: University of Oklahoma Press, 1990), 58–60.

12. Jeremy Adelman and Stephen Aron, "From Borderlands to Borders: Empires, Nation-States, and the Peoples in between in North American History," *American Historical Review* 104, no. 3 (1999): 838.

13. James D. Richardson, *A Compilation of the Messages and Papers of the Presidents, 1789–1897*, 10 vols. (Washington, DC: Government Printing Office, 1896–1999), 7:2961–2967; 5:435–436, 469.

14. Forsyth to Marcy, November 8, 1856, in enclosure to Pierce, National Archives, Diplomatic Despatches to Mexico, cited in Olliff, *Reforma Mexico and the United States*, 69.

15. Thomas David Schoonover, *Dollars over Dominion: The Triumph of Liberalism in Mexican-United States Relations, 1861–1867* (Baton Rouge: Louisiana State University Press, 1978).

16. Quoted in *The True Northerner* (Paw Paw, Michigan), April 23, 1858.

17. Carlos Butterfield, *United States and Mexican Mail Steamship Line, and Statistics of Mexico* (New York: J. A. H. Hasbrouck, 1859), 86.

18. "Mexico and Mr. Cox," *Cincinnati Daily Press*, March 26, 1860; Samuel Cox, *Eight Years in Congress from 1857 to 1865: Memoir and Speeches* (New York: Appleton, 1865), 129. Also see "Coxicological Expansion," *Cincinnati Daily Press*, March 26, 1860.

19. For example, *Richmond* (VA) *Enquirer,* August 27, 1858; *The Spirit of Democracy* (Woodsfield, OH), September 8, 1858; *Orleans Independent Standard* (Irasburgh, VT), August 27, 1858.

20. *Harper's Weekly,* April 30, 1859.

21. Richardson, *Messages and Papers,* 7:3095–3097.

22. Marcela Terrazas y Basante, "Ganado, armas y cautivos: Tráfico y comercio il sito en la frontera norte de Mexico, 1848–1882," *Mexican Studies* 35, no. 2 (2019): 171–203 (accessed July 26, 2021), and "Efectos del nuevo lindero. Indios, mexicanos y norteamericanos ante la frontera establecida al término de la guerra entre México y Estados Unidos" (The effects of a new boundary: Indians, Mexicans, and North Americans and the border established after the Mexican-American War), *Norteamérica: Revista Académica del CISAN-UNAM* 11, no. 1 (2016): 75–96.

23. *New York Herald*, October 18, 1859.

24. *New York Herald*, October 18, 1859.

25. *New York Herald*, October 18, 1859.

26. "Gov. Wise and the Harper's Ferry Banditti," *Register* (Raleigh, NC), November 5, 1859.

27. See Jerry Thompson, *Cortina: Defending the Mexican Name in Texas* (College Station: Texas A&M University Press, 2007), 62–63.

28. Mary Ryan, *Civic Wars: Democracy and Public Life in the American City during the Nineteenth Century* (Berkeley: University of California Press, 1997), 136; Phillip S. Paludan, "The American Civil War Considered as a Crisis in Law and Order," *The American Historical Review* 77, no. 4 (1972): 1013–1034.

29. Richardson, *Messages and Papers,* 7:3098.

30. Thompson, *Cortina,* 74. Upon arrival in late March, he scurried around chasing "alarms about Cortinas" but found them all "false," and "the frontier on the river quiet." Lee to Cooper, March 24, 1860, and April 11, 1860, in John Jenkins, *Robert E. Lee on the Rio Grande* (Austin, TX: Jenkins Publishing, 1988), 11, 17–18.

31. Quoted in Sam Houston to John Floyd, April 14, 1860, *Writings of Sam Houston,* 8:19.

32. See Houston to John Floyd, February 15, 1860, in *Writings of Sam Houston,* 7:478–479. To Jacob Thompson, February 17, 1860 (ibid., 480–482); and to James Buchanan, February 17, 1860 (ibid., 482).

33. Thompson, *Cortina,* 93.

34. *Congressional Globe,* Senate, 36th Congress, 1st session, 939.

35. *Congressional Globe,* Senate, 36th Congress, 1st session, 942.

36. *Congressional Globe,* Senate, 36th Congress, 1st session, 938, 942.

37. See Senators Hale and Wilson comments, *Congressional Globe,* Senate, 36th Congress, 1st session, 1142–1144.

38. April 18, 1860, *Congressional Globe,* House, 36th Congress, 1st sess., Appendix, 240 (Hamilton), 290 (Otero). For Republicans see *Congressional Globe,* House, 36th Congress; 1st sess., Appendix, 237 (Olin).

39. John G. Parkhurst, *Official Proceeding of the Democratic National Convention held in 1860 at Charleston and Baltimore* (Cleveland: Nevin's Print, 1860), 62. The Texas delegation caucused with Yancey in Charleston and marched out with the rest of the Lower South delegates at Charleston in protest.
40. *The Daily Exchange* (Baltimore), June 20, 1860.
41. *Cincinnati Daily Press,* June 6, 1860.
42. *New-York Daily Tribune,* June 16, 1860.
43. *Richmond Enquirer,* June 19, 1860.
44. Olliff, *Reforma Mexico and the United States*, 143-144; Pearl T. Ponce, "'As Dead as Julius Caesar': The Rejection of the McLane-Ocampo Treaty," *Civil War History* 53, no. 4 (2007): 342-378.
45. Ponce, "'As Dead as Julius Caesar,'" 374-375.
46. *New York Times,* January 25, 1860, 4; "Americanizing Mexico," *New York Times,* March 23, 1860.
47. *New-York Daily Tribune,* April 12, 1860, 4.
48. *New Orleans Daily Picayune,* June 5, 1860, 2. *Augusta Sentinel,* February 24, 1860; cited in Ponce, "'As Dead as Julius Caesar,'" 351. For more on the racist undercurrent of anti-imperialism see Eric Love, *Race over Empire: Racism and U.S. Imperialism, 1865-1900* (Chapel Hill: University of North Carolina Press, 2004).
49. See Ponce, "'As Dead as Julius Caesar,'" 374-375.
50. "President's Message," *Buchanan County* (Iowa) *Guardian,* January 5, 1860.
51. "The 'Sick Man' of America," *New York Herald,* September 3, 1860.
52. See Ponce, "'As Dead as Julius Caesar.'" For a discussion of Mexican views see Robert N. Sinkin, *The Mexican Reform, 1855-1876: A Study in Liberal Nation-Building* (Austin: Institute of Latin American Studies, 1979), 153-157, and Paolo Riguzzi, *Reciprocidad imposible?: la política del comercio entre México y Estados Unidos, 1857-1938* (Zinacantepec, Estado de México: El Colegio Mexiquense: Instituto Mora, 2003).
53. Cited in *Nebraska Advertiser* (Brownville, NE), March 29, 1860, 2. See also *Vermont Phœnix* (Brattleboro, VT), June 9, 1860.
54. *New York Herald,* June 5, 1860, 6.
55. Donald E. Reynolds, *Texas Terror: The Slave Insurrection Panic of 1860 and the Secession of the Lower South* (Baton Rouge: Louisiana State University Press, 2007), 32.
56. William R. Manning, *Diplomatic Correspondence of the United States: Inter-American Affairs, 1831-1860* (Washington, DC: Carnegie Endowment for International Peace, 1932), 9:287-288.
57. Reprinted in *Boston Post,* August 28, 1860, 2. Yusuf Abdulrahman Nzibo, "Relations between Great Britain and Mexico, 1820-1870" (PhD diss., University of Glasgow, 1979), chap. 9.
58. Reprinted in "The South and the Union," *North American and United States Gazette* (Philadelphia), October 19, 1860.
59. Phillip E. Myers, *Caution and Cooperation: The American Civil War in British-American Relations* (Kent, OH: Kent State University Press, 2008), chap. 1; Sam Walter Haynes, *Unfinished Revolution: The Early American Republic in a British World* (Charlottesville: University of Virginia Press, 2010), chap. 12; Elisa Tamarkin, *Anglo-*

philia: Deference, Devotion, and Antebellum America (Chicago: University of Chicago Press, 2008); F. K. Prochaska, *The Eagle and the Crown: Americans and the British Monarchy* (New Haven, CT: Yale University Press, 2008), esp. 43–81; Duncan Campbell, *Unlikely Allies: Britain, America and the Victorian Origins of the Special Relationship* (London: Bloomsbury Academic, 2008).

60. Robert E. Ankli, "The Reciprocity Treaty of 1854," *Canadian Journal of Economics / Revue Canadienne d'Economique* 4, no. 1 (1971): 1–20; Lawrence H. Officer and Lawrence B. Smith, "The Canadian-American Reciprocity Treaty of 1855 to 1866," *Journal of Economic History* 28, no. 4 (1968): 598–623; Charles Callan Tansill, *The Canadian Reciprocity Treaty of 1854* (Baltimore: Johns Hopkins University Press, 1922).

61. William Henry Seward, "Oration at Columbus, Ohio, September 14, 1853—The Destiny of America," *The Works of William H. Seward*, new ed., vol. 4 (Boston: Houghton, Mifflin, 1888), 124 and "Political Equality the National Idea," Saint Paul (MN), September 18, 1860, ibid. 333. In Minnesota Seward favorably contrasted Canada's "excellent states to be hereafter admitted into the American Union" with the "rapid decay and dissolution" of Spanish American Republics.

62. *Globe*, September 25, 1857, cited in Sydney F. Wise and Robert Craig Brown, *Canada Views the United States: Nineteenth-Century Political Attitudes* (Seattle: University of Washington Press, 1967), 81.

63. The prince's primary escort during the trip, the colonial secretary and Duke of Newcastle, wrote home to Russell about the "rapidly growing affection for England, which I am thoroughly convinced this visit will speedily ripen into a firm and (if properly watched and fostered) an enduring attachment." John Martineau, *The Life of Henry Pelham, Fifth Duke of Newcastle, 1811–1864* (London: John Murray, 1908), 299–300.

64. On the whole, the American press applauded what the *Atlas and Bee* termed the "sensible prince's" decision to avoid the religiously motivated demonstrations of a "silly people." See "A Sensible Prince and a Silly People," *Bangor Daily Whig & Courier* (Bangor, ME), September 11, 1860.

65. "The Prince of Wales and the Presidential Election," *New York Herald*, September 15, 1860, 6.

66. "A True Prince Coming," and "The Coming Prince," *New York Times*, May 9, 1860.

67. Lyons to Newcastle, May 14, 1860, Sir Richard Bickerton (Second Lord) Lyons Papers, Arundel Castle, Box 212. Material from Arundel Castle Archives reproduced by kind permission of his Grace the Duke of Norfolk.

68. "Disorder reigned supreme" and "Chaos had come again," *The Globe* (Toronto), September 25, 1860; N. A. Woods, *The Prince of Wales in Canada and the United States* (London: Bradbury and Evans, 1861), 280; *London Times*, September 22, 1860.

69. See Radforth, *Royal Spectacle*, esp. 313–324. After the royal tour was complete the *Herald* correspondent, British-born Kinahan Cornwallis concluded that in the U.S. "there was a universal desire to pay him respect and do him honor. The enthusiasm was even greater than that displayed by the people of the British Provinces." Kinahan Cornwallis, *Royalty in the New World, or the Prince of Wales in America* ... (New York: M. Doolady, 1860), 163, 174.

70. Ryan, *Civic Wars*, 136.

71. Radforth, *Royal Spectacle*, 319.
72. *New York Times*, October 5, 1860.
73. Radforth, *Royal Spectacle*, 334; Prochaska, *The Eagle and the Crown*, 76.
74. "An Unfortunate Mistake," *Boston Daily Advertiser*, September 12, 1860.
75. Prochaska, *The Eagle and the Crown*, 69.
76. "Welcome to the Prince," *New York Herald*, October 12, 1860.
77. *Daily Advertiser* (Detroit), September 21, 1860.
78. Radforth, *Royal Spectacle*, 358.
79. Radford, *Royal Spectacle*, 360. *Evening Post* (New York), October 15, 1860.
80. Radforth, *Royal Spectacle*, 330–335, quote 333; "The Prince and the Ladies," *Harper's Weekly*, October 13, 1860; "Ode on the Departure of the Prince of Wales," *Punch Magazine* (London), July 21, 1860, and the cartoon "The Next Dance," October 20, 1860.
81. Cornwallis, *Royalty in the New World*, 245.
82. *New York Times*, November 6 and October 26, 1860; Radforth, *Royal Spectacle*, 324.
83. James Buchanan, "Fourth Annual Message," *The American Presidency Project*, http://www.presidency.ucsb.edu/ws/index.php?pid=29501 (accessed September 18, 2018).
84. Cited in Adrian Robert Brettle, "The Fortunes of War: Confederate Expansionist Ambitions during the American Civil War" (PhD diss., University of Virginia, 2014), 25.
85. Dwight L. Dumond, ed., *Southern Editorials on Secession* (New York: Century, 1931), 442.
86. David C. Keehn, *Knights of the Golden Circle: Secret Empire, Southern Secession, Civil War* (Baton Rouge: Louisiana State University Press, 2013), 113–170.
87. John H. Reagan, "State of the Union. Speech . . . Delivered in the House of Representatives, January 15, 1861," in *Southern Pamphlets on Secession, November 1860–April 1861*, ed. Jon L. Wakelyn (Chapel Hill: University of North Carolina Press, 1996), 154, 150.
88. "Declaration of Causes: February 2, 1861: A declaration of the causes which impel the State of Texas to secede from the Union," Texas State Library and Archives Commission, https://www.tsl.texas.gov/ref/abouttx/secession/2feb1861.html (accessed August 14, 2018).
89. "Declaration of Causes."
90. Reagan, "State of the Union," 150.
91. "The Commission to Washington—The Virginia and Kentucky Resolutions," *Louisville* (KY) *Daily Journal*, February 1, 1861.
92. "Speech before a Union Mass Meeting, Austin, Texas, September 22, 1860," in *Writings of Sam Houston*, 8:153.
93. For charge and rebuttal see "The Policy of Aggression," *New Orleans Daily Crescent*, December 14, 1860, in Dumond, ed., *Southern Editorials*, 332.
94. "Views suggested by imminent danger," Winfield Scott to Abraham Lincoln, October 29, 1860, Abraham Lincoln papers: Series 1. General Correspondence, Library of Congress, https://www.loc.gov/resource/mal.0418800/?sp=2&r=-0.043,0.572,1.379,1.027,0 (accessed August 29, 2018).
95. Roy Basler, ed., *The Collected Works of Abraham Lincoln*, online edition, 4:175–176, https://quod.lib.umich.edu/l/lincoln/lincoln4/1:274?rgn=div1;view=fulltext (accessed

September 1, 2018). Iowa Representative Grimes agreed fearing "how rapidly are we following in the footsteps of the governments of Mexico and South America!" See William Salter, *The Life of James W. Grimes: Governor of Iowa, 1854–1858; a Senator of the United States, 1859–1869* (New York: D. Appleton, 1876), 135. This suggests a precursor to the fears of "mexicanization" that Gregory P. Downs has recently found. See Downs, "The Mexicanization of American Politics: The United States' Transnational Path from Civil War to Stabilization," *American Historical Review* 117, no. 2 (2012): 387–409.

96. Stephen Arnold Douglas, *Speech of Senator Douglas, before the Legislature of Illinois, April 25, 1861, in Compliance with a Joint Resolution of the Two Houses* ([n.p.], 1861), 3, http://hdl.handle.net/2027/loc.ark:/13960/t6154qd7f.

97. Downs, "The Mexicanization of American Politics."

98. Scott to Lincoln, October 29, 1860, Abraham Lincoln papers: Series 1. General Correspondence, Library of Congress, https://www.loc.gov/resource/mal.0418800/?sp=2&r=-0.043,0.572,1.379,1.027,0 (accessed August 29, 2018).

99. *The North-Carolinian* (Fayetteville, NC), February 16, 1861.

100. Mr. Toombs to John Picket, May 17, 1861, in James D. Richardson and Allan Nevins, *The Messages and Papers of Jefferson Davis and the Confederacy, Including Diplomatic Correspondence, 1861–1865* (New York: Chelsea House-R. Hector, 1966), 21.

101. Howard C. Perkins, ed., *Northern Editorials on Secession* (New York: D. Appleton-Century, 1942), 1:423–424.

102. *Daily Boston Traveller,* April 5, 1861, in Perkins, ed., *Northern Editorials,* 2:961–962.

103. *The Local News* (Alexandria, VA), November 26, 1861.

104. *Daily Democrat and News* (Davenport, IA), February 26, 1861.

105. Still, the paper quickly assured its New York readers that the real "seat of empire" would remain the "great free city," now capable of more easily harnessing the wealth of multiple confederacies. See "The Free Confederacy of the North," *New York Herald,* February 1, 1861.

106. *New York Herald*, February 17, 1861.

107. "Shall We Have Mexico!" *New York Times,* December 26, 1860, in Perkins, ed., *Northern Editorials,* 2:957–959.

108. "The Attitude of England," *Daily Whig and Republican* (Quincy, IL), March 14, 1861, in Perkins, *Northern Editorials,* 2:959.

109. Anonymous, *The New England Tour of H.R.H. the Prince of Wales*, 3rd ed. (Boston: Bee Printing, 1860), 3–4.

110. R. J. de Cordova, *The Prince's Visit: A Humorous Description* (New York: B. Fordham, 1861), 76–77.

111. Montgomery, "Reannealing of the Heart Ties."

5

"The Pirates and Their Abettors in This Province"

Sovereignty, Violence, and Confederate Operations in Britain's Atlantic Colonies, 1863–1865

Beau Cleland

In the early hours of December 7, 1863, Orin Schaffer lay dying on the deck of the U.S.-flagged merchant steamship *Chesapeake*, en route from New York to Portland, Maine. His fatal wound came from a pistol shot, but the finger on the trigger belonged to a British subject, not a Confederate. Schaffer died before dawn, and the same British hands threw his body overboard. The attack on the *Chesapeake*, like several others in the same period, was privately organized and executed across international boundaries without state sanction, which placed the attackers firmly in the filibustering tradition of the mid-nineteenth century. Schaffer's death, and the subsequent escape from justice by "the pirates and their abettors in this province," as the American vice-consul in Halifax put it, demonstrated that some British North Americans were not merely observers of the American Civil War but active participants on the Confederate side.[1] Their actions in the *Chesapeake* attack and its aftermath reflected the increasing independence of the settler colonies of British North America and the colonists' ability to circumvent British neutrality and law in support of the rebellion. The Confederate government seized upon events like this hijacking as an opportunity to then leverage its informal colonial network into something more activist and sinister, by turning British neutrality and the contested sovereignty of the settler colonies into a weapon against the Union.

This essay is centered on the hijacking of the *Chesapeake* by British subjects, mostly colonials from New Brunswick and Nova Scotia, and a spate of copycat attacks that followed it in 1864 and 1865. Historian Aaron Sheehan-Dean writes that "the nature of nationalism in mid-nineteenth-century America required believers to pledge adherence to standards of conduct" that tended to limit violence, and that international norms, morality, and diplomatic pressure "compelled the Confederacy to participate in the war as a state rather than a guerilla republic."[2] The cases of the *Chesapeake* and others provide a compelling challenge to this framing. When the combatants, in whole or in part, on these expeditions were not citizens or even residents of the belligerent polities, those standards of conduct were not so rigid. When the Confederacy lent its assistance to these ventures, it discarded state norms and behaved as a "guerilla republic." The transnational nature of the irregular conflict on the maritime periphery of North America, unlike much of the domestic guerilla war, brought even minor incidents to the direct attention of the highest Confederate authorities, particularly Jefferson Davis, Judah Benjamin, and Stephen Mallory, because it involved a critical neutral power.[3] Such events also attracted the notice of senior British colonial and imperial authorities, as well as those of the Union. The murders that occurred during these incidents, because of their location and the perpetrators, brought forth complicated questions of international law, intra-imperial sovereignty, and the use and abuse of neutrality. Disputes arose over the obligation of colonial courts to uphold imperial primacy over foreign affairs, and over how traditional understandings of the rights and duties of neutrals should shift in response to attacks that attempted to fuse privateering and filibustering into a new species of international maritime violence.

The Confederacy's operatives abroad took advantage of the divided sovereignty inherent in the British colonies, seeking opportunities to exploit British neutrality in the war against the United States. These Confederates showed a savvy ability to identify sympathetic locals, including within colonial governments, and solicit their aid. As in Bermuda and the Bahamas, local merchants in places like Halifax worked with Confederates openly, despite taking liberties with British neutrality law. Local authorities guarded their judicial prerogatives from imperial interference, even when the cases involved matters that fell ostensibly under London's authority, such as neutrality violations. Colonial courts repeatedly freed the perpetrators of raids and acts of piracy that were launched from British North American soil, often against the wishes of Crown officials, and residents also sheltered and protected fugitives from capture. The Confederate government seized upon this opening to launch further informal military and covert operations from the soil and waters of British North America and sought in many cases to extend the protection of belligerent status to attackers who did not qualify for it under Confederate laws such as the Partisan Ranger Act or as privateers under the law of nations.

Confederate ambivalence toward direct control over informal diplomatic relations and trade created an environment, particularly in Nova Scotia and New Brunswick, that promoted and legitimized freelance action by both Confederate citizens and British subjects, with unpredictable consequences. What began as commercial and logistical support moved, by late 1863, toward paramilitary operations that bore a significant resemblance to earlier patterns of filibustering—private, international military adventures not done at the behest of a state and launched with the tacit support of the local populace. The possibility of filibustering greatly concerned British officials from the earliest days of the war, particularly in the aftermath of William Walker's last attempt in Central America in 1860.[4] Fears of filibustering reappeared during and after the *Trent* crisis, although it was *northern* filibustering that initially worried British observers most.[5] When pro-Southern quasi-private warfare sprang up and threatened open conflict along the northern U.S. border in 1863 and 1864, imperial officials in London and North America discovered, to their alarm and frustration, that local courts prevented effective action to stop further raids and failed to bring to justice those responsible for violations of British neutrality and international law. The relative political maturity of Nova Scotia in some respects enabled rather than dissuaded violations of British neutrality.

Confederate engagement with the British Empire occurred almost entirely within what historians have variously termed the "Anglo world," "Greater Britain," or the British World.[6] The "Settler Revolution" of the nineteenth-century Anglo world—the phenomenal growth and development of British settler colonies, and, in the case of the United States, former colonies, in comparison to the rest of the world—shaped the power relations between colony and metropole in the course of creating "a politically divided but culturally and economically united intercontinental system."[7] Upper and Lower Canada, for example, received self-governing status relatively quickly after the rebellions of 1837–1838, while imperial officials spent decades considering whether to reduce Jamaica to direct control in response to both the intransigence of the white minority government and unrest of its majority Black population.[8] Whether settler colonies received responsible government as a benign nod to their right to British institutions or as a piece of *realpolitik* to keep them within the empire without violence is immaterial, although it seems clear that race informed British assumptions about colonial self-government.[9] The result in either case was that colonies such as Nova Scotia, New Brunswick, and the United Province of Canada exercised political independence within the British Empire to a degree unseen since the American Revolution. The Confederate rebellion found opportunity in that independence.

Between 1841 and the opening of the Civil War the imperial government conceded sovereignty in British North America over most issues of internal legislation, the courts, and revenue to colonial legislatures and judges. One scholar suggests that "from the 1850s self-government [in British settler colonies] became so well-established that governors were titular figures whose administrative power was severely circumscribed," and that in order to shield themselves from local critics they chose to "portray themselves as merely the symbolic representatives of the British monarch, or even as defenders of the abstract notion of sovereignty."[10] Confederates and locals both took opportunistic advantage of this sovereignty gap, particularly in areas like the enforcement of neutrality laws and extradition, to launch raids against the Union and shelter themselves from the consequences. British municipal laws dealing with areas not expressly delegated to colonial governments, such as the 1819 Foreign Enlistment Act, could, depending on their wording, apply to all British subjects and territory, the colonies included.[11] Yet the British government relied on colonial courts and police forces for enforcement, which provided frequent opportunity for lax or nonexistent observance of the law.[12]

The northern colonies provided other attractions for the Confederacy. British North America was too far north to be a major entrepot for blockade running, although some ships managed to run into Confederate ports from the Maritime colonies, mainly Nova Scotia and New Brunswick, and the two colonies were frequently listed as the false destination of blockade runners as they attempted to enter the Confederacy.[13] Nova Scotia, and the port of Halifax in particular, assumed an important role for the Confederacy as a communications and transit hub that the Royal Navy sheltered, albeit unintentionally. Because the North American squadron's main base and summer headquarters were at Halifax, a substantial garrison and naval presence discouraged the U.S. Navy from aggressively interfering with trade. Local political conditions in Nova Scotia also proved favorable for the Confederacy, not least because "[Nova Scotian] politics remained essentially a struggle between members of the mercantile and professional elites."[14] The Confederacy found important friends among both groups, and economic hardship made some influential Halifax merchants particularly receptive to aiding the Confederacy.

Merchants made some of the earliest connections between the Confederacy and Halifax, as they did elsewhere in the colonies. Prewar ties and shipping routes provided one avenue for such arrangements. Shortly after U.S. President Abraham Lincoln declared the blockade of the Confederacy in 1861, a Savannah firm led by Andrew Low, a merchant and banker of English birth, proposed running in provisions purchased in Halifax under cover of their British nationality, acting on the erroneous assumption that this would shield them from capture.[15] In other cases family and interpersonal connections drew Southerners and Nova Scotian merchants together.[16] The Confederate government also attempted to arrange the purchase of arms and equipment within British North America, although the meager returns discouraged much further effort along those lines after 1861.[17] The quest for economic gain along with a romantic view of the Confederacy's efforts seem to have attracted others to their cause, notably Alexander Keith Jr., a nephew of his more famous brewer and merchant namesake.[18]

Support for the Confederacy among the Haligonian elite was not restricted to merchants. Prominent physician Dr. William J. Almon supported the Confederacy in word and deed, sending a son to fight in the rebel army, and physically aiding the escape of a prisoner in the so-called *Chesapeake* affair of the winter of 1863–1864.[19] The provincial attorney general, William Alexander Henry, and the provincial secretary, Charles Tupper—both powerful members of the Nova Scotia Executive Council—also openly professed Confederate sympathies.[20] Likewise, Thomas Connolly, the Catholic archbishop of Halifax, materially aided Confederate efforts in the colony, hosting Southern agents and officers and providing them with introductions and pleas for support from Catholics across British North America. Connolly's stance may have merely echoed the Vatican's sympathy for the Confederacy, but he may also have been troubled by the lack of opportunity accorded Irish Catholics in the United States, something he publicly wrote about in the months after the Civil War ended.[21] These men formed a key portion of an informal pro-Confederate network that lent their efforts and influence to promoting the fortunes of the rebellion, even in defiance of the imperial government. Their actions, especially in the aftermath of the *Chesapeake* affair, showed the limits of imperial influence over British North Americans and the advantages of what might be termed Confederate soft power in the colonies.

The importance of this "soft" power derived in large part from the ad hoc nature of the Confederate state, especially in the early months of the Civil War. The recruitment of friendly and influential colonial subjects, who acted independently of the Confederate government but generally in its interest, helped counterbalance some of the institutional weakness of the young State Department. The Confederate tendency toward dispersed, informal diplomacy was on full display in British North America, as white Southerners crisscrossed the provinces, representing themselves as agents of Confederate governments at all levels, regardless of their actual authority to do so. Some were relatively prominent men, like Raphael Semmes and Dr. Luke Blackburn, and destined for fame (or infamy), but others were unsavory figures like Vernon Locke and John C. Braine, a smuggler and a con artist, respectively. The chaotic first months after secession reflected the South's sudden loss of the bureaucratic framework, procedures, and relative discipline of the U.S. State Department, and its inadequate replacement by first a multiplicity of relatively independent states, followed by a newly formed Confederate State Department. The State Department suffered from a revolving door of secretaries until Judah P. Benjamin took charge in March of 1862, and throughout its existence the department struggled to gain and maintain a monopoly over Confederate foreign policy.[22]

This tenuous control, and the freelance agents whom it encouraged, influenced the development of the pro-Confederate network in Nova Scotia. George N. Sanders, formerly a Kentucky Democratic politician and U.S. consul in London, was the most prominent example of such unofficial agents. He quickly engaged in a continuing series of informal negotiations, contracts, and other endeavors on the Confederacy's behalf, to the intense frustration of officials in Richmond because he held no official position with the government. Sanders's early efforts bore some fruit, particularly by gaining the interest of Benjamin Wier, a Halifax merchant and politician with a checkered past who later served as one of the first members of the new Senate of Canada.[23] Private connections and profit-seeking first brought Wier into the Confederate orbit. Sanders arranged a contract with Wier's firm for a courier and transport service between the Confederacy and Halifax, under the cover of schooner service with Baltimore. Sanders seems to have done so of his own volition, and not as a paid agent of the Confederacy, as evidenced by the government's later refusal to compensate him or his son Lewis for their efforts. Sanders succeeded in getting the Confederate government to adopt his scheme, but the transport line fell apart after Union authorities discovered it.[24]

Wier and Company provided a variety of services for the Confederacy, including forwarding and receiving cargo and letters, ship repair (vital, since key blockade-running hubs at Bermuda and the Bahamas lacked most of the necessary facilities for major repairs to steamships), and later served as the terminus of the Canadian portion of the Confederacy's network to send escaped prisoners of war back to the South. Wier's activities were well known to Union and British authorities, but the latter did little to restrain them, as his activities stayed largely within the letter of imperial law (the Foreign Enlistment Act and neutrality did not preclude repair and communications services for a belligerent power). Wier and his fellow Maritime Confederate supporters severely tested that forbearance in the winter of 1863–1864, as they placed themselves squarely in the middle of a military, diplomatic, and legal battle over the fate of the steamer *Chesapeake*.

Perhaps no event better illustrates the Confederate exploitation of private initiative, divided sovereignty, and local sympathies than the so-called "second *Chesapeake* affair" (the first one being, in Nova Scotian memory, the capture of the USS *Chesapeake* by the HMS *Shannon* during the War of 1812).[25] This was not a random attack. Rather, it can be traced to Confederate promotion of privateering and adventurism in the earliest days of the war and to Confederate Secretary of the Navy Stephen Russell Mallory's ongoing quest "to create a branch of naval warfare which shall enable us to unite and employ private enterprise and capital against the enemy."[26] Private military action had a long history in British colonies and in North America generally, and the Civil War provided opportunity to those inclined to resume that tradition of unauthorized violence, often characterized by a loose interpretation of maritime law and open defiance of the government in London.[27] The attack on the *Chesapeake* represented a foreseeable, although unauthorized, extension of the logic of informal diplomacy and privatized warfare in the colonies.

A privateer is a privately owned vessel authorized by a sovereign to attack the shipping and property of an enemy power. This authorization was typically granted by a commission or a letter of marque and reprisal issued by a government, and ships and other property captured under a letter of marque could be sold only by following a strict procedure—usually involving an appearance before an admiralty court. Failure to do so was to commit piracy. Both the United States and the Confederacy had clauses in their constitutions authorizing the use of letters of marque, and privateers had constituted the bulk of American naval force in previous wars.[28] Britain and the major powers of Europe agreed to end privateering in the settlement following the Crimean War, but the United States never signed the agreement. In 1861 Confederate government officials had hoped privateers might even the naval imbalance with the United States, but a lack of ships and the unwillingness of European powers to admit prizes (i.e., captured ships) into their ports dampened their effectiveness.[29] And, as was nearly inevitable with letters of marque, certain captains chose to abuse their authority and engaged in outright piracy.[30]

The man chiefly responsible for the attack on the *Chesapeake* was Vernon Guyon Locke, originally of Sandy Point, Nova Scotia. Locke, born in 1827, was a sailor and captain who worked on vessels based in ports up and down the North American coast from Nova Scotia to North Carolina. When the Civil War began, his sympathies lay with the South, as did his instinct for personal gain, and he obtained access to a letter of marque from the owner of the privateer schooner *Retribution*. Locke, who often used the alias John Parker, from his first moments as a privateer was either ignorant or contemptuous of British neutrality and international law.[31] Like most Confederate privateers, he captured few prizes and faced the nearly insurmountable difficulty of trying to sail a captured vessel through the blockade and into a Confederate port to be sold as a prize. The Queen's neutrality proclamation of 1861 forbade ships of either side from bringing ships or cargo captured as prizes into British ports, and the other major powers followed suit, effectively leaving Confederate commerce raiders the option of burning their captures or trying to bring them through the blockade.[32] One of Locke's first captures, the *J. P. Ellicott*, in fact escaped when the ship's crew rose up against the prize crew and reclaimed their vessel.[33]

Locke responded to this difficulty by running his next prize, the American schooner *Hanover*, ashore in one of the outlying islands of the Bahamas and bringing its cargo separately to Nassau for sale. He then loaded the *Hanover* with a cargo of salt for an attempt to run the blockade.[34] These actions were patently illegal by both British and Confederate law, but questions of legality did not slow down Locke, then or later. He subsequently seized the brig *Emily Fisher* and repeated his effort to land the cargo, allegedly in the presence of a local official on Long Cay who refused to intervene.[35] By ignorance or complicity, local Bahamian officials aided Locke in violating British neutrality.

Local sympathy, enhanced by Confederate informal diplomacy, helped Locke repeatedly during his colorful career. He escaped justice for his role in the *Hanover* affair by working with local friends in the Bahamas to conceal his identity and the character of his prize. Pressure from British and Union authorities eventually forced Bahamian officials to arrest Locke as he loitered in Nassau in May 1863. The local criminal court was not scheduled to resume until October, so the locals granted Locke the "surprisingly small and insignificant" bail of £200. William Seward protested, correctly, that Locke would gladly lose such a sum and skip town.[36] Even the Colonial Office remarked that the bail situation seemed to open Bahamian authorities to suspicion of collusion, and, like clockwork, when the court resumed its session Locke failed to appear. The Colonial Office was furious with the Bahamas' governor Charles Bayley, and the colonial secretary, the Duke of Newcastle, personally demanded an explanation.[37] Given the openly pro-Confederate proclivities of the Bahamian authorities, including Bayley and the attorney general, in earlier cases, it is unsurprising that officials made no meaningful effort to keep Locke from fleeing the colony, and ultimately neither suffered for their laxity.[38]

Locke's escape from the Bahamas made it clear to him and his associates that they could rely on a widespread network of friends and local officials to carry out legally dubious raiding and shelter them from the consequences, seemingly heedless of the lack of approval from the Confederate government. He even managed to sell the *Retribution* to a blockade-running firm before taking his leave of Nassau, which likely helped fund his next adventure.[39] If local authorities in the Bahamas had shielded him from British law and Union capture, Locke could certainly expect the same or greater assistance in his native province. He was not disappointed.

In early November 1863 Locke found his way to St. John, New Brunswick, from Nassau, and fell in with John Clibbon Braine, another British subject with ties to privateering and raiding.[40] Locke and Braine gathered a group of young men from Nova Scotia and New Brunswick and hatched a plan to seize an American steamship on the high seas and convert it into a privateer by using the commission and letter of marque from the *Retribution*, which Locke retained when he sold the ship. Locke offered his recruits shares of any spoils or prizes as an inducement to join the expedition.[41] They planned to maintain the legality of their attack by renaming their target the *Retribution II* once they gained possession of it, or perhaps they merely hoped to confuse anyone who might examine the ship's papers. Locke and Braine seemed either ignorant or heedless of the rule that letters of marque applied to specific ships regardless of the name and were not transferable.[42] The group determined that the *Chesapeake*, a fast steamer that plied regularly up the New England coast, fit their needs. In an era that often openly celebrated filibustering, yet another party prepared itself to cross a foreign frontier for military action.[43]

Locke remained in New Brunswick while Braine led a group to New York and took passage, with weapons concealed in their baggage, on the *Chesapeake*, which was bound for Portland, Maine, with an assorted cargo. The ship left port on December 5, with Braine and a party of about twelve companions on board. Just after midnight on the 7th, while the ship was off Cape Cod, the group attacked. The hijackers shot Orin Schaffer, the ship's second engineer, three times as he tried to escape from the engine room. The attackers wounded two other crewmen and narrowly missed the captain, and within a few minutes they had control of the *Chesapeake* "in the name of the Southern Confederacy."[44] The hijackers steamed into the Bay of Fundy, between New Brunswick and Nova Scotia, and there rendezvoused with Locke, who took command.[45]

The operation, which started smoothly, soon began to unravel in the face of logistical difficulties and poor decisions. The boat that carried Locke out also ferried most of the *Chesapeake*'s remaining crew ashore at St. John on the morning of December 9, where they immediately reported the attack to the Union consul.

His telegraph communication quickly reached U.S. authorities, and several warships began hunting for the missing ship. The *Chesapeake*, moreover, did not have enough coal remaining to reach a friendly port like St. George's, Bermuda, or Wilmington, North Carolina. Locke (under the alias John Parker) sailed up the coast, making several stops in desperate search of coal and selling portions of the cargo as they went.[46] During one of these stops, Braine left the ship and escaped capture by the American vice-consul in Liverpool, Nova Scotia, with the aid of local citizens.[47] The *Chesapeake* reached Mud Cove, near Sambro, Nova Scotia, on December 16, where it anchored to await a supply of coal sent from Wier in Halifax. On the morning of December 17, the USS *Ella and Annie* recaptured the *Chesapeake* near the Sambro harbor entrance and caught one pirate in his sleep on board the coaling schooner anchored nearby along with two Halifax men from its crew. The other attackers fled ashore. After a ten-day search in foul winter weather, the Union again possessed the *Chesapeake*.

In his enthusiasm to nab the pirates, the American captain actually violated British neutrality by seizing the ship within British territorial waters, which at the time extended one marine league, roughly three miles, from shore. The Union naval commander on the scene, Commander A. G. Clary of the USS *Dacotah* quickly realized the seriousness of the situation and ordered the *Ella and Annie* to proceed to Halifax with the *Chesapeake* so that the seizure could be adjudicated. When the small flotilla arrived in Halifax, word spread quickly among local authorities, the British garrison, and the populace that the *Chesapeake* had been seized in British waters and that, furthermore, the U.S. Navy held several local men as prisoners on board their ship. The very real possibility of a diplomatic rupture or even armed conflict hung over Halifax harbor.

The official response to the arrival of the *Chesapeake* fell mainly to the garrison commander and acting governor, Maj. Gen. Charles Hastings Doyle. Local politicians also involved themselves, particularly Dr. Charles Tupper, in his role as the provincial secretary. Doyle, like the other colonial administrators of British North America, had severely circumscribed powers. He could issue arrest warrants, for example, but their execution relied on local police forces and magistrates, and any warrant remained subject to habeas corpus proceedings and the decisions of the independent colonial judicial system. Colonists across the Western Hemisphere agitated for greater control over their own affairs throughout the first half of the nineteenth century, but the imperial government curtailed its own authority only haltingly and unevenly, especially in the turmoil following the end of slavery in the British Empire in 1834.[48] Upper and Lower Canada experienced small rebellions led by populist reformers in 1837 and 1838, respectively, augmented by American filibusters.[49] The government quickly put down both, but in their aftermath reformers in London and British North America argued that granting increased self-government under the British flag was preferable to forced independence and likely annexation by the United States.[50]

After a great deal of agitation in the 1840s and 1850s, the imperial government granted British North America the principle of responsible government. The imperial government retained authority over external matters, the form of government, and public lands and resources. By necessity, the "problem of sovereignty was solved without precision, but with faith in the good sense and goodwill of all concerned" and the assumption that "there would be no great clashes over the demarcation of imperial and colonial questions."[51] Historian Phillip Buckner argues that responsible government in fact increased the power of the colonial executive (though not necessarily the governor) by imposing some form of party discipline on the elected assembly, and that it doubled as "a means of securing collaboration of the colonial elites in the perpetuation of Imperial rule."[52] Nova Scotia, the first colony to be granted responsible government, tested this faith in good sense and goodwill during the American Civil War. Imperial authorities quickly discovered that their local collaborators did not hesitate to defy them if it suited their desire for justice (or personal gain). Imperial sovereignty over foreign policy in the colonies proved far less supreme and unchallenged than the architects of responsible government expected.

The *Chesapeake* affair immediately confronted Doyle with the challenge of navigating this division in sovereignty. The breach of British territorial waters by a United States warship clearly fell under crown responsibility as a matter of foreign policy, as did, at least on its face, the extradition, under the 1842 Webster-Ashburton treaty, of the men accused of piracy and murder. Colonial courts, however, bore responsibility for adjudicating both the fate of the *Chesapeake* and its captors, a difficult task as the practical application of the treaty had yet to be tested in 1863, and no one had ever been extradited under its terms. To further complicate matters, colonial courts had jurisdiction over local violations of imperial laws, such as the Foreign Enlistment Act, that inevitably had international repercussions. If colonial judges and juries differed with the Crown on how to handle the fallout of the hijacking, then a conflict loomed over the hazy boundaries of authority in British North America. The Confederate government and its local supporters acted quickly to bring such a conflict to life.

After the furor over British courts' attempted intervention in the extradition trial of George Anderson of 1860–1861, a fugitive slave wanted in Missouri, imperial officials acted cautiously when interacting with colonial courts. British North

Americans overwhelmingly resented London's attempted interference in that earlier case, despite the public's deep sympathy for the escaped slave Anderson and strong opposition to his potential return to bondage.[53] Any imperial attempt to force a particular outcome onto the Maritime colonies' courts and public in the case of the *Chesapeake*'s captors could produce a similar, or even stronger, response. Doyle and the Colonial Office could press for arrests and prosecutions, but they could not directly interfere in the proceedings. As the U.S. warships entered Halifax harbor with the recaptured *Chesapeake*, the potential for conflict between Britain and the United States, and between London and the colonies, approached its peak.

Doyle demanded that the U.S. Navy hand over to local authorities the *Chesapeake* and the men captured along with it so that each could face the appropriate legal proceedings. Rumors abounded that the *Ella and Annie* and *Dacotah* might try to escape Halifax with their prisoners, and that the garrison had been ordered to fire on them if they attempted to do so. Both rumors were false, but they reflect the real tension of the moment and the distinct possibility that intemperate behavior on either side might escalate a minor breach of neutrality into a potentially deadly incident. The tension only increased as several more American warships that had taken part in the hunt for the *Chesapeake* arrived at Halifax.

The American prize crew duly handed the *Chesapeake* over into British custody without incident, although Doyle had the ship docked at the Queen's Wharf under armed guard to prevent any further mischief. Commander Clary agreed to Doyle's demand to hand over the prisoners and ordered a boat to transfer them ashore at 1 p.m. the next day. The prisoner transfer seemed poised to go off smoothly until local sentiment and the Confederate network in Halifax intervened. Unwilling to accept as legitimate the Americans' capture of George Wade, the pirate found asleep on the coaling schooner, Doyle asked them to deliver Wade to a police constable on the wharf along with the two Halifax men from the schooner's crew. A crowd, angry that the Yankees had seized local men from British waters, waited as the American boat approached, and as Wade stepped onto the wharf, Confederate supporter William J. Almon told him to jump into a waiting rowboat. Wade needed no further encouragement. He leaped into the boat, and two oarsmen quickly pulled away from the wharf. Almon, Alexander Keith Jr., and Dr. Peleg Smith blocked the constable's attempt to aim his pistol at the escaping pirate, and the constable could only watch in frustration as the boat rowed away across the harbor and disappeared.[54]

The interference of three wealthy, prominent Haligonians in a prisoner transfer was hardly accidental, and it infuriated both Doyle and the Americans. All three publicly supported the Confederacy, and now they openly defied British authority to aid the escape of a colonial subject who had engaged in violence on behalf of the rebellion. Their actions, however, stemmed not just from pro-Confederate sentiment, but from their peculiar sense of local patriotism. A wide swath of the Maritime population did not support the prosecution (and potential extradition) of a local man whom the Americans had seized while in violation of Nova Scotian, and by extension British, territory and neutrality. They did not care that international law and British treaty obligations required otherwise. The stage was set for a conflict between colonial public opinion and imperial sovereignty.

The motivations of the pirates themselves is more difficult to ascertain, although it seems likely that the chance for monetary gain and adventure encouraged some of them. Few beyond Locke and Henry A. Parr seemed to have any significant ties to the South. Braine demonstrated a commitment to conducting attacks for the rebellion, though they usually involved the opportunity for personal gain, and his personal account of the *Chesapeake* seizure was filled with obvious lies about his own role and the legitimacy of the action.[55] A pro-Northern newspaper in Saint John described some of the attackers (after the capture) as being "of the very worst species of 'roughs' at that, regular jailbirds."[56] A witness who attended Braine's recruiting meetings in Saint John testified that volunteers were offered a share of the voyage's spoils and promised that they "would be protected" by the Confederate government, presumably from piracy charges.[57] Other witness testimony suggested that the volunteers were "proposed to enter the Confederate service," but no pay was on offer.[58] It seems likely therefore that the volunteers understood they were operating as privateers or pirates, within a "no prey, no pay" system, and not as regularly enlisted members of the Confederate armed forces. In the absence of other evidence, it appears that the colonial volunteers for the *Chesapeake* attack were chiefly motivated by the prospect of gain, and perhaps a chance at adventure in the long privateering tradition of the Maritime provinces. As occasionally happened in earlier conflicts, this put colonial residents at odds with imperial inclinations.

The first point of contention between imperial and local authority was the fate of three of the pirates captured in New Brunswick. Although the ringleaders of the attack, Locke, Braine, and Parr, remained at large, the New Brunswick authorities seized three local men who had not had the diligence or foresight to stay hidden. New Brunswick Lieutenant-Governor Arthur Gordon, in issuing the warrants for their arrest, plainly believed his power was circumscribed, and that once he issued the warrant the matter lay entirely in the hands of local magistrates.⁵⁹ The pirates' initial appearance before a St. John police magistrate in January 1864 raised a series of difficulties for imperial authorities over jurisdictional and legal technicalities that repeated themselves in subsequent cases across British North America. Confederate sympathizers in Halifax and New Brunswick arranged for two prominent attorneys, including John Hamilton Gray, a former premier of New Brunswick, to defend the accused. They contested the standing of a lowly police magistrate to hear an extradition case, as well as the propriety and wording of the arrest warrant. The police magistrate seemed poised to grant extradition, while the pro-Confederate network had friends on the bench of the New Brunswick higher courts, so it was in their interest to get the case moved. They also argued that the men should be given the chance to prove they acted as legitimate combatants and that even if they had been guilty of piracy they should be tried in British courts. A variety of witnesses appeared on the defendants' behalf, including Dr. Luke Blackburn, posing as a disinterested party, present merely to testify to the veracity of Jefferson Davis's and Judah P. Benjamin's signatures on "Parker's" commission.⁶⁰

The magistrate rejected all these claims and ordered the men held in jail, pending an appeal. Their attorneys promptly appealed to the New Brunswick Supreme Court, where Justice William Johnston Ritchie agreed to hear the case. Ritchie, a future chief justice of the Supreme Court of Canada, was closely connected to the pro-Confederate elite in the Maritimes.⁶¹ His brother, John W. Ritchie, had already consulted with Benjamin Wier about the case and represented the Confederate government before the Halifax vice-admiralty court when the *Chesapeake* came up for trial. Justice Ritchie was also the brother-in-law of W. J. Almon. After two weeks of hearings, Ritchie indicated that his ruling would favor the defense. He ruled that not only were the arrest warrants improperly filed, but the application for extradition itself was invalid because the American consul had made it rather than the United States government. This was specious: The consul represented the United States government and held an exequatur from the Queen to that effect, and furthermore he was in telegraphic communication with the State Department in Washington. Ritchie concluded by rejecting the men's arrest for piracy because the police magistrate improperly worded his own arrest warrant. He admonished the pirates for violating the Foreign Enlistment Act but did nothing else about their obvious crime, and ordered the men released on a writ of habeas corpus.⁶² Ritchie thus managed to undermine both British municipal laws restricting unsanctioned military activity as well as the treaty designed to ease cross-border tensions in North America, all in the service of protecting local men who more or less admitted to being guilty of a crime.

The Colonial Office anticipated that local courts might not cooperate and directed Lieutenant-Governor Gordon to prepare new warrants in the event of the pirates' release.[63] Gordon instructed provincial Attorney General John Mercer to do so three days before the trial ended, but Mercer ignored the directive. The new warrants did not arrive, and despite a mountain of evidence that the three had been complicit in violations of both municipal and international law, the hijackers walked out of the St. John jail on March 10, 1864, as free men and promptly disappeared. It seems clear that the provincial courts and authorities, particularly Mercer and Ritchie, could have held the *Chesapeake* raiders on the evidence available by simply issuing a new warrant and ordering their immediate re-arrest. Through deliberate inaction they turned a botched and inept act of piracy into a marginal success for the Confederacy because they demonstrated that attacks planned, recruited, and launched from British soil could expect some level of protection from local authorities against imperial law or extradition to the United States. The interpersonal connections of the Confederate informal commercial-diplomatic network, extending through Ritchie, ensured the escape of the attackers.

The Confederate network in Halifax, meanwhile, worked in the vice-admiralty court to gain legal cover for the seizure of the *Chesapeake* by having it declared an act of war or legitimate privateering rather than simply piracy. John W. Ritchie and Benjamin Wier alerted Confederate authorities of the raid and pending trials as quickly as they could, via their connection with Maj. Norman S. Walker, the chief Confederate officer in Bermuda. Walker forwarded the news to Judah P. Benjamin and Jefferson Davis through the blockade. Wier told them he had secured the legal advice of "Mr [J. W.] Ritchie . . . one of our very best lawyers, and also a friend to Southern independence," for the captured men and hoped to secure some sort of evidence from Richmond that they acted as legitimate combatants in order to prevent their extradition to the United States.[64] Ritchie suggested that the capture might be found legitimate by the local admiralty court and the ship could be awarded to the Confederacy as a result.[65]

The trial of the *Chesapeake* opened to intense interest. The provincial attorney general, James William Johnston, represented the Crown, while Ritchie appeared on behalf of the Confederacy despite not having any formal appointment as their agent. Johnston, himself a Confederate sympathizer and uncle by marriage to William J. Almon, felt that the case should not have come to the court at all, and he remained relatively passive during the proceedings. Ritchie, appearing as an *amicus curia* rather than a formal Confederate representative, argued that the *Chesapeake* should be considered a lawful prize because it had been captured by Confederate citizens—a dubious claim at best since only one of the attackers, Canadian-born Parr, had lived for any length of time in the South.[66] The presiding judge, Alexander Stewart, rejected this claim out of hand as irrelevant and exclaimed that "this Court has no prize jurisdiction" over Union or Confederate captures, and he could not entertain mere "[v]ague assertions and rumours" that the seizure was a legitimate act of war, since the attackers did not see fit to appear and make their claim before the court.[67] Stewart therefore had no choice but to dismiss any latent claim to the vessel.

Stewart made this decision not least because Confederate encounters in other colonial possessions had set a precedent for neutrality violations involving captured ships and cargoes that the imperial government was eager to avoid repeating. Locke's earlier escapades in the Bahamas had been augmented by further incidents around the globe. The CSS *Alabama* had carried a prize into Cape Town in violation of the Queen's neutrality proclamation and attempted the sale through subterfuge of the cargo of others in Mauritius. Officials in the Cape Colony and Mauritius initially abetted these attempts to avoid British neutrality regulations, but the Colonial Office sent clear guidance to colonial ports around the world, including Halifax, that further such incidents would not be tolerated. Doyle made sure that Stewart saw the relevant documents from the Colonial Office before the *Chesapeake* came to trial.[68] Any prizes brought into a colonial port that had not been condemned already by a Confederate admiralty court were to be seized and returned to their owner without trial.[69] In fact, just before the *Chesapeake* hearing began, the Royal Navy seized the CSS *Tuscaloosa*, formerly the American bark *Conrad*, in Cape Town on the same order. The *Conrad* had been captured months earlier at sea by the CSS *Alabama* and converted into a cruiser without appearing before a prize court.[70] Stewart made no decision as to the legal status of the captors themselves but emphasized that "the *Chesapeake*, if a prize at all, is an *uncondemned prize*" and the act of bringing such a vessel into a neutral port was an offense so grave that it "*ipso facto* subjects that prize to forfeiture."[71] Stewart released the ship and its cargo to their owners, prompting Doyle to write privately (and prematurely) to Lord Lyons in Washington that "the closing scene of the Chesapeake has at last taken place."[72] The *Chesapeake* appeared before the court primarily because of the American violation of British territorial waters during its recapture, however, and Judge Stewart left the legality of the seizure itself in question. His ruling did not proscribe future ship hijackings, but instead clung narrowly to the confines of imperial policy regarding prize ships. The window for further attacks remained open.

Nova Scotian authorities, having disposed of the case of the *Chesapeake* before the vice-admiralty court, still had to deal with the fallout of George Wade's escape from custody. Although the trial of William J. Almon, Alexander Keith Jr., and P. W. Smith before a Halifax municipal court was purely domestic, the outcome had potential consequences for British neutrality and foreign policy. If another local court failed to punish the abettors (at least in American eyes) of a murderous attack on a civilian ship, it might encourage further hijackings and sour still-fragile Anglo-American relations. The hearings attracted intense public interest on both sides of the border, and it illustrated the inherent conflict between popular opinion in the colonies and official British policy.

The nature of Halifax's lower criminal court practically guaranteed that the case's outcome would be controversial. Elected city officials heard cases in Halifax and decided what, if any, charges the defendants would face, rather than a professional judge or a grand jury. In this instance the mayor, Philip Carteret Hill, also served as chief magistrate. Hill came from the same "Tory-Anglican-merchant establishment" of Halifax that had produced Almon, Ritchie, and many other Confederate sympathizers, and his impartiality in the case was questionable at best.[73] After some delay, the trial opened on 11 January 1864. As an indication of the imperial government's acute interest in the case, Doyle took the unusual step of ordering the provincial attorney general to be present at the proceedings and answer questions about the events on the Queen's Wharf on the day of Wade's escape. When testimony closed, Smith reluctantly ruled that the three should appear before the Halifax County Supreme Court in the spring session, but only on the lesser charge of interfering with a police officer rather than the far more serious count of aiding the escape of a prisoner. The defendants walked free after giving a small bond.[74]

During the Supreme Court's next session, a grand jury reviewed the case referred from Halifax, and it dismissed the charges due to a supposed lack of evidence. This confirmed the suspicions of many observers that no jury in staunchly pro-Confederate Halifax would convict local men for aiding the rebellion. Doyle remarked privately to Lord Lyons that "I strongly believe that Dr. Almon is so popular a person, and that there are so many sympathetic with the Southern Cause here, it will be very difficult to find a Jury who will agree in their finding. Nous verrons!"[75] By the end of spring, 1864, everyone involved with the capture of the *Chesapeake* and the escape of the hijackers had either eluded pursuit or been acquitted altogether. The almost complete lack of personal consequences assured future attacks from neutral soil, and the near absence of diplomatic trouble for the Confederacy encouraged further sponsorship of unconventional warfare from British territory.

When Davis and the cabinet in Richmond learned of the *Chesapeake* affair, they were unaware that most of the legal proceedings in the Maritimes that would determine the ship's fate were already underway. Nevertheless, Davis and Stephen Mallory immediately recognized the potential windfall that a favorable decision in the Halifax admiralty court could provide. If the capture received legal sanction on British soil, it opened the way for an expanded campaign of hijacking against Union shipping that would be protected by law as legitimate privateering. This could re-ignite Confederate privateering and perhaps meet Davis's heretofore unfulfilled expectations for it. The "piratical" attacks on ships like the *Chesapeake, Roanoke,* and *Salvador,* to give three examples of varying legality, were not spontaneous crimes, invented out of thin air by their perpetrators. The Confederate government accepted the importance and legitimacy of privatized warfare such as privateering from the very beginning, and this preference for engaging private capital for the war at sea lasted throughout the war, although its form changed dramatically with the military and financial situation. Jefferson Davis, like most leading public figures in the Confederacy, expected privateers to form the bulwark of the South's naval forces. This widespread assumption did not survive British neutrality laws and the Foreign Enlistment Act, which crippled privateering by respectively closing off access to British ports and admiralty courts and preventing easy purchase of armed steamships. The former certainly caused the greatest hardship for would-be privateers, who could not carry their captured prizes into British ports. Confederate privateers also lacked easily accessible prize courts, without which they could not legally sell the vessels and cargoes they captured. Prize vessels thus had to run the Union blockade, which proved exceedingly difficult. Privateering proved unappealing to crews and owners who could not easily be paid, and the few ships and crews who attempted it generally had brief and unspectacular careers after the summer of 1861.[76]

In response to the lackluster results of its privateers, the Confederate government tried several approaches to make up for its naval weakness. An overseas purchasing program to buy from European shipyards met with mixed success. Commerce raiders like the *Alabama* and *Florida* hurt Union merchant shipping, but their success and the corresponding diplomatic uproar drove the Palmerston government to enforce the Foreign Enlistment Act stringently against further Confederate ships being built covertly in British yards.[77] Very few of the

European-built warships intended for the Confederate Navy ever reached their hands. As a corollary to this program, some Confederate officials and private citizens advocated an unconventional approach to naval warfare as a way to avoid the restrictions of formal privateering while still attracting private capital to fund and operate ships.

Southerners began proposing unconventional attacks at sea almost as soon as the war started. Many would-be privateers could not meet the conditions of Confederate law, which required a vessel to be on hand in a Confederate port and a substantial bond as a guarantee against misconduct before the government could issue a letter of marque. To avoid this, a Charleston resident named David Riker wrote the Confederate government in July 1861 and proposed to go to Havana and hijack a steamship bound from there to New York. Robert Toombs, then secretary of state, did not definitively reject the idea, but urged Riker and his men to obtain commissions in the state militia in order to protect themselves from piracy charges.[78] Their plan never materialized, but the attack on the *Roanoke* three years later was almost identical, except that the hijackers were led by a British subject. By 1864, the Confederate government turned haltingly to encouraging hijackings and providing them with enough official cover to prevent the participants from being hanged as pirates or spies (not always successfully).[79] The problem with this method, of course, was that it was usually illegal. Either the attacking parties were guilty of launching attacks, as bona fide servicemen, from neutral territory, or they were guilty, as civilians without a letter of marque, of piracy. The parties of men who engaged in seizing merchant ships at gunpoint, unsurprisingly, did not place a high priority on observing diplomatic and legal niceties, and even the attacks conducted by bona fide Confederate servicemen usually broke the neutrality laws of their points of origin.[80] The participants relied on the inability or unwillingness of their neutral hosts to prevent the attacks and prosecute them afterward.

The news of the *Chesapeake* attack came to Richmond at a time when the Davis administration was experimenting with unconventional naval warfare and actively seeking new opportunities to seize ships by subterfuge. Confederate raiding parties had already used the technique with success against Union shipping in places like the Chesapeake estuary, and extending the practice beyond internal waterways seemed only logical. In early 1862, in the very midst of passing responsibility for government blockade running to merchant firms in Charleston and Nassau, Secretary of the Navy Stephen Mallory strongly and repeatedly advocated the use of a privatized "provisional navy" specifically organized to raid in this fashion.⁸¹ Mallory lobbied Congress successfully, and it passed a law creating the new organization, dubbed the "Volunteer Navy," on 18 April 1863, which Davis signed a few days later.⁸²

The new organization suffered, however, under some of the same restrictions that had choked off privateering, particularly the requirement to commission ships in a Confederate port, which made it exceedingly difficult to obtain suitable vessels. In the winter of 1863–1864 Mallory, now less tied to long-standing antebellum norms for privateering, convinced Congress to modify the bill to permit ships to be commissioned abroad, during the same session in which they dramatically tightened controls over blockade running.⁸³ While the actual participation in the Volunteer Navy program was slim, Mallory's advocacy for it, and Congress's acquiescence demonstrated an increased willingness to cede oversight of violence to private parties at a time when government control over all aspects of the war tended to increase. Mallory in particular provided encouragement for this quasi-private raiding even when it fell outside the purview of the Navy. He encouraged groups interested in operating as "independent river guerilla parties" in the West who sought to use government sanction to "secure to them the rights of prisoners of war, if captured," and offered to facilitate their applications to President Davis.⁸⁴ The *Chesapeake* affair and the events that followed demonstrated that Mallory and Davis had overcome any earlier hesitation about extending this style of warfare beyond Confederate shores. The legal and political environment in Richmond increasingly favored covert raiding, private initiative, and the use (and potential abuse) of neutral territory.

Davis, in earlier instances, refused permission for such operations. Mallory and others presented him with plans to attack the prisoner-of-war camp at Johnson's Island on several occasions in 1862 and early 1863. The proposals required the use of Canadian territory, and Davis, who still clung to hopes of recognition and intervention, did not wish to antagonize the British government. By the late summer of 1863 he abandoned his opposition in response to events abroad. British authorities acted, in Davis's mind, as pro-Union partisans in a number of cases, particularly the seizure of the so-called Laird rams—ironclad warships meant for the Confederacy that were under construction at the Laird shipyard near Liverpool.⁸⁵ The seizure of the Laird rams and the increasingly obvious unwillingness of the British government to recognize the Confederacy removed much of Davis's reluctance to violate British territory and sensibilities.⁸⁶ This was augmented by increasing Confederate hopes that France would emerge as their best chance for recognition, intervention, and the construction of warships.⁸⁷ Respect for neutrality, which had animated Confederate discourse on diplomacy and relations with Britain, suddenly became far less of a stumbling block for those who wished to take more direct action against Union targets on the periphery of North America.

Attacks like that on the *Chesapeake* dovetailed with this increased appetite for unconventional violence. Private military expeditions against countries nominally at peace with the organizing nation—filibustering—commonly aided efforts at empire building, and the Civil War was no exception.[88] Historians have struggled on occasion to define filibustering from other forms of interstate violence, not least because filibustering expeditions often received tacit encouragement and support from governments. Robert May defines the term *filibuster* rather tightly, emphasizing the private nature of the expedition as the most important characteristic; thus any attack that received "implicit or explicit permission" from their government "failed the test of privacy."[89] Yet numerous antebellum filibustering attacks received just such support from governments, from American attacks against Spanish Florida to Narciso López's failed expedition to Cuba. In the case of the expedition against Florida, it is likely that President James Madison himself approved of the operation.[90] So many of these private expeditions received some sort of quiet government approval that it seems more practical, therefore, to classify filibustering inclusively according to the relative *extent* and openness of government knowledge and approval, rather than their complete absence. Pro-Confederate filibustering fits neatly into this modified category. The government in Richmond often did not know of these attacks in advance, but nevertheless accepted the casual invocation of legitimacy by their organizers, and cabinet officials in Richmond, especially Mallory, as shown below, promoted them on numerous occasions. Vernon Locke waved around a Confederate letter of marque to persuade British colonists to join him in attacking a country with whom their own government was formally at peace. This was just as much a filibustering endeavor as the parties of Americans who joined with the Patriotes and Hunters' Lodges during the Canadian rebellions of 1837–1838. Groups of armed men from these societies crossed the border in the opposite direction, from the United States into Canada, to aid a rebellion in an ostensibly friendly territory.[91] John C. Braine and Thomas Hogg later took similar actions by using volunteer commissions in the Confederate Navy, signed by Mallory, to attract crews for hijacking missions in neutral territory. The Civil War–era expeditions in British North America joined an often overlooked history of private, international violence along the northern frontier.

The *Chesapeake* was not the only example of maritime filibustering for the rebellion. Just weeks earlier Thomas Hogg, a Confederate citizen, and a party that included several British subjects hijacked the American merchant ship *Joseph R. Gerrity* out of Matamoras, Mexico, and sailed it into British Honduras (modern-day Belize). Hogg illegally sold the ship and cargo, then made his escape when British officials learned the truth and attempted to arrest him.[92] A similar attack from Canada in the fall of 1863 using Confederate naval officers was aborted at the last moment after being betrayed by an informant. They planned to seize a steamer on Lake Erie and liberate the prisoner-of-war camp at Johnson's Island, Ohio.[93] When British authorities arrested several seamen involved in the capture of the *Gerrity* in Liverpool, James Mason, inspired by Confederate support for the *Chesapeake*'s captors, funded their legal defense, thereby demonstrating a willingness to legitimize filibustering and piracy ex post facto.[94] These incidents received remarkably broad support from Confederates who commented upon them. Confederate agent Norman Walker, passing word from Bermuda, expressed disapproval of the *Chesapeake* attack's methods but recommended that the government support the captors nonetheless. His wife, Georgiana, commenting privately, disapproved of the hijacking but stopped short of condemning it.[95] Clearly, Benjamin, Mason, and Davis agreed, and virtually no one in a position of power recommended that the Confederate government openly disavow the attacks, although some officials did attempt to prevent attacks that were plainly illegal. By early 1864, the Confederate cabinet demonstrated a robust appetite for unconventional naval warfare and a tolerance for filibustering on its behalf, and the events in the Maritime provinces seemed ripe for exploitation in the service of building a slaveholding empire.

To that end, Davis dispatched University of Virginia law professor James P. Holcombe to Halifax, seeking some advantage in the pending trials over the ship and its captors, and to arrange a network to transport home escaped Confederate prisoners of war. Before Holcombe arrived, however, the Halifax vice-admiralty court released the *Chesapeake* back to its owners, thwarting Davis's hopes. Nonetheless, Holcombe expressed great concern that the hijackers, now fugitives, should receive Confederate support, because they "imperiled life and liberty in an enterprise of great hazard, which they honestly believed was invested with the sanction of law." In part because of the hijackers' "generous sympathy with our cause," Holcombe urged that the government give, ex post facto, official sanction for the raid.[96] The filibustering tail wagged the dog of Confederate foreign policy, as Davis and Benjamin agreed to provide such evidence.[97] The Confederate government supported these raiders out of a sense of moral obligation to those who took up arms on their behalf but also because they offered a cheap and disruptive weapon against Union commerce and naval power. The utter failure of British courts to successfully prosecute the attackers in the *Gerrity* and *Chesapeake* attacks for either piracy or violating the Foreign Enlistment Act provided no disincentive for acknowledging or sponsoring further raids. More followed in short order.

In October 1864, the residents of St. George's, Bermuda, watched as the United States–flagged mail steamship *Roanoke* burned to the waterline and sank a short distance outside of the harbor. This catastrophe was no accident. A group of hijackers—pirates, according to American authorities—set the ship ablaze deliberately after Bermudian officials denied them entry to the port at St. George's. Awakened by the *Chesapeake* case and a further hijacking on the Great Lakes that September, the Colonial Office scrambled for a way to characterize these attacks. They were "a new feature which has sprung up in the present American war," and "the like was not practised in the previous conflicts of Civilized Nations."[98] Led by John C. Braine of the *Chesapeake* attack, the bulk of the party that seized the *Roanoke* in the name of the Confederacy, despite their claims to the contrary, had no official sanction or commission in the Confederate armed forces, and acted as private citizens.[99] Many of them were British subjects as well. The *Roanoke* was one of at least seven attacks scattered around the North American maritime periphery, from the Pacific coast of Panama up to the Great Lakes, with a similar modus operandi but vastly different levels of official sanction. The attackers in this hybrid of filibustering and privateering, with the example of the *Chesapeake* before them, counted on neutral sites in the colonies to shelter them before and after their attacks.

In the case of the *Roanoke*, the locals rewarded this faith. Braine, fresh from his *Chesapeake* adventure and a visit to Richmond, presented himself to Charles Helm, the Confederate consul in Havana. He asked Helm for assistance in carrying out his plan to seize the *Roanoke*, which he claimed had the approval of the government. Braine misled Helm—he had an acting master's commission in the Confederate Navy, provided by Mallory as a shield against hanging, but Mallory had approved seizing a ship from a northern port, not from Cuba.[100] Helm thought Braine's plan to launch an attack from Havana was both illegal and ill-advised, but he could not prevent the expedition's departure. Braine and his men seized the *Roanoke* on September 28, shortly after it departed Havana en route to New York. Helm wrote to Benjamin, greatly concerned that Davis or Mallory might actually have approved this plan, and pointed directly to the portions of the law of nations that this kind of action violated.[101] He cited Vattel, Kent's *Commentaries*, and Wheaton as all forbidding any attempt to set on foot an armed expedition, on land or sea, from neutral territory, even if the violence actually occurred beyond the limits of neutral land or waters, and he urged any future hijacking attacks to originate from a Union port. Helm also reported, erroneously, that he had dissuaded Thomas Hogg (captor of the *Gerrity*) from undertaking a similar venture. Hogg's mission had the full support of Mallory, as it turned out. In a stark demonstration of the impossibility of restraining these attacks, Hogg actually gave Braine and his men weapons, money, and exit passes from the Spanish authorities that enabled them to carry out the attack.[102]

Braine took the *Roanoke* to Bermuda, where he received reinforcements and assistance from locals and the Confederate office in St. George's. Bermuda authorities refused to allow the ship into the harbor, their pro-Southern proclivities dampened by pressure from London to crack down on violations of neutrality rules, although they did not seize the ship as an illegal prize as policy required. Out of fuel, Braine chose to burn the ship and merrily went ashore with the passengers and crew. Braine claimed that he and his men held commissions in the Confederate service, which was true only for Braine himself, the men having been recruited in Havana, and applicable only for a legitimate mission to New York, and he did not disclose that his mission was not only unauthorized but actively resisted by the Confederate consul in Havana.[103] On the other hand, the Confederate office in St. George's, which certainly knew of Braine's misdeeds in the *Chesapeake* case, hired a ship in a futile attempt to refuel the *Roanoke* at sea and recruited crew members to go aboard and join Braine.[104] Bermudan authorities decided they would not arrest or prosecute the hijackers, who lingered for some time, boasting of their exploits. Crown lawyers initially decided the seizure, while reprehensible, was not piracy, assuming Braine's commission was real, although Colonial Secretary Edward Cardwell scolded Lieutenant-Governor William Hamley for failing to properly enforce the Foreign Enlistment Act and the rules against prize vessels entering British ports.[105] Before he could be arrested for these related crimes Braine disappeared, off in search of another victim, while authorities in London and Washington raged at his easy escape from justice.

Braine struck again in Chesapeake Bay late in the war. In April 1865 he led a party that captured the schooner *St. Mary* by feigning distress in a small yawl, and then seizing the ship after being helped aboard by its crew. Braine evaded capture and made it to the Bahamas, where he sold part of the ship's cargo illegally. The improbably named Rawson W. Rawson, who had recently arrived to replace Charles Bayley as governor of the Bahamas, proved just as willing as his predecessor and his counterpart in Bermuda to take Braine at his word and to ignore the *Chesapeake* attack (inexcusable, especially since Vernon Locke was on trial in Nassau at the time for that very event). Rawson refused requests from the

U.S. consul to arrest Braine because he considered the *St. Mary* a legitimate prize, and that its entry into British waters, normally prohibited, was allowable because the ship was supposedly in distress. Not surprisingly, the Nassau court acquitted Locke, and he and Braine went their separate ways, to the disgust of Union and British imperial officials.[106]

In contrast to Braine's self-directed raiding, the attack on the Pacific mail steamship *Salvador* quite certainly had the approval and support of the Confederate government. The *Salvador* ran regularly between Panama and California, often carrying gold, and Hogg persuaded Stephen Mallory to support an attack. The party was to board the ship in Panama and, like the others, seize the ship once it reached international waters and either convert it into a cruiser to attack further vessels or destroy it and make their escape. An informant tipped off the Union Navy, and a substantial group of warships awaited the *Salvador* off the Pacific coast of Panama. On 10 November 1864, Union sailors boarded the ship and arrested Hogg and his men before they could even make their attempt. The hijacking attempt with the greatest official legitimacy, ironically, failed most ignominiously. The *Salvador* was not the last such attack, but the war ended before the Confederate Navy could organize any more on such official terms. The *Salvador*'s hijackers, unlike Braine and Locke, had to face trial in an American court in San Francisco.[107] Lacking a friendly colonial judge, they were convicted and had death sentences commuted to substantial stays in prison.

This fusion of filibustering and privateering was evidence of a North American cultural tradition of transnational private violence. This was a continuity, from the Hunters' Lodges of the 1837–1838 Canadian rebellion, to William Walker, to postbellum Fenian raiders, of what one might call grassroots foreign policy activists, engaging in violence in support of (if not at the behest of) an aspiring secession movement.[108] This species of raiding also points to an enduring link between adventurism and private capital. Though driven by different circumstances, Southern support for Walker's Central American filibusters before the war was mirrored in 1863 and 1864 by Stephen Mallory, who, more than any other Confederate leader, promoted the fusion of private capital and violent means. After the war, the phenomenon reappeared in places like Baja California, where filibusters once again made themselves a nuisance with the support of English land speculators.[109] The cataclysmic war and concurrent state expansion of 1861–1865 obscured this habit of private violence, but it certainly did not kill it.

The actions of private adventurers and filibusters shaped the Confederate government's behavior in the colonies and at sea, in large part because of the government's continued reliance on private parties to manage affairs in the region.

James Mason took his cues from the trials in the Maritime colonies and funded the defense of the men on trial in England for seizing the *Gerrity*. Stephen Mallory promoted further hijacking operations because they offered the opportunity for minimal risk offensive actions with a good chance of success, and these attacks suited his desire to further engage private enterprise in the war at sea. In the months that followed the *Chesapeake* affair, hijackers claimed several more ships as victims, from Panama, across the British West Indies, and even on the Great Lakes. The attackers claimed Confederate authorization as cover for their deeds, truthfully in some cases, falsely in others. The Confederate government proved more willing, as their military situation worsened and the Union's "hard hand of war" struck home, to authorize or legitimize increasingly wild attempts at freelance diplomacy and violence on the British periphery of North America. The resulting chaos and public outcry demonstrated the depth and inordinate effect of the pro-Confederate networks across British America, as a relative handful of people caused problems, for both Britain and the Union, all out of proportion to their numbers.

Notes

1. British North American participation in the war on the Union side has been the subject of great contention, and although true numbers are probably impossible to determine, it is certain that large numbers, perhaps in the low thousands, served in the Union army. See Robin W. Winks, *The Civil War Years: Canada and the United States*, 4th ed. (Montreal: McGill-Queen's University Press, 1998), 177–185. Quote is found in Nathaniel Gunnison to Charles Tupper, 23 December 1863, in *Papers Relating to Foreign Affairs, Accompanying the Annual Message of the President to the Second Session Thirty-eighth Congress* (Washington, DC: Government Printing Office, 1865), 487. Hereinafter cited as FRUS 1864.

2. Aaron Sheehan-Dean, *The Calculus of Violence: How Americans Fought the Civil War* (Cambridge, MA: Harvard University Press, 2018), 357.

3. Daniel E. Sutherland, *A Savage Conflict: The Decisive Role of Guerrillas in the American Civil War* (Chapel Hill: University of North Carolina Press, 2009), 270; Sheehan-Dean, *Calculus of Violence*, 72–76.

4. Milne to Secretary of the Admiralty, 2 October 1860, Admiralty Letters Book, MLN 104/1, Milne Papers, National Maritime Museum, Greenwich, UK (hereinafter abbreviated as MM). Milne repeatedly sent ships to Central America in response to rumored filibustering attacks even after the Civil War began.

5. Sir Alexander Milne to the Secretary of the Admiralty, 2 May 1860, 26 July 1860, 13 August 1860, and 7 September 1860, MLN 104/1, Milne Papers, MM; Lord Lyons to Lord John Russell, 31 December 1861, box 107, Private Correspondence, Lyons Papers, Arundel Castle Archive, Arundel, UK.

6. James Belich, *Replenishing the Earth: The Settler Revolution and the Rise of the Anglo-World, 1783–1939* (New York: Oxford University Press, 2009), 1–14; Phillip A. Buckner and R. Douglas Francis, *Rediscovering the British World* (Calgary: University of Calgary Press, 2005), 1–19; Charles Wentworth Dilke, *Greater Britain: A Record of Travel in English-Speaking Countries* (London: Macmillan, 1888).

7. Belich, *Replenishing the Earth*, 9.

8. John Manning Ward, *Colonial Self-Government: The British Experience, 1759–1856* (London: Macmillan, 1976), 111–123.

9. Many scholars of British imperialism, focused on Britain's Asian and African colonies, assumed political control as the chief motive for devolving political power, particularly to "collaborating elites." Ronald Robinson, "Non-European Foundations of European Imperialism: Sketch for a Theory of Collaboration," in *Studies in the Theory of Imperialism*, ed. Roger Owen and Bob Sutcliffe (London: Longman, 1972), 120–126.

10. Mark Francis, *Governors and Settlers: Images of Authority in the British Colonies, 1820–60* (London: Macmillan, 1992), 1, 8.

11. In the context of international law, "municipal" refers to a country's domestic laws that are operative within its own borders, not to local or city government.

12. Tyler Wentzell, "Mercenaries and Adventurers: Canada and the Foreign Enlistment Act in the Nineteenth Century," *Canadian Military History* 23, no. 2 (2014): 1–21.

13. Stephen R. Wise, *Lifeline of the Confederacy: Blockade Running during the Civil War* (Columbia: University of South Carolina Press, 1988), 191–192; Greg Marquis, *In Armageddon's Shadow: The Civil War and Canada's Maritime Provinces* (Montreal: McGill-Queen's University Press, 1998), 244–255. Manifests for outbound blockade runners frequently listed St. John or Halifax as their false destination. See, for example, the shipping notices in the *Nassau Guardian* for almost any period between 1862 and 1865.

14. Phillip A. Buckner, "The 1860s: An End and a Beginning," in *The Atlantic Region to Confederation: A History*, ed. Phillip A. Buckner and John G. Reid (Toronto: University of Toronto Press, 1994), 371.

15. Andrew Low and Co. to Leroy P. Walker, 24 April 1861, in *War of the Rebellion: A Compilation of the Official Records of the Union and Confederate Armies*, 128 vols. (Washington, DC: Government Printing Office, 1880–1901), ser. 4, vol. 1, 237. Hereinafter cited as OR.

16. Roger S. Durham, *High Seas and Yankee Gunboats: A Blockade-Running Adventure from the Diary of James Dickson* (Columbia: University of South Carolina Press, 2005), 31–40.

17. Report of the Secretary of War, n.d. (February 1861), OR ser. 4, vol. 1, 958.

18. Ann Larrabee, *The Dynamite Fiend* (Halifax, NS: Nimbus, 2005), chaps. 2 and 3; Marquis, *In Armageddon's Shadow*, 88–96; Michael J. Turner, *Stonewall Jackson, Beresford Hope, and the Meaning of the American Civil War in Britain* (Baton Rouge: Louisiana State University Press, 2020), 2–3. Marquis found substantial (though far from unanimous) support across the Maritimes for the Confederacy, with frequent comparisons made between them and others attempting to throw off the "yoke" of foreign domination, such as Italy or Poland, whereas Turner highlights the importance of the romantic view of Confederate heroism in attracting British support.

19. Allan E. Marble, "Almon, William Johnston," in *Dictionary of Canadian Biography* (University of Toronto/Université Laval, 2003), http://www.biographi.ca/en/bio/almon_william_johnston_13E.html. Almon also had an indirect connection to slavery. His father and some other family members received compensation for slaves on a Jamaica estate after West Indian emancipation. "William Bruce Almon," Legacies of British Slave-ownership database, http://wwwdepts-live.ucl.ac.uk/lbs/person/view/46486 (accessed 14 August 2019).

20. Francis I. W. Jones, "A Hot Southern Town: Confederate Sympathizers in Halifax during the American Civil War," *Journal of the Royal Nova Scotia Historical Society* 2 (1999): 56.

21. Thomas L. Connolly, "The Archbishop of Halifax on the Irish in British and Republican America," in *The Irish Position in British and Republican North America: A Letter to the Editors of the Irish Press Irrespective of Party*, by Thomas D'Arcy McGee, 2nd ed. (Montreal: M. Longmoore, 1866), Appendix B.

22. William C. Davis, *Look Away! A History of the Confederate States of America* (New York: Free Press, 2002), 85–88.

23. David A. Sutherland, "Wier, Benjamin," in *Dictionary of Canadian Biography*, http://www.biographi.ca/en/bio/wier_benjamin_9E.html (accessed 19 June 2019).

24. Judah P. Benjamin to George N. Sanders, 28 October 1862, Reel 12, Confederate States of America Records, Library of Congress Manuscript Division, Washington, DC. Hereinafter cited as CSAR. Benjamin to Jefferson Davis, 30 March 1864, Reel 13, CSAR.

25. Troy Bickham, *The Weight of Vengeance: The United States, the British Empire, and the War of 1812* (New York: Oxford University Press, 2012), 126–128.

26. Stephen Mallory to Jefferson Davis, 6 January 1862, *The Official Records of the Union and Confederate Navies in the War of the Rebellion*, 30 vols. (Washington, DC: Government Printing Office, 1894–1922), ser. 2, vol. 2, 124. Hereinafter cited as ORN followed by series and volume.

27. Mark G. Hanna, *Pirate Nests and the Rise of the British Empire, 1570–1740* (Chapel Hill: University of North Carolina Press, 2015), 183–221.

28. Bickham, *Weight of Vengeance*, 128–129.

29. Jan Lemnitzer, *Power, Law, and the End of Privateering* (London: Palgrave Macmillan, 2014), 115–138.

30. It is difficult to overstate how common it was to abuse letters of marque in the preceding centuries. See Lauren Benton, "Toward a New Legal History of Piracy: Maritime Legalities and the Myth of Universal Jurisdiction," *International Journal of Maritime History* 23, no. 1 (2011): 225–240; Hanna, *Pirate Nests and the Rise of the British Empire, 1570–1740*, passim.

31. The real John Parker, the original captain of the *Retribution*, died of yellow fever in 1861, and Locke assumed his name in order to take over the privateer commission. Thomas B. Power to N. Irwin, 22 February 1864, reel 9, CSAR.

32. Marquis, *In Armageddon's Shadow*, 135–136.

33. "The Rebel Pirate Retribution," *New York Times*, 13 March 1863.

34. William H. Seward to Lord Lyons, 4 April 1863, in *Message of the President of the United States, and accompanying documents, to the two houses of Congress, at the commencement of the first session of the thirty-eighth Congress, Part I* (Washington, DC: Government Printing Office, 1864), 1:547; John Burnside to Charles Nesbitt, 20 April 1863, ibid., 1:641–643. Hereinafter cited as FRUS 1863.

35. Affidavit of Isaac R. Staples, in *Correspondence Concerning Claims Against Great Britain*, vol. 6 (Washington, DC: Government Printing Office, 1871), 736; United States, *The Case of the United States, Laid Before the Tribunal of Arbitration, Convened at Geneva under the provisions of the treaty between the United States of America and Her Majesty the Queen of Great Britain, concluded at Washington, May 8, 1871* (Leipzig: F. A. Brockhaus, 1872), 261.

36. Seward to Lyons, 10 November 1863, FRUS 1863, Supplement, cxxviii. Other sources place the bail as low as £100.

37. Bayley to Newcastle, 31 October 1863, f364–365, CO 23/172, CO 23: Original Correspondence, Bahamas, The National Archives, Kew, United Kingdom. Hereinafter abbreviated as TNA.

38. Bayley to Newcastle, 22 August 1863, f67–69, CO 23/172, TNA. For further context see Beau Cleland, "Between King Cotton and Queen Victoria: Confederate Informal Diplomacy and Privatized Violence in British America during the American Civil War" (PhD diss., University of Calgary, 2019), 114–128.

39. *Case of the United States*, 261.

40. Marquis, *In Armageddon's Shadow*, 139–141. Some publications write Braine's name as "Brain," but as the vast majority of sources spell it in the former fashion, I have adhered to the more common spelling.

41. New Brunswick Vice-Admiralty Court and Alfred A. Stockton, *Reports of Cases Decided in the Vice-Admiralty Court of New Brunswick from 1879 to 1891: With an Introduction on Admiralty Jurisdiction* (St. John: J. & A. McMillan, 1894), 236–238.

42. James M. Matthews, ed., *The Statutes at Large of the Provisional Government of the Confederate States of America, from the Institution of the Government, February 8, 1861, to Its Termination, February 18, 1862, Inclusive. Arranged in Chronological Order. Together with the Constitution for the Provisional Government, and the Permanent Constitution of the Confederate States, and the Treaties Concluded by the Confederate States with Indian Tribes* (Richmond: R. M. Smith, 1864), 100–104.

43. See, for example, Laurence Oliphant, *Patriots and Filibusters, or, Incidents of Exploratory Travel* (London and Edinburgh: W. Blackwood and Sons, 1860), 132–242. *Blackwood's Magazine* published the book serially in its issues.

44. ORN ser. 1, vol. 2, 1096, 536–538. In some correspondence Schaffer's first name is spelled "Owen." Some pro-Confederate accounts claimed Schaffer fired shots at his attackers, wounding one, but none of the crew's statements suggest that they were armed or expecting any sort of attack. Any wounded pirates likely came by their injuries through their own negligence.

45. The narrative of the capture of the *Chesapeake* is compiled from ORN, ser. 1, vol. 2, 512–660. For two good but slightly differing summaries, see Winks, *The Civil War Years*, chapter 12, and Marquis, *In Armageddon's Shadow*, chapters 6 and 7.

46. Marquis, *In Armageddon's Shadow*, 152–154.

47. Nathaniel Gunnison to W. H. Seward, 14 December 1863, ORN ser. 1, vol. 2, 523. Joseph Davis to Gunnison, 14 December 1863, in House of Commons, *North America No. 9 (1864): Papers Relating to the Seizure of the United States' Steamer "Chesapeake"* (London: Harrison and Sons, 1864), 15.

48. Ward, *Colonial Self-Government*, 34–37, 111–123.

49. Recent scholarship ties the Canadian rebellions to the broader Atlantic revolutionary movements of the nineteenth century, as well as the democratic Chartist movement in Britain. Michael Ducharme, "Closing the Last Chapter of the Atlantic Revolution: The 1837–1838 Rebellions in Upper and Lower Canada," *Proceedings of the American Antiquarian Society* 116, no. 2 (2007): 413–430.

50. Ward, *Colonial Self-Government*, 60–65, 172–175. Ward suggests that the "Durham Report," published in the aftermath of the rebellions, was less important in the eventual grant of responsible government than broader changes in British society and attitudes toward settler colonies.

51. Ward, *Colonial Self-Government*, 174.

52. Phillip A. Buckner, *The Transition to Responsible Government: British Policy in British North America, 1815–1850* (Westport, CT: Greenwood Press, 1985), 6, 355. Quote is from p. 6.

53. Patrick Brode, *The Odyssey of John Anderson* (Toronto: University of Toronto Press, 1989), 67–82.

54. Marquis, *In Armageddon's Shadow*, 172. Charles Hastings Doyle to the Duke of Newcastle, 23 December 1863, in *Papers Relating to the Seizure of the United States' Steamer "Chesapeake,"* 10–13.

55. Marquis, *In Armageddon's Shadow*, 173–174.

56. Saint John *Globe*, 10 December 1863, quoted in Marquis, *In Armageddon's Shadow*, 147.

57. Testimony of Charles Watters, in *"The Chesapeake." The Case of David Collins, et al., prisoners arrested under the provisions of the Imperial Act, 6 & 7 Vic., Cap. 76, on a charge of piracy* . . . (Saint John, NB: J. & A. McMillan, 1864), 16–17.

58. *The Chesapeake*, 16–18. Quote is from p. 18.

59. Arthur Gordon to the Duke of Newcastle, 1 January 1864, in *Papers Relating to the Seizure of the United States' Steamer "Chesapeake,"* 34–35.

60. Marquis, *In Armageddon's Shadow*, 186–187.

61. Gordon Bale, *Chief Justice William Johnston Ritchie: Responsible Government and Judicial Review* (Ottawa: Carleton University Press, 1991), 85–89.

62. Marquis, *In Armageddon's Shadow*, 192–193.

63. Winks, *The Civil War Years*, 259–262.

64. B. Wier to Maj. Norman S. Walker, 5 January 1864, reel 9, CSAR.

65. J.W. Ritchie to B. Wier, 5 January 1864, reel 9, CSAR.

66. Marquis, *In Armageddon's Shadow*, 145.

67. Report of Proceedings in the Vice Admiralty Court of Nova Scotia, regarding the "Chesapeake," 15 February 1864, in *Papers Relating to the Seizure of the United States' Steamer "Chesapeake,"* 83–85.

68. Doyle to Newcastle, 18 February 1864, in *Papers Relating to the Seizure of the United States' Steamer "Chesapeake,"* 81.

69. Marquis, *In Armageddon's Shadow*, 198–199. See the correspondence surrounding the cargo of the *Sea Bride* in Mauritius, W. R. G. Mellen to Edward Rushworth, 4 February 1864, FRUS 1864, 564–565.

70. Rear Admiral Sir Baldwin Walker to Lt. John Low, 27 December 1863, in C.S.S. Tuscaloosa Logs, W. S. Hoole Special Collections Library, University of Alabama, Tuscaloosa, Alabama.

71. Decision of Judge Alexander Stewart, enclosed in William H. Seward to Charles Francis Adams, 24 February 1864, FRUS 1864, 198–199.

72. Charles Hastings Doyle to Lord Lyons, 17 February 1864, Box 123, Letters Received, Lyons Papers.

73. Marquis, *In Armageddon's Shadow*, 206–207.

74. Lewis Hutt to City Marshal of Halifax, 21 December 1863, FRUS 1864, 484–485. Marquis, *In Armageddon's Shadow*, 209. J. W. Johnston to Doyle, 13 January 1864, in *Papers Relating to the Seizure of the United States' Steamer "Chesapeake,"* 60–62.

75. Doyle to Lyons, 17 February 1864, Box 123, Letters Received, Lyons Papers. "Nous verrons" translates roughly as "we shall see."

76. William Morrison Robinson, *The Confederate Privateers* (Columbia: University of South Carolina Press, 1928).

77. Frank J. Merli, *Great Britain and the Confederate Navy, 1861–1865* (Bloomington: Indiana University Press, 1970), 257. Merli argues that enforcement against Confederate ships was ad hoc and driven by diplomatic and political necessity rather than a stringent interpretation of law.

78. David Riker to Robert Toombs, 18 July 1861, in reel 12, CSAR.

79. John Yates Beall, a Southerner, was hanged for his role in ship hijackings and other clandestine attacks. A Union military tribunal did not accept a commission from Jefferson Davis as sufficient to excuse his actions. On the other hand, John C. Braine repeatedly escaped justice in colonial courts by claiming he was in the Confederate service. See John Y. Beall, *Memoir of John Yates Beall: His life; trial; correspondence; diary; and private manuscript found among his papers, including his own account of the raid on Lake Erie* (Montreal: John Lovell, 1865). W. G. Hamley to Edward Cardwell, 28 October 1864, ORN ser. 1, vol. 3, 243–247.

80. Winks, *The Civil War Years*, 287–291. Men who could credibly claim to be Confederates led the September 1864 attack on the *Philo Parsons*.

81. Mallory to Davis, 6 January 1862, ORN ser. 2, vol. 2, 124–125. Mallory to Davis, 27 February 1862, ORN ser. 2, vol. 2, 153.

82. W. W. Lester, *A Digest of the Military and Naval Laws of the Confederate States . . . Analytically Arranged* (Richmond: Evans and Cogswell, 1864), 211–214. Congress also created a provisional navy, but this structure served as a way to promote junior officers by merit rather than seniority. They dubbed the quasi-privateering body the "Volunteer Navy" to differentiate the two.

83. Confederate States of America, *Journal of the Congress of the Confederate States of America, 1861–1865*, vol. 3 (Washington, DC: Government Printing Office, 1904), 681.

It is unclear how international law would have treated such a vessel, although assuming it was purchased rather than captured, the commission and letter of marque might have been legal—the CSS *Alabama* obtained a legal commission without entering a Confederate port.

84. Mallory to Col. E. C. Cabell, 10 September 1863, OR ser. 1, vol. 22, part 2, 1001–1002.

85. Merli, *Great Britain and the Confederate Navy, 1861–1865*, 195–210.

86. Jefferson Davis, message to Congress, 2 May 1864, in James D. Richardson, ed., *The Messages and Papers of Jefferson Davis and the Confederacy, 1861–1865*, vol. 1 (New York: Chelsea House, 1983), 230–231.

87. Warren F. Spencer, *The Confederate Navy in Europe* (Tuscaloosa: University of Alabama Press, 1983), 170–173; Howard Jones, *Blue and Gray Diplomacy: A History of Union and Confederate Foreign Relations* (Chapel Hill: University of North Carolina Press, 2010), 307–314.

88. Dominic Alessio, "Filibustering from Africa to the Americas: Non-State Actors and Empire," *Small Wars and Insurgencies* 27, no. 6 (2016): 1044–1066.

89. Robert E. May, *Manifest Destiny's Underworld: Filibustering in Antebellum America* (Chapel Hill: University of North Carolina Press, 2002), xv. May also defines filibustering as an American phenomenon, but it seems obvious that the practice is not limited to any particular nation.

90. James G. Cusick, *The Other War of 1812: The Patriot War and the American Invasion of Spanish East Florida* (Athens: University of Georgia Press, 2007), 33–37.

91. Amy S. Greenberg, *Manifest Manhood and the Antebellum American Empire* (New York: Cambridge University Press, 2010), 30.

92. Thomas E. Hogg to J. P. Benjamin, 3 May 1864, ORN ser. 2, vol. 3, 1111–1112.

93. Winks, *The Civil War Years*, 146–152. The first plot was far more advanced than many contemporary observers and subsequent historians realized, and its leaders canceled it only at the last moment. George W. Gift to Ellen Shackleford, 16 November 1863, in the George W. Gift papers #1152, Southern Historical Collection, The Wilson Library, University of North Carolina at Chapel Hill.

94. James Mason to J. P. Benjamin, 12 April 1864, ORN ser. 2, vol. 3, 1082–1084.

95. Norman Walker to J. P. Benjamin, 15 January 1864, reel 9, CSAR; Georgiana Gholson Walker, *The Private Journal of Georgiana Gholson Walker, 1862–1865, With Selections from the Post-War Years, 1865–1876*, ed. Dwight Franklin Henderson (Tuscaloosa: Confederate Publishing Company, 1963), 61.

96. James P. Holcombe to J. P. Benjamin, 1 April 1864, ORN ser. 2, vol. 3, 1072–1073.

97. See, for example, Benjamin to P. H. Aylett, 2 March 1864, ORN ser. 2, vol. 3, 1044.

98. Note of Thomas F. Elliot, Under-Secretary of State, 11 January 1865, f47, CO 37/193, TNA.

99. Braine had obtained an acting master's commission from Mallory under false pretenses, but most of the party was recruited in Havana and was not in the Confederate service.

100. J. P. Benjamin to Charles J. Helm, 13 September 1864, ORN ser. 1, vol. 3, 239–240.

101. Helm to Benjamin, 17 August 1864, ORN ser. 1, vol. 3, 234–237.

102. Francis X. Holbrook, "A Mosby or a Quantrill? The Civil War Career of John Clibbon Braine," *American Neptune* 33, no. 3 (1973): 205–206.

103. Charles J. Helm to Don Domingo Dulce, 21 November 1863, ORN ser. 1, vol. 3, 242–243.

104. S. Brownlow Gray to William G. Hamley, 24 October 1864, ORN ser. 1, vol. 3, 244–247.

105. Cardwell to Hamley, 16 January 1865, ORN ser. 1, vol. 3, 247–248.

106. Holbrook, "A Mosby or a Quantrill?" 209–211.

107. Alexander S. Cano, "The Salvador Affair: Anatomy of a Confederate Naval Expedition to Central America" (MA thesis, Angelo State University, 2006), 77–97.

108. Michel Gobat, *Empire by Invitation: William Walker and Manifest Destiny in Central America* (Cambridge, MA: Harvard University Press, 2018), 2–11.

109. May, *Manifest Destiny's Underworld*, 287.

6

"A Long-Cherished Plan"

Detroit and the U.S. Annexation of Canada during the Nineteenth Century

John W. Quist

With a population of just over 45,000 in 1860, Detroit was the nineteenth largest city in the United States. But located across the Detroit River from Windsor, Ontario (known as Upper Canada before 1841 and Canada West from 1841 to 1867),[1] Detroit ranked, after Buffalo, as the second largest U.S. city bordering Canada. Unsurprisingly, nineteenth-century Detroiters knew Canada—and followed Canadian affairs (as well as developments throughout British North America)—better than most U.S. residents. Detroiters' views on Canada can thus provide an instructive window into the broader U.S. debate regarding Canada and Canadian annexation.[2]

This essay examines nineteenth-century Detroiters' views on the U.S. annexation of Canada, primarily through their partisan newspapers—the Democratic *Detroit Free Press*, the Republican *Detroit Advertiser and Tribune*, and the Republican *Detroit Post*—and the city's, and arguably the state's, most important politician during the Civil War years, Republican U.S. Senator Zachariah Chandler. After providing some context, it will focus on the half-dozen years following the American Civil War, as it was then that U.S. talk of annexing Canada loomed largest. Relations between Great Britain and Canada plummeted during the Civil War and contributed to the growth of annexationist sentiment in the U.S. with some, Chandler being the most important, arguing that the nation should settle its grievances with Britain by annexing part or all of Canada.[3]

The U.S. withdrawal from the 1854 Reciprocity Treaty in 1866 also contributed to Americans' talk of Canadian annexation, with both those favoring and opposing the Reciprocity Treaty—free traders and protectionists—arguing that their respective position would further that aim. Detroit's Democrats and Republicans, who argued vigorously over a host of issues, expected that Canada would one day become part of the United States—"a long-cherished plan," according to the *Detroit Free Press*.[4] They saw Canadian Confederation as a minor distraction in view of their expectation of Canadians' incorporation into the United States. For the most part, annexationists believed these developments would occur through peaceful means, and supposed annexation would be something that Canadians would welcome.

Although the Treaty of Washington (1871) and the subsequent settlement of the *Alabama* claims caused the most vocal annexationist talk to diminish, Detroiters—and Americans generally—continued to speak of Canadian annexation during the decades that followed. At the same time, U.S. interest in annexing Canada often reflected words Americans heard—and read—coming from north of their border, as Canadians throughout British North America spoke often of joining the United States. As one twentieth-century scholar on the topic explained, "Annexationism was much more prominent in [Canada and its colonial antecedents] than in the [United States]." Or, as the *New York Times* put it in 1865 during a week when Canadian annexation was a much-discussed topic: "We should not, in fact, know that it [annexation] was ever thought of by anybody, if we did not from time to time learn of it from the Canadian papers."[5]

Several factors on both sides of the border converged to make many nineteenth-century Americans eager to annex Canada, though this essay will focus on the U.S. side of the ledger. For one thing, many English-speaking Canadians were a generation—or less—removed from the United States, which encouraged U.S. residents to conclude, incorrectly, that Canada was filled with thousands of Americans in all but name, who were eager to live once again under the stars and stripes. Many in the U.S. also believed exaggerated reports that French-speaking Canadians were dissatisfied with the British and wanted to join the United States. Numerous Americans also held the conviction that U.S. institutions would inevitably prevail across North America—and beyond—with some in the U.S. trying to accelerate the process by fostering dissent and rebellion against the British in Canada. And recognizing British challenges in defending such a vast area as Canada, many nineteenth-century Americans expected that British efforts to defend Canada against a U.S. invasion would ultimately fail.

Nineteenth-century Detroiters mostly concerned themselves with trade and with the economic opportunities that Canada offered, particularly after the reciprocity trade agreement of 1854 more broadly opened cross-border trade. While Detroit's connections through the Atlantic world were initially fostered by the Erie Canal's completion in 1825 (by which water trade moved from Detroit, through Lake Erie, to the canal's western terminus in Buffalo, New York), the high costs for traveling along the Erie Canal eventually caused Detroit merchants to favor, or at least consider, shipping by way of Ontario's Welland Canal and the St. Lawrence River. Additionally, the Great Western Railroad's opening in 1854, linking Buffalo with Windsor, and the Grand Trunk Railway, connecting Michigan to New England across Ontario in 1859 (through a line that ran to Port Huron, Michigan) provided Detroiters with faster passenger and freight transportation than did the water route or the rail lines that ran through Ohio. In short, by the mid-nineteenth century Detroit and southern Ontario had grown economically dependent on each other.[6]

Accompanying that economic activity were tensions that extended back to the eighteenth century—tensions that often stemmed from Americans' hostility to Great Britain and from Americans' expectations that Canadians longed to be liberated from the British. Before Americans had formally declared their independence, they invaded Quebec in the hope of adding a fourteenth colony to the rebellion. Six years later, the U.S. Articles of Confederation provided generous terms for Canada's admission to the U.S. Confederation that the Articles offered to "no other colony."[7] When the United States invaded Canada during the War of 1812, Americans learned, to their surprise, that Canadians mostly saw them as aggressive conquerors rather than as liberators.[8] Some Americans—including two parties of raiders from Detroit, each numbering over one hundred—also assisted those Canadians trying to throw off British rule in 1837–1838, a move that led Martin Van Buren to issue a presidential proclamation threatening to prosecute Americans who aided the insurgents. Van Buren further resisted American annexationists' calls to assist the insurgents after the Canadian authorities destroyed the American ship *Caroline*.[9]

Van Buren's response to the *Caroline* Affair illustrates how, by the late 1830s, U.S. officials saw Canadian annexation as a fringe movement. Much of this reluctance regarding Canadian annexation stemmed from the Missouri Crisis of 1819–1821, as sectional disagreements over slavery caused major politicians to eschew adding additional territory to the United States. This aversion toward annexation changed, though, following the treaty signed on April 12, 1844, that provided for Texas's annexation to the United States. Although the U.S. Senate rejected this treaty in June 1844, the national Democratic Party embraced Texas annexation, along with the entirety of the disputed Oregon country. Whigs, in contrast, prioritized eastern economic development over territorial expansion, and largely opposed Texas annexation. Not long thereafter they criticized the Mexican War, with many, if not most, Northern Whigs fearing the prospect of slavery spreading to territory annexed from Mexico.[10]

Yet after their defeat in the 1844 election and Democrats' success in seizing over half of Mexico, some Whigs—Northern Whigs in particular—began speaking more boldly of annexing Canada to the United States. Northern Whig voices favoring the annexation of Canada included the *Detroit Advertiser*, whose editors declared in 1845 they had "personally no objections, but . . . would be glad to see" Canada's annexation sooner rather than later. Its political rival, the *Detroit Free Press*, a strong proponent of Texas annexation, soon thereafter declared that, among Whig papers, the *Advertiser* held the "honor of first proposing annexation with Canada."[11] Because they favored having the United States be an ethnically and racially homogeneous country, Whigs felt fewer misgivings about annexing Canada and the rest of British North America than they did Mexico. Since Canadians—at least English-speaking Canadians—did not seem that much different from Americans, Canada's prospective incorporation stood congruent with Whigs' vision of the United States.[12]

During the sectional debates that preceded and followed the Mexican War's outbreak, Northern Whigs also recognized that annexing slave-free Canada would counterbalance territory acquired from Mexico or elsewhere (such as Cuba) amenable to slave-based agriculture.[13] Other Whigs used an argument especially attractive in Michigan—that southern Ontario "separates Michigan from New York," and gave Britain a presence in the Great Lakes and the power "to stop our merchantmen whenever she pleases."[14] In 1849 the *Detroit Free Press* protested the emerging Whig embrace of annexation, called annexation "a great democratic doctrine," reminded its readers of Whigs' previous opposition to annexation, and declared that a future Democratic administration—and not a Whig one—would "admit in due time[,] into this glorious Union[,] both Canada and Cuba."[15] Developments during the next two decades demonstrated the continued bipartisan appeal of Canadian annexation.

The growth of U.S. sectionalism during the 1850s effectively shelved discussion in Detroit—and the United States—regarding the annexation of Canada. Even more important in shifting the conversation away from annexation was the 1854 Elgin-Marcy Treaty between the United States and Great Britain, more commonly known in the nineteenth century as the Reciprocity Treaty. The treaty provided for free trade of raw materials, U.S. access to British North American fishing grounds, and it opened the St. Lawrence River to American ships on equal terms with British and Canadian ships.[16] Reciprocity increased the trade between the United States and British North America, with nineteenth-century Canadians thereafter concluding that their growing prosperity stemmed from trade with the U.S.[17] Consequently, talk within Canada regarding annexation to the United States—which Montreal merchants fostered after Britain repealed its Corn Laws in 1846—decreased. Americans followed suit and spoke little of annexing Canada.[18]

Mid-nineteenth-century Canadians managed their internal affairs, thanks to the British Act of Union in 1840 that unified Upper and Lower Canada (Ontario and Quebec) into the United Province of Canada in 1841, and a market revolution similar to one that had started earlier in the United States.[19] Meanwhile, Great Britain continued to control Canada's foreign affairs, resulting in Americans derisively referencing Canadians as "colonists" despite Canada's semi-independent status. Consequently Canada became entangled in the deteriorating relations between the U.S. and Britain during the Civil War, stemming largely from Britain's recognition of the Confederacy as a belligerent, though not a nation, and the construction of Confederate raiding ships in British ports. Not surprisingly, the long-standing hostility of the Northern U.S. public toward Britain escalated.[20] Soon, that antagonism led to increased U.S. talk regarding the annexation of Upper and Lower Canada (today's Ontario and Quebec) as well as Britain's other North American colonies.

With only the Detroit River separating them from Canada, Michigan residents, Detroiters in particular, felt these international tensions acutely. During the *Trent* affair[21] Michigan's Republican governor, Austin Blair, called for a preemptive invasion of Canada in his January 1862 annual message. He declared that the "British government has concealed designs, and only seeks a pretext for a rupture." Blair thought Michiganians needed "a full supply of arms . . . and a powerful war machine upon the great lakes. Michigan is to be defended, if it comes to that, not upon her own ground, but upon the soil of Canada."[22] And with milder tones, the less bellicose Democratic *Detroit Free Press* reported later that year, "An uneasy feeling has prevailed in this city for some time; an undefined apprehension that Britain is on the eve of the contest with the United States, in which, of course, Canada would be involved."[23]

Notwithstanding the thousands of Canadians who served in the Union army,[24] Canada became the home to Confederate agents and Confederate soldiers who escaped from Northern prisons, a large contingent of whom resided in Windsor.[25] Desperately hoping to turn the tide in the war in late 1864, Confederate agents launched two attacks on the United States from Canada. In September, Confederates hijacked a Detroit ship, the *Philo Parsons*, south of Windsor and unsuccessfully attempted to liberate Confederate prisoners from Ohio's Johnson Island in Lake Erie.[26] More frightening was the attack that Confederates launched on St. Albans, Vermont, from Quebec the following month that involved arson, robberies of three banks, and one civilian death. After the St. Albans' raiders' arrest in Quebec, a local Canadian judge released the prisoners on December 13, 1864. Canadian-American relations, and British-American relations, thereafter worsened, with Americans' charging British and Canadian authorities with assisting the Confederacy.

Two days after the release of these prisoners, a belligerent *Free Press* headline asked, "What Can Be Done to Protect Us from Canada?" Because Canadians had failed to control people living within their borders, Americans had the right, according to the *Free Press*, of obtaining redress if Canadian "citizens, subjects or denizens come across the border and commit crimes against us." Events made plain that "we are now drifting into a war—not with England, unless she elects to take part in it—but with Canada." The *Free Press* called upon President Lincoln to "declare a complete and absolute non-intercourse with the Canadian provinces.... No person should be permitted to come into the States without a passport, showing who and what he is." Nonintercourse would be a serious inconvenience to Detroit, but complete nonintercourse was preferable to war. "We can subsist without Canada."[27]

Republican U.S. Senator and Detroit resident Zachariah Chandler went further. Speaking in the U.S. Senate on December 14, 1864, Chandler reported complaints from Detroiters regarding Canadian authorities and the cross-border crime coming from Canada. Besides insisting on the militarization of the Canadian border (partially fulfilled with the mustering of the Michigan 30th Infantry the following month), Chandler foreshadowed his later calls for Canadian annexation by also urging the U.S. secretary of state "to demand from the British government payment in full for [U.S.] ships and cargoes" destroyed by English-built Confederate raiders.[28]

Three days after Chandler's speech, U.S. Secretary of State William Seward imposed passport controls on the U.S.-Canadian border—controls so rigidly enforced that the *Free Press* changed its mind and joined with the Republican *Advertiser and Tribune* in calling for the passport restrictions to be repealed. They declared that costs to Detroit business were too great, and the protections offered by passport control were minimal. Although Seward rescinded this passport order in early March 1865, Detroiters' frightened response to Confederate raids from Canada and their insistence upon ending passport controls exhibited their complicated relationship with Canadians, who stood as neighbors, economic partners, and potential adversaries.[29] These plummeting relations between the U.S. and Britain/British North America affected annexation discussions during the half-dozen years following the U.S. Civil War.

The passport controversy and the Confederate threat in Canada fueled the renewed local and national debate regarding the Reciprocity Treaty of 1854. Negotiated by Democrats during the Franklin Pierce administration, the treaty underlined that party's free trade ideals. American protectionists—primarily Whigs in 1854, but Republicans soon thereafter—opposed this free trade accord, as did American manufacturers and New York merchants, who believed that the treaty diverted western trade to the St. Lawrence River.[30] Neither the U.S. nor Great Britain had the power to terminate the treaty for ten years following its implementation on March 16, 1855, but afterward abrogation could occur when one party gave a year's notice of its intention to withdraw.[31]

To be sure, the increased Republican control of the federal government following the 1864 elections would have challenged the treaty's continuation even if the U.S. lacked war-related grievances against Britain and Canada. Congressional opposition to Reciprocity began to coalesce in May 1864 when House Republicans nearly passed a resolution calling for the Reciprocity Treaty's termination. After the *Philo Parsons* hijacking and the St. Albans Raid, prospects for the treaty's future looked bleak once Congress returned in December 1864.[32] Just days after the session's start, the House approved a resolution charging President Abraham Lincoln to announce the country's withdrawal from the Reciprocity Treaty.[33] The Senate debated the House resolution the following month, at which time Senator Zachariah Chandler argued for the treaty's termination by insisting that it initially aimed to

> give the people of Canada the full benefit of the American market without taxation, in order to prevent them from carrying out the scheme which was then almost generally advocated in Canada, of annexation to the United States. From the date of the adoption of the treaty until to-day that feeling, that desire for annexation and incorporation with the United States has . . . become extinct, and the great mass of the people of Canada are to-day in sympathy with the rebellion against this Government.[34]

On January 18, 1865, the House and Senate issued a joint resolution that terminated the Reciprocity Treaty. On March 17, 1865, the U.S. State Department gave Britain notice that the U.S. would withdraw from the treaty in one year.[35]

This retreat from Reciprocity began a debate in Detroit that followed party lines yet revealed a common understanding that Canada would—or should— become part of the United States. Both opponents and proponents of Reciprocity argued that their position made Canada's annexation more likely. John F. Potter, the U.S. consul general at Montreal, echoed Chandler's argument—that Reciprocity had diminished annexationist sentiment in Canada—in a speech Potter delivered at a Detroit commercial convention in July 1865. The convention, which hosted 450 delegates from across North America, aimed to underline reciprocity's advantages with an eye toward persuading American officials to reconsider their withdrawal from the treaty.[36] Speaking contrary to the convention's purpose, Potter expressed his belief "that in two years from the abrogation of the Reciprocity Treaty, the people of Canada themselves will apply for admission to the United States." After Canadians in the room angrily protested, Potter repeated himself and added, "I may say I came here with the consent of my own government, to express my views on reciprocity."

Widely reported in the United States and Canada, Potter's speech generally met with disapproval but represented an aggressive annexationist position found among some Republicans.[37] The *Free Press*, which favored continuing Reciprocity and free trade generally, depicted Potter's position as restricting trade to Canada in a way that would so seriously injure Canadians "that they would be glad to resort to Annexation in order to overcome their difficulties." Yet in its criticism of Potter the *Free Press* revealed a different vision regarding annexation: It should only occur voluntarily and be "based on mutual love and respect"—sentiments that would result from "mutual free trade and intercourse." By developing a "community of interests . . . so bound together as to render an interruption of them an evil to be dreaded," the "two peoples" would "become one" and "annexation" would naturally and gradually follow. Potter's intemperate language, the *Free Press* added, effectively halted "the progress of public opinion" in both the U.S. and Canada toward annexation.[38]

The Republican *Advertiser and Tribune* opposed the Reciprocity Treaty (although not nearly as much as the *Free Press* favored it) and regularly ran editorials and essays criticizing free trade and favoring protectionism.[39] Yet the *Advertiser and Tribune* likewise condemned Potter and "all this talk about coercing Canada to become a portion of the American Union." While the *Advertiser and Tribune* held that it would be better for the United States to control the Great Lakes' outlet to the Atlantic, its editor thought that annexation should occur only when "one side of the border [was] as well-improved, as populous, and as enterprising as the other." Were they to be annexed, Canadians should "be with us in heart, as well as by political relations."[40] Despite being politically aligned with the most aggressive annexationists, the *Advertiser and Tribune* rejected coercive annexation. In contrast to the *Free Press*, though, it did not advance an agenda to unite Canada with the U.S. It was content to wait for Canadians to improve themselves until they would be worthy to join the Union. Like its Democratic adversary, the *Advertiser and Tribune* envisioned a voluntary continental union as beneficial.

Proponents of a peaceful path to annexation received a severe blow in 1866 when the Fenians, an Irish American group dedicated to liberating Ireland from Britain, openly prepared to invade Canada from the United States. The Fenians hoped this invasion would draw British troops to Canada and then inspire the Irish to revolt against British rule. Although Fenians had spoken of invading Canada for several decades, they were most active in 1866 when they enlisted numerous former Union soldiers into their cause.[41] The Fenians initially planned for a coordinated invasion along the Canadian-U.S. border from Detroit to Eastport, Maine, on June 1, 1866. The only significant invasion point, though, was from Buffalo, New York, to Fort Erie, Ontario, which Canadian and British troops quickly suppressed, with American officials thereafter arresting Fenian leaders in the U.S.[42]

The Fenian invasion raised international tensions and caused Canadians to militarize their border, briefly, at Windsor. Both the *Free Press* and the *Advertiser and Tribune* condemned the raids, with the *Free Press* complaining beforehand that John Potter's comments the previous year and Fenian plans to invade Canada "made the Provincials peculiarly sensitive. Their common sense tells them that the continued danger of a collision with the [United] States and the crippled state of the commerce, are but a poor compensation for being regarded as bastard Britons." Canadians stubbornly refused to dissolve their connection with Britain, "and even the prospect of permanent peace and the full development of their great natural resources will hardly bring them to join Uncle Sam's family."[43]

In contrast, the newly formed *Detroit Post*, a Republican newspaper aligned with Senator Zachariah Chandler, complained that President Andrew Johnson bowed to British calls to arrest Fenians remaining in the U.S. rather than demanding compensation for Canadian and British actions during the Civil War. The U.S. needed to enforce its "claims either in an indirect way by following the precedent of English neutrality, or in a direct way, by making a final demand with the alternative of war." By frequently repeating how the Fenian invasion demonstrated Canada's vulnerability to invasion, the *Post* also made clear how U.S. claims against Britain could lead to Canadian annexation.[44]

Canadianist historians generally acknowledge how the American Civil War, coupled with the perception of the United States as an aggressive and expansionistic power, played key roles in confederating Britain's North American colonies in 1867.[45] The Detroit newspapers reported on developments in British North America leading toward Confederation and editorially noted when British North Americans questioned Confederation and favored U.S. annexation. The *Free Press*, which claimed to be following Canadian developments with "no little interest" cited an 1866 Episcopal sermon in Kingston, Ontario, as evidence of growing annexationist sentiment in Canada and added that conversions to annexationism were on the rise in Montreal—just one of many occasions when the *Post* and the *Free Press* argued that Canadian support for annexation was active and growing. The *Advertiser and Tribune* continued to believe annexation would be desirable for the United States and Canada, but lamented that Canadians remained regrettably cool to the idea.[46]

Canadian Confederation did little to change Detroiters' perception that annexation was either the likely or best outcome. Of the city's newspapers, the *Post* addressed Confederation most directly. Noting Confederation Day—July 1, 1867—with a lead editorial, the *Post* welcomed "the advent of the new Dominion," but doubted Canada's long-term prospects. Its government had too many appointive offices, and the "lack of enterprise among its people . . . and the distinctions of caste will materially retard its development."[47] Previously, the same paper had concluded that the prospective government of Canada, headed by the governor-general, created a "Kingdom" at odds with the Monroe Doctrine.[48] Suggesting that most capable Canadians flocked to the United States, the *Post* expected that Canada would eventually become part of the U.S.

Neither the *Free Press* nor the *Advertiser and Tribune* printed much regarding Confederation Day, and generally downplayed its importance. While the *Free Press* often commented on the emerging Canadian Confederation—and noted how newspapers in other cities ignored these developments[49]—the *Advertiser and Tribune* glibly summarized its position by noting that "the people of the United States do not care the flip of a copper whether the proposed confederation is established or not." The latter devoted more editorial space to the execution of Mexico's Maximilian and described the Confederation activities in Windsor as a local celebration, much as it would a Sunday school convention.[50] Despite the *Free Press*'s occasional anxiety regarding Confederation and the steps that preceded it, the *Advertiser and Tribune*'s indifference to Confederation appears to be consistent with how most Americans viewed this development. While the *Post*, the *Free Press*, and the *Advertiser and Tribune* did not view Canadian Confederation as momentous, neither did they see it as an obstacle that would interfere with their desired objective of Canadian annexation—an objective that all three papers saw occurring through a peaceful, rather than a violent, process.

It was also through the prospect of Canadian annexation—or at least the annexation of territory that became part of Canada—that Detroiters reacted to the announcement of the Alaska purchase in March 1867. Editorially, the *Free Press* had little to say about the Alaska purchase and reported some of the initial negative press on the topic. The *Post* and the *Advertiser and Tribune*, in contrast, greeted the news with pleasant surprise. After months of criticizing William Seward for his positions and actions regarding Reconstruction, the *Advertiser and Tribune* congratulated the secretary of state for negotiating the deal. It explained that Seward's annexationist ideas were well known and that he had been keenly interested in annexing Mexico and Canada. Besides noting the advantages Alaska would offer the U.S. in the event of a war with Britain, the paper argued that possession of Alaska made it easier for the United States to wrest control of British Columbia from Britain and then have the U.S. control "the entire Pacific Coast line" between the Washington territory and Alaska. Similarly, the *Post* praised the purchase as a "check to the scheme of British empire on this continent" and as a "menace" to Britain because of the U.S. desire to link Alaska to the rest of the country: "Of course we should not always remain content to be separated from part of our territory and people by a foreign jurisdiction."[51]

The Alaska Purchase caused Detroiters to devote greater attention to British Columbia. The *Free Press* reported how British Columbians debated whether they should seek annexation to the United States or join the then-emerging Canadian Confederation. The *Free Press* optimistically added: "It is certain that the advantages of annexation would be more immediately felt than those of an admission into the new British North American Confederacy." The *Post* argued for British Columbian annexation more vigorously: "The Northwest will never belong to Canada, but will soon be a part of the United States." And within weeks of the Alaskan purchase, the *Post* reported that the Johnson administration had begun discussing internally "a project to negotiate with the British of the entire western half of the British possessions on this continent. . . . Of course part of the price would be paid in the surrender of the *Alabama* claims."[52]

The *Detroit Post*'s sentiments regarding the annexation of British Columbia, and of Canada, echoed those of its chief sponsor, Zachariah Chandler. Blaming the British for the Confederate attacks from Canada and incensed about the Confederate raiders constructed at English shipyards, Chandler, more than any other public figure in the U.S., continued to raise the prospect of Canadian annexation as compensation for U.S. losses. In particular, he saw Canada as a suitable reparation for the *Alabama* claims—named for the damages that Union shipping had incurred from British-built Confederate raiders like the CSS *Alabama* between 1862 and 1864.[53]

In his December 1864 Senate speech, previously described, Chandler called upon the British to compensate the United States for damages to its shipping. In January 1866 Chandler raised the topic again in the U.S. Senate. Referring to his resolution from December 1864, Chandler noted that the British had not only refused to pay the U.S., they had also closed the door to negotiations. Considering several remedies, including the prospect of war, he added, "We might seize Canada, and say that we would take land in payment . . . and hold it until payment was made." Instead, Chandler chose what he called "a peaceful remedy": withdrawing the U.S. minister (ambassador) and ending economic relations, resulting in "absolute nonintercourse with Great Britain" and Canada—a move Chandler believed would foster Canadian annexation.[54]

Reaction to Chandler's proposal was widespread and mixed, with his party's newspaper, the *Advertiser and Tribune*, calling it "cutting off one's nose to spite one's face" and assessing the damage such measures would inflict on Americans: "It means prostrating our own business interests to punish a neighbor."[55] This blatant criticism of Chandler led to an open break between Michigan's largest Republican newspaper and the state's senior U.S. senator, also a Republican. Two months later, Chandler and his political allies established the *Detroit Post*, which took a more radical position on Reconstruction politics than did its crosstown Republican rival. Chandler hired Carl Schurz, a former Civil War general and future U.S. senator, to be its first editor. For the next eleven years Detroit hosted two Republican newspapers, with the *Post* offering Chandler the assurance that his positions would be aired. And during the first five years of its publication, the *Post* consistently called for Canadian annexation.[56]

In December 1867, Chandler continued to seek U.S. compensation from Britain for the *Alabama* claims by calling upon Congress to repeal the neutrality laws, thus opening the door to having the U.S. assist any nation that might be at war with Britain. Speaking in the Senate, Chandler even offered a resolution "to preserve neutrality between the Government of Great Britain and the King of Abyssinia" that would foster the U.S. construction of ships that Abyssinia could use against British commerce. Chandler also calculated that the U.S. losses from British actions during the Civil War amounted to $2 billion. Given Britain's continued refusal to compensate the United States, Chandler moved beyond nonintercourse to embrace a proposal he had rejected in 1866: that the U.S. regard "every acre of land that Great Britain owns on this continent or the adjacent islands" as now being mortgaged to the U.S.[57]

Efforts to settle the *Alabama* claims during the waning days of the Johnson administration failed,[58] and with matters still unresolved in 1869, Chandler raised the stakes higher. In another Senate address Chandler recounted his previous speeches on the topic and asked why the U.S. should continue to conduct futile negotiations with Britain. After restating the mortgage he declared the U.S.

had upon Canada, Chandler argued that the U.S. could not "afford to have an enemy and an enemy's base so near. . . . It is a national necessity that we should own these British possessions." Chandler hoped that negotiations would resolve these differences, but if "England insists upon having war, let that war be short, sharp, and decisive." Chandler then offered Michigan troops to perform the task: "If that war comes . . . sixty thousand veteran soldiers of Michigan will take the contract to take possession of the Canadas in thirty days" without the assistance of soldiers from other states. And with over two million battle-hardened veterans in the U.S., Chandler further boasted that the U.S. had more veteran soldiers "than all the rest of the world put together."[59]

This time the *Advertiser and Tribune* defended Chandler's remarks (even as Chandler's newspaper, the *Post*, did not defend the senator)—going so far as to call, uncharacteristically, the "Dominion . . . a standing menace to our institutions."[60] In contrast, the *Free Press* called Chandler a "clown and a buffoon" for threatening to have the U.S. invade Canada and for insisting on taking Canada in exchange for the *Alabama* claims. It bolstered its charge by running excerpts from newspapers across the North that shared its view.[61] Undeterred, Chandler aggressively continued to champion Canadian annexation and sometimes did so without connecting them to the unsettled *Alabama* claims.

Soon, Chandler's imperialistic demands extended beyond Canada. In 1870 Chandler announced in the U.S. Senate that he wanted to enlarge U.S. domestic commerce by extending U.S. borders and absorbing the Caribbean Islands, Hawaii, Canada, Santo Domingo, and Colombia. U.S. control of these areas, Chandler explained, would make the rest of the world an American tributary. Also of interest to Chandler, the editors of the *Detroit Post*, and others, was the Red River country of present-day Manitoba, then under the control of the Hudson's Bay Company. The U.S. settlers residing there and some of the French-speaking Métis objected to the transfer of the region from the Hudson's Bay Company to the new Confederated government. Both Chandler and his fellow Michigan senator, Detroiter Jacob Howard, promoted the Red River region's annexation to the U.S., with Chandler introducing a bill into Congress calling for Manitoba's statehood. Addressing this matter in the Senate, Chandler asserted, "This continent is ours, and we may as well notify the world . . . that we will fight for our own if we must."[62]

After William Seward proposed having the U.S. annex the Bahamas or British Columbia to settle the *Alabama* claims, his successor as secretary of state, Hamilton Fish, initially proposed resolving differences with Britain through Canadian annexation. Fish enjoyed the support of President Ulysses S. Grant in this matter, who briefly endorsed the idea in cabinet meetings. Ultimately Grant and Fish rejected Chandler's approach, also favored by U.S. Senator Charles Sumner of Massachusetts, of protracting the negotiations until Britain relinquished Canada. Besides favoring stronger ties with Britain, Fish also recognized that annexation lacked majority support in Canada and realized that the British would refuse to surrender Canada so long as most Canadians opposed annexation.[63]

In early 1871, news leaked that the *Alabama* claims were "on the point of settlement" with a "satisfactory conclusion" at hand. By this time, observers understood that the final sticking point between Britain and the U.S. rested on U.S. access to Canadian fisheries, not on annexation. Realizing that an opportunity to annex at least a portion of British North America was slipping away, outgoing Michigan Senator Jacob Howard introduced a resolution into the U.S. Senate that called upon the commissioners then settling the *Alabama* claims to recognize that British possessions in North America were "an obstacle to the permanent harmony of the two Governments and a standing incitement to persons anxious to involve them in war." Howard's resolution would have the Senate "earnestly recommend that the commission may, in any settlement suggested by them, embrace the cession to the United States" of "British possessions as lies to the westward of Hudson's bay." Howard's resolution failed to garner support and the Senate eventually referred the resolution to the Foreign Relations Committee, where it died.[64]

The Treaty of Washington (1871) led to international arbitration that finally settled the *Alabama* claims, with the United States receiving a cash payment of $15.5 million from Britain rather than land. Detroit newspapers—and newspapers throughout the country—regarded the treaty as a victory and said nothing about the lack of Canadian territory in the deal. Before even examining the treaty's text, the *Detroit Post* announced in a headline that the treaty was "highly favorable to the United States," and then afterward declared it "comprehensive, moderate, and well executed. It is equally just and unambiguous. It is a new and noble starting point for both parties." The *Free Press* similarly hoped that the Senate would ratify the treaty. That ratification occurred on May 24, 1871, by a 50–12 vote, with both Michigan senators, Zachariah Chandler and Thomas W. Ferry, siding with the majority. Despite his reservations, the wily Chandler demonstrated his loyalty to the Grant administration by privately promising Hamilton Fish to work for the treaty's ratification and to "help through the House and Senate any [supportive] legislation." Chandler then lobbied other senators to ratify the treaty, without amendments, and thereafter stopped speaking of Canadian annexation.[65]

Zachariah Chandler's rapid retreat from being an aggressive proponent of Canadian annexation should not cause us to see annexation as a mere tool used in pursuit of greater political objectives. By 1871, Americans' continued interest in Canadian annexation, even if often fueled by Canadian politics, had been a feature of American political life for decades. And the Treaty of Washington did not end American discussion of the question. Within days of the Senate ratification, the *Detroit Post* expected that Canadian annexation "will be brought about by the Canadians themselves rather than by any annexation party either in this country or that," and added that the greater prosperity in the United States would compel Canadians to unite with the United States. American discussions regarding the topic continued to follow the Canadian lead. As Donald F. Warner has shown, annexationism rose again in Canada during the 1880s and early 1890s, particularly whenever Canadians perceived that their alignment with Britain deprived them of the economic prosperity they believed to be more abundant in the U.S.[66] Although Detroit newspapers occasionally raised the prospect of Canadian annexation,[67] the issue never again had the resonance in Detroit as it did during the half-dozen years following the Civil War, when annexationism asserted itself as a way to settle scores with Britain.

More importantly, the U.S. withdrawal from the Reciprocity Treaty in 1866 showed how both free traders and protectionists, Democrats and Republicans, believed that Canada would—or should—eventually become part of the United States. Canadians would eventually realize, Americans believed, that incorporation into the U.S. would be to their unquestioned advantage. And most American annexationists held that Canada would become American peacefully and not through military conquest. Part of this belief stemmed from the American conviction that, despite national crises over slavery and fighting a devastating Civil War, their society was the world's best and that it would become dominant throughout North America, and beyond. Besides, Canadians seemed so similar to Americans. This American conviction regarding Canadian annexation also stemmed from Americans' failure to understand Canadians.

Notes

1. Throughout this essay I generally use the terms *Ontario* and *Quebec* rather than their pre-1867 names.

2. Before 1867, *Canada* meant the United Province of Canada, which included Ontario and Quebec. With Confederation in 1867, Canada thereafter also included New Brunswick and Nova Scotia. Other British North American colonies—Prince Edward Island, Newfoundland, and British Columbia—later became part of Canada, as did the

Hudson's Bay Company's territories of Rupert's Land and the North-Western Territory (now the provinces of Alberta, Manitoba, and Saskatchewan and the Yukon Territory, Northwest Territory, and Nunavut). Robert Bothwell, *Your Country, My Country: A Unified History of the United States and Canada* (New York: Oxford University Press, 2015), 117–118.

3. In "The Story of an Illusion: The Plan to Trade the *Alabama* claims for Canada," *Civil War History* 15, no. 4 (1969): 332–348, Doris W. Dashew underlines Charles Sumner's role in favoring Canadian annexation. As my essay demonstrates, Chandler's long-standing support for Canadian annexation preceded Sumner's heralding of annexation from 1869 to 1871, which Dashew emphasizes.

4. *Detroit Free Press*, February 4, 1867.

5. Donald F. Warner, *The Idea of Continental Union: Agitation for the Annexation of Canada to the United States, 1849–1893* (Lexington: University of Kentucky Press, 1960), vi; *New York Times*, July 22, 1865. See also ibid., May 5, 1879: "It is a little singular that most of the talk about Canadian annexation comes from the other side of the boundary."

6. J. G. Snell, "H. H. Emmons, Detroit's Agent in Canadian-American Relations, 1864–1866," *Michigan History* 56, no. 4 (1972): 302–303; F. Clever Bald, *Michigan in Four Centuries* (New York: Harper and Brothers, 1954), 247.

7. Robert Middlekauff, *The American Revolution, 1763–1789* (New York: Oxford University Press, 1982), 304–308; Winton U. Solberg, ed., *The Federal Convention and the Formation of the Union of the American States* (Indianapolis: Bobbs-Merrill, 1958), 50.

8. Bothwell, *Your Country, My Country*, 84–86; Arthur R. M. Lower, *Canadians in the Making: A Social History of Canada* (Toronto: Longmans, Green, 1958), 173–178; J. M. S. Careless, *Canada: A Story of Challenge* (Toronto: Macmillan of Canada, 1963), 131–134; Harry L. Coles, *The War of 1812* (Chicago: University of Chicago Press, 1965).

9. James D. Richardson, ed., *A Compilation of the Messages and Papers of the Presidents, 1789–1897*, vol. 3 (Washington, DC: Government Printing Office, 1896), 481; Major L. Wilson, *The Presidency of Martin Van Buren* (Lawrence: University of Kansas Press, 1984), 157–162; Marc L. Harris, "The Meaning of Patriot: The Canadian Rebellion and American Republicanism, 1837–39," *Michigan Historical Review* 23, no. 1 (1997): 33–69; Bothwell, *Your Country*, 97–98; Willis F. Dunbar and George S. May, *Michigan: A History of the Wolverine State*, rev. ed. (Grand Rapids, MI: William B. Eerdmans, 1980), 282–284.

10. On Texas annexation, see Daniel Walker Howe, *What Hath God Wrought: The Transformation of America, 1815–1848* (New York: Oxford University Press, 2007), 677–690. Regarding Whigs' opposition to territorial expansion and their preference for building the nation's economy and infrastructure instead, see Michael A. Morrison, "Westward the Curse of Empire: Texas Annexation and the American Whig Party," *Journal of the Early Republic* 10, no. 2 (1990): 221–249; Major L. Wilson, *Space, Time, and Freedom: The Quest for Nationality and the Irrepressible Conflict, 1815–1861* (Westport, CT: Greenwood Press, 1974), 115–117; Jeffrey G. Charnley, "Swords into Plowshares: A Hope Unfulfilled: Michigan Opposition to the Mexican War, 1846–1848," *The Old Northwest* 8, no. 3 (1982): 199–222.

11. *Detroit Advertiser*, as quoted in *Detroit Free Press*, April 8, 1845; *Detroit Free Press*, June 6, 1845.

12. Wilson, *Space, Time, and Freedom*, 115; Albert K. Weinberg, *Manifest Destiny: A Study of Nationalistic Expansionism in American History* (Baltimore: Johns Hopkins University Press, 1935), 359–363. Regarding the Whig embrace of imperialism by the late 1840s, see Daniel Walker Howe, *The Political Culture of the American Whigs* (Chicago: University of Chicago Press, 1979), 145–146.

13. One contemporary reported that Lewis Cass, a Detroit resident and Democratic aspirant for the presidency, recognized this logic and used it for initially opposing the Texas annexation in April 1844: "If we annexed Texas to please the South, we should be forced into a war with England to annex Canada to please the North." *The Cass Platform* (Washington, DC, [1848]), 7. By 1848 Michigan's antislavery Free Soilers were beginning to embrace Canadian annexation. *True Democrat* (Ann Arbor), November 23, 1848. Turning the logic of antislavery Northerners on its head, the *New York Times* later recommended that the South endorse Canadian annexation as a way to "enlarge the hunting ground for runaway slaves." *New York Times*, July 23, 1852.

14. *National Intelligencer*, May 20, 1845. These comments notwithstanding, the Rush-Bagot Agreement of 1818 largely demilitarized the Great Lakes. Thomas A. Bailey, *A Diplomatic History of the American People*, 6th ed. (New York: Appleton-Century-Crofts, 1958), 158–159.

15. *Detroit Free Press*, July 25, 1849. Regarding the Whig embrace of annexing Canada in the late 1840s—demonstrated most vocally by Winfield Scott's embrace of the idea in 1849 (see *Saratoga Whig* [New York], July 6, 1849)—and for the broader mid-nineteenth-century discussion, see Cephas D. Allin and George M. Jones, *Annexation, Preferential Trade, and Reciprocity; an Outline of the Canadian Annexation Movement of 1849–50, with Special Reference to the Questions of Preferential Trade and Reciprocity* (Toronto: Musson Book Company, 1912), 375. Americans embracing Canadian annexation at this time were, in turn, responding to Canadians, Montreal merchants in particular, who were despondent over their economic prospects following Britain's repeal of its Corn Laws in 1846—a move that destroyed the privileged market Canadian grain enjoyed in Britain. Warner, *Continental Union*, 1–34.

16. Lawrence H. Officer and Lawrence B. Smith, "The Canadian-American Reciprocity Treaty of 1855 to 1866," *Journal of Economic History* 28, no. 4 (1968): 598–623.

17. Contrary to the view of nineteenth-century Canadians, economic historians argue that Canadian prosperity stemmed from U.S. demand caused by the Civil War, railroad construction, and other factors, rather than from the treaty itself. Officer and Smith, "Canadian-American Reciprocity Treaty."

18. Warner, *Continental Union*, 1–34; Joe Patterson Smith, *The Republican Expansionists of the Early Reconstruction Era* (Chicago: University of Chicago Libraries, 1933), 5.

19. Careless, *Canada*, 188–227.

20. Howard Jones, *Blue and Gray Diplomacy: A History of Union and Confederate Foreign Relations* (Chapel Hill: University of North Carolina Press, 2010).

21. The *Trent* Affair occurred after a U.S. warship, the USS *San Jacinto*, forcibly halted the RMS *Trent* in November 1861 and seized Confederate envoys James M. Mason and John Slidell. Mason and Slidell were traveling on the *Trent* to Great Britain and France, respectively, seeking Confederate recognition. After relations between the U.S. and

Britain further deteriorated and the British government began to make plans for war against the U.S., the Lincoln administration released Mason and Slidell to a British naval vessel in January 1862. Mason and Slidell then continued their journey but never secured Confederate recognition. Jones, *Blue and Gray Diplomacy*, 83–111.

22. Blair's message of January 2, 1862 in *Joint Documents of the State of Michigan for the Year 1861* (Lansing: John A. Kerr, 1862), 4. In response to the rising tensions stemming from the *Trent* Affair, Zachariah Chandler privately hoped that by March 1862 the U.S. could "spare 200,000 troops for the conquest of Canada." Chandler to Henry W. Lord, November 16, 1861, quoted in Paul Taylor, *"Old Slow Town": Detroit during the Civil War* (Detroit: Wayne State University Press, 2013), 113. Such fears and threats worried British officials, who recognized that Canadian defense of an American invasion would be challenging, if not impossible, given the long and porous Canadian border.

23. *Detroit Free Press*, November 9, 1862.

24. Robin W. Winks, *Canada and the United States: The Civil War Years*, 4th ed. (Montreal: McGill-Queens University Press, 1998), 178–205, makes clear that, despite the difficult relations between the U.S. and the Canadian governments, more Canadians volunteered for the Union army than for the Confederates. Phillip Buckner holds that between "thirty-five and fifty thousand British Americans fought in the American Civil War, mainly in the northern forces." Buckner, "British North America and a Continent in Dissolution: The American Civil War in the Making of Canadian Confederation," *Journal of the Civil War Era* 7, no. 4 (2017): 527–528.

25. Martin J. Havran, "Windsor and Detroit Relations during the Civil War," *Michigan History* 38, no. 4 (1954): 371–389.

26. *Detroit Advertiser and Tribune*, September 21, 1864; Frank B. Woodford, *Father Abraham's Children: Michigan Episodes in the Civil War* (Detroit: Wayne State University Press, 1961), 137–148; Taylor, *"Old Slow Town,"* 167–174.

27. *Detroit Free Press*, December 15, 1864. For other examples of the *Free Press*'s alarm regarding Confederates attacking the U.S. from Canada, see October 27 and December 8, 1864.

28. *Congressional Globe*, 38th Congress, 2nd session, 33, 34 (December 14, 1864). *Detroit Advertiser and Tribune*, December 15, 16, 1864; John Robertson, *Michigan in the War*, rev. ed. (Lansing: W. S. George, 1882), 485–487.

29. *Papers Relating to Foreign Affairs, Accompanying the Annual Message of the President to the First Session, Thirty-Ninth Congress,* Part 1 (Washington, DC: Government Printing Office, 1866), 54; Richardson, *Compilation of the Messages and Papers of the Presidents*, 6:282; *Detroit Free Press*, December 23, 1864, January 1, 4, 5, 10, 18, 22, March 10, 1865; *Detroit Advertiser and Tribune*, December 26, 1864, January 2, 10, 14, 16, 27, 30, 1865.

30. Warner, *Continental Union*, 35. Officer and Smith, "Canadian-American Reciprocity Treaty," however, argue that Reciprocity directed Canadian trade to New York and diminished traffic along the St. Lawrence.

31. Richardson, *Compilation of the Messages and Papers of the Presidents*, 5:325–326; Charles C. Tansill, *The Canadian Reciprocity Treaty of 1854* (Baltimore: Johns Hopkins University Press, 1922), 79, 92.

32. Lester Burrell Shippee, *Canadian-American Relations, 1849–1874* (New Haven, CT: Yale University Press, 1939), 173–178.

33. *Congressional Globe*, 38th Congress, 2nd session, 32, 33 (December 13, 1864).

34. *Congressional Globe*, 38th Congress, 2nd session, 230 (January 12, 1865). A dedicated champion of a protective tariff, Chandler would have likely opposed reciprocity regardless of the Civil War's course. Mary Karl George, *Zachariah Chandler: A Political Biography* (East Lansing: Michigan State University Press, 1969), 209–214.

35. Winks, *Civil War Years*, 346; George P. Sanger, ed., *The Statutes at Large, Treaties, and Proclamations of the United States of America from December 1863 to December 1865* (Boston: Little, Brown, 1866), 13:566.

36. *Proceedings of the Commercial Convention, Held in Detroit, July 11th, 12th, 13th and 14th, 1865* (Detroit: Advertiser and Tribune Company, 1865).

37. *New York Times*, July 21, 1865. Potter's speech was first reported by the *Free Press*, July 16, 1865, and the *Tribune and Advertiser*, July 17, 1865. Countering Potter's assertion that he was expressing the sentiments of higher-ranking officials in the State Department, U.S. Senator and Detroit native Jacob Howard said Potter's claims were "totally unfounded" (*Proceedings of the Commercial Convention*, 274). Regarding the widespread comment that Potter's speech elicited, see *New York Times*, July 17, 21, 22, 1865, November 13, 1867; *Detroit Free Press*, July 21, 31, 1865; *Detroit Advertiser and Tribune*, July 21, 23, 27, 1865; Smith, *Republican Expansionists*, 61–62.

38. *Detroit Free Press*, July 16, 1865. For other examples of the *Free Press* favoring the annexation of Canada through free trade, see March 26, 1865, June 7, 14, 1869 (in another version of the free trade argument, the *Free Press* [February 4, 1867] urged Detroiters to construct a tunnel under the Detroit River that would remove the water barrier and speed the path to annexation). Speaking at the Detroit Commercial Convention, James Joy, a Detroit Republican, argued that free trade was a better tool for annexing Canada than revoking Reciprocity. *Proceedings of the Commercial Convention*, 153–154. And over two years following the Detroit convention, the *New York Times* (November 13, 1867) insisted that Potter's indiscretion had "silenced" Canadians favoring annexation and further held that free trade was the surer path toward Canadian annexation.

39. *Detroit Advertiser and Tribune*, January 20, 1865 (a mild repudiation of Reciprocity and the paper's only editorial on the topic). For *Advertiser and Tribune*'s rejection of free trade and embrace of a protective tariff, see July 27, December 1, 1865, January 4, 6, 10, July 9, 1866. The latter essay insists that Canadians were in fact protectionists despite their free trade talk.

40. *Detroit Advertiser and Tribune*, July 17, 1865. See also July 15, 1865.

41. Shippee, *Canadian-American Relations*, 213–239; Warner, *Continental Union*, 50, 54, 123, 131, 169; Winks, *Civil War Years*, 322–326, 370–371; Smith, *Republican Expansionists*, 73–98.

42. Smith, *Republican Expansionists*, 82; Shippee, *Canadian-American Relations*, 227. See also Mitchell Snay, *Fenians, Freedmen, and Southern Whites: Race and Nationality in the Era of Reconstruction* (Baton Rouge: Louisiana State University Press, 2007); Brian Jenkins, *Fenians and Anglo-American Relations during Reconstruction* (Ithaca, NY: Cornell University Press, 1969); Christopher Klein, *When the Irish Invaded Canada: The*

Incredible True Story of the Civil War Veterans Who Fought for Ireland's Freedom (New York: Doubleday, 2019).

43. *Detroit Free Press*, April 8, 1866.

44. *Detroit Post*, June 8, 10, 12, 1866. Regarding the weakness of Canadian defenses, see July 6, 17, August 15, November 26, 1866. The *Free Press*, the *Advertiser and Tribune*, and the *Post* reported on the Fenian invasion, its aftermath, and local reactions—in both Detroit and Windsor—throughout June 1866.

45. Buckner, "The American Civil War in the Making of Canadian Confederation," 512–540; Winks, *Civil War Years*, 338–339, and passim; Bothwell, *Your Country*, 111–121.

46. *Detroit Free Press*, November 28, 1866. The *Post* and the *Free Press* happily reported growing Canadian sentiment favoring annexation frequently—even after Confederation (particularly in Nova Scotia, where anti-Confederation sentiment remained strong). See *Post*, July 12, 17, November 27, 28, December 11, 1866, January 5, 1867, May 7, June 20, July 27, September 2, November 11, 1868, April 16, 22, May 8, 19, June 1, 5, November 18, December 31, 1869, January 25, 1870; *Free Press*, March 26, 1865, July 13, December 27, 30, 1866, March 14, May 26, 1867, August 23, 1868, June 7, 14, September 13, November 16, 1869, and December 30, 1879. For the *Advertiser and Tribune*'s view that most Canadians opposed annexation, and that Canadians favoring Confederation attacked their opponents as being annexationists, see July 11, 27, October 6, 1865, July 9, 1866, and May 5, 1869.

47. *Detroit Post*, July 1, 1867. See also February 28, March 18, 28, May 24, June 14, 15, 22, July 2, 1867.

48. *Detroit Post*, February 28, 1867. The *Free Press* also complained that the forthcoming Dominion had the look of a kingdom—a troubling appearance to anti-monarchical Americans (*Detroit Free Press*, February 27, March 2, 1867). Within weeks, a joint resolution advanced by Congressional representative Nathaniel Banks of Massachusetts passed the United States House and Senate—practically without debate—expressing their "extreme solicitude" at the "confederation of states on this continent, extending from ocean to ocean" that was "founded on monarchical principles" (*Papers Relating to Foreign Affairs Accompanying the Annual Message of the President to the Second Session, Fortieth Congress*, Part I [Washington, DC: Government Printing Office, 1868], 77–78). The resolution appears to have mostly reflected the views of Banks, who in 1866 had submitted a bill to the House of Representatives that called for the annexation of Britain's North American provinces to the United States. Although Congress never voted on Banks's annexation bill, the *Post*, *Free Press* and *Advertiser and Tribune* commented on it, with the *Post* (July 6, 1866) and the *Free Press* (July 13, 1866) seeing the bill as a way of provoking an annexationist discussion. The *Advertiser and Tribune* (July 9, 1866) ridiculed Banks's proposal as being unreasonable while also acknowledging that the bill's terms for annexation would "be advantageous to both parties." See also Warner, *Continental Union*, 65–67, and Smith, *Republican Expansionists*, 111–112, citing how Zachariah Chandler, in March 1867, linked the unwelcome prospect of Canadian Confederation with his effort to repeal the neutrality laws.

49. See, for example, *Detroit Free Press*, June 16, November 28, 1866, February 27, March 2, June 8, June 28, 1867.

50. *Detroit Advertiser and Tribune*, June 19, July 1, July 2, 1867. For an example of how the *Advertiser and Tribune* reported Windsor news as local news, see December 2, 1867.

51. *Detroit Free Press*, March 31, April 2, 1867; *Detroit Advertiser and Tribune*, April 4, 5, 1867; *Detroit Post*, April 2,1867.

52. *Detroit Free Press*, May 26, 1867; *Detroit Post*, April 22, 25, 1867, December 30, 31, 1869, January 5, June 20, 1870. William Seward saw the Alaskan purchase as a step toward acquiring British Columbia. Despite pro-annexationist reports from British Columbia, residents there generally opposed annexation to the U.S. British Columbia became Canada's sixth province in 1871. David E. Shi, "Seward's Attempt to Annex British Columbia, 1865–1869," *Pacific Historical Review* 47, no. 2 (1978): 217–238.

53. George, *Chandler*, 141; Adrian Cook, *The Alabama Claims: American Politics and Anglo-American Relations, 1865–1872* (Ithaca, NY: Cornell University Press, 1975).

54. *Congressional Globe*, 39th Congress, 1st session, 226–227 (January 15, 1866).

55. *Detroit Advertiser and Tribune*, January 17, 19, 20, 1866.

56. George, *Chandler*, 141; Hans L. Trefousse, *Carl Schurz: A Biography* (Knoxville: University of Tennessee Press, 1982), 162–163; Silas Farmer, *History of Detroit and Wayne County and Early Michigan: A Chronological Cyclopedia of the Past and Present*, 3rd ed. (New York: Munsell and Company, 1890), 684–685. Schurz edited the *Post* from April 1866 until April 1867 (*Detroit Post*, April 5, 1866, April 6, 13, 1867), in which he advanced Canadian annexation, a position he continued to hold for decades thereafter. Dashew, "Story of an Illusion," 33; *Detroit Post*, March 18, 1867; *Harper's Monthly* 87 (October 1893): 737–746. Regarding the break between Chandler and the *Advertiser and Tribune*, see George, *Chandler*, 141; *Advertiser and Tribune*, January 17, 19, 20, 1866; Joanna Elizabeth Schneider, "The Reaction of Michigan Republicans to Civil War Financial Legislation" (MA Thesis, Wayne State University, 1963), 40–42. In 1869, the *Advertiser and Tribune* editor explained that his opposition to Chandler (including the paper's attempt to defeat Chandler's senate reelection bid in 1868–1869) was strictly personal, declared Chandler to be responsible for that opposition, and complained about Chandler's control of the state's Republican party. Ibid., 40–41. The *Post*, in contrast, insisted on its editorial independence, reported that Chandler was merely one—and not the largest—of the newspaper's three hundred stockholders from across Michigan, and that the *Post* launched in 1866 because the *Advertiser and Tribune's* "editors were unfaithful to the Republican party" through their opposition to a national bank system. *Detroit Post*, November 25, 26, 1868; see also March 6, March 19, 1871.

57. *Congressional Globe*, 40th Congress, 2nd session, 83–84 (December 9, 1867); *Detroit Free Press*, December 10, 1867; *Detroit Post*, December 12, 14, 1867. Regarding Chandler's proposal in March 1867 to repeal the neutrality laws, see Smith, *Republican Expansionists*, 111–112. For a broader examination of U.S. sentiment favoring Canadian annexation as a way to settle the *Alabama* claims, see Dashew, "Story of an Illusion."

58. Glyndon G. Van Deusen, *William Henry Seward* (New York: Oxford University Press, 1967), 507–510; Cook, *Alabama Claims*, 43–72.

59. *Congressional Globe*, 41st Congress, Special Session of the Senate, 730 (April 19, 1869); Cook, *Alabama Claims*, 80–84. Chandler's *Detroit Post* often reminded its readers of Canada's inability to defend itself against the U.S. and that Canadians were vulnerable

to a U.S. invasion so long as the U.S. and Britain remained on unfriendly terms, July 17, August 15, November 28, 1866, July 1, 1867, May 30, 31, October 14, 1870.

60. *Detroit Advertiser and Tribune*, April 21, 1869. See also April 23, 26, 1869 (the *Post*, April 20, 1869, printed Chandler's speech without comment). The *Advertiser and Tribune's* defense of Chandler seems particularly out of place given the paper's vigorous effort to defeat Chandler's reelection bid the previous January and its continued criticism of Chandler on patronage. George, *Chandler*, 170–173; *Detroit Post*, April 21, 22, 1869.

61. *Detroit Free Press*, April 23, May 1, 1869.

62. George, *Chandler*, 183; *Proposed Annexation of Winnipeg. Speech of Hon. Zachariah Chandler of Michigan in the Senate of the United States, April 22, 1870* (Washington, DC: Congressional Globe, 1870), 3; Donald F. Warner, "Drang Nach Norden: The United States and the Riel Rebellion," *Mississippi Valley Historical Review* 39, no. 4 (1953): 693–712; Alvin C. Gluek Jr., *Minnesota and the Manifest Destiny of the Canadian Northwest: A Study in Canadian-American Relations* (Toronto: University of Toronto Press, 1965); *Congressional Globe*, 41st Congress, 2nd session, Appendix, 404–410 (May 28, 1870); *New York Times*, May 29, 1870. Regarding the *Detroit Post's* calls for the U.S. annexation of the Red River Country, see December 5, 29, 30, 1869, January 5, 25, 26, 27, April 21, May 27, 1870.

63. Van Deusen, *Seward*, 505; Allan Nevins, *Hamilton Fish: The Inner History of the Grant Administration* (New York: Dodd, Mead, 1936), 383–399; Dashew, "Story of an Illusion," 344–348; Shi, "Seward's Attempt to Annex British Columbia"; William S. McFeely, *Grant: A Biography* (New York: W. W. Norton, 1981), 347–348.

64. *Detroit Post*, January 27, February 20, 1871; *Congressional Globe*, 41st Congress, 3rd session, 1382 (February 18, 1871), 1459 (February 21, 1871).

65. *Detroit Post*, May 9, 13, 1871; *Detroit Free Press* May 17, 1871; Nevins, *Fish*, 470–493; Cook, *Alabama Claims*, 41, 47, 112–113, 159–161, 174, 187, 200–201, 204; *Senate Executive Journal*, 42nd Congress, special session, 108 (May 24, 1871).

66. *Detroit Post*, May 27, 1871; Warner, *Continental Union*, 142–256; P. Bender, "The Annexation of Canada," *North American Review* 139 (July 1, 1884): 42–50.

67. *Detroit Free Press*, December 30, 1879, June 28, 1884; Warner, *Continental Union*, 177, 191, 198, 202, 207, 216–217. Regarding U.S. interest in Canadian annexation during the late nineteenth and early twentieth centuries, see *New York Times*, May 5, December 27, 1879; Warner, *Continental Union*, 142–256; Weinberg, *Manifest Destiny*, 363–381.

7

From Memphis to Mexico

The U.S. Army's Assertion of Sovereignty during Reconstruction

Andrew L. Slap

Questions about sovereignty were central to the reconstruction of the United States after the Civil War. Much of the focus at the time and since has been on the debates over the relationship between the federal government and the states. Republicans offered several different reasons for why the federal government had the authority to remake the Southern states. The reserve clause of the Constitution guaranteeing each state a republican form of government soon became the most popular. Senator Charles Sumner declared it "the sleeping giant of the Constitution," and explained "there is no other clause which gives to Congress such supreme power over the states." President Andrew Johnson and many Democrats, of course, objected to Sumner's interpretation both of the Constitution and where sovereignty lay. While vetoing a Reconstruction bill from Congress, Johnson contended that it was "an absorption and assumption of power by the General Government which, if acquiesced in, must sap and destroy our federative system of limited power, and break down the barriers which preserve the rights of the States. It is another step, or rather stride, towards centralization and the concentration of all legislative powers in the National Government."[1]

The contest over the relative sovereignty of the federal government and the states became enmeshed in a related and highly visible fight over which branch of the federal government had the authority to control Reconstruction. The long battle between the Republican-controlled Congress and President Johnson, a lifelong Democrat, for control of Reconstruction finally ended with the impeachment of Johnson in 1867 and the implementation of Congressional Reconstruction with the creation of military governments in the former Confederate states. These well-studied battles over political and constitutional authority during Reconstruction are important, but so much focus on them has obscured other sources and levels of contested sovereignty in this turbulent time. The Civil War fostered the rise of a new force in the contest over sovereignty, the United States

Army. Empowered by its role in an intranational conflict, the U.S. Army began acting autonomously and asserting its sovereignty throughout the North American continent, from the municipal level in places like Memphis, Tennessee, to the international in Mexico.

The U.S. Army had a long history of involvement in conflicts over sovereignty, both domestic and foreign, dating from well before the Civil War. To promote the sovereignty of the national government the United States of America's first secretary of the treasury, Alexander Hamilton, created an extensive economic program, which included an excise tax on whiskey. When some Pennsylvanians resisted in the so-called Whiskey Rebellion of 1794, President George Washington personally led a federalized militia force to compel obedience, because, as he wrote to a former Revolutionary War comrade, "[T]he daring and factious spirit which has arisen to overturn the laws, and to subvert the Constitution, ought to be subdued. If this is not done, there is an end of, and we may bid adieu to all government in this Country." Washington was far from the only president to use the United States military in this way. President John Adams sent the federal military forces to help quell the so-called Fries's Rebellion in Pennsylvania in 1799, and in 1857 President James Buchanan sent a U.S. Army force to assert national sovereignty over the Mormons in Utah.[2]

The U.S. Army also quickly established a tradition of ignoring Mexican sovereignty by crossing the national border while the two countries were at peace. The first time was in 1830, when President Andrew Jackson ordered U.S. Army forces to protect traders near the border, and a major took 200 U.S. soldiers into Mexico to rescue a caravan. Incidents like this continued for decades, right up until the Civil War. As Brian Schoen's chapter explores in more detail, in 1859 the chaotic, three-sided First Cortina War broke out, with the U.S. and Mexican armies fighting the forces of outlaw Juan Cortina. Dissatisfied with Mexican efforts, a U.S. Army officer led his soldiers across the border to attack Cortina, causing Mexican officials to send a lengthy letter protesting against the violation of Mexican sovereignty. In response, President Buchanan's administration sent Robert E. Lee, then a colonel in the U.S. Army, to the Mexican border with two letters signed by the secretary of war. One letter authorized Lee to pursue enemy raiders "beyond the limits of the United States," and the other ordered him to break up the outlaw forces in Mexico if the Mexicans failed to do so themselves. Lee soon sent troops into Mexico, resulting in an inadvertent firefight between the U.S. Army and the Mexican Guardia Nacional.[3]

These antebellum cases of the U.S. military's involvement in conflicts over sovereignty varied in time, location, and many other details. There is, however, one important constant. The army operated at either the direct or at least implied orders of the executive branch. Most Americans would take this for granted. The Department of Defense published an article in the early twentieth century that started, "Civilian control of the military is so ingrained in America that we hardly give it a second thought." According to the article, "The country survived the Civil War with the idea of civilian control of the military still intact." Historians have generally concurred, with Marcus Cunliffe concluding that "[w]ithin the American military heritage was a habitual assumption that soldiers must always defer to civilians: They always had done." During the Civil War, however, there were many examples of generals exerting their own authority against the wishes of the president and civilian government.[4]

George B. McClellan had been a rising star in the army before resigning in 1857 to become a railroad executive. When the Civil War began, he was quickly brought back to the United States Army as a major general, one of the highest-ranking officers in the service. After the Union defeat at the First Battle of Bull Run in July 1861, Lincoln gave McClellan command of the Union armies around Washington, DC, including the powerful Army of the Potomac. Within a week he wrote his wife;

> I find myself in a new and strange position here—Presdt, Cabinet, Genl Scott & all deferring to me—by some strange operation of magic I seem to have become the power of the land. . . . I almost think that were I to win some small success now I could become Dictator or anything else that might please me—but nothing of that kind would please me—therefore I won't be Dictator. Admirable self-denial!

The self-denial did not last long. According to one historian, by the fall of 1861 McClellan's "ignorance of the constitutional relationship between general and commander-in-chief [was] becoming apparent." Lincoln was patient with McClellan's self-aggrandizement but met with him in July of 1862 to discuss the army's slow progress. McClellan presented Lincoln with a lengthy letter, which Lincoln immediately read in front of his general. McClellan started by stating that as president, Lincoln had the Constitutional responsibility and authority for directing "civil and military policy." The general then, however, lectured the president for five paragraphs on what that civil and military policy should be, including a warning that "a declaration of radical views, especially upon slavery, will rapidly disintegrate our present armies."[5]

McClellan was far from the only Union general who tried to dictate policy to the civilian government or thought about becoming a dictator. John C. Frémont had long been involved in both the military and in politics. An army officer famous for his expeditions exploring the West, Frémont had also married Jessie Benton, the daughter of powerful Missouri United States Senator Thomas Hart Benton and, in 1856, ran as the first Republican nominee for president. Lincoln appointed Frémont Union Army major general in May 1861 and soon promoted him commander of the Department of the West. Frémont faced pressure both from guerrillas in Missouri and Republicans who wanted him to move against slavery. In August 1861 Frémont took the extraordinary step of declaring martial law without consulting Lincoln. The declaration included the execution of guerrillas caught behind Union lines and the emancipation of slaves belonging to Confederates. Lincoln asked Frémont to modify the declaration, which the general refused to do. Eventually Lincoln publicly ordered him to modify the declaration and soon relieved Frémont of command.

Joseph Hooker, like McClellan and Frémont, had served in the army before the Civil War but at the outbreak of fighting was a civilian. Lincoln appointed him a brigadier general in August 1861, and Hooker quickly gained attention with his aggressiveness in combat. Lincoln had been searching for an aggressive general to command the Army of the Potomac and decided to try Hooker in January 1863. When Lincoln appointed him commander of the Army of the Potomac, the president handed Hooker a letter with advice. Part of it concerned the fact that a *New York Times* army correspondent had reported to his editor that Hooker had "denounced the commanding general as incompetent, and the President and Government at Washington as imbecile and 'played out.'" In addition, Hooker thought nothing would go right "until we had a dictator, and the sooner the better." Lincoln explained in the letter that

> I have heard, in such way as to believe it, of your recently saying that both the Army and the Government needed a Dictator. Of course it was not for this, but in spite of it, that I have given you the command. Only those generals who gain success can set up dictators. What I now ask of you is military success, and I will risk the dictatorship.[6]

While the previous men were failures as generals, even the most successful and famous Union generals overstepped their constitutional bounds to try to dictate policy. Ulysses S. Grant had graduated from West Point and fought in the

Mexican-American War of 1846, but less than a decade later resigned his commission and then struggled as a civilian. Grant's lack of success and connections meant that at the beginning of the war he could only obtain a commission as a colonel in the Ohio volunteers. He quickly showed his skill and tenacity in command, and in January 1864 Lincoln appointed him general of the entire Union Army, answerable only to the president. In the last days of the war, while fleeing the recently captured Confederate capital of Richmond, General Robert E. Lee wrote to Grant for peace. A month earlier, however, Abraham Lincoln had warned Grant that politicians and not generals would set the terms of peace. Secretary of War Edwin Stanton had explained to Grant that President Lincoln "instructs me to say that you are not to decide, discuss, or confer upon any political question. Such questions the President holds in his own hands." Grant therefore repeatedly asked for Lee to surrender the Army of Northern Virginia insisting that "I have no authority to treat on the subject of peace." Grant's staff officer Horace Porter later recalled that "General Grant kept steadily in mind the fact that he was simply a soldier, and could deal only with hostile armies. He could not negotiate a treaty of peace without transcending his authority."

But was Grant really being a simple soldier at the surrender, nobly maintaining military obedience to civilian control? Joan Waugh, for one, has argued that Grant's agreement with Lee "went beyond a purely military surrender" and that he "intruded into political reconstruction by defining the conditions and consequences of the parole he was offering to the soldiers of the major Confederate army in the field." She also notes General William T. Sherman went even further than Grant a few weeks later by negotiating a general treaty of peace with General Joseph E. Johnson in North Carolina that he was later forced to modify.[7]

Reconstruction and Andrew Johnson's ascendancy to the presidency only intensified the U.S. Army's independent involvement in matters of sovereignty. Johnson declared the insurrection in his home state of Tennessee officially suppressed on June 13, 1865, though he added that this did not impair regulations for "the exercise of military law in cases where it shall be necessary for the general public safety and welfare during the existing insurrection." In his first Presidential Address on December 4, 1865, Johnson spent several paragraphs explaining his dislike of military rule and his happiness that civilian courts were operating throughout much of the South. Some members of the U.S. Army, though, apparently did not get the message from their commander in chief.[8]

Formal military rule ended in Memphis, Tennessee, on July 3, 1865, and by the fall of that year there was a functioning city government, including a civilian police force and courts. The city, however, had two parallel and rival sets of law enforcement. The U.S. Army still sent patrols of soldiers through the city, and military commissions tried civilians for a variety of offenses. The composition of the two forces made the situation even more violent, for the only army units in Memphis were African American regiments and the police force was overwhelmingly Irish. These groups' years of mutual antipathy led to repeated, problematic instances when the police arrested soldiers or soldiers arrested police officers. Just ten days after Johnson's Presidential Address, police officer John J. Magevney was brought before a military commission for assaulting some African American soldiers in Memphis. Magevney insisted that "the commission has no jurisdiction to hear and determine the offence charged," but to no avail as the trial proceeded. At the end of trial he once again called into question the legitimacy of the military commission, arguing, "I was tried by the Police Commission and had to pay the damages caused by said shooting which amounts to $30 which under the circumstances I think it very hard to be tried for it the second time." Magevney was found not guilty, but while the trial was underway another Memphis police officer, Michael Mulloney, shot a Black civilian, Billy Clark, while trying to arrest him. General John E. Smith ordered an investigation and trial by a military commission. Mulloney was found guilty of involuntary manslaughter in January 1866 and sentenced "to be confined at hard labor for the period of two years, at such penitentiary as the General Commanding may direct."[9]

Johnson tried to make the situation clear to the army in his April 2, 1866, proclamation "Declaring the Insurrection in Certain Southern States to be at an End." Here he stated that the former rebellious states had "given satisfactory evidence that they acquiesce in this sovereign and important resolution of national unity" and that "military occupation, martial law, military tribunals, and the suspension of... habeas corpus" should only be allowed "for repelling invasion or suppressing insurrection or rebellion." Apparently, this declaration was not clear enough. A month later Johnson felt compelled to issue an executive order specially dealing with military commissions. Dripping with sarcasm, the order begins: "Whereas some military commanders are embarrassed by doubts as to the operation of the proclamation of the President dated the 2d day of April, 1866, upon trials by military courts-martial and military officers; to remove such doubts—It is ordered by the President, That hereafter, whenever offenses committed by civilians are to be tried where civil tribunals are in existence which can try them, their cases are not authorized to be, and will not be, brought before military courts-martial or commissions."[10]

Ironically, the very day that Johnson reminded the army about the primacy of civilian control, May 1, 1866, the Memphis Race Massacre started. Three days of violence began with a small conflict between a few Irish policemen and African American soldiers who had just been mustered out of the army. Soon a white mob led by the police were attacking African Americans throughout south Memphis, particularly targeting the families of soldiers. Some soldiers pleaded with General George Stoneman, commander of the Department of Tennessee and stationed in Memphis, to intervene. Stoneman was a West Point graduate who was renowned for leading daring cavalry raids during the Civil War with thousands of troops. In Memphis, however, he had less than a hundred and fifty soldiers remaining under his authority and did not think it was sufficient to contain the violence. He later testified that he did not initially know the extent of the violence, which resulted in forty-eight people killed (forty-six Blacks and two whites) while at least five Black women were raped and over a hundred buildings burned.[11]

Eventually Stoneman did decide that the army should take control of the situation. He wrote to the mayor and sheriff that "I had determined to take the thing into my own hands, and that I should set all civil authority aside." He declared martial law and "put some pickets in town, placed a guard of about thirty men on Main street near the square, and of a few men at two or three other points, with instructions to disperse any party seen or heard of assembling together for any purpose whatever." He excluded the police force from this assembly ban "so long as they can be relied upon as preservers of the peace." Even after the massacre was over, Stoneman continued to exercise control in Memphis. He ordered that a commission be formed to investigate the massacre and also wrote a letter to the mayor of Memphis making clear who was truly in charge of the city. He warned:

> I have to assure you, and through you the people of Memphis, that if they cannot govern themselves as a law-abiding and Christian community, they will be governed, and that hereafter it will be my duty and privilege to see that there are no more riotous proceedings or conduct either on the part of the whites or blacks or city authorities.

So much for the President's orders to return Southern communities to civilian control.[12]

At the same time, President Johnson was also having difficulty with the army's independent actions with Mexico, which were causing difficulties with the administration's relations with France. Throughout much of the Civil War, Confederate cruisers had resupplied in French ports, and French shipyards also built ironclads intended for sale to the Confederates. Secretary of State William H.

Seward had managed to convince the French not to sell the ironclads to the Confederates, partly by threatening that the United States would intervene in France's ongoing attempt to take over Mexico. Conflict in Mexico between conservative monarchists and republican liberals had opened the door for European intervention. In late 1861 France sent soldiers to Mexico, and by 1864 the French had conquered much of Mexico and installed Archduke Ferdinand Maximilian as emperor there in 1864. The Mexican President Benito Juárez continued to hold on to the northern part of the country but was under great pressure. While Seward wanted the French and Maximillian out of Mexico, he purposefully did not take any actions to involve the United States in Juárez's struggle that would lead to war with a European power. The difficulty was that General Ulysses S. Grant preferred force.[13]

Grant had a long history with Mexico, having fought in the Mexican-American War in 1846 as a young lieutenant. This experience gave him an appreciation for the country, but he came to hate the war itself. In 1879 he told a reporter, "I do not think there was ever a more wicked war than that waged by the United States on Mexico," which was the United States' first war against another republic. Many historians have argued that a combination of guilt, a commitment to republicanism, and a personal friendship with Juárez's representative in Washington led Grant to be committed to returning Juárez and his Liberal government to power. Grant certainly saw the French invasion of Mexico as interrelated with the Civil War, which fits with the growing trend of historians like Thomas Bender and Don Doyle to place the Civil War in a larger global fight for liberal and republican governments in the mid-nineteenth century. It is ironic, though, to see how far a general would usurp civilian control in the name of republican ends.[14]

The disagreement between Seward and Grant over how to approach the French intervention in Mexico became clear when the two met in the summer of 1864. Grant soon began a campaign to convince others in the government that the Confederates would escape across the border or seek French military aid, making it necessary to force the French out of Mexico if the United States were truly to end the Civil War. In January of 1865, Grant turned from words to actions. With the approval of Stanton, Grant sent General Lew Wallace down to the border, where he crossed into Mexico and met with representatives of President Juárez. When Lincoln learned of the mission, he admonished Wallace to tell Secretary of State Seward about it. At the same time Grant advised the commander of the Department of the Pacific, General Irvin McDowell, that if Confederate forces invaded California from Mexico that rather than just defend the border of the United States, it would be justified to take and hold Mexican territory.

According to historian William E. Hardy, Grant "had begun to cross the boundary of military command into the realm of policymaking."[15]

Grant's attempts to subvert Seward's foreign policy escalated in the summer of 1865. Initially, Grant had hoped that the new President, Andrew Johnson, shared his position and would make the administration more aggressive toward the French in Mexico, particularly with increasing concerns about the defeated Confederates taking refuge south of the border. Johnson, however, was more interested in Reconstruction and delegated foreign policy to Seward. In response Grant decided to act on his own, and according to one historian "kept his commander in chief and the secretary of state in the dark about his motives in increasing the number of American soldiers near the Texas-Mexican border."[16]

In May 1865 Grant ordered General Philip Sheridan to command U.S. Army forces west of the Mississippi River. Sheridan had graduated from West Point in 1853 and became a career army officer, though when the Civil War started he was still a first lieutenant. Like Grant, he quickly demonstrated aggressiveness and skill that led to promotion to major general within two years. Both men had also made their reputations in the Western theater. When Grant was made commander of all Union armies at the beginning of 1864 he went east to supervise personally the Army of the Potomac. He soon summoned Sheridan east to command the Cavalry Corps of the Army of the Potomac and the two of them formed a close relationship; Grant knew from wartime experience he could depend on Sheridan. After receiving his formal orders to head to the Mexican border, Sheridan had a private meeting with Grant in May 1865. Sheridan later recalled:

> At this same interview he informed me that there was an additional motive in sending me to the new command, a motive not explained by the instructions themselves, and went on to say that, as a matter of fact, he looked upon the invasion of Mexico by Maximilian as a part of the rebellion itself, because of the encouragement that invasion had received from the Confederacy, and that our success in putting down that secession would never be complete till the French and the Austrian invaders were compelled to quit the territory of our sister republic. With regard to this matter, though, he said it would be necessary for me to act with great circumspection, since the Secretary of State, Mr. Seward, was much opposed to the use of our troops along the border in any active way that would be likely to involve us in a war with European powers.[17]

Clearly, Grant was ordering Sheridan to follow a policy directly against the wishes of the secretary of state. One historian has insisted that in doing so, "Grant was essentially contemplating getting the U.S. involved in a war in Mexico on his own initiative."[18]

Sheridan followed Grant's instructions, positioning large military units in southern Texas and stationing most of an army corps directly on the border with Mexico. He even asked for more troops to be sent to Texas "to concentrate at available points in the state enough to move against the invaders of Mexico if occasion demanded." Sheridan himself spent most of June 1865 on the border to convince the French that he might attack and sent scouts into Mexico. The scouts told Sheridan where his forces could most effectively make demonstrations along the border. Sheridan did all of this while knowing that it was not what Seward wanted, recalling that the secretary of state was "unalterably opposed to any act likely to involve us in war." The French minister in Washington complained to Seward about Sheridan's threatening posture and incursions into Mexican territory. Seward in turn asked Secretary of War Stanton to prohibit the army from operating against the French in Mexico without approval by the State Department. Warned by Grant about the order, Sheridan backed down, but only temporarily.[19]

By September 1865 Sheridan had once again grown impatient with Seward's diplomacy. The general galloped to the border with a regiment of cavalry and began open communication with Mexican President Juárez. The purpose was to spread rumors that the United States Army was working with Juárez and would soon invade Mexico to help the Liberals against the French. Sheridan worked to convince the French of his hostile intentions, ordering a pontoon train to the border and increasing troop activity. The plan worked, with the French becoming so alarmed that they withdrew their troops, not just from the border but from most of northern Mexico. Sheridan used the absence of French forces to begin supplying the Liberal forces with arms and ammunition by leaving them on the U.S. side of the river to fall into their hands. The French minister once again complained to Seward in October, writing, "It would be difficult for neutrality to be more openly violated, and that facts more grave should occur to contradict the assertions which your excellency has given me in the name of your government." Seward replied asking that the minister "accept, sir, a renewed assurance of my highest consideration" and promising that Sheridan had been instructed to preserve neutrality. Seward also once again brought Sheridan temporarily to heel.[20]

Sheridan complained about "the slow and poky methods of our State Department" while finding ways to circumvent them. He explained that "in truth, it was often very difficult to restrain officers and men from crossing the Rio Grande with hostile purpose," but of course the soldiers knew what their general wanted.

A United States Army colonel temporarily occupied the Mexican border town of Matamoros to protect neutral merchants. Grant and Sheridan repeatedly asked permission up the chain of command to Secretary of War Stanton and President Johnson to sell arms to the forces of President Juárez, only to have their civilian superiors repeatedly refuse. Still, Sheridan acknowledged later that "during the winter and spring of 1866 we continued covertly supplying arms and ammunition to the Liberals—sending as many as 30,000 muskets from Baton Rouge Arsenal alone." The army accomplished such supply missions many times, thereby secretly disobeying the directives of the nation's civilian leadership to dictate their own foreign policy for the United States.[21]

The actions of the army helped make the intervention in Mexico too costly and dangerous for the French, convincing them to withdraw their soldiers. Even in victory, though, generals continued to place themselves above their civilian superiors. President Johnson stated that Grant should accompany the United States Minister to Mexico for negotiations in a cabinet meeting in October 1866. Grant told his commander in chief that "he did not think it expedient for him to go out of the country," a refusal that left Johnson "surprised and a little disconcerted." Clearly there were multiple contests over sovereignty in Mexico that year. While Maximilian and Juárez fought to see who would control Mexico, the United States Army and its highest-ranking general struggled to wrest control of foreign policy away from civilian politicians.[22]

Soon, of course, Grant would become president himself, and the tables would turn. During his first term a massive fire devastated Chicago in October 1871. The fire lasted for three days, destroying over 17,000 buildings and leaving almost 75,000 people homeless. Even worse, an Illinois paper declared that "beside the distress, the panic, and the selfishness produced by imminent danger, crime was rife" and that there was "murder and plunder on all sides." The Chicago and Illinois governments did not have the resources to cope with the disaster. Fortunately, General Sheridan was then stationed in Chicago. As commander of the huge Division of the Missouri, which stretched from Canada to Mexico, Sheridan controlled more than half of the United States Army's soldiers. He quickly sent for seven companies of infantry, as well as tents and rations for civilians. By the second day of the fire prominent citizens beseeched Sheridan and the mayor for the general to take command of the city, to which they both agreed. The mayor issued a proclamation declaring "the preservation of the good order and peace of the city is hereby entrusted to Lieutenant General P. H. Sheridan, United States Army," after which Sheridan declared martial law. The only problem was that the major did not have the authority to issue such a proclamation. According to article IV, section 4 of the Constitution, the United States could protect a state against domestic violence only "on application of the Legislature, or of the Executive," of that state, and thus Sheridan had unconstitutionally taken military control of the city.[23]

The governor of Illinois, John M. Palmer, appreciated Sheridan's help, but was also jealous of his constitutional prerogatives and bore a personal grudge from when they served together during the Civil War. Palmer tried to have the troops removed as quickly as possible, but events conspired to make the situation worse. William T. Sherman, now Commanding General of the United States Army, added to the controversy by explicitly ordering four additional companies of infantry to Chicago "to act as police." Palmer complained to Grant to no avail. Eventually the governor appealed to the state legislature. "The General commanding the army seems also to have fallen into the dangerous error of supposing that his official military powers are paramount to the constitution and the laws," Palmer told the legislature, and "I must protest against such interference, because it will establish a precedent dangerous to liberty, because it familiarizes the people with military rule, and inspires them with distrust of the capability of civil government." People from across the country sent letters of support to Palmer, including one from Indiana which warned "that ere long, and everywhere, the military will supersede the civil authorities of the whole country."[24]

Military rule did become more common throughout the North American continent in the 1860s. Rachel St. John explains that the battles for control of the U.S.-Mexico "border would continue into the 1880s as settlers, soldiers, filibusters, and Native peoples fought to defend, displace, and defy the boundary line and the sovereign limits it signified." These international and transnational struggles over sovereignty, though, were also part of internal conflicts over sovereignty. The fights in the United States during Reconstruction over the relative power of the states and the nation or the President and Congress are well known. The Civil War, however, had familiarized the U.S. Army and its generals with more power and autonomy than they had been accustomed to wielding in the antebellum period. The border between the military and civilian worlds had certainly been permeable before the war, with successful generals even being elected president fairly often. General Winfield Scott had actually remained in the military while he sought the presidential nomination of the Whig party twice in the 1840s and when he ran as the Whig candidate in 1852. This practice continued during the Civil War, as Frémont considered running against Lincoln for the Republican nomination in 1864, and that year McClellan ran for president against Lincoln as a Democrat. McClellan remained in the military until election day and was depicted in uniform in campaign posters. During the Civil War the borders between civil and military authority then crumbled, as generals asserted independent authority to set government policy. While there may have been some influence from politicians appointed as generals during the conflict, it is notable that all but one of the generals discussed in this essay graduated from West Point and all were professional soldiers. The army has often been considered an instrument of sovereignty, but at least during the Civil War era the army appropriated sovereignty to itself.[25]

Notes

1. Charles Sumner, *Congressional Globe*, 40th Congress, 1st session, 614; Andrew Johnson, "Veto Message of Civil Rights Bill," quoted in Eric Foner, *Reconstruction: America's Unfinished Revolution, 1863–1877* (New York: Harper & Row, 1988), 250.

2. George Washington to Daniel Morgan, October 8, 1794, The George Washington Papers, Ser. 4, General Correspondence, Library of Congress, Digital Collections, https://www.loc.gov/item/mgw439084/.

3. Matt M. Matthews, *The U.S. Army on the Mexican Border: A Historical Perspective* (Fort Leavenworth, Kansas: Combat Studies Institute Press, 2007), 1–4; Clarence C. Clendenen, *Blood on the Border: The United States Army and the Mexican Irregulars* (Toronto: Macmillan, 1969), 33–40.

4. Jim Garamone, "Why Civilian Control of the Military?" *American Forces Press Service* (May 2, 2001), https://www.veteransadvantage.com/blog/military-veterans-news/cover-story-why-civilian-control-military (accessed July 26, 2022; originally published on defense.gov, accessed May 16, 2018). Marcus Cunliffe, *Soldiers and Civilians: The Martial Spirit in America, 1775–1865* (New York: Free Press, 1968), 438. The classic work on civil control of the military is Samuel P. Huntington, *The Soldier and the State: The Theory and Politics of Civil Military Relations* (Cambridge, MA: Harvard University Press, 1957). Huntington writes little about the Civil War or Reconstruction.

5. James A. Rawley, *Abraham Lincoln and a Nation Worth Fighting For* (Lincoln: University of Nebraska Press, 2003), 67; George B. McClellan to Abraham Lincoln, July 7, 1862, in *The Political History of the United States of America during the Great Rebellion, from November 6, 1860, to July 4, 1864*, ed. Edward McPherson (Washington, DC: Philip and Solomons, 1864), 385–386.

6. Abraham Lincoln to Major General Hooker, January 26, 1863, quoted in Stephen W. Sears, *Chancellorsville* (New York: Houghton Mifflin, 1996), 57; also see p. 21.

7. Greg P. Downs, *After Appomattox: Military Occupation and the Ends of War* (Cambridge, MA: Harvard University Press, 2015), 1; Horace Porter, *Campaigning with Grant* (New York: Century, 1897), 465; Joan Waugh, "'I Only Knew What Was in My Mind': Ulysses S. Grant and the Meaning of Appomattox," *Journal of the Civil War Era* 2, no. 3 (2012): 29–31.

8. Andrew Johnson, "Proclamation 137—Removing Trade Restrictions on Confederate States Lying East of the Mississippi River," June 13, 1865, online by Gerhard Peters

and John T. Woolley, *The American Presidency Project*, https://www.presidency.ucsb.edu/documents/proclamation-137-removing-trade-restrictions-confederate-states-lying-east-the-mississippi; Andrew Johnson, "First Annual Message," December 4, 1865, online by Gerhard Peters and John T. Woolley, *The American Presidency Project*, https://www.presidency.ucsb.edu/documents/first-annual-message-10 (accessed July 26, 2022).

9. Military Commission of John J. Magevney, MM 3338, and Military Commission of Michael Mulloney, MM 3455, both in RG 153, National Archives, Washington, DC.

10. Andrew Johnson: "Proclamation 153—Declaring the Insurrection in Certain Southern States to be at an End," April 2, 1866, online by Gerhard Peters and John T. Woolley, *The American Presidency Project*, https://www.presidency.ucsb.edu/documents/proclamation-153-declaring-the-insurrection-certain-southern-states-be-end; Andrew Johnson: "Executive Order—General Orders: 26—Order in Relation to Trials by Military Courts and Commissions," May 1, 1866, online by Gerhard Peters and John T. Woolley, *The American Presidency Project*, https://www.presidency.ucsb.edu/documents/executive-order-general-orders-26-order-relation-trials-military-courts-and-commissions.

11. *Reports of the Select Committee on the Memphis Riots and Massacres* (Washington, DC: Government Printing Office, 1866), 2–3, 34–36. Hereafter referred to as RSC. Also see Steven V. Ash, *A Massacre in Memphis: The Riot That Shook the Nation One Year After the Civil War* (New York: Hill and Wang, 2013).

12. *RSC*, 51–53.

13. Glyndon G. Van Deusen, *William Henry Seward* (New York: Oxford University Press, 1967), 365–370; Matthews, *The U.S. Army on the Mexican Border*, 41–45.

14. Amy Greenberg, *A Wicked War: Polk, Clay, Lincoln, and the 1846 U.S. Invasion of Mexico* (New York: Knopf, 2012), 274, xiii; Thomas Bender, *A Nation Among Nations: America's Place in World History* (New York: Hill & Wang, 2006), 122–123, 133; Don H. Doyle, *The Cause of All Nations: An International History of the American Civil War* (New York: Basic Books, 2015), 8. For historians on why Grant supported Juárez, see Brooks D. Simpson, *Let Us Have Peace: Ulysses S. Grant and the Politics of War and Reconstruction, 1861–68* (Chapel Hill: University of North Carolina Press, 1991), 103, 112; and Jean Edward Smith, *Grant* (New York: Simon & Schuster, 2001), 415.

15. Andrew F. Rolle, *The Lost Cause: The Confederate Exodus to Mexico* (Norman: University of Oklahoma Press, 1965), 215, 217; William E. Hardy, "South of the Border: Ulysses S. Grant and the French Intervention," *Civil War History* 54, no. 1 (2008): 66, 69–70. See also William L. Richter, *The Army in Texas during Reconstruction, 1865–1870* (College Station: Texas A&M University Press, 1987).

16. Hardy, "South of the Border," 64, 66, 72, 74. For more on defeated Confederates fleeing to Mexico see Todd W. Wahlstrom, *The Southern Exodus to Mexico: Migration across the Borderlands after the American Civil War* (Lincoln: University of Nebraska Press, 2015).

17. Philip H. Sheridan, *Personal Memoirs of P. H. Sheridan, Volume II* (New York: Charles L. Webster, 1888), 210.

18. Albert Joseph Griffin Jr., "Intelligence versus Impulse: William H. Seward and the Threat of War with France over Mexico, 1861–1867" (Ph.D diss., University of New Hampshire, 2003), 118–119.

19. Sheridan, *Personal Memoirs, Volume II*, 213–215; Matthews, *The U.S. Army on the Mexican Border*, 43–44; Hardy, "South of the Border," 75.

20. Sheridan, *Personal Memoirs, Volume II*, 215–216; Matthews, *The U.S. Army on the Mexican Border*, 44–45; The Marquis de Montholon to Mr. Seward, October 19, 1865, in *Executive Documents Printed by the Order of the House of Representatives during the First Session of the Thirty-Ninth Congress, 1865–66, Volume 1* (Washington, DC: Government Printing Office, 1866), 339; Mr. Seward to the Marquis de Montholon, October 31, 1865, in *Executive Documents*, 339; Mr. Seward to the Marquis de Montholon, November 10, 1865, in *Executive Documents*, 340.

21. Sheridan, *Personal Memoirs, Volume II*, 217, 224–226; Matthews, *The U.S. Army on the Mexican Border*, 45; William Marvel, *Lincoln's Autocrat: The Life of Edwin Stanton* (Chapel Hill: University of North Carolina Press, 2015).

22. Gideon Welles, *Diary of Gideon Welles: Secretary of the Navy under Lincoln and Johnson: With an Introduction by John T. Morse, Jr. Volume 2* (Boston: Houghton Mifflin, 1911), 621.

23. Andrew L. Slap, "'The Strong Arm of the Military Power of the United States': The Chicago Fire, the Constitution, and Reconstruction," *Civil War History* 47, no. 2 (2001): 146–147, 150–152.

24. Slap, "'The Strong Arm of the Military Power,'" 154–158.

25. Rachel C. St. John, *Line in the Sand: A History of the Western U.S.-Mexico Border* (Princeton, NJ: Princeton University Press, 2011), 37.

8

"Hold the Fort"

Securing the Soldiers' State in Nineteenth-Century America

Susan-Mary Grant

The cover of one of the most influential works on the American state in the Civil War era, Richard Franklin Bensel's *Yankee Leviathan*, showed a grainy black and white image, the details of which were, at first glance, hard to identify.[1] Bensel's publishers provided little guidance in this regard, describing it simply as "a depiction of Washington, D.C., drawn by Thomas Nast." Printed in *Harper's Weekly*, exactly one month before polling day in the controversial election of 1876, Nast's sketch included the Capitol Building, certainly, but Washington, DC, was only figuratively, not physically its subject. Titled "Hold the Fort: The spirit of the war revived," and further subtitled "The War was not, and shall not be a failure," Nast's image foregrounded a line of Union graves, each guarded by the ghost of a Union soldier. (See Figure 2.) This was not the first time that Nast had invoked the Union dead for political effect. During the 1864 election campaign, his "Compromise with the South" image made clear the potential cost of Republican defeat at the polls that Fall in its implicit assertion that Democratic victory would render Union soldiers' sacrifice worthless. (See Figure 3.) Over a decade later, in the year not just of America's centennial but of the defeat of federal forces by Lakota Sioux and Cheyenne troops at Little Bighorn in southern Montana, Nast was again inviting his viewers to locate the value of the Union and the strength of the American state in its soldiers' sacrifice—state sovereignty, in short, secured by those who died, as Lincoln put it, that the "nation might live."[2]

The defeat of America's national forces at Little Bighorn forms the introduction to a more recent study of modern statehood, Charles Maier's *Leviathan 2.0*. It does so largely in order to highlight one moment in history when an Indigenous community "resisted the encroachments of the modern state, with its aspirations for territorial expansion, its exploitation of steam and steel, and its highly developed organization of government." George Armstrong Custer's American troops were fighting, and that day dying, on the frontiers of the United States, operating on the margins of that state's geographical reach into what had only

Figure 2. Thomas Nast, "Hold the Fort: The spirit of the war revived; The war was not, and shall not be, a failure," *Harper's Weekly*, October 7, 1876. Courtesy of the Library of Congress Prints and Photographs, LC-USZ62-114832.

Figure 3. Thomas Nast, "Compromise with the South," dedicated to the Chicago Convention, *Harper's Weekly*, September 3, 1864. Courtesy of the Library of Congress Prints and Photographs, digital ID cph.3a00743.

recently been designated Montana Territory out of land previously part of Indian Country. They were staking a claim for state sovereignty at the limits of its legality.[3]

The future state of Montana had, as hindsight reveals, been secured by treaties ultimately worth less to their Indigenous signatories than the paper they were written on. And Custer's ill-fated "Last Stand" was in reality a cadaveric spasm in a conflict for Indigenous survival, one for which time and technology had already prepared the script—in Maier's words, a "transitional sort of conflict" that did not simply "expand the power of the encroaching state" but prefigured the "new genocidal type of assault that would flourish in the twentieth century." Custer's unfortunate troops, in effect, formed part of a wider global pattern of state reconstitution in the second half of the nineteenth century, even as their temporarily victorious opponents were making their own "last stand for indigenous political autonomy."[4]

For Maier, the fascination, and the focus of his study, resides in the "tempo of change" across an era of state reconstruction that affected the Western Hemisphere after 1850 in Europe as much as in North America. The costs of that reconstruction, prompted and directed as it was by armed conflict, are not ignored, and the willingness of both "liberal nation builders" and generals to countenance "the use of explosives, lethal flying metal splinters, maiming of young bodies, and destruction of property" is highlighted as significant in the emergence of the modern state. Largely absent from this analysis, however, and referenced only obliquely in an intriguing aside concerning the "vibrations of unseen energy" within global space, is the emotional component of the newly reconstituted nation-states, what might be termed their spiritual sovereignty—the crucial link between any state and its population, and one largely determined by the dead.[5] This is a surprising lacuna given that long before, but to an even greater extent since, the publication of Benedict Anderson's famous thesis on nationalism and the "ghostly *national* imaginings" that saturate the modern state, scholars have evinced a fascination with the relationship between the dead of war and those states in whose name they died. Most recently, for example, Shannon Bontrager has explored the link between the war dead, cultural memory, and the rise of an aggressive imperialistic republicanism in the years between the Gettysburg Address and the spring of 1921, when Congress authorized the creation of the Unknown Soldier memorial in Arlington. Death and burial practices in the military, he argues, "exposed a key landscape where agents of nation and empire collaborated to define who belonged" in the nation. But it went further than that. As America's borders expanded and encroached ever further West into and across Indigenous land, usurping what had been Indigenous sacred space, white settlers effectively "used death as a tool of colonialism."[6]

Both Anderson and Bontrager link nationalism solely with the dead, but in the case of America's civil war it is not just the war dead but also the war wounded that attract scholarly interest. In studies that range widely over the many and various wounds of war, their costs to the individual and to the state, and their debilitating personal, and sometimes political, consequences, historians have worked to shed light on what is sometimes referred to as the "dark side" of the Civil War. In some respects, this is intended as a counterpoise to what Gary Gallagher has termed the "Appomattox Syndrome," the "assumption that United States victory was somehow preordained." In others, it qualifies and questions the national narrative of the trajectory of that victory as a positive transitional one: from slavery to freedom, states' rights to state sovereignty, Union to nation.[7]

In both cases, however, the focus is less directly on federal state apparatus than it is on the citizens themselves, on their understanding of the state, their loyalty to it, their dissent from it, their expectations of it in respect to post-conflict care, and their class, race, and gender roles within it. Such studies often deploy a gendered lens, specifically masculinity, as a means of interrogating the evolving relationship between citizen and state in the mid-nineteenth century. This approach is of particular value to our understanding of state sovereignty, arguably more so if it builds on and is situated beyond the antebellum era and deploys the binary paradigm as defined by historian Amy Greenberg. The "two preeminent and dueling mid-century masculinities: *restrained manhood* and *martial manhood*" that she identified were both outward-directed constructs, aspects of performative masculinity dependent upon the shifting balance of gender, class, and race relations to structure and sustain them. And she identified a martial inflection to American expansion long before the Civil War raised, and arguably resolved, the question of state sovereignty and, subsequently, facilitated America's further expansion westward. Over the course of the Civil War, inevitably, these variants of masculinity became increasingly influenced by military and, above all, national assumptions that, this chapter argues, went beyond the individual and located martial manhood as the cornerstone of the federal state.[8]

This chapter further proposes that a more complete understanding of the ways in which martial manhood served as the link between the spatial and the spiritual dimensions of state sovereignty can be achieved if we pursue the debate to its borders, but also consider these borders from other than a United States perspective. It pursues Anthony Giddens's argument that nationalism is "the cultural sensibility of sovereignty, the concomitant of the co-ordination of administrative power within the bounded nation-state." Therefore, in this context borders are not meant simply as the geopolitical limits of the American state, but rather borders in their broadest sense, what Frances Stonor Saunders calls "philosophies of space, credibility contests, latitudes of neurosis, signatures to the social contract, soothing containments, scars." In the American case martial manhood, refined in the conflict between Union and Confederacy during the Civil War, was further qualified both during the war and after 1865 at the borders of the nation and against Indigenous nations. In this respect, the rapid demobilization of the Civil War armies, and subsequent reduction of the nation's military forces, may have obscured the extent to which the nineteenth-century United States was moving toward what was, paradoxically in an American context, a twentieth-century socialist ideal: the Armed Nation in which "every man [was] a citizen and every citizen a soldier."[9]

Sovereignty without Centralization

With the threat of civil war looming over the United States, in the year of John Brown's ill-fated raid on Harpers Ferry, one of Brown's supporters, the Unitarian minister and active abolitionist Thomas Wentworth Higginson, shared with the American public his musings on the subject of civil conflict in the form of an essay on the English experience over two hundred years before. "There is no such chemical solvent as war," Higginson warned; "where it finds a mingling of two alien elements, it leaves them permanently severed."[10]

In the same year, and similarly seeking a conciliatory approach to the subject of national division, the popular magazine *Godey's Lady's Book* took the opportunity presented by Thanksgiving Day to contemplate the sentiments supporting the American state; these, it asserted, had little to do with "national loyalty" or "national pride," but were purely practical. "An angry man hesitates to get his house on fire," it proposed, "because in every room is one of his own sleeping children. In these United States are scattered broadcast, growing up side by side with the natural productions, or else grafted on the ancient trees, the universal Yankee nation." This was an exclusive version of inclusivity, of course. Ethnically defined against both Indigenous and African Americans and, increasingly for Northerners, culturally defined against the white South, the idea of national sovereignty was, as *Godey's* had suggested, more about patriotic pragmatism than about the political state. And it was, above all, vague. In theory, vague enough to apply to almost anyone; in practice so vague as to appear invisible to many. Foreign visitors were especially bemused. "During my short sojourn in this country I have never yet met any person who could show me where the sovereignty of the Union resides," observed London *Times* correspondent William Howard Russell during the American Civil War. "General Prentiss, however, and his Illinois volunteers," he continued, "are quite ready to fight for it."[11]

It is unlikely that Russell had singled out Illinois for any other reason than that, on his return from the South in the summer of 1861, he had met briefly with General Benjamin Mayberry Prentiss, then in command of the Union forces around Cairo, Illinois.[12] Yet it was peculiarly apposite that this was the state he selected as his example of Union resolve, the one that boasted the motto "State Sovereignty, National Union." In that order. This motto, furthermore, had been authorized in the year of the debates over what became the Missouri Compromise. The specter of sectional schism and states' rights hovered over even this, one of the most symbolic of Union states, the state of Abraham Lincoln, during and after the Civil War.

In this context, it may not be surprising that these three, diverse voices, speaking to us from very different vantage points around the Civil War, spoke as one on the subject of American state sovereignty and that they located it—or in Russell's case, failed to locate it—not in the bureaucratic or political structures of the state but in the rather more diffuse sentiments that, they all clearly concurred, lay beneath and supported the obvious, outward symbols of statehood. Such sentiments, *Godey's* believed, possibly more in hope than expectation, trumped sectionalism; for Higginson they were imperiled, perhaps forever, by civil conflict; and for Russell, there simply was no other explanation that he could detect for volunteering to fight for the Union than the evidence provided by the act of fighting itself.

On the subject of the Confederacy, however, Russell seemed less bemused. Secession, it appeared to him, was a more obvious cause to rally around, albeit in the name of an as-yet-theoretical, or arguably rogue state, sovereignty. "Young ladies sing for it; old ladies pray for it; young men are dying to fight for it; old men are ready to demonstrate it," he noted, writing only days after Fort Sumter fell. Secession's strength lay in opposition—indeed, in precisely the kind of division that Higginson had warned was intrinsic to civil conflict. "The utter contempt and loathing for the venerated Stars and Stripes, the abhorrence of the very words United States, the intense hatred of the Yankees," underpinned it and, in Russell's view, would inevitably destroy a Union that "has gone to pieces, never to be put together again." Later in the war, as Confederate victory seemed less likely, Russell presented secession as the ghost at the federal feast, the specter haunting state sovereignty. "In this Confederate flag there is a meaning which cannot die," he predicted; "it marks the birthplace of a new nationality" that, even in defeat, would leave "indelible colors in the political atmosphere."[13]

By the end of the Civil War, and with the Union triumphant, it may have seemed to contemporary observers, contra Russell's opinion, that the ghost had finally been laid to rest, that in the defeat of secession, sovereignty had finally been secured and a state—a truly national, modern state—created. Later scholars, primarily interested in the transformation of the federal state, certainly thought so. For Bensel, the American state was "a mere shell" on the eve of the war, "a government with only a token administrative presence in most of the nation and whose sovereignty was interpreted by the central administration as contingent on the consent of the individual states." The modern state emerged, he argued, "from the wreckage of the Civil War." Gregory Downs and Kate Masur, by contrast, rejected Bensel's postwar "Yankee Leviathan" in favor of the "Stockade State," one "hard pressed to extend its sovereignty throughout the land." Stephen Skowronek, in a similar vein, emphasized the wider social, demographic, environmental and administrative forces at work in late-nineteenth-century America. He located the impetus for the emergence of the modern state in the alliterative combination of "*crisis, class conflict,* and *complexity.*" This, he proposed, whatever it was in practice, was only "concentrated on a national scale for the first time in American history between 1877 and 1920." For Maier, but also Steven Hahn, writing from a global and a hemispheric perspective, respectively, American state expansion was tied to the scramble for both destiny and empire, an imperative that Hahn regards as America's colonial inheritance, and Maier locates in a wider narrative driven by "the most efficient engine of expansion and governance that the world had seen for centuries: the modern nation-state."[14]

In the process of nuancing this narrative and writing America into the world, however, we may have delineated a limited legislative landscape in ways that sometimes obscure the grassroots sentiments, secular and spiritual, about state and nation that populated that landscape, informed the politics predicated on it, and served as the catalyst for a nationalism that revolved around not just the pain but also the potency of conflict in the construction of modern America. The practical, political, and personal parameters of that modernity have formed the fulcrum of scholarly debate for decades, but not necessarily the same debate. As Peter Parish once pointed out, mid-nineteenth-century America can often seem divided, and not just along a North-South axis. On the one hand, we have "the great drama surrounding slavery, expansion, North-South rivalry, secession, Civil War, and Reconstruction." On the other, the "long-term social, economic, and cultural changes arising from industrialization, urbanization, and large-scale immigration" dominates. The war is central to the first narrative, rather more diffuse throughout the second.[15]

In purely legislative terms, certainly, the war was productive of expanded government power on several levels. This is not surprising. In historical terms, in almost all nation-states, it "was war, and preparations for war, that provided the most energizing stimulus for the concentration of administrative resources and fiscal reorganization." America was no different in this aspect of its state formation than the European nations were at around the same time as the Civil War. The federal government's budget, along with the number of civilian workers it employed, quintupled over the course of the war; and in the case of the latter the shift was more dramatic than it seemed, as out of some 36,700 employees on the eve of the war, over 30,000 were local postmasters. Both military and nonmilitary legislation alike revealed "congressional initiative" on a wide range of national legislation affecting tariffs through taxes to the transcontinental railroad. At the same time, the practicalities of war revealed a greater emphasis and reliance on voluntary, private initiative than subsequent wars sustained. Both on the battlefield and off, be it in the form of medical and material support for the Union armies as provided by the United States Sanitary Commission, supply of the troops via the growth of arms manufacturing, or maintenance of morale among both soldiers and civilians through the publications of propaganda agencies such as the Loyal Publication Society, national power expanded, but it did so along largely private lines. In many respects, indeed, the Civil War was, as Parish once described it, "a private enterprise war, with very little governmental direction of the economy or of much of the war effort."[16]

Pursuing this point, we have tended to locate the Civil War as unique within America's historical continuum, situated on the cusp between union and nation, slavery and freedom, an individualistic antebellum laissez-faire liberalism and a "new industrial discipline" that defined the Gilded Age and beyond. Underpinning this is the concomitant shift in America's popular and political landscape that the war apparently produced. Out of an antebellum patchwork pattern of patriotism predicated on local loyalties and state sentiment, it is widely argued, the war forged the groundwork for a modern, fully functioning and, crucially, free-labor federal state. So not only was the Civil War "the crucial American drama," it was the cornerstone of American modernity, the catalyst for what Alan Trachtenberg famously termed the "incorporation of America," a process driven and defined by the North's stand against secession, against states' rights, against the South, and against slavery.[17]

Contemporary opinion did not always concur. There remained contrary voices suggesting that the relationship between the Civil War and national authority was more complex than it seemed, and that military victory had not necessarily secured state sovereignty. For E. L. Godkin, the editor of *The Nation*, the American state after the Civil War was in much the same position as it had been before it: It represented "sovereignty without centralization." Godkin viewed this in a relatively positive light, however, as the necessary context for "consolidation without despotism, nationality under democratic forms." His view, if not necessarily the sentiment behind it, was echoed by the noted author H. G. Wells, who concluded that "the typical American has no 'sense of the state.' I do not mean that he is not passionately and vigorously patriotic," Wells qualified, but "he sees the world in fragments." Scholars, similarly, primarily focused on the detail as opposed to the bigger picture of the American state in the Civil War era, and have tended to emphasize the importance of this fragmentation to American power and governance, in Frank Towers's words "its diffusion among a dizzying mix of local, state and federal authorities and private and semi-private agencies." What nineteenth-century Americans preferred, according to Brian Balogh, was that "the national government enable rather than command." And both of these perspectives were earlier explored, albeit from a different angle, by Peter Dobkin

Hall, who posited that private organizations, rather than a powerful central state, underpinned American "political economic and cultural nationality."[18]

These various interpretations of the frequently uneasy political balance between, and relative understandings of state sovereignty and national union in the Civil War era have often implied too clear a distinction between the two. In part this may be because decentralized states were becoming the norm rather than the exception at this time. The idea of popular sovereignty, radical in the eighteenth century when it was conceived, played out in both constructive and destructive ways in the nineteenth. The imperative to present the American Civil War as a unique driver of modernity in terms of central state sovereignty, therefore, must be qualified by an appreciation of the fact that regional rebellions against centralized authority typified the nineteenth century. Indeed, Americans need only have glanced south to witness several, indeed many, examples of such uprisings in Latin American nations: in Argentina, for example, where the battle between the *unitarios* and the *federalistas* persisted across the century, or Uruguay, long divided between Montevideo and its rural hinterland, and, of course, Mexico, where "the Federalist-versus-Centralist battle took up much of the first half of the century and arguably still played a role in the twentieth."[19]

The issue for historians now, given the direction of travel of Civil War–era scholarship and its emphasis on the war's "dark side" and its appalling human cost, is not one of comparison, but one of synthesis and cohesion. If the American state was all but invisible in the nineteenth century, at best fragmented and at worse fractured beyond repair by the Civil War, then we must consider what it was that strengthened that state in the war's aftermath. Because if the Confederacy's tombstone, as Frank Owsley once famously argued, might have borne the epitaph "died of states' rights," it does not necessarily follow that the banner of the Union carried the "blueprint for modern America" in quite the way that we have long supposed.[20] If we wish to assess the ways in which the Civil War shifted "the American governmental concept from one of federalism to one of nationalism," we need to move beyond the limitations of legislative change to consider what else shifted over the course of the conflict in terms of how the state was conceptualized, not just politically, or even practically, but psychologically and spiritually.[21]

One place to begin may be with the soldiers themselves and the state structure that they found themselves in at the war's outset, because that structure was not one geared toward fighting a nineteenth-century conflict, not least because it was predicated on a previous century's assumptions about and fear of standing armies. Operating under eighteenth-century legislation—"two militia acts of ancient vintage—nothing more" was what the Union had to go on—hardly an assertion of federal state authority designed to inspire or command loyalty to that state in 1861. The limitations became obvious when even those volunteers who were first to offer their services in the initial call for militia to protect Washington after the fall of Fort Sumter did so with one eye on the implications. Many refused to take the oath of allegiance, as then Assistant Adjutant-General Irvin McDowell reported, because of "the uncertainty they felt of the position they would occupy after being mustered in." "They had the impression," he observed, that taking the oath "would make regular soldiers of them." The situation was not helped by the crowds that had gathered and who encouraged the would-be recruits "not to take the oath."[22]

Even when the war was fully underway and the three-year regiments were raised and in the field, it was by no means entirely self-evident where the chain of command led or where a soldier's loyalties lay. And loyalty was by no means a straightforward matter. We tend to think about Civil War volunteers on the East Coast, heading off toward the James Peninsula and McClellan's ill-fated campaign to seize Richmond. Sometimes we consider soldiers in the West, fighting a very different kind of campaign to secure the Mississippi River. Rarely, however, do we bring into play those troops who were not, at first, engaged in fighting the Confederacy at all, but were deployed against the Indigenous nations in states such as Wisconsin and Minnesota. Such was the experience of Chauncey H. Cooke, who was uneasy at being directed to fight against Indigenous peoples, some of whom he was personally familiar with. Initially enthusiastic to sign up and fight for the Union, Cooke found himself enrolled in the 25th Wisconsin Infantry that was engaged in General Pope's 1862 campaign against the Oceti Sakowin in Minnesota. He was not the only one in his regiment, he reported to his mother, who had not enlisted to fight the Indigenous peoples but "to fight rebels" and was unhappy with the situation. He reminded her of one Oceti Sakowin leader "who has been to our place so many times with his hunting party who was so good to us," and recalled his father commenting that "if a few Indian contractors were scalped, there would be no trouble." He also mentioned the Bishop of Minnesota, Henry Benjamin Whipple, an advocate for Indigenous rights, who "said the government had not kept its promise" and that was why Indigenous people "had no blankets and no rations" and had taken up arms.[23]

Although Cooke never actually saw action in this campaign (he contracted measles), his letters reveal a real disquiet about his regiment's potential engagement with a people whom he not only regarded as friends and neighbors but as victims of the federal government. His views were not popular in his regiment, but he felt sufficiently strongly about the matter to return often to "the wrongdoing of the government" in regard to Indigenous nations. For others, in regiments fighting in the South, the issue was enslavement, and the lack of clarity and consistency when it came to helping, or not, fugitives. One example—but there were many—affected the 20th Massachusetts, one of whose officers had been accused in the press of returning fugitive slaves to their enslavers. John A. Andrew, the governor of Massachusetts, sought to censure the officer concerned for bringing disgrace on the state. He was roundly rebuffed by George B. McClellan, however, who reminded Andrew that the

> volunteer regiments from the different States of the Union when accepted and mustered into the service of the United States become a portion of the Federal Army and are as entirely removed from the authority of the governors of the several States as are the troops of the regular army. As discipline in the service can only be maintained by the strictest observance of military subordination nothing could be more detrimental than that any interference should be allowed outside the constituted authorities.[24]

McClellan was in no doubt about the range and remit of "the constituted authorities" during the Civil War. There was no room, in his opinion, for challenges to federal state sovereignty in the Army of the Potomac. Nevertheless, there were many such challenges, and the sectional, and indeed personal, "tendencies operating against centralization of government at the outbreak of the Civil War" were not necessarily diminished by its end. The question of loyalty to the Union has exercised historians for many years, but even here recent research has revealed an unsettled, contested landscape upon which the borders of belonging to the nation were recalibrated on the home front as much as on the battlefield as "[d]isparate groups struggled to control its meaning." Yet as John Hutchinson reminds us, as the world moved from established empires to one of nation-states, the contours of these states and the nationalism that shaped them were often determined by conflict. And inevitably a "heightened sense of nationhood" can often be detected in wartime. It is to the "competing repertoires" that result that scholars should turn to locate the support structures and the shape of the modern state.[25]

In pursuit of some of these repertoires, Matthew Gallman has drawn our attention to the links between antebellum advice literature and wartime patriotic tracts: Both, he argues, established military duty during the Civil War as essentially about the establishment of societal borders as both "credibility contests" and "soothing containments," borders defined by antebellum class assumptions and social sensibilities that determined who was, and who was not part of the nation. In essence, it created a federal focus. In this regard, Caroline Janney has complicated our understanding of the period by emphasizing the ways in which the fragmented perspective continued to distract the federal focus throughout the postbellum era in the "lingering acrimony" that pertained between North and South. This inhered not just in the political battles in Congress but informed the wider cultural and social struggle to stabilize the federal state. Her thesis therefore prompts us to ask different questions, to examine the conflict from different angles. It is not necessarily an acceptance of the validity, far less the virtue, of the idea of Confederate nationalism to use it as a reminder that, in historical terms, the successful securing of state sovereignty for one group of individuals has usually involved the loss of same for another, and that in the case of the United States, this had been the pattern from the start. Consequently, so far from exacerbating sectional tensions, as Janney has proposed, and hampering the nation's achievement of "its true potential greatness," it was in fact the open "wounds of war" that enabled the nation to come together again in the gradually dawning realization, after 1865, that in violence, not voluntarism, lay the sovereignty and the security of the American state.[26]

Landscapes of Conflict

"War," observed Oliver Wendell Holmes Sr., "is a very old story, but it is a new one to this generation of Americans." For previous generations, he noted, war meant the Revolution. The War of 1812 barely impacted on their memory, and "everybody knows that the Mexican business did not concern us much." No, Holmes stressed, "war is a new thing to all of us who are not in the last quarter of their century." For Holmes, as for others, the first and most significant transformation for their nation occurred when thousands of citizens voluntarily became citizen-soldiers and the potential military power of the federal state became, for the first time for that generation, fully visible. It is worth emphasizing this point, not least because the complex realities of raising regiments where federal authority was concerned, the problems identified by Shannon and others, may serve to disguise, or at least distract from the impact this had at the time. Few of these problems were visible to the outside observer; or even to the soldiers themselves in many cases. What was evident, however, was the new, very visible landscape of war. British journalists Edward Dicey, the correspondent for the *Spectator*, and Russell of the *Times* were certainly stunned by it. The "scene before my eyes,"

Dicey reported, "was one of war," an endless "military panorama [that] seemed to be unrolling itself ceaselessly" across Washington, DC. All around the city, Dicey reported, "every hillside seemed covered with camps," whose "white tents caught your eye on all sides," while across the river, "the great army of the Potomac stretched miles away, right up to the advanced posts of the Confederates south of the far-famed Manassas. The numbers were so vast," he commented, "that it was hard to realize them."[27]

"The Federal armies," Russell observed, were "luxurious in the matter of baggage, and canteens, and private stores," and this accumulated paraphernalia of war lent the entire enterprise a rather unmilitary air. The "scene is delightful," Elisha Hunt Rhodes of the Second Rhode Island Volunteers noted; the "ships are gaily decorated with flags, and it looks more like a pleasure excursion than an army looking for the enemy." Nevertheless, if the opening scenes of the war seemed to replicate the pageantry more typically associated with Fourth of July parades and a Revolutionary tradition shorn, by 1861, of most of its discomfiting internecine elements, not everyone was enthused by the sight. For author Nathaniel Hawthorne, the image of "lines of soldiers, with shouldered muskets" in Washington put him "in mind of similar spectacles at the gates of European cities. It was not without sorrow," he reported, "that we saw the free circulation of the nation's life-blood (at the very heart, moreover) clogged with such strictures as these, which have caused chronic diseases in almost all countries save our own. Will the time ever come again, in America," he asked, "when we may live half a score of years without once seeing the likeness of a soldier, except it be in the festal march of a company on its summer tour? Not in this generation, I fear" he concluded, "nor in the next, nor till the Millennium."[28]

Hawthorne's view was that this was no temporary transference of authority, in fact, but a fundamental transformation at the heart of the state. He did not envisage a military dictatorship, of course, nor even a vast extension of the regular army. What he perceived was a more subtle but nonetheless significant sea change at the grass roots of American society. "Even supposing the war should end tomorrow," he suggested,

> and the army melt into the masses of the population within the year, what an incalculable preponderance will there be of military titles and pretensions for at least half a century to come! Every country-neighborhood will have its general or two, its three or four colonels, half a dozen majors, and captains without end—besides non-commissioned officers and privates, more than the recruiting-offices ever knew of—all with their campaign-stories, which

will become the staple of fireside-talk forevermore. Military merit, or rather, since that is not so readily estimated, military notoriety, will be the measure of all claims to civil distinction. One bullet-headed general will succeed another in the Presidential chair; and veterans will hold the offices at home and abroad, and sit in Congress and the State legislatures, and fill all the avenues of public life.

And yet this version of the future that Hawthorne envisaged for the nation after the Civil War was not, in his opinion, necessarily a bad thing. It may, he argued, "substitute something more real and genuine, instead of the many shams on which men have heretofore founded their claims to public regard." And, from the perspective of 1862, when the war was not yet going the Union's way, he advised his fellow Northerners to turn their thoughts to that future "and assume the military button before it is too late."[29]

In some respects, of course, the American state had long had its federal finger on the military button. Although the antebellum state had little obvious impact either on individual states or the citizens thereof, and although to them it may have been both fragmented and invisible, lacked many of the traditional state structures and was, in John Murrin's pithy phrase, "a roof without walls," that was only the perspective from the inside looking out. From the outside looking in, the American state was powerful, destructive, and even if it appeared fragmented to some, it nevertheless sustained a robust and coherent military presence on its frontiers. The line of forts in Texas, begun in 1851 and stretching from Fort Worth in the north to Fort Duncan on the Rio Grande, was perhaps the most obvious physical example of central state intervention in the lives of incomer and Indigene alike in the settlement of the frontier and the extension of the nation.[30]

In this respect, the United States prior to the Civil War was operating in ways similar to state formation in the era of absolutism in early modern Europe. Where it differed was that it was not pursuing "a theory of achievable equilibrium," far less acknowledging "the legitimacy of other states." America's legitimacy was, too often, defined by contempt for that of others. This may not have been the ideal espoused by the nation's Founding Fathers, and in particular Jefferson, whose desire for a future landscape comprising "free and independent Americans," in the plural, all enjoying "the right of self-government," posited a rather different path than the one his nation chose to pursue. In its geographical expansion, the emergence of the sovereign state in North America had, until the Civil War, never been "a purely internal affair," but was constructed via an ongoing process whereby "previously existing frontiers were not only altered, but significantly altered towards becoming borders," a process that, again, the United States shared with Europe. In America, however, treaties with other sovereign nations, negotiated in order to "establish peace and alliances with American Indian nations" had, by the nineteenth century, become little more than a "vehicle for acquiring land" as America's own national identity became increasingly directed toward the geographical "expansion of the nation-state." In effect, and prior to the Civil War, the United States was heavily invested in the process of becoming what Giddens has termed "a bordered power-container." But this shift in emphasis was barely visible to those eastern elites whose focus was mainly internally directed: on the South, on slavery, and on the constitutional implications of state sovereignty in the context of sectionalism and secession.[31]

Decades prior to the Civil War, political theorist Francis Lieber, later famous for his *Code for the Government of Armies in the Field* (1863), argued that the United States did not need centralization but nationalization. And he defined this in organic terms, as "the diffusion of the same life blood through a system of arteries, throughout the body politic." Yet this, along with the full implications of the modern state with, in Maier's words, "its exploitation of steam and steel," only became feasible, to the elites at least, with the outbreak of war. For Holmes, when he perceived his nation's military potential, he echoed Lieber and interpreted it in organic terms. The "whole nation is now penetrated by the ramifications of a network of iron nerves which flash sensation and volition backward and forward to and from towns and provinces as if they were organs and limbs of a single living body," he observed.[32]

Interpreting war in organic terms, as a "system of iron muscles which . . . move the limbs of the mighty organism one upon another," Holmes was also attuned to the nationalizing potential of this living machine, its ability to reveal to Americans "that we are one people." Given the situation at the time of writing, this was stretching matters somewhat. Nevertheless, with his eye firmly, indeed exclusively, on the Free States, he observed that while it "is easy to say that a man is a man in Maine or Minnesota," it was "not so easy to feel it, all through our bones and marrow. The camp," he concluded, "is deprovincializing us very fast," and revealing "how fairly the real manhood of a country is distributed over its surface." As Holmes's musings indicate, although the martial side of the nation was, in some respects, ever-present in the national memory of the Revolution, even if less so in personal memories of the Mexican-American War, it did not dominate contemporary consciousness until Civil War recruitment began, until that sea of white tents began to dominate the landscape around Washington, and

General George B. McClellan began what turned out to be the very protracted process of moving the Army of the Potomac to the James Peninsula.[33]

Arguably it was at that moment, and in that landscape that the transformation of the American state really began, in a process that cannot be described or even defined politically or purely in terms of legislative change, but one that permeated all aspects of American social and cultural life for the remainder of the nineteenth century and, arguably, established the groundwork for its global military role after that. As a nation created through violence, the United States by the mid-nineteenth century was also a nation whose national narrative disguised that violence with a veneer of voluntarism. It downplayed the more unsettling aspects of citizen-soldier service by invoking a classical precedent, the famous Roman consul, Lucius Quinctius Cincinnatus, whose willingness to abandon the ploughshare for the sword in defense of Rome, and, crucially, reverse the process once the Republic was saved, was presented as the ideal to which the New World Republic aspired. This "symbolic link between patriotism and the plough" served simultaneously as exemplar and, for the Civil War generation, an excuse for a form of "martial citizenship" that, in theory at least, applied to Union and Confederate alike. In Holmes's words, the war disproved those who "believed the old valor of Revolutionary times had died out from among us."[34]

Holmes's perspective, both a validation of and veneration for a state secured by its soldiers, seemed to apply only to the Union side in the war's immediate aftermath. Union soldiers could more obviously express pride in having "vindicated their right to be ranked with their illustrious sires in the great brotherhood of Cincinnatus, or *sons of the soil*. Victorious and scar-worn veterans," one newspaper proposed, "they have returned home and mingle with their fellow-citizens in all the honorable pursuits of private life." John A. Logan, one of the founders of the Union veterans' organization, the Grand Army of the Republic, reinforced the point by highlighting the significance of the volunteer soldier to the Union cause: "One day he was a civilian quietly following the plow," he observed, and "upon the next he became a soldier, knowing no fear and carrying a whole destroying battery in his trusty rifle."[35]

Yet this description was equally applicable to the Confederate soldier. And it became, in time, a significant stepping-stone on the road to reunion, not because it permitted former foes to shake hands across stone walls and put their animosities behind them, but precisely because it mattered not at all whether they did or not. The lines between Union and Confederate may, as Thomas Wentworth Higginson had suggested was the case in civil conflict, have been drawn deeper, but the fact was that they were drawn on the same page. Persistent mutual loathing across the former sectional divide neither challenged nor changed the Cincinnatian paradigm for the Civil War generation, because its essence lay not in the state but in the soldier, not in the cause, but in the conflict, not in an ill-defined antebellum Union, but in a robust and reconstructed American nation that, having asserted its sovereignty over internal rebellion, could turn its attention to the question of how best to keep it safe in the future. This is a point often overlooked, largely because there is, perhaps for obvious reasons, a finality in the way in which scholars, even those looking through a wide-angle lens, approach America's civil conflict as one that, in Maier's words, "sealed the transformation of the North American nation-state."[36]

From the perspective of the time, that a transformation had taken place was indisputable, but it was not necessarily secure; far less had it secured a unified nation. Barely a few months after Lee's surrender at Appomattox, Benjamin Butler was feeling pessimistic about the war's outcome. Dismayed at the lack of support for the former slaves, he shared his concerns with Benjamin Wade. "All is wrong," he complained; "we are losing the just results of this four year struggle." The North, in his opinion, needed to wake up "from the dream of brotherly Union where brotherly love is not." To another he confessed how "soured, so disgusted, so sick of the wrong being done to the dead and living by the apathy of the country" he was. So far from the war inculcating a stronger sense of coherence across the newly reunited states, it had already been relegated to history. Notably, it was Confederate prison camps that Butler singled out as problematic in this respect. "Libby, Belle Isle, Salisbury, Millen, are all forgotten," he bemoaned, and "Andersonville only kept in remembrance by the trial of a miserable cur who only did his master's bidding. That, too, will fade away," he believed, "and the opportunity to make a homogeneous people united as are the East and the West is lost, and I fear for ever."[37]

Ghosts of the Union . . . and the Confederacy

For Butler, what was swiftly being forgotten in the months after the Civil War was a combination of the moral imperative of emancipation and the immorality of Confederate prison camps. In a sense, he was critiquing the swift severing of a bond that, he had believed, was forged between state and citizen, in particular the citizen-soldier of the Union armies, between 1861 and 1865. Two decades later, however, Civil War memory had taken on a very different hue. Most famously enunciated by Civil War veteran and future Supreme Court Justice Oliver

Wendell Holmes Jr., Civil War memory had by that point become inflected by a robust strain of martial masculinity recently described as in essence a "sentimental culture" that not only enshrined "extreme courage" but downplayed "the war's most grotesque elements." Holmes summed up this strain of sentiment when, in 1884 on the occasion of Memorial Day, he invoked the Civil War dead. "For one hour, twice a year at least,—at the regimental dinner, where the ghosts sit at table more numerous than the living, and on this day when we decorate their graves," he intoned, "the dead come back and live with us." On that occasion, Holmes was addressing Union veterans, but more notable, a decade later, was his injunction to students at Harvard in 1895 to "keep the soldier's faith against the doubts of civil life." By this point, the Civil War seemed almost a distant memory, and one that Holmes, at least, believed was fading fast. "We do not save traditions in this country," he complained. "The regiments whose battle-flags were not large enough to hold the names of the battles they had fought vanished with the surrender of Lee," he declared, "although their memories inherited would have made heroes for a century."[38]

In fact, in the context of the times, Holmes's was rather an unusual assertion, for two reasons. First, by 1895 the country was awash with Civil War monuments and memoirs, some of which appeared in the hugely popular "Battles and Leaders" series inaugurated by *Century Magazine* in 1884. Second, even if the popular memory of the war was, as Holmes charged, on the wane, the political power of the Civil War generation was waxing strong. Membership of the Union veterans' organization, the Grand Army of the Republic (GAR), was approaching half a million. Every elected Republican president since 1868 had been a Civil War officer. And in the year after Holmes's address, the political clout of the Civil War was confirmed. Voters in the 1896 election were presented with the choice between Democrat William Jennings Bryan, born in the year of Lincoln's election, and the Republican former Union Army major, William McKinley, whose campaign was supported by several of his Civil War comrades: Oliver Otis Howard, who had lost an arm in the Peninsula Campaign, and Dan Sickles, who had lost a leg at Gettysburg. The Republicans, clearly, were banking on the fact that the Civil War generation would keep the soldier's faith—faith in their efficacy as a political party if nothing else.

Faith, of course, is a mutable, multivalent construct. And Holmes's late-nineteenth-century interpretation of what the soldier's faith might involve was neither universal nor necessarily focused on the idea of sovereign state integrity. It bore little obvious relation, indeed, to the sentiments expressed by those who joined up to fight in 1861, being conceptualized, as it was in 1895, as a counterpoint to commerce rather than confidence in national union. In sentiment, it bore comparison with Confederate commemoration, structured as that had long been around the dead, and designed, in those terms, to evoke sacrifice and suffering as the spiritual heart of the nation. Yet the martial masculinity evoked in Holmes's expressions of regret that "war is out of fashion," his argument that the nation's "military prowess and strength" be replenished and reinforced by "dangerous sport," and his blunt and rather callous comment that if the result was that "once in a while . . . a neck is broken," this should not be viewed "as a waste, but as a price well paid for the breeding of a race fit for headship and command" did not meet with universal approval. Indeed, it was met with appalled criticism at the time by, among others, the New York *Evening Post*, which dismissed it as "sentimental jingoism" designed "to glorify war and the war spirit." The newspaper expressed horrified amazement that "a Judge of the Massachusetts Supreme Court" should encourage warfare "on the ground that if you put it off too long, your character runs down and you get too fond of money."[39]

Holmes's variant of martial masculinity was perhaps inevitably an elite construction, grounded in a Boston Brahmin upbringing. And with its surreal evocation of the North as "a place hung about by dark mists, out of which come the pale shine of dragon's scales, and the cry of fighting men, and the sound of swords," it was, frankly, medieval—seemingly out of touch with both the times and the country. But it was not simply Holmes's apparently pro-war sentiments that upset some of his contemporaries. It was his reaching for a moral equivalence between the respective causes of the Union and the Confederacy, his suggestion that "those who stood against us held just as sacred convictions that were the opposite of ours." His former comrade in the Twentieth Massachusetts, abolitionist Pen Hallowell, tackled him directly. He warned of "the sentimental sophistry" that encouraged Union and Confederacy to be commemorated equally as Americans, arguing that this was to "degrade the war to the level of a mere fratricidal strife for the display of military prowess and strength." As scholars have shown fairly conclusively, however, by the closing years of the nineteenth century, that was largely what had happened. African American troops, who had hoped as their predecessors had hoped, to lever the citizen-service tradition into acceptance in the nation, were, over time, excluded from a narrative designed to heal sectional rifts, and did not achieve racial inclusion. In this respect, the nationalist borders that underpinned state sovereignty became barriers, constructed to defend a social imaginary that was not yet fully inclusive of all citizen-soldiers.[40]

In the years between the Civil War and Holmes's notorious Harvard Memorial Day speech, other borders came into play in the defense of state sovereignty.

Holmes's nation had not entirely laid down the sword; and barely three years later it was about to take it up again in a war with Spain, although obviously Holmes's critics could not know that in 1895. And where it had been fighting was on the borders of its state sovereignty, against Indigenous nations who still held their own claims to sovereignty, fighting undertaken and directed, in many cases, by those who had only recently been engaged in the Civil War.

In facing the challenge posed to state sovereignty by secession, the federal government could and did refute any suggestion that the Confederacy was, or was likely to be, in any sense a separate nation. Ben Butler perhaps put it best when explaining to former comrade William Duff Telfer that to "take the ground that the rebels are aliens" would be to "admit the right of secession." "The rebels by their acts are public enemies," Butler pointed out, "not less enemies because they are citizens, and not less citizens . . . because they are traitors." The same argument could not be advanced in respect of those whose claim to sovereignty, although threatened, was valid. Instead, it was simply elided in a developing discourse that defined the Indigenous nations as threats to American state sovereignty, reinforced by the argument that these nations were unsuited to such a mode of government. "In all our relations with the Indians we have persistently carried out the idea that they were a sovereign people," observed Bishop Henry Whipple. But given that "a nation cannot exist within a nation," this proved to be a "fatal step" for the Indigenous nations' future within a United States whose white populations' "refusal to accept Indians as persons was enshrined by the drafters of declarations and constitutions on parchment, by sculptors in stone, by painters on canvas, by folklorists in legends, and by writers in print."[41]

The military experiences of those on the frontier after, as during the Civil War, are generally deemed to have been downplayed in the national narrative, overshadowed politically but also culturally by the conflict between the Union and the Confederacy. This is not wholly accurate, not least because in many cases those concerned, from Chauncey Cooke onward, were the same individuals but mainly because post–Civil War political debate, when not dealing with the practicalities of Reconstruction, devoted a lot of attention to the relationship between the military and the Indigenous nations, and between the military and the American state. In the process, many of the class tensions inherent in the soldier/state relationship were exposed, but many more were resolved as the United States moved toward and beyond its centennial celebrations and into an era that, it has been argued, witnessed the rise of a new national militarism. In this post–Civil War period, the struggle between civilian and military control of the frontier was underpinned, but eventually resolved, by a national narrative that both secured sectional reconciliation, on white terms, and the image of the soldier in the American state.[42]

Several of the contemporary debates revolved around the need to reduce the size of the military in the wake of the Civil War and Reconstruction, a traditional discussion in a nation long suspicious of standing armies and not yet reconciled to the need for one. Opposing calls for such a reduction, the territorial delegate for what was then the Arizona Territory, Richard McCormick, argued against such a move. "Though a soldier in time of peace is like a chimney in summer," he quoted, "yet what wise man would pluck down his chimney because his almanac tells him it is the middle of June." James Nesmith from Oregon was similarly unhappy at the idea, drawing attention to the nation's "constantly extending frontier" and the growing need to defend the white, settler population against the "constant state of turmoil and war" with the Indigenous nations. He was not, however, uncritical of the military, which he described as an "aristocratic institution" populated by men who were "pillars of State in time of war and perhaps its caterpillars in times of peace. But I do know," he emphasized, "that so far as we on the frontier have been brought in contact with them we regard them as an absolute necessity."[43]

Opposing these arguments, however, Henry Banning from Ohio, who had served as a Union infantry officer during the Civil War, proposed that a Regular Army was no longer necessary because almost every American man was now, in effect, a soldier. At the outbreak of the Civil War, he noted, "our people were ignorant of military drill and discipline. A call to arms brought to the field an army of men who knew little of the use of arms and nothing of the art of war." The situation in 1874, Banning argued, was very different. "Now we are a nation of soldiers," he averred, "drilled, disciplined veterans, whose five years' experience in the field would be worth more in actual war than twenty years' West Point training—soldiers who fought with Grant, Sherman, Thomas, Sheridan and McClellan; soldiers who fought with Lee, Jackson, Longstreet and Hood." Banning was perhaps being more optimistic than realistic when he proposed that any future conflict would "bring immediately to the field five hundred thousand trained soldiers from the North and South . . . who had fought against each other, but who would now go to battle like brothers." His perspective, bolstered as it was by the more typical, sentimental rhetoric surrounding martial masculinity and military patriotism in defense of America in the later nineteenth century, was more widespread than we might suppose.[44]

Banning's opinion, that "hard experience" in war was of inestimably greater value to the United States, and to that end the most important initiative the nation could pursue would be "to create and educate the private soldier," was not an isolated one. It spoke to the class concerns of fellow politicians such as Nesmith as well as echoed the views of others, such as Harris Plaisted, Union officer from and future governor of Maine. Plaisted supported the idea of founding a Military Professorship at Waterville College in Maine on the grounds that it was in tune with "the spirit of the times" and because it was more "republican" to disperse military training across the nation than to have it concentrated at West Point. "The army is to be a power in the country quite different from what it has been," Plaisted noted, and because of this "West Point, as the sole manufactory of army officers ought to be abolished." What Plaisted advocated was the encouragement of "military instruction" and "discipline" across the nation. That way, he argued, "Army Officers would then be more free from class imbecility, conceit, and prejudice, and imbued with more liberal and patriotic sentiments." Believing strongly in "the determination and patriotism of the people" in securing state sovereignty in the Civil War, for Plaisted the future security of that sovereignty, and the safety of the Republic, lay in a diffused martial spirit firmly grounded in "the sentiments of the people."[45]

In this respect, the United States deviated from the nation-building norm as that pertained across Europe. "All traditional states have laid claim to the formalized monopoly over the means of violence within their territories," Giddens notes, but "it is only within nation-states that this claim characteristically becomes more or less successful." In America it was clearly less successful, as evidenced by the traditional suspicion the nation evinced toward standing armies, the essentially private nature of the Civil War, the hostility expressed by those unwilling to join up because they believed this meant joining the Regular Army. Defined and defended by the Civil War generation, state sovereignty in the United States in the years immediately following the Civil War was as fragmented and as invisible as it always had seemed to some. Only this time it was its new, martial support structures that were invisible. And foreigners remained as bemused as ever. In 1882, the *North American Review* published an article by Scottish war correspondent Archibald Forbes on the American Army. It began with an anecdote of Forbes's meeting with a German who detailed all the wonders he had witnessed in this New World Republic. But it was the one thing that he had not seen that puzzled him: the Army. "Where is the garrison of New York? Where the garrison of Washington?" he is reported as asking. "Where are its legions, where its masses of infantrymen.... Why, there was not so much as a solitary sentry on the Schloss of the President."[46]

Forbes expressed himself unsurprised. "Of no nation which maintains a standing army are the troops so little *en evidence* as are those of the United States," he commented. "Probably two-thirds of the population of the republic never saw so much of its army as a company of line infantry." On this last point Forbes may have been, in 1882, statistically accurate, but he was missing one crucial, generational point: Many of those now in control of the nation, the politicians and the businessmen, the judges and the Supreme Court Justices, had seen a great deal of the army and were unlikely to forget it. It was for that reason that they sought to inculcate a martial spirit among the populace, a citizen-soldier tradition that functioned as well on the frontier as at the heart of the nation—a democratic, republican militarism that made of every man a soldier, but not a soldier within a separate, Regular Army. It was as Senator Albert Beveridge put it at the turn of the new century: "All this nation is a standing army. There is a soldier in the breast of every free man." If the Regular Army had a role in the Republic, the future mayor of Chicago, Carter Harrison, commented the year following the end of Reconstruction and the removal of federal troops from the states of the former Confederacy, it was as a "nucleus around which is to be nurtured an American martial spirit." Standing armies, in his opinion, "do not encourage martial spirit among a people." On the contrary, the "people forget how to fight when they have hired soldiers to do their battles." Ultimately, it came down to one thing, best summed up by William Phillips, Republican Representative from Kansas: The American people could ill-afford to "neglect the martial spirit which gave us our Government and which may be able to maintain it."[47]

Conclusion

In seeking the "blueprint for modern America" through the transformation of the state in the mid-nineteenth century, we have for many years focused on the rise of the political and military machine, highlighting those aspects of it that conform most closely to state development in other nations, mainly, but not exclusively, European nations. And in the case of the Civil War, the emphasis has too often been on the rapid demobilization of its citizen armies, the postwar reduction in the strength of its regular armed forces, and the apparent dissolution or diminution of many of those institutional structures associated with the temporarily expanded military machine, be that the Army Medical Bureau or the voluntary, civilian organizations such as the USSC. We have taken at face value the insistence of contemporary American politicians and spokesmen that the United States was intrinsically hostile to the idea of centralized military power and the later assertions of European scholars that the "social pressures favoring a monopolization of force" in the United States have always "been weak in comparison with those in European societies." We have consequently assumed that America was in some ways the exception to Max Weber's assertion that establishing the legitimate use of violence was the first and most crucial requirement for the modern nation-state. We have therefore assumed that at all levels and at almost all times America conformed to Henry Clay's wish that it never be "in that complete state of preparation for war for which some contend; that is, that we should constantly have a large standing army, well disciplined, and always ready to act." There were doubtless many occasions in the nation's history up to and including the Civil War when America's military leaders rather wished it were otherwise, but in fact America had always been prepared for war.[48]

Violence, not voluntarism, was America's birthright, as it is that of most, if not all, nation-states. And the apparent battle between state sovereignty and national union took place within that foundational reality. It is certainly true that by the nineteenth century, and in the context of what was by then a well-ingrained *mythos* surrounding the Revolution and those who secured the nation's independence by force, many of the nation's religious and secular spokesmen were engaged in downplaying the violence of the nation's founding in their quest to formulate and fix the "New Man" in the "New World." They, possibly intentionally, focused on the non-military aspects of the civic ideal, emphasized virtue rather than violence, and thereby abbreviated the "Machiavellian moment" to conform to a dialogue driven more by religious precepts than by secular ones.

In the search for the animating spark that would energize a national outlook and secure the republican state, antebellum writers and thinkers frankly floundered in the face of a fragmented nation, falling back on such evocative but essentially vague descriptions of the "spirituality" of the state. The Civil War forced a reassessment, and a secularization of this antebellum spiritual vagueness. At the grassroots level, it also served as a conflict that trumped all other concerns, be these related to the fate of Indigenous peoples on the frontier as well as in the nation, or that of the formerly enslaved within the already recognized borders of the state. Chauncey Cooke remained unhappy at what he was being asked to do in Minnesota, but his new identity as a soldier ensured that he adhered to the maxim that "military orders must be obeyed." Governor Andrew of Massachusetts was both angered and embarrassed that Massachusetts troops might be guilty of returning fugitives to their enslavers, but McClellan taught him a sharp lesson about where power lay in a nation at war. For both, the borders of that nation, and the experience of securing them, were inherently scarred, as Frances Stonor Saunders proposed; and insofar as they were also credibility contests, this was a test the nation won only because it forced Americans to consider

Machiavelli's question: "In what man ought the country to look for greater loyalty than in that man who has promised to die for her?" Not so much a transformation as an acceptance of a hitherto uncomfortable tradition of citizen service in the name of the nation, this shift in the concept of the state represented the climax of the drive toward nationalism, toward modernity, that located the heart of the body politic and the spark that animated its existence as a state, in the soldier.[49]

Notes

1. Richard Franklin Bensel, *Yankee Leviathan: The Origins of Central State Authority in America, 1859–1877* (New York: Cambridge University Press, 1990).

2. Abraham Lincoln, "Address Delivered at the Dedication of the Cemetery at Gettysburg," November 19, 1863, in Roy P. Basler, ed., *The Collected Works of Abraham Lincoln*, vol. 7 (New Brunswick, NJ: Rutgers University Press, 1953), 23.

3. Charles S. Maier, *Leviathan 2.0: Inventing Modern Statehood* (Cambridge, MA: Harvard University Press, 2012), 2.

4. Maier, *Leviathan 2.0*, 5, 95.

5. Maier, *Leviathan 2.0*, 79, 102.

6. Benedict Anderson, *Imagined Communities: Reflections on the Origin and Spread of Nationalism*, rev. ed. (London: Verso, 1992), 9; Shannon Bontrager, *Death at the Edges of Empire: Fallen Soldiers, Cultural Memory, and the Making of an American Nation, 1863–1921* (Lincoln: University of Nebraska Press, 2020), 4, 9.

7. Gary Gallagher, Foreword to Robert M. Sandow, ed., *Contested Loyalty: Debates over Patriotism in the Civil War North* (New York: Fordham University Press, 2018), vii. The historiographical fascination with the dead of the Civil War arguably began with Drew Gilpin Faust, *This Republic of Suffering: Death and the American Civil* War (New York: Alfred A. Knopf, 2008), and Mark S. Schantz, *Awaiting the Heavenly Country: The Civil War and America's Culture of Death* (Ithaca, NY: Cornell University Press, 2008), although there were several earlier studies that focused on this, including William Blair, *Cities of the Dead: Contesting the Memory of the Civil War in the South, 1865–1914* (Chapel Hill: University of North Carolina Press, 2004); Drew Gilpin Faust, *"A Riddle of Death": Mortality and Meaning in the American Civil War* (Gettysburg, PA: Gettysburg College, 1995); Susan-Mary Grant, "Raising the Dead: War, Memory and American National Identity," *Nations and Nationalism* 2, no. 4 (2005): 509–529, and "Patriot Graves: American National Identity and the Civil War Dead," *American Nineteenth Century History* 5, no. 3 (2004): 74–100; Edward Tabor Linenthal, *Sacred Ground: Americans and Their Battlefields* (Urbana: University of Illinois Press, 1991); Monro MacCloskey, *Hallowed Ground: Our National Cemeteries* (New York: Richards Rosen Press, 1968); and Carolyn Marvin and David W. Ingle, *Blood Sacrifice and the Nation: Totem Rituals and the American Flag* (New York: Cambridge University Press, 1999). John R. Neff, *Honoring the Civil War Dead: Commemoration and the Problem of Reconciliation* (Lawrence: University Press of Kansas, 2005), introduced the problem of national state stability in the Civil War's aftermath, a subject developed further in Caroline Janney, *Remember-*

ing the Civil War: Reunion and the Limits of Reconciliation (Chapel Hill: University of North Carolina Press, 2013). The debate over both the dead and the wounded, and their longer-term impact on the state began with J. David Hacker, "A Census-Based Count of the Civil War Dead," *Civil War History* 7, no. 4 (2011): 307–348; Nicholas Marshall, "The Great Exaggeration: Death and the Civil War," *Journal of the Civil War Era* 4, no. 1 (2014): 3–27; and see Hacker's response, "Has the Demographic Impact of Civil War Deaths Been Exaggerated?" *Civil War History* 60, no. 4 (2014): 453–458; Megan Kate Nelson, *Ruin Nation: Destruction and the American Civil War* (Athens: University of Georgia Press, 2012); Brian Matthew Jordan, *Marching Home: Union Veterans and Their Unending Civil War* (New York: Liveright, 2016); Brian Craig Miller, *Empty Sleeves: Amputation in the Civil War South* (Athens: University of Georgia Press, 2015); Sarah Handley-Cousins, "'Wrestling at the gates of Death': Joshua Lawrence Chamberlain and Nonvisible Disability in the Post–Civil War North," *Journal of the Civil War Era*, 6, no. 2 (2016): 220–242; and Michael C. C. Adams, *Living Hell: The Dark Side of the Civil War* (Baltimore: Johns Hopkins University Press, 2014), ix.

8. Amy S. Greenberg, *Manifest Manhood and the Antebellum American Empire* (Cambridge: Cambridge University Press, 2005), 11, 21. An earlier study that argued for a new, postwar martial spirit among American men was Joe Dubbert, *A Man's Place: Masculinity in Transition* (New York: Prentice Hall, 1979). Other studies of shifts in masculinity in and beyond the Civil War era include E. Anthony Rotundo, *American Manhood: Transformations in Masculinity from the Revolution to the Modern Era* (New York: Basic Books, 1993), 222–241; Gail Bederman, *Manliness and Civilization: A Cultural History of Gender and Race in the United States, 1880–1917* (Chicago: University of Chicago Press, 1995), 5–7; Mark C. Carnes and Clyde Griffen, eds., *Meanings for Manhood: Constructions of Masculinity in Victorian America* (Chicago: University of Chicago Press, 1990), 10–11; Karen Bourrier, *The Measure of Manliness: Disability and Masculinity in the Mid-Victorian Novel* (Ann Arbor: University of Michigan Press, 2015), 8–10; Lorien Foote, *The Gentlemen and the Roughs: Manhood, Honor, and Violence in the Union Army* (New York: New York University Press, 2010), 1. For further development of these ideas in a Civil War context, see also J. Matthew Gallman, *Defining Duty in the Civil War: Personal Choice, Popular Culture, and the Union Home Front* (Chapel Hill: University of North Carolina Press, 2015); and Kanisorn Wongsrichanalai, *Northern Character: College-Educated New Englanders, Honor, Nationalism, and Leadership in the Civil War Era* (New York: Fordham University Press, 2016).

9. Anthony Giddens, *Nation-State and Violence* (Cambridge: Polity Press, 1985), 219; Frances Stonor Saunders, "Where on Earth are you?" *London Review of Books* 3 (March 2016); Harry Quelch, "Socialism, Militarism, and Mr. Haldane's Scheme," *The Social Democrat* 11, 4 (1907): 200–207, 207; see also Quelch, *Social-Democracy and the Armed Nation* (London: Twentieth Century Press, 1900), and Marilyn Lake, "Mission Impossible: How Men Gave Birth to the Australian Nation—Nationalism, Gender and Other Seminal Acts," *Gender and History* 4, no. 3 (1992): 305–322. At the close of the Civil War in April 1865, the Union Army comprised over 1 million officers and men. By the end of that year, some 800,000 of these were mustered out. Of those who remained to "occupy" the South, by January 1866 their number had diminished from some 270,000 to 87,550.

Figures from Mark L. Bradley, *The Army and Reconstruction, 1865–1877* (Washington, DC: Center of Military History, US Army, 2015), 15. And see the debate a decade later over further reduction, on fiscal grounds, of the armed forces, e.g., *Congressional Record*, 43rd Congress, 1st Session (May 28, 1874), 4350–4366; (May 29, 1874), 4393–4397.

10. Thomas Wentworth Higginson, "A Charge with Prince Rupert" first appeared in the *Atlantic Monthly* in 1859, and was reprinted in Higginson, *Atlantic Essays* (Boston: James R. Osgood, 1871), 129–130, 131–132, 135.

11. *Godey's Lady's Book* 59 (November 1859): 466; William Howard Russell, *My Diary North and South* (New York: T. O. H. P. Burnham, 1863), 338.

12. Martin Crawford, ed., *William Howard Russell's Civil War: Private Diary and Letters, 1861–1862* (Athens: University of Georgia Press, 1992), 73.

13. Russell, *Diary North and South*, 105–106, 216.

14. Bensel, *Yankee Leviathan*, ix; Gregory P. Downs and Kate Masur, eds., *The World the Civil War Made* (Chapel Hill: University of North Carolina Press, 2015), 3; Stephen Skowronek, *Building a New American State: The Expansion of National Administrative Capacities, 1877–1920* (New York: Cambridge University Press, 1982), 9–10; Steven Hahn, *A Nation without Borders: The United States and Its World in an Age of Civil Wars, 1830–1910* (2016; repr., New York: Penguin Books, 2017), 1–2, 6; Maier, *Leviathan 2.0*, 5. See also Samuel P. Huntington, *Political Order in Changing Societies* (New Haven, CT: Yale University Press, 1968); Anthony Giddens, *The Nation-State and Violence* (Cambridge: Polity Press, 1985); and John Hutchinson, *Nationalism and War* (Oxford: Oxford University Press, 2017).

15. Peter J. Parish, "The Importance of Federalism," in Peter J. Parish, *The North and the Nation in the Era of the Civil War*, ed. Adam I. P. Smith and Susan-Mary Grant (New York: Fordham University Press, 2003), 108.

16. Giddens, *Nation-State and Violence*, 112; Joseph G. Dawson III, "The First of the Modern Wars," in *Themes of the American Civil War: The War Between the States*. ed. Susan-Mary Grant and Brian Holden Reid (New York: Routledge, 2010), 78; Parish, "The Importance of Federalism," 97, 102.

17. Alan Trachtenberg, *Reading American Photographs: Images as History: Matthew Brady to Walker Evans* (1989; repr., New York: Hill and Wang, 1999), 109; Allan Nevins, *Ordeal of the Union* (1947–1971; repr., New York: Collier Books, 1992), vol. 4, *The War for the Union*, 271–273; George M. Fredrickson, *The Inner Civil War: Northern Intellectuals and the Crisis of the Union* (New York: Harper and Row, 1965); Richard D. Brown, *Modernization: The Transformation of American Life, 1600–1865* (1976; repr., Prospect Heights, IL: Waveland Press, 1988), 159; Alan Trachtenberg, *The Incorporation of America: Culture and Society in the Gilded Age* (1982; repr., New York: Hill and Wang, 2007).

18. Godkin quoted in Parish, "The Importance of Federalism," 108–109; H. G. Wells, *The Future in America: A Search After Realities* (New York: Harper and Brothers, 1906), 153–154, 205; Frank Towers, "Party Politics and the Sectional Crisis: A Twenty-Year Renaissance in the Study of Antebellum Political History," in *The Routledge History of Nineteenth-Century America*, ed. Jonathan Daniel Wells (New York: Routledge, 2018), 130; Brian Balogh, *A Government Out of Sight: The Mystery of National Authority in Nineteenth-Century America* (New York: Cambridge University Press, 2009), 3.

19. Miguel Angel Centeno, *Blood and Debt: War and the Nation-State in Latin America* (University Park: Pennsylvania State University Press, 2002), 62; Peter Dobkin Hall, *The Organization of American Culture, 1700–1900: Private Institutions, Elites, and the Origins of American Nationality* (New York: New York University Press, 1984), 1.

20. Frank Owsley, *States Rights in the Confederacy* (Chicago: University of Chicago Press, 1925); Leonard P. Curry, *Blueprint for Modern America: Nonmilitary Legislation of the First Civil War Congress* (Nashville, TN: Vanderbilt University Press, 1968); Heather Cox Richardson, *The Greatest Nation of the Earth: Republican Economic Policies during the Civil War* (Cambridge, MA: Harvard University Press, 1997); George M. Fredrickson, "Blue Over Gray: Sources of Success and Failure in the Civil War," in *A Nation Divided: Problems and Issues of the Civil War and Reconstruction*, ed. George M. Fredrickson (Minneapolis: Burgess Publishing, 1975), 57–80.

21. Curry, *Blueprint for Modern America*, 250.

22. Fred A. Shannon, *The Organization and Administration of the Union Army, 1861–1865* (1928; repr., ACLS ebook, 2008), 1:29; Irvin McDowell to Lorenzo Thomas, April 11, 1861, *Official Records of the War of the Rebellion (ORA)*, Series I, 51:322–323.

23. Chauncey H. Cooke to mother, September 21, 1862, in Cooke, "A Badger Boy in Blue: The Letters of Chauncey H. Cooke," *Wisconsin Magazine of History* 4, no. 2 (1920): 80.

24. Cooke to mother, October 20, 1862, "A Badger Boy in Blue," 85; this particular controversy over fugitives is covered in *ORA*, Series 2, 1:784–799 in the correspondence between Governor Andrew, Secretary of War, Simon Cameron, and McClellan; quotation from McClellan to Andrews, December 20, 1861, ibid., 791.

25. Fred A. Shannon, "State Rights and the Union Army," *Mississippi Valley Historical Review* 12, no. 1 (1925): 52, 71. In support of this point, it is worth recalling that David Potter argued that "in the North as well as in the South there were deep sectional impulses, and support or nonsupport of the Union was sometimes a matter of sectional tactics rather than of national loyalty," in "The Historian's Use of Nationalism and Vice Versa," *American Historical Review* 67, no. 4 (1962): 941. The issue of states' rights as a Northern phenomenon has been more recently revisited for the antebellum era in Michael Woods, "'Tell Us Something about State Rights': Northern Republicans, States' Rights, and the Coming of the Civil War," *Journal of the Civil War Era* 7, no. 2 (2017): 242–268, esp. 243; Sandow, *Contested Loyalty*, 2; Edward L. Ayers, *Loyalty and America's Civil War* (Gettysburg, PA: Gettysburg College, 2010); John Hutchinson, *Nationalism and War* (Oxford: Oxford University Press, 2017), 2, 86. The literature on loyalty and patriotism in relation to the Civil War is voluminous and covers works that focus largely on the political arena alongside those that range broadly over the theme of loyalty and patriotism among both the elites and the masses. Earlier studies include Frank L. Klement, *The Copperheads in the Middle West* (Chicago: University of Chicago Press, 1960) and Richard Orr Curry, *A House Divided: A Study of Statehood Politics and the Copperhead Movement in West Virginia* (Pittsburgh: University of Pittsburgh Press, 1964). Both works were revisited and their findings revised by Jennifer L. Weber in *Copperheads: The Rise and Fall of Lincoln's Opponents in the North* (New York: Oxford University Press, 2006). A broader view of loyalty is taken by Robert M. Sandow in

Deserter Country: Civil War Opposition in the Pennsylvania Appalachians (New York: Fordham University Press, 2009). Works that adopt a cultural/intellectual approach began with George M. Fredrickson, *The Inner Civil War: Northern Intellectuals and the Crisis of the Union* (1965; repr., New York: Harper Torchbooks, 1968), but also include Melinda Lawson, *Patriot Fires: Forging a New American Nationalism in the Civil War North* (Lawrence: University Press of Kansas, 2002), and, taking the argument into the postwar period, Cecilia Elizabeth O'Leary, *To Die For: The Paradox of American Patriotism* (Princeton, NJ: Princeton University Press, 1999), and Edward J. Blum, *Reforging the White Republic: Race, Religion, and American Nationalism, 1865–1898* (Baton Rouge: Louisiana State University Press, 2005).

26. Gallman, *Defining Duty in the Civil War*; Saunders, "Where on Earth Are You?" 207; Janney, *Remembering the Civil War*, 6.

27. Oliver Wendell Holmes Sr., "Bread and the Newspaper," *Atlantic Monthly* 8, no. 47 (1861): 348; Edward Dicey, *Spectator of America* (Athens: University of Georgia Press, 1989), 142–143.

28. Russell, *My Diary North and South*, 546; Elisha Hunt Rhodes, *All For the Union: The Civil War Diary and Letters of Elisha Hunt Rhodes*, ed. Robert Hunt Rhodes (New York: Vintage Books, 1991), 53; Nathaniel Hawthorne, "Chiefly about War-Matters," *Atlantic Monthly* 10, no. 57 (1862): 57, 44–45.

29. Hawthorne, "Chiefly about War-Matters," 45.

30. John Murrin, "A Roof without Walls: The Dilemma of American National Identity," in *Beyond Confederation: Origins of the Constitution and American National Identity*, ed. Richard Beeman, Stephan Botein, and Edward C. Carter II (Chapel Hill: University of North Carolina Press, 1987), 333–348. See also Parish, "The Distinctiveness of American Nationalism," in Parish, *The North and the Nation*, 57–70, esp. 58–59; and Susan-Mary Grant, "When Was the First New Nation? Locating America in a National Context," in *When Is the Nation? Towards an Understanding of Theories of Nationalism*, ed. Atsuko Ichijo and Gordana Uzelac (London: Routledge, 2005), 157–176.

31. Giddens, *Nation-State and Violence*, 87, 89; Jefferson quoted in J. P. Dunn, *Massacres of the Mountains: A History of the Indian Wars of the Far West* (New York: Harper and Brothers, 1886), 46; Heidi Kiiwetinepinesiik Stark, "Marked by Fire: Anishinaabe Articulations of Nationhood in Treaty Making with the United States and Canada," *American Indian Quarterly* 36, no. 2 (2012): 126; Giddens, *Nation-State and Violence*, 120.

32. Maier, *Leviathan 2.0*, 2; Francis Lieber, *Manual of Political Ethics* (Boston: Charles C. Little and James Brown, 1839), 2:497; Holmes, "Bread and the Newspaper," 348.

33. Holmes, "Bread and the Newspaper," 350.

34. Edward T. Linenthal, *Changing Images of the Warrior Hero in America: A History of Popular Symbolism* (New York: Edwin Mellen Press, 1982), 51–52; Michael Kammen, *A Season of Youth: The American Revolution and the Historical Imagination* (New York: Alfred A. Knopf, 1978), 100; R. Claire Snyder, *Citizen-Soldiers and Manly Warriors: Military Service and Gender in the Civic Republican Tradition* (Lanham, MA: Rowman & Littlefield, 1999), 86; Patrick J. Kelly, *Creating a National Home: Building the Veterans' Welfare State, 1860–1900* (Cambridge, MA: Harvard University Press, 1997), 2; Holmes, "Bread and the Newspaper," 349.

35. Anon, "The Soldier's Union," *Vincennes Times*, June 30, 1866; John Alexander Logan, *The Volunteer Soldier of America* (Chicago: R. S. Peale, 1887) 105.
36. Maier, *Leviathan 2.0*, 117.
37. Benjamin F. Butler to Benjamin F. Wade, July 20, 1865, in *Private and Official Correspondence of Gen. Benjamin F. Butler during the Period of the Civil War* (Private Printing, 1917), 5:642; to General Turner, October 20, 1865, 675.
38. Peter S. Carmichael, *The War for the Common Soldier: How Men Thought, Fought, and Survived in Civil War Armies* (Chapel Hill: University of North Carolina Press, 2018), 230; Oliver Wendell Holmes Jr., "Memorial Day Address, May 30 1884," in *Oliver Wendell Holmes: Occasional Speeches*, ed. Mark DeWolfe Howe (Cambridge, MA: Belknap Press of Harvard University Press, 1962), 9; Oliver Wendell Holmes Jr., "Memorial Day Address, May 30 1895," in *The Essential Holmes: Selections from the Letters, Speeches, Judicial Opinions, and Other Writings of Oliver Wendell Holmes, Jr.*, ed. Richard A. Posner (1992; repr., Chicago: University of Chicago Press, 1996), 87–95.
39. Holmes, "Memorial Day Address, 1895," 73–74, 78, 80–81; Anon, "Sentimental Jingoism," *Evening Post* (New York), December 16, 1895; Anon, "Force as a Moral Instrument," *Evening Post* (New York), December 17," 1895.
40. Holmes, "Memorial Day Address, 1895," 80; N. P. Hallowell, *An Address by . . . Delivered on Memorial Day, May 30, 1896 at a Meeting Called by the Graduating Class of Harvard University* (Boston: Little, Brown, 1896), 6–8. On the class dimensions of Civil War armies the best work is Lorien Foote, *The Gentlemen and the Roughs: Violence, Honor, and Manhood in the Union Army* (New York: New York University Press, 2010). And on the racial dimensions of Civil War commemoration see Nina Silber, *The Romance of Reunion: Northerners and the South, 1865–1900* (Chapel Hill: University of North Carolina Press, 1993); David W. Blight, *Race and Reunion: The Civil War in American Memory* (Cambridge, MA: Harvard University Press, 2001); and David W. Blight, *Beyond the Battlefield: Race, Memory, and the American Civil War* (Amherst: University of Massachusetts Press, 2002).
41. Benjamin Butler to William Duff Telfer, December 18, 1866, in Butler, *Private and Official Correspondence*, 5:716; Henry Benjamin Whipple, *Lights and Shadows of a Long Episcopate* (London: Macmillan, 1899), 124; Richard Drinnon, *Facing West: The Metaphysics of Indian Hating and Empire Building* (Minneapolis: University of Minnesota Press, 1980), 213. For a discussion of the impact of the Civil War on the Cherokee Nation and its parallel internecine divisions see William G. McLoughlin, *After the Trail of Tears: The Cherokees' Struggle for Sovereignty, 1839–1880* (Chapel Hill: University of North Carolina Press, 1993), chap. 8.
42. See, for example, Jerome A. Greene, *Indian War Veterans: Memories of Army Life and Campaigns in the West, 1864–1898* (New York: Savas Beatie, 2007); Roger Possner, *The Rise of Militarism in the Progressive Era, 1900–1914* (Jefferson, NC: McFarland, 2009).
43. R. C. McCormick in the House of Representatives, May 29, 1874, *Congressional Record*, 43rd Congress, 1st Session, 4341; James Nesmith, May 28, 1874, 4359–4360. A fresh approach to the long-standing debate in the United States over military power can be found in Pieter Spierenburg, "Democracy Came Too Early: A Tentative Historical

Explanation for the Problem of American Homicide," *American Historical Review* 111, no. 1 (2006): 104–114.

44. Henry B. Banning, House, May 28, 1874, *Congressional Record*, 43rd Congress, 1st Session, 4362.

45. Banning, House, May 28, 1874, *Congressional Record*, 43rd Congress, 1st Session, 4363; Harris M. Plaisted to Benjamin Butler, October 1, 1865, in Butler, *Private and Official Correspondence*, 5:666.

46. Giddens, *Nation-State and Violence*, 120; Archibald Forbes, "The United States Army," *North American Review* 135, no. 309 (1882): 127.

47. Forbes, "United States Army," 127; Beveridge quoted in Possner, *Rise of Militarism*, 1; Carter H. Harrison, in the Committee of the Whole (H.R. Bill 4867), *Congressional Record*, 45th Congress, 2nd Session, May 21, 1878, 3638; William A. Phillips, in the Committee of the Whole (H.R. Bill 4867), *Congressional Record*, 45th Congress, 2nd Session, May 21, 1878, 3616.

48. Piter Spierenburg, "Democracy Came Too Early: A Tentative Explanation for the Problem of American Homicide," *American Historical Review* 111, no. 1 (2006): 104–114, 113; Henry Clay, House of Representatives, March 13, 1818, in *The Life and Speeches of the Hon. Henry Clay* (New York: Van Amringe and Bixby, 1844), 1:309–310.

49. Cooke to mother, September 21, 1862, "Badger Boy in Blue," 80; Saunders, "Where on Earth Are You?"; Niccolò Machiavelli, *The Art of War*, trans. Henry Neville (Crete: Heraklion Press, 2013) ix.

Conclusion

Law and Order in Nineteenth-Century North America

Brian Schoen and Frank Towers

A half century ago Phillip Paludan urged scholars to consider the American Civil War as a crisis of law and order. The article fit within the dichotomies that modernization theory was then generating, but it was not dependent on them, perhaps explaining its historiographic staying power. Paludan argued that Southerners' dedication to tradition and commitment to slavery's security made them fearful of anything that threatened to take power out of their hands. For white Northerners too, Paludan argued, political stability mattered, as secession would "produce disorder, anarchy, and a general disrespect for democratic government." According to Paludan, they went to war to prevent the destabilization of not just the Union, but what they, and he, saw as the primary level of political life—local communities. Secessionists and Unionists felt compelled to fight for self-government and ordered liberty, as they differently understood them. According to Paludan, "The order of a society depends on more than the rigid enforcement of all of its laws. It depends on maintaining an enduring consensus about a people's fundamental goals and beliefs, and hence on the success of the institutions created to secure this consensus."[1] Nineteenth-century Americans of diverse outlooks would have agreed.

Paludan defined a "political order" as the "institutions [that] provide the means for resolving intergroup conflicts, for utilizing the power of government to achieve the ambitions of society, and for preserving whatever freedom its citizens demand."[2] For Northerners "secession and the firing on Sumter provoked a crisis in which all these things seemed threatened."[3] Although using different terms, Paludan's case for the Civil War as a crisis over law and order resonates with this volume's interest in sovereignty (understood as claims to rule as well as the actual exercise of governing power). The resemblance between his work, produced half a century ago, and this volume serves as a reminder that at some level there is nothing new under the sun in historiography. At the same time, a look back to an earlier era's interest in questions of sovereignty reveals important changes in perspective stemming from a shift to questions about the nation-state and the international dimensions of civil wars.

Focused primarily on the North, Paludan examined its tradition of democratic self-government and its residents' fear that it would be overthrown if secession triumphed. Our authors have looked outward beyond the United States' border, and more often than not they have found hopes for a new and more stable sovereign order driving their subjects' behavior. In this respect, earlier scholarship that looked within the nation for clues to what broke it apart encountered a thick discourse of foreboding around the dissolution of the Union. As Elizabeth Varon and others have shown, by 1860 leading advocates of secession in the South and emancipation in the North had come around to embracing disunion as a means for waging revolution, but the moderates in the middle continued to prophesy the horrors of civil war should the Union fall.[4] In this respect, a continental geographic perspective makes a difference not only in uncovering patterns that crossed national boundaries, but also in recapturing the optimism and ambition, as well as the fear, built into the imperial projects of Americans of diverse political and regional identification.

This volume shifts away from Paludan in another way. He, like many of his peers, significantly downplayed antebellum Americans' consciousness of the nation-state, and as a result, he concluded that the actual threat to Northern communities was more abstract than real.[5] A deep current of scholarship on Southern secessionism has similarly stressed the irrationality of slaveholders' concerns about Republicans' desire or their ability to threaten slavery, especially given the presumed weakness of the federal apparatus.[6] Nineteenth-century white Americans may have preferred their government to be more "out of sight" than European states were or than the twentieth-century federal government would become.[7] Yet as this volume shows, they still expected their government to do certain things and especially to pursue national interests in a chaotic world and to preserve law and order on a continent experiencing multiple sovereignty crises.[8]

Indeed, a continental approach shows that expectations for the nation-state often outpaced what was feasible. As John Craig Hammond has demonstrated, the national government's aptitude for empire-building fueled the imagination of both free-soil and slave expansionists. Yet the national power was incapable of consolidating power or fully realizing more ambitious schemes. Domestic disagreement surely contributed to that, yet the European imperial presence in Canada and Latin America coupled with still-powerful Plains Indian nations evidenced that continental domination was not manifestly destined. In a sense, the comparative actual weakness of the antebellum federal state elevated the national government's significance as Americans pursued the sometimes overlapping but often countervailing desires of territorial conquest and geopolitical stability. Ironically, a common goal in the pro- and antislavery plans for westward expansion was a stronger federal government that could carry out these competing agendas, be it a federally enforced slave code in the territories or a federally imposed ban on the further extension of slavery westward.

As noted in the introduction, such aspirational claims for sovereign powers are more typical of the term's usage in everyday politics than are sober discussions of what government can actually do. As a case in point, Americans were quite sure that they could do a better job than their Mexican predecessors in taming the Southwest. As Alice Baumgartner demonstrates, however, Americans were initially no more capable of securing the southern border than their Mexican counterparts, leaving continued opportunities for Indians, fugitive slaves, and those escaping peonage. In fact, by 1854 the U.S. government conceded their inability to tame the border, paying the Mexicans' extra money to get out of complying with Article 11 of the 1848 treaty, which had made the U.S. responsible for halting Indian cross-border raids.[9] Amy Greenberg shows that William Walker, who knew a thing or two about filibusters into Mexico, presumed his whiteness and support from other Americans would be sufficient to stabilize a precarious situation within Central America. In an ironic sense he was correct, but only because United States officials could not thwart his efforts, which generated enough local resistance to push several Latin American states, with British aid, to consolidate national authority. As Brian Schoen shows, continued uncertainty across and along the Mexican border, and a deep desire to create order on it, exacerbated the sectional conflict and framed Americans' own descent into civil war.

The war was born out of divisions over what the U.S.'s fundamental purpose on the world stage was, but also the desire to better police internal and international borders and to control white and black movement, thought, and political action.[10] The fighting itself, however, only deepened and broadened the problem. Guerrilla fighting offers one much-studied example of the devolution into community disorder. Fighting, especially in Kentucky, Missouri, and Kansas, devolved into personal violence and retribution that constrained the ability of individuals to stay neutral.[11] Beau Cleland's piece demonstrates that the war also created community divisions outside of the United States, while testing the limits of neutrality on the war's international front. Confederate sympathizers' brazen actions generated significant tension with the Union, opening up legal questions about what responsibilities belligerents and neutral powers had amid a civil war.

The Confederacy's desperation led it to embrace illegal actions, which rippled throughout the Atlantic. Westminster pursued a careful form of neutrality, and Confederate privateers would have been jailed on the spot had Parliament's rules on neutrality been strictly observed. Yet Cleland's article reminds us that this mattered little to many in the Maritime provinces.[12]

In this respect, a North American focus opens up insights into the role, not of the British and French Empires, but of the rich historiography on nineteenth-century Canada, Mexico, and Native Peoples.[13] The appearance of the French-ified Mexican Conservative army in Andrew Slap's piece reminds us that similar dynamics as Cleland and Greenberg have described await further exploration on the United States' southern border. These essays implicitly show the value of transnational histories that look to provinces rather than to capitals in assessing what borders meant and how these competing imperial projects played out on the ground in places like Michigan, Nova Scotia, and Matamoros. This isn't to say that the center did not matter. Otherwise, the Michiganders' hopes for Canadian annexation that Quist showed continued after the war, might have led to greater action. But Washington officials recognized that Canadian Confederation signaled the will of most Canadians, making annexation a futile effort. They pressed for peace and neutrality over acquisition and instability. Yet what is evidenced in these chapters is that national governments, even when they could define the terms and goals, could not guarantee that outcomes would align. They seldom did.[14]

By moving the question of sovereignty out of legal history and into a broader social and political perspective on the period, this volume also seeks to show how claims to power and legitimacy drove the conflicts of the period and shaped the postwar settlement. This intent is perhaps best exemplified in Susan-Mary Grant's closing essay that links the seemingly coldly rational and constitutional question of the state's authority to the heated, deeply emotional debate over what the nation owes its veterans, and what role that sacrifice played in maintaining the postwar government's legitimacy. In doing so, Grant takes Paludan's question about a war over law and order into the conceptual terrain of nationalism, loss, and gender.

It is common currency to suggest that the American Civil War re-established the rule of law in the United States and created a unified nation. Union victory signaled that the framework of Union would prevail over state-sponsored secession, and Black freedom over slavery. It is also possible that, as Heather Cox Richardson has suggested, white Americans found a semblance of cohesion through the conquest of the West.[15] Yet the supposed triumph of order is only apparent if one's reference point is the chaotic world created by the rivalry between the Confederacy and Union and the potential for perpetual warfare had the Union not won the war. To reference Paludan's criterion, "Consensus about a people's fundamental goals and beliefs" proved elusive, and "hence the success of the institutions" remained precarious. Americans debated, created, and then in many instances subverted a second founding. Americans continued to fret about what Gregory Downs has called the "Mexicanization of their Politics" as violence continued in the American South and on the Great Plains, where Indian empires had reasserted themselves.[16]

Collectively, the chapters in this volume suggest that American definitions of power and the perception of law and order were always contested and inextricably linked to friction points far removed from the traditional conceived loci of politics. They illustrate the reality that Americans filtered their own experiences and problems through the lens not only of their assets and vulnerabilities within the United States, but also through connections and conflicts at and over its borders. We hope that this volume illustrates the benefits of studying the U.S. Civil War era as part of a broader crisis of sovereignty in mid-nineteenth-century North America.

Notes

1. Phillip S. Paludan, "The American Civil War Considered as a Crisis in Law and Order," *American Historical Review* 77, no. 4 (1972): 1013–1034, (anarchy) 1017, (consensus) 1013.

2. Paludan, "American Civil War," 114.

3. Paludan, 114.

4. Elizabeth Varon, *Disunion! The Coming of the American Civil War, 1789–1859* (Chapel Hill: University of North Carolina Press, 2008); Jason Phillips, *Looming Civil War: How Nineteenth-Century Americans Imagined the Future* (New York: Oxford University Press, 2018); Adam I. P. Smith, *The Stormy Present: Conservatism and the Problem of Slavery in Northern Politics, 1846–1865* (Chapel Hill: University of North Carolina Press, 2017); Michael E. Woods, "Charleston, City of Mourners: Anticipation of Civil War in the Cradle of Secession," *Civil War History* 67, no. 1 (2021): 7–28. There is also a good bit of literature highlighting the crisis of law and order built into the war. See, for example, Mary P. Ryan, *Civic Wars: Democracy and Public Life in the American City during the Nineteenth Century* (Berkeley: University of California Press, 1997); Jennifer L. Weber, *Copperheads: The Rise and Fall of Lincoln's Opponents in the North* (New York: Oxford University Press, 2006); Chandra Manning, *What This Cruel War Was Over: Soldiers, Slavery and the Civil War* (New York: Vintage, 2007); Daniel E. Sutherland, *A Savage Conflict: The Decisive Role of Guerrillas in the American Civil War* (Chapel Hill: University of North Carolina Press, 2009); Randolph Roth, *American Homicide* (Cambridge, MA: Harvard University Press, 2009); William A. Blair, *With Malice toward*

Some: Treason and Loyalty in the Civil War Era (Chapel Hill: University of North Carolina Press, 2014).

5. Paludan, "American Civil War," 1019.

6. The thesis that white Southerners exaggerated the danger of Lincoln's election originated with border South Unionists in the secession crisis. It has manifested in scholarship that emphasizes the contingency of the war, as opposed to its inevitability. For representative examples see David M. Potter, *The Impending Crisis: America before the Civil War, 1848–1861*, comp. and ed. Don E. Fehrenbacher (1976; repr., New York: Harper Perennial, 2011), 454; Edward L. Ayers, *In the Presence of Mine Enemies: The Civil War in the Heart of America, 1859–1863* (New York: W. W. Norton, 2003), 150–160; William W. Freehling, *The Road to Disunion: Volume II: Secessionists Triumphant* (New York: Oxford University Press, 2007), 352–374.

7. Brian Balogh, *A Government Out of Sight: The Mystery of National Authority in Nineteenth-Century America* (Cambridge, UK: Cambridge University Press, 2009).

8. Jay Sexton, "The Civil War and U.S. World Power," in *American Civil Wars: The United States, Latin America, Europe, and the Crisis of the 1860s*, ed. Don H. Doyle (Chapel Hill: University of North Carolina Press, 2017), 29.

9. Brian DeLay, *War of a Thousand Deserts: Indian Raids and the U.S.-Mexican War* (New Haven, CT: Yale University Press, 2009), xiii–xxii.

10. Elliot West, "Reconstructing Race," *Western Historical Quarterly* 34, no. 1 (2003): 6–26; Andrew Lang, *A Contest of Civilizations: Exposing the Crisis of American Exceptionalism in the Civil War Era* (Chapel Hill: University of North Carolina Press, 2021).

11. Sutherland, *A Savage Conflict*.

12. Beau Darl Cleland, "Between King Cotton and Queen Victoria: Confederate Informal Diplomacy and Privatized Violence in British America during the American Civil War" (PhD diss., University of Calgary, 2019). For more on neutrality see Stuart S. Bernath, *Squall across the Atlantic: American Civil War Prize Cases and Diplomacy*, 1st ed. (Berkeley: University of California Press, 1970); Richard Little, "British Neutrality versus Offshore Balancing in the American Civil War: The English School Strikes Back," *Security Studies* 16, no. 1 (2007): 68–95; Frank J. Merli, *The Alabama, British Neutrality, and the American Civil War* (Bloomington: Indiana University Press, 2004); J. Lemnitzer, *Power, Law and the End of Privateering* (New York: Palgrave, 2014); Stephen C. Neff, *Justice in Blue and Gray: A Legal History of the Civil War* (Cambridge, MA: Harvard University Press, 2010); Brian Schoen, "The Civil War in Europe," in *The Cambridge History of the American Civil War: vol. 2: Affairs of the State*, ed. Aaron Sheehan-Dean (New York: Cambridge University Press, 2019), 342–365.

13. West, "Reconstructing Race." For additional examples and further discussion see chapters in *Remaking North American Sovereignty: State Transformation in the 1860s*, ed. Jewel Spangler and Frank Towers (New York: Fordham University Press, 2020).

14. There are some synthetic works that have seen the broad periods through a continental perspective. See Steven Hahn, *A Nation without Borders: The United States and Its World in an Age of Civil Wars, 1830–1910* (New York: Viking, 2016); Jay Sexton, *The Monroe Doctrine: Empire and Nation in Nineteenth-Century America* (New York: Hill and Wang, 2011).

15. Heather Cox Richardson, *West from Appomattox: The Reconstruction of America after the Civil War* (New Haven, CT: Yale University Press, 2008).
16. Gregory P. Downs, "The Mexicanization of American Politics: The United States' Transnational Path from Civil War to Stabilization," *American Historical Review* 117, no. 2 (2012): 387–409; Pekka Hämäläinen, *The Comanche Empire* (New Haven, CT: Yale University Press, 2008).

Acknowledgments

This is the second volume of essays to emerge from the conference "Remaking North American Sovereignty: Towards a Continental History of State Transformation in the 1860s," held from July 30 through August 1, 2015, in Banff, Alberta, Canada. The editors thank all of those involved for their patience with us and for sticking with the project.

Although he is not included in the volume, none of this would have happened without the early support and insight of William Allen Blair. Ferree Professor Emeritus of Middle American History at Pennsylvania State University, Bill worked for many years as the editor of the journal *Civil War History* and then founded and edited the *Journal of the Civil War Era*. He also served as director of the Richards Center for the Study of the Civil War Era. Bill has been at the forefront of expanding the field of American Civil War studies and was very excited about the idea of pulling together scholars from different national historical traditions to think about the 1860s as one common story. He also convinced the Richards Center to provide crucial funding for the Banff conference and then shepherded some of the papers into print in a special issue of the *Journal of the Civil War Era*. Everyone involved in this project owes him a debt.

The collaborations that made this book go well beyond Bill, however. The Banff conference and the ideas that inform this book owe a great deal to the conference organizing committee members Lindsay Campbell, Gregory P. Downs, Patrick Kelly, Amelia Kiddle, Paul Quigley, Brian Schoen, Jay Sexton, and Andrew Slap. Matt Isham and Barby Singer at the Richards Center for the Civil War Era stepped in to help manage the logistical challenges of an international conference.

The Banff conference benefited from generous funding from Canada's Social Sciences and Humanities Research Council, The Virginia Center for the Civil War (VCCW), and, at the University of Calgary, the Centre for Military and Strategic Studies (CMSS), the Latin American Research Centre (LARC), the Department of History, and the Faculty of Arts. In this search for funding we especially thank Paul Quigley, director of the VCCW, David Bercuson, longtime director of CMSS, and Hendrik Kraay, who was simultaneously running LARC and serving as head of the Department of History.

Moving from the conference to this edited volume would not have happened without Andrew L. Slap, editor of the Reconstructing America series at Fordham University Press. Andy not only got involved early on, committing to the project before he saw any chapters, he also presented a paper at the conference which he has revised for this volume. We also thank Fredric Nachbaur, director of Fordham University Press, and Eric Newman, the Press's managing editor.

In addition to readers of individual chapters, we extend special thanks to Erika Pani and Andre Fleche for their insightful comments on the entire manuscript.

Taylor and Francis publishers permitted the publication of a revised version of John Craig Hammond's article "Inveterate Imperialists: Contested Imperialisms, North American History, and the Coming of the U.S. Civil War," which appeared in *American Nineteenth-Century History* in 2021.

On behalf of everyone involved with the meeting at Banff, the editors want to acknowledge the contribution of Tony Kaye and express their sorrow at his untimely death in 2017. Tony's paper for that meeting, "Understandings of Sovereignty among Slave Rebels and Abolitionists, 1829–1848," looked across the Americas to uncover a theory of sovereignty expressed in the culture of rumor used by slave rebels. It was a fascinating study that typified Tony's innovative understanding of the history of slavery. He gave a great deal to the profession and is missed by his peers.

We dedicate this book to our students, all of them, whom we have taught in our careers. Graduate students were an important component of the Banff conference (for example, Alice Baumgartner and Beau Cleland participated in the meeting while working on their doctorates), and the themes of this book developed out of our collective efforts to broaden our teaching beyond a narrowly conceived national history of the United States to one that encompasses the full range of world history. Thinking about how to bring those insights to students, and being challenged by them to address questions we had never thought of, has made our scholarship not only better but also a lot more fun.

Contributors

Alice L. Baumgartner is an assistant professor of history at the University of Southern California. She is the author of *South to Freedom: Runaway Slaves to Mexico and the Road to the Civil War* (Basic Books, 2020).

Beau Cleland is an assistant professor of history at the University of Calgary. He is the author of "Sustaining the Confederacy: Informal Diplomacy, Anglo-Confederate Relations, and Blockade Running in the Bahamas" for the *Journal of Southern History* (forthcoming, 2023). He previously served as an officer in the United States Army, with service in Iraq and Afghanistan.

Susan-Mary Grant is a professor of American history at Newcastle University, UK. She is the author of *The Concise History of the United States of America* (Cambridge University Press, 2012) and most recently *Oliver Wendell Holmes, Jr.: Civil War Soldier, Supreme Court Justice* (Routledge, 2015). She is a Fellow of the Massachusetts Historical Society and is working on a book about Civil War veterans.

Amy S. Greenberg is George Winfree Professor of History at Penn State University. She is the author of five books, including *A Wicked War: Polk, Clay, Lincoln and the 1846 U.S. Invasion of Mexico* (Knopf, 2012), *Manifest Destiny and American Territorial Expansion: A Brief History with Documents* (Bedford/St. Martin's, 2012), and, most recently, *Lady First: The World of First Lady Sarah Polk* (Knopf, 2019).

John Craig Hammond is an associate professor of history and assistant director of academic affairs at Penn State New Kensington in suburban Pittsburgh. He is the author and editor of numerous works on slavery and empire in North American history. Most recently, he is co-editor, with Jeffrey Pasley, of volume 1 of *A Fire Bell in the Past: The Missouri Crisis at 200* (University of Missouri Press, 2021).

John W. Quist is a professor of history at Shippensburg University. He is the author of *Restless Visionaries: The Social Roots of Antebellum Reform in Alabama and Michigan* (Louisiana State University Press, 1998) and the editor or co-editor of several volumes, including *James Buchanan and the Coming of the Civil War* (University Press of Florida, 2013) and *Michigan's War: The Civil War in Documents* (Ohio University Press, 2019).

Brian Schoen is the James Richard Hamilton/Baker and Hostetler Professor of Humanities and chair of the Department of History at Ohio University. He is author of *The Fragile Fabric of Union: Cotton, Federal Politics, and the Global Origins of the Civil War* (Johns

Hopkins University Press, 2009) and several recent book chapters, articles, and edited anthologies on the early American Republic and Civil War Era.

Andrew L. Slap is a professor of history at East Tennessee State University. He is the author of *The Doom of Reconstruction: The Liberal Republican Movement in the Civil War Era* (Fordham University Press, 2006), as well as the editor or co-editor of several anthologies, including *Reconstructing Appalachia: The Civil War's Aftermath* (University Press of Kentucky, 2010); *This Distracted and Anarchical People: New Answers for Old Questions about the Civil War Era North* (Fordham University Press, 2013); and *Confederate Cities: The Urban South during the Civil War Era* (University of Chicago Press, 2015). He is also the editor of Fordham's series Reconstructing America, of which this volume is the latest entry.

Jewel L. Spangler is an associate professor and head of the Department of History at the University of Calgary. She is the author of *Virginians Reborn* (University of Virginia Press, 2008) and co-editor of *Remaking North American Sovereignty: State Transformation in the 1860s* (Fordham University Press, 2020). Her current project is a microhistory titled "The Richmond Theatre Fire of 1811 in History and Memory."

Frank Towers is a professor of history at the University of Calgary. He is the author of *The Urban South and the Coming of the Civil War* (University of Virginia Press, 2004) and the co-editor of *The Old South's Modern Worlds* (Oxford University Press, 2011), *Confederate Cities* (University of Chicago Press, 2015), and *Remaking North American Sovereignty* (Fordham University Press, 2020).

Index

Adams, John, 175
African Americans, 8; as British allies, 43; citizenship for, 54–55; in Memphis, 179–80; in Mexican-American War, 24, 33n37; Prince visit and, 101; as rivals, 47; in troops, 208
Agamben, Georgio, 78
Alabama, CSS: legality of, 149n83; merchant shipping hurt by, 136; neutrality violated by, 134. See also *Alabama* claims
Alabama claims, 12, 153; Bahamas or British Columbia annexation for, 164; Canadian annexation and, 162–65; settlement of, 165; Treaty of Washington and, 165. See also *Alabama*, CSS
Alabama Platform, 96
Alaska purchase, 161–62, 172n52
Albert (Prince), 100–1
Alger, William Rounseville, 37
Almon, William J., 123; Doyle on, 135, 149n75; slavery and, 146n19; trial of, 135; Wade, G., intercepted by, 130
Alta California, 24, 29
Americanization: in Mexico, 36–37; in Nicaragua, 71–72
American Revolution, 57
American state: as blueprint, 212; borders in, 193; Civil War memory in, 206–7; contemporary views of, 212–13; dead and, 192, 214n7; expansion in, 196, 204; ghosts of the Union and Confederacy in, 206–12; landscapes of conflict in, 201–6; legitimacy of, 203; martial citizenship in, 205–6, 212; military in, 203, 210–12, 215n9; nationalism in, 204; sentiments supporting, 194; as shell, 195; soldiers' sacrifice for, 189, *190*, *191*; sovereignty without centralization in, 193–201; transformation of, 204, 206, 214; violence in, 213
Anderson, Benedict, 192
Anderson, George, 129–30
Andrew, John A., 200, 213
Apache, 2, 89
"Appomattox Syndrome," 192
Arista, Mariano, 24
Army, U.S., 174; executive branch controlling, 176; French Intervention and, 180–84; generals in, 176–78; in Memphis, 178–79; in Mexico, 175, 180–81; presidential candidates in, 185–86; presidential use of, 175
Articles of Confederation, U.S., 154
Atlantic, 2, 6

Balogh, Brian, 197
Banks, Nathaniel, 171n48
Banning, Henry, 210–11
Basson, Lauren L., 80n7
Battle of San Jacinto, 23
Baumgartner, Alice, 8–9, 223
Bayley, Charles, 126, 142
Beal, Bob, 84n62
Beall, John Yates, 149n79
Bell, John, 99
Bender, Thomas, 181
Benjamin, Judah P., 120; in Confederate State Department, 124; for filibustering, 140
Bensel, Richard Franklin, 189, 195
Benton, Jessie, 177
Benton, Thomas Hart, 177
Berrien, John, 29–30

Beveridge, Albert, 212
Bickley, George, 37
Bilbau, Francisco, 71
Blackburn, Luke, 123, 132
Blackfoot, 2
Blacks. *See* African Americans
Blair, Austin, 156
Blair, Francis, Jr., 55
Blair, William, 80n9
blockade runners, 122, 145n13
Bontrager, Shannon, 192
borders, 2, 5; in American state, 193; definitions of, 193; societal, 200–1; as uncertain, 89; U.S.-Mexico, 88, 185, 223
Boyce, William, 91
Bradburn, Juan Davis, 22
Bradbury, James W., 25
Braine, John Clibbon, 123, 147n40; attacks by, 131; capture of, 128; *Chesapeake* seized by, 127; Confederate protection for, 131, 141–43, 149n79; escape by, 128, 131, 142; filibustering by, 139; with Locke, V., 127; *Roanoke* seized by, 141–42, 150n99; *St. Mary* seized by, 142–43
Breckinridge, John, 99
Britain, 2, 7; neutrality of, 11–12; slavery abolished by, 46
British Act of Union (1840), 156
British Empire, 5, 7; Canada in, 100; Confederacy and, 120–21, 145n18; municipal laws of, 122, 145n11; political control of, 121, 145n9; slavery in, 128
British North America, 2, 7, 43; challenges for, 86; colonial administrators of, 128; Confederacy in, 122–23; responsible government in, 129, 148n50; sovereignty in, 121–22; in Union army, 144n1; and U.S. Civil War, 119. *See also* Canada
Brodhead, Richard, 25
Brown, Charles H., 81n13
Brown, John, 93–94, 193–94
Bruyneel, Kevin, 78, 81n11
Bryan, William Jennings, 207

Buchanan, James, 11, 50; annual message from, 92–95, 104; on expansion, 89; flip-flop by, 92; for Mexican protectorate, 91–92; on Prince visit, 101; truce denied by, 99; U.S. Army used by, 175; on Walker, W., 73
Buckner, Phillip, 129, 169n24
Burbank, Jane, 42
Butler, Anthony, 21–22
Butler, Benjamin, 206, 209

Calhoun, John C., 25–26
Canada, 2, 8, 166n2; blockade runners in, 122, 145n13; Britain controlling, 156, 160; British Act of Union (1840) in, 156; in British Empire, 100; Confederates in, 156–57, 169n24; Confederation Day in, 161; Detroit trade with, 153–54; ethnic divisions in, 66; expansionism in, 74–76; Fenian invasion of, 160; First Nations peoples in, 65; nonintercourse with, 157, 163; Northern state with, 109–10; Northwest in, 79; passport controls with, 157; princes and provinces in, 99–104; railroad in, 75–76, 78; reformer rebellions in, 121, 128–29, 139, 143, 148n49; regionalism in, 77; religion in, 100; self-governing in, 121–22; state formation in, 78–79. *See also* British North America; Métis; Riel, Louis
Canadian annexation, 12, 37; *Alabama* claims and, 162–65; Alaska purchase and, 161–62; assumptions about, 153; Banks bills for, 171n48; British Columbia in, 162, 172n52; Canadians for, 153, 160–61; capital for, 109, 118n105; *Detroit Advertiser* for, 155; historical tensions influencing, 154; Mexican-American War and, 155; press on, 152, 167n5; Reciprocity Treaty influencing, 152, 155, 158–59, 168n17; shelving of, 155; Texas annexation influencing, 154; trade influencing, 153–54, 168n15, 170n38; as voluntary, 159, 166; Whigs for, 154–55, 168n15

INDEX 235

Canadian Confederation, 10, 12, 166n2; Canadian annexation and, 161; Manitoba in, 65, 77; Métis joining of, 76–77
Canadian Pacific Railway, 67, 75, 77–78
capitalism, 5–6
Cardwell, Edward, 142
Caribbean, 2, 38; as borderland, 46; colonization of, 54–55
Caroline, 154
Cass, Lewis, 90, 168n13
Central America, 47; competition in, 70; Walker, W., impact on, 72–74
Chamorro, Violeta Barrios de, 71
Chandler, Zachariah, 12, 152; compensation demanded by, 157, 160, 162–63; invasion threats by, 164, 169n22; mortgage claims by, 163; for nonintercourse, 163; press and, 163, 172n56; against Reciprocity Treaty, 158, 170n34; on Treaty of Washington, 165
Chesapeake, 12; affair of, 123–24, 129–30; attackers in, 131–32; attack of, 119–20, 125, 127–28; Braine on, 127; in British territorial waters, 128; colonial courts on, 129–33; as lawful prize, 133–34; Locke, V., attacking, 125, 127–28; pirate trial for, 131–33, 135; prisoner transfer from, 130–31; privateering on, 136; prosecution failure for, 140–41; recapture of, 128; release of, 140; Schaffer death on, 119, 127; trial about, 133–34
Chicago, 184–85
Cincinnatus, Lucius Quinctius, 205
Clark, Billy, 179
Clary, A. G., 128, 130
Clay, Henry, 26, 108
Clayton-Bulwer Treaty (1850), 70
Cleland, Beau, 11–12, 223–24
Code for the Government of Armies in the Field (Lieber), 204
Codell, Julie, 67
Cold War, 4–5
colonies, 4, 7
colonization, 54, 63n33

Comanche, 2, 42, 89
Compendium of The Impending Crisis (Helper), 94
Compromise of 1850, 45
"Compromise with the South" (Nast), 189, 191
Confederacy, 3–4; attacks by, 156; Bahamian support for, 126–27; blockade of, 122, 126; British Empire and, 120–21, 145n18; in British North America, 122–23; in Canada, 156–57, 169n24; European-built ships for, 136–38; filibustering for, 139–40, 143–44, 224; French support for, 180; ghosts of, 206–12; as guerrilla republic, 119–20; hijackings encouraged by, 137, 143, 149n80; privateers for, 125, 136–37; soft power of, 123–24; unofficial agents for, 124. *See also* secession
Confederate prison camps, 206
Confederate State Department, 124
Conkling, Roscoe, 51–52
Connolly, Thomas, 123
Conrad, 134
Cooke, Chauncey H., 199–200, 213
Cooper, Frederick, 42
Cordova, Raphael J. de, 110–11
Corn Laws, 168n15
Cornwallis, Kinahan, 116n69
Cortina, Juan: raid by, 92–93; rumors about, 95; U.S. Army attacking, 175
Corwin, Thomas, 108, 110
Costa Rica, 70–71; nationalism in, 72; Walker, W., impact on, 72, 74
Cox, Samuel, 91
Crimean War, 91, 100, 125
Crittenden Amendments, 51
Cuba, 7, 46–47
Cunliffe, Marcus, 176
Custer, George Armstrong, 189, 191

Daily Louisville Democrat, 36
Dashew, Doris W., 167n3
Davis, David Brion, 29

Davis, Jefferson, 12; amendment proposed by, 27; on *Chesapeake* affair, 136; emissaries by, 108; for filibustering, 140; hesitation by, 138; on slaves, 49; on Texas border, 96
Delay, Brian, 42
Detroit: Alaska purchase and, 161–62; on Canadian annexation, 152–53; commercial convention in, 158–59; Edward (Prince) in, 12, 101; Erie Canal and, 153; international tensions felt in, 156; as large, 152; against passport controls, 157; press in, 152; trade with, 153–54. *See also* Chandler, Zachariah
Detroit Advertiser and Tribune: on Alaska purchase, 162; for Canadian Annexation, 155; on Canadian Confederation, 161; Chandler criticized by, 163; Chandler defended by, 164, 173n60; on Fenian raids, 160; on Potter's speech, 159; against Reciprocity Treaty, 159; on Reforma War, 90; as Republican, 152, 163
Detroit Free Press: on *Alabama* claims, 165; on Alaska purchase, 161–62; on apprehension in Detroit, 156; on British Columbia annexation, 162; for Canadian Annexation, 152, 155, 159, 170n38, 171n46; on Canadian Confederation, 161; Chandler criticized by, 164; as Democratic, 152; on *Detroit Advertiser*, 155; on disunion, 109; on Fenian raids, 160; on nonintercourse with Canada, 157; on Potter's speech, 159; on pro-annexationist sentiment, 160–61
Detroit Post: on *Alabama* claims, 165; on Alaska purchase, 162; for Canadian annexation, 163, 171n46; on Canadian Confederation, 161; on Canadian vulnerability, 164, 172n59; with Chandler, 160; establishment of, 163, 172n56; as Republican, 152, 163
Dicey, Edward, 201–2
Doolittle, James, 53

Douglas, Stephen, 36, 96, 108
Downs, Gregory, 20, 117n95, 195, 225
Doyle, Charles Hastings: on Almon, 135, 149n75; in *Chesapeake* affair, 128–29, 134; demands by, 130
Doyle, Don, 181
Dred Scott v. Sanford, 9, 27–28, 50
Drescher, Seymour, 29
Durham Report, 148n50

Edling, Max, 42
Edward (Prince), 11, 85–86; in American imagination, 99–104, 116n63; in Detroit, 12, 101; disorder around, 101, 116n64; on election night, 102; in New England, 110; in New York, 102; in Richmond, 103–4; U.S. enthusiasm for, 110, 116n69; in Washington, DC, 103; women and, 102–3
Elgin-Marcy Treaty. *See* Reciprocity Treaty (1854)
Ella and Annie, 128
empire. *See* imperialism
Erie Canal, 153
exceptionalism, 86
expatriation, 68, 81n17

Fenians, 160
Ferry, Thomas W., 165
Fessenden, William, 96
filibustering: British concerned about, 121; Brown, C., definition of, 81n13; *Chesapeake* attack as, 119; for Confederacy, 139–40, 143–44, 224; definitions of, 139, 150n89; government support for, 139; replacement of, 40–41; by Walker, W., 10
First Nations peoples. *See* Indians
Fish, Hamilton, 12, 164–65
Foner, Eric, 30n1
Forbes, Archibald, 211–12
Ford, John "Rip," 31n2
Foreign Enlistment Act (1819), 122, 124; colonial courts on, 129; enforcement of,

INDEX 237

136–37; pirates violating, 132; privateering crippled by, 136
Forsyth, John, 90
Fort Sumter, 85, 108
Foster, Eden Burroughs, 50
France, 2, 7; Confederacy supported by, 180; Mexico intervention by, 85–86, 181–83; slavery abolished by, 46
free negro empire, 46–47
free white labor, 53–54
Frémont, John C., 177
French Intervention. *See* France
fugitive slaves, 8–9; extradition of, 21–22; freedom in Mexico for, 20–21; legal status uncertain for, 19–22; from Louisiana, 21–22; in Mexican-American War, 24, 33n37; passports for, 24

Gadsden, James, 73–74
Gadsden Purchase. *See* Treaty of Mesilla
Galeano, Eduardo, 72
Gallagher, Gary, 192
Gallman, Matthew, 200–201
GAR. *See* Grand Army of the Republic
Gay, Sydney Howard, 30n1
gender, 5; martial manhood in, 13, 73, 193, 208; sovereignty and, 192–93
Gerrity, 140–41, 144, 150n93
Giddens, Anthony: on nationalism, 193; on power, 204; on violence, 211
Gobat, Michel, 72
Godey's Lady's Book, 194–95
Godkin, E. L., 197
Golden Circle, 47
Gold Rush, 69–70
Gordon, Arthur: power of, 131–32; warrants ordered by, 131, 133
Grand Army of the Republic (GAR), 207
Grant, George M., 75–76
Grant, Susan-Mary, 13, 224
Grant, Ulysses S., 12–13; Fish supported by, 164–65; on French Intervention, 181–83; as general, 177–78; Juárez supported by, 181–82; as president, 184

Gray, John Hamilton, 132
Great Plains, 2
Green, Benjamin, 23
Greenberg, Amy, 10, 193, 223
Gregg, David L., 74
Grimes, James W., 117n95
Grinberg, Keila, 34

Hahn, Steven, 8, 196
Hale, James, 51
Hale, Nathan, 102
Hall, Peter Dobkin, 197–98
Hallowell, Pen, 208
Hämäläinen, Pekka, 42
Hamilton, Alexander, 175
Hamilton, Andrew Jackson, 96
Hamley, William, 142
Hammond, John Craig, 9–10, 87, 222
Hammond, James Henry, 97
Hannegan, Edward D., 30
Hanover, 126
Hardy, William E., 182
Harrison, Carter, 212
Hawaii, 74
Hawthorne, Nathaniel, 202–3
Heintzelman, Sam, 95
Helm, Charles, 141–42
Helper, Hinton, 94
Henry, William Alexander, 123
Higginson, Thomas Wentworth, 194–95, 205–6
Hill, Philip Carteret, 135
Hogg, Thomas: hijacking by, 139–40; Mallory supporting, 142; seizures attempted by, 143
Holcombe, James P., 140
"Hold the Fort" (Nast), 189, *190*
Holmes, Oliver Wendell, Sr., 201; on Civil War memory, 206–7; on martial masculinity, 208; on military potential, 204; on soldier's faith, 207–8; on valor, 205
homo sacer, 78
Honduras, 66, 70
Hooker, Joseph, 177

Houston, Sam, 91; inaugural address by, 95; objections by, 105; on political independence, 87–88; on Southern constitutional party, 107; on Treaty of Guadalupe, 89
Howard, Jacob, 164–65, 170n37
Hutchinson, John, 200

imperialism, 5; American, 8–10; colonization in, 54–55; fiscal policies in, 42–43; free negro empire in, 46–47; French, 7; in Golden Circle, 47; hierarchies in, 39–40; historical analysis of, 40–42; ideals in, 38–39, 44–45; Northerner in, 48; sectional conflict in, 38–39, 44, 48; slavery and, 37–38, 44; Southern pro-slavery, 38, 45, 47–52, 56, 57n1. *See also* Americanization; Southernization
Indians, 7–8; as British allies, 43; buffalo and, 76; at Little Bighorn, 189, 191; in Manitoba, 65; soldiers against, 199–200; as sovereign people, 209. *See also* Apache; Comanche; Métis
Indigenous Americans. *See* Indians
Ireland, 7

Jackson, Andrew, 175
Janney, Caroline, 201
Jefferson, Thomas, 203
Johnson, Andrew, 13, 160; for civilian control, 179–80; delegation by, 182; impeachment of, 174; presidential address by, 178
Johnson, Joseph E., 178
Johnston, James William, 133
Joseph R. Gerrity, 140
Joy, James, 170n38
J. P. Ellicott, 126
Juárez, Benito, 11; government formed by, 90; Grant, U., support for, 181–82; plans by, 88

Kansas-Nebraska Act, 50
Karp, Matthew, 58n6

Keith, Alexander, Jr., 123, 130, 135
Kellogg, William, 107
Knights of the Golden Circle, 93; justification by, 46; morphing of, 105; press about, 36–37
Kramer, Paul A., 39

Laird rams, 138
Lamar, Mirabeau Buonaparte, 71
Lane, Harriet, 103
Latin America, 10; influence of, 21; uprisings in, 198
Laviña, José Francisco, 21, 32n12
Lee, Robert E., 95, 114n30; in Mexico, 175; peace requested by, 178
legal portability, 9
Lemmon vs. the People of New York, 50
letter of marque, 125; abuse of, 146n30; Locke, V., misuse of, 127
Leviathan 2.0 (Maier), 189
Lieber, Francis, 204
Liholiho, Alexander, 74
Lincoln, Abraham, 8, 48; blockade by, 122; colonization and, 54, 63n33; election of, 103; on empire, 53; Frémont and, 177; Hooker and, 177; irrational fears about, 222, 226n6; McClellan and, 176; against Mexican annexation, 110; on Reciprocity Treaty, 158; on secession, 107–8; warning by, 49, 51
Little Bighorn, 189, 191
Locke, John, 23
Locke, Vernon Guyon, 123; bail for, 126, 147n36; *Chesapeake* attacked by, 125, 127–28; escape by, 126–27; filibustering by, 139; as at large, 131; letter of marque misused by, 127; neutrality violated by, 126; as John Parker, 125, 128, 132, 146n31; as privateer, 125–26; *Retribution* and, 125–26, 146n31; ships captured by, 126; trial of, 142–43
Logan, John A., 205
Logan, William H., 22
López, Narciso, 139

Louisiana, 21–22
Low, Andrew, 122
Lyons (Lord), 99

Machiavelli, Niccolò, 214
Macleod, Rod, 84n62
Madison, James, 139
Magee, John L., 49
Magevney, John J., 179
Maier, Charles, 3; on Civil War, 206; on expansion, 196; *Leviathan 2.0* by, 189; on Little Bighorn, 189, 191; on nationalization, 204; on tempo of change, 191–92; on transformation, 206
Mallory, Stephen Russell, 120, 125; on *Chesapeake* affair, 136; filibustering promoted by, 139, 143–44; Hogg supported by, 142; for provisional navy, 137–38; seizure approved by, 141
Manifest Destiny, 12; evolution of, 69; replacement of, 40–41
Marquis, Greg, 145n18
martial manhood, 13; Holmes on, 208; in masculinity duality, 193; Walker, W., in, 73
Mason, James Murray, 168n21; for border protection, 96; for filibustering, 140, 144; McLane-Ocampo treaty pulled by, 97
Masur, Kate, 195
Mata, José María, 88, 92–93
Maximilian, Ferdinand, 2, 13, 181
May, Robert E., 58n6; on expansionism, 87; on filibustering, 73, 139, 150n89
McClellan, George B., 176; on power, 213; as presidential candidate, 185–86; on volunteer regiments, 200
McCormick, Richard, 210
McDowell, Irvin, 181, 199
McKinley, William, 207
McKinney, Thomas Freeman, 28
McLane, Robert, 92, 97

McLane-Ocampo Treaty, 11, 94–95; failure of, 97–98, 111; secret executive session for, 96–97; support for, 97, 110
Memphis: African Americans in, 179–80; law enforcement in, 178–79; martial law in, 180; military rule in, 178; U.S. Army in, 178–79
Memphis Race Massacre, 179–80
Mercer, John, 133
Merli, Frank J., 149n77
Métis, 10, 65, 76–77. *See also* Riel, Louis
Mexican-American War, 2, 7, 20; Canadian annexation and, 155; fallout from, 9; fugitive slaves in, 24, 33n37; Mexican Cession in, 24–27; purpose of, 45–46; uncertainty after, 88
Mexicanization, 117n95, 225
Mexico, 2, 7–8; Americanization in, 36–37; as cautionary tale, 107–8; challenges for, 86; Constitution of 1857 in, 34n54; disorder in, 86–87; on extradition of slaves, 21–22; French Intervention in, 85–86, 181–83; impact of, 29; inconsistencies in, 30; independence of, 20–21, 23; as protectorate, 89–91, 110; slave passports from, 24; slavery abolished in, 21, 23–25, 28–29, 31n9, 89; slaves escaping to, 19, 21, 23, 29, 31n2; slaves protected in, 9, 19–20, 23; Southernization in, 36–37; sovereignty of, 175; support for, 23; territories conquered from, 24–25; U.S. Army in, 175, 180–81; U.S. press about, 93; victory in, 110; Walker, W., invasion of, 69–70, 74. *See also* fugitive slaves; Reforma War
Milne, Alexander, 144n4
Mississippi Valley plantation complex, 45–46
Missouri Compromise: Mexican Cession and, 26; overturning of, 27, 29
Missouri Crisis (1819–1821), 154
Mitchel, John, 47
modernization, 5
Montgomery, Skye, 111

Mora, Juan Rafael, 70, 72
Morton, Desmond, 79
Mulloney, Michael, 179
Murrin, John, 203

Nast, Thomas: "Compromise with the South" by, 189, *191*; "Hold the Fort" by, 189, *190*
national authority, 196–97
nationalism, 3, 6, 13; in American state, 204; dead and, 192; inclusivity in, 194; sovereignty and, 193–94; standards of conduct in, 119–20
Native Americans. *See* Indians
Nesmith, James, 210–11
neutrality: abuse of, 120; Locke, V., violation of, 126; Queen's proclamation of, 126
Neutrality Act (1794), 28
Nicaragua, 10; Americanization in, 71–72; civil war in, 70; press in, 67; slavery in, 71; treaties with, 99; Walker, W., as president of, 70–71; Walker, W., conquering of, 65–66; war in, 71
North America, 2–3; America as imperial power in, 41–42; crises in, 86; intertwined republics in, 87–99; Prince of Wales visit to, 85–86; secession and sovereignty reimagined for, 104–12
Nuevo México, 24, 29

Ocampo, Melchor, 88, 97
Olmsted, Frederick Law, 31n2
Ortega, Daniel, 71
Otero, Mariano, 96
Owram, Doug, 74
Owsley, Frank, 198

Palmer, John M., 185
Paludan, Phillip, 221–22, 225
Parish, Peter, 196–97
Parker, John, 146n31. *See also* Locke, Vernon Guyon
Parkman, Francis, 4

Parr, Henry A., 131
Parrish, Isaac, 25
Partisan Ranger Act, 120
Phillips, William, 212
Philo Parsons, 149n80, 156, 158
Pickett, John, 108
Piedras, José de las, 22
Pierce, Franklin, 157–58
pirates: capture of, 131–32; *Chesapeake* attacked by, 119; Foreign Enlistment Act violated by, 132; motivations of, 131; vs. privateers, 125. See also *Chesapeake*
Plaisted, Harris, 211
political order, 221
Ponce, Pearl, 97–98
Porter, Horace, 178
Potter, John F., 158–59, 170n37, 217n25
Prentiss, Benjamin Mayberry, 194
Prince of Wales. *See* Edward (Prince)
The Prince's Visit (Cordova), 110–11
privateers: on *Chesapeake*, 136; for Confederacy, 125, 136–37; Locke, V., as, 125–26

Quist, John, 11–12

Radforth, Ian, 103
Rawson, Rawson W., 142–43
Reagan, John, 96, 105–6
Reciprocity Treaty (1854), 99–100, 169n30; Canadian annexation influenced by, 155, 168n17; Chandler against, 158, 170n34; debate about, 157–58; termination of, 158–59; U.S. withdrawal from, 152, 166
Reconstruction, 8; control of, 13; costs of, 191–92; Greater, 7; reserve clause and, 174; sovereignty in, 174
Reforma War, 11, 85–86; lead up to, 88; U.S. view of, 90–91
Reid, Jennifer, 66
reserve clause, 174
Retribution, 125–26, 146n31
Rhodes, Elisha Hunt, 202

INDEX 241

Richardson, Heather Cox, 224
Riel, Louis, 10, 65; as American, 66, 79, 80n7, 81n17; background of, 65; context for, 74–75; execution of, 66–67, 77, 79, 81nn11,18; impact of, 77–79, 84n62; Métis helped by, 76–77; as Napoleonic, 66, 80n8; press used by, 67–68; state consolidation and, 69; state formation and, 78–79, 84n69
Riker, David, 137
Rio Grande War, 95, 111
Ritchie, John W.: as brother, 132; as Confederate representative, 133–34
Ritchie, William Johnston, 132–33
Rivington, Alex, 76
Roanoke: attack on, 137, 141–42, 150n99; burning of, 141–42
Rodríguez, Maria Regina, 32n12
Romero, Matías, 110
Russell, John, 100
Russell, William Howard, 194–95; on landscape of war, 201–2; on secession, 195; on sovereignty lacking, 194
Russian Empire, 42
Ryan, Mary, 101

Salvador, 143
Sanders, George N., 124
Santa Anna, Antonio López de, 20, 22–23
Santamaría, Juan, 72
Saunders, Frances Stonor, 193, 213
Schaffer, Orin, 119, 127, 147n44
Schlereth, Eric, 68
Schoen, Brian, 10–11, 223
Schurz, Carl, 163, 172n56
Scott, Dred. See *Dred Scott v. Sanford*
Scott, James C., 19
Scott, Winfield, 95; on new confederacies, 108; as presidential candidate, 185; on secession, 107
secession: border instability justifying, 105; chaos after, 123–24; Declaration of Causes for, 106; Northern views on, 107–8; racism in, 106; sovereignty haunted by, 195; sovereignty reimagined and, 104–12; vote for, 107
Second World War. See World War II
sectional conflict, 38–39, 44, 48
Seminoles, 19, 43
Semmes, Raphael, 123
Settler Revolution, 121
Seward, William, 13, 51, 100; on Alaskan purchase, 172n52; annexing proposition by, 37, 164; on free labor, 52, 54; French Intervention and, 180–81, 183; on Locke, V., 126; on northern confederacy, 109, 116n61; for passport controls, 157; promises by, 54; war promoted by, 104
Sexton, Jay, 39
Sheehan-Dean, Aaron, 119
Sheridan, Philip, 13; arms supplied by, 183–84; in Chicago, 184–85; Grant, U., meeting with, 182; at Mexican border, 183
Sherman, William T., 178, 185
Sibaja, Luis Fernando, 72
Siebert, Wilbur H., 30n1
Sioux, 2
Skowronek, Stephen, 195–96
Slap, Andrew, 13, 224
slaveholders: concerns of, 21–22; demands by, 44, 49; disunion by, 56; fears of, 28, 45, 60n18, 61n22; imperialism by, 38, 45, 47–52, 56, 57n1; legal portability by, 9; rights of, 26; Slave Power of, 38, 50. See also imperialism
slavery, 5–6, 9; Almon and, 146n19; in British Empire, 128; Crittenden Amendments about, 51; empire for, 36, 38, 46–47, 49–51; expansionists for, 36; imperialism and, 37–38, 44; legal protections for, 28–29; Mexican abolition of, 23; in Mexican Cession, 24–27; Mexico influencing, 88; in Mississippi Valley plantation complex, 45–46; movements against, 45; politics of, 44, 60n18; splintering effect of, 86

slaves, 4; Davis, J., on, 49; insurrection by, 93–94; Mexican protection of, 9, 19–20, 23; protection of, 49. *See also* African Americans; fugitive slaves
Slidell, John, 168n21
Smith, John E., 179
Smith, Peleg, 130, 135
social contract, 22–23
South America, 2
Southernization, 36–37, 46
sovereignty, 1, 3, 6; aspirational claims for, 222–23; in British North America, 121–22; without centralization, 193–201; construction of, 112; crisis of, 86; gender and, 192–93; of Indians, 209; nationalism and, 193–94; North America reimagining of, 104–12; in periphery, 85; in Reconstruction, 174; secession haunting of, 195; spiritual, 192, 213; as vague, 194
Spain, 7; Cuba controlled by, 46; Mexican independence from, 20–21, 23; San Domingo seized by, 109
Stanton, Edwin, 178, 183
state consolidation: government expansion through, 68–69; Manifest Destiny and, 69; state-sanctioned murder and, 67, 80n9
state power, 6, 40; in conflicts, 42; for expansion, 43–45; fiscal policies and, 42–43; national union and, 197–98; uses of, 53; weakness of, 44
Stewart, Alexander, 134
St. John, Rachel, 185
St. Mary, 142–43
Stone, Lewis Maxwell, 105
Stoneman, George, 13, 180
Sumner, Charles, 165, 167n3, 174

Taney, Roger, 27–28
Taylor, Alan, 3, 57
Taylor, Quintard, 31n2
Telfer, William Duff, 209
Texas, 7; annexation of, 24, 45, 154, 168n13; Cortina raid in, 92–93; fears in, 98–99; fires in, 98; Independence of, 9; New Mexico Territory in, 45; Rangers in, 93, 95; as "rebellious colony," 23; Rio Grande War in, 95, 111; slave capture in, 28; slave flight from, 45–46; Volunteer Regiment bill in, 95–96. *See also* secession
Texas Revolution, 20; Battle of San Jacinto in, 23; social contract in, 22–23
Toombs, Robert, 48; on Crittenden Amendments, 51; promise by, 49–50; Riker encouraged by, 137
Towers, Frank, 197
Trachtenberg, Alan, 197
treaties, 2; Clayton-Bulwer Treaty, 70; McLane-Ocampo Treaty, 11; Treaty of Mesilla, 88; Webster-Ashburton treaty, 129. *See also* Reciprocity Treaty (1854)
Treaty of Guadalupe Hidalgo, 20, 88–89, 92
Treaty of Mesilla, 88
Treaty of Washington (1871), 153, 165
Trent Affair, 121, 156, 168n21
Tupper, Charles, 123, 128
Turner, Michael J., 145n18
Tuscaloosa, CSS, 134
Tyler, Ronnie C., 31n2

Underground Railroad, 19, 30n1
Underwood, Joseph, 30
Urrea, José, 23
U.S.-Mexico War. *See* Mexican-American War

Van Buren, Martin, 154
Vanderbilt, Cornelius, 10; Nicaraguan invasion financed by, 70; as spurned, 66, 71
Varon, Elizabeth, 222
Volunteer Navy, 137–38, 149n82

Wade, Benjamin, 110, 206
Wade, George, 130, 135
Waite, Kevin, 58n6

Walker, Norman S., 133, 140
Walker, William, 10; background of, 65; British views on, 121; Central America impacted by, 72–74; Costa Rica impacted by, 72, 74; critics of, 71–72; execution of, 65–67; fame of, 69–70; impact of, 72–74, 223; martial manhood of, 73; Mexico invaded by, 69–70, 74; as Napoleonic, 66, 80n8; Nicaragua conquered by, 65–66, 70–71; press used by, 67; Southern support for, 143; state consolidation and, 69; U.S. impacted by, 73–74
Wallace, Lew, 181
Ward, John Manning, 148n50
War for Independence, U.S., 41
Warner, Donald F., 166
War of 1812, 154
Washburne, Elihu, 51
Washington, George, 175
Waugh, Joan, 178
Weber, Max, 213

Webster-Ashburton treaty, 129
Wells, H. G., 197
West, Elliot, 7
West, U.S., 2, 5, 7
Wheeler, John H., 71
Whipple, Henry Benjamin, 199, 209
Whiskey Rebellion (1794), 175
Wier, Benjamin, 124, 133
Wigfall, Louis, 95, 97
Wilmot, David, 25, 29, 50
Wilmot Proviso, 25–26; debates about, 29–30; traction of, 88
Wise, Henry, 45
World War II, 5
Wyatt-Brown, Bertram, 73

Yancey, William, 96, 107, 115n39
Yankee Leviathan (Bensel), 189, 195

Zuloaga (General), 90

Reconstructing America
Andrew L. Slap, series editor

Hans L. Trefousse, *Impeachment of a President: Andrew Johnson, the Blacks, and Reconstruction.*

Richard Paul Fuke, *Imperfect Equality: African Americans and the Confines of White Ideology in Post-Emancipation Maryland.*

Ruth Currie-McDaniel, *Carpetbagger of Conscience: A Biography of John Emory Bryant.*

Paul A. Cimbala and Randall M. Miller, eds., *The Freedmen's Bureau and Reconstruction: Reconsiderations.*

Herman Belz, *A New Birth of Freedom: The Republican Party and Freedmen's Rights, 1861 to 1866.*

Robert Michael Goldman, *"A Free Ballot and a Fair Count": The Department of Justice and the Enforcement of Voting Rights in the South, 1877–1893.*

Ruth Douglas Currie, ed., *Emma Spaulding Bryant: Civil War Bride, Carpetbagger's Wife, Ardent Feminist—Letters, 1860–1900.*

Robert Francis Engs, *Freedom's First Generation: Black Hampton, Virginia, 1861–1890.*

Robert F. Kaczorowski, *The Politics of Judicial Interpretation: The Federal Courts, Department of Justice, and Civil Rights, 1866–1876.*

John Syrett, *The Civil War Confiscation Acts: Failing to Reconstruct the South.*

Michael Les Benedict, *Preserving the Constitution: Essays on Politics and the Constitution in the Reconstruction Era.*

Andrew L. Slap, *The Doom of Reconstruction: The Liberal Republicans in the Civil War Era.*

Edmund L. Drago, *Confederate Phoenix: Rebel Children and Their Families in South Carolina*.

Mary Farmer-Kaiser, *Freedwomen and the Freedmen's Bureau: Race, Gender, and Public Policy in the Age of Emancipation*.

Paul A. Cimbala and Randall Miller, eds., *The Great Task Remaining Before Us: Reconstruction as America's Continuing Civil War*.

John A. Casey Jr., *New Men: Reconstructing the Image of the Veteran in Late-Nineteenth-Century American Literature and Culture*.

Hilary Green, *Educational Reconstruction: African American Schools in the Urban South, 1865–1890*.

Christopher B. Bean, *Too Great a Burden to Bear: The Struggle and Failure of the Freedmen's Bureau in Texas*.

David E. Goldberg, *The Retreats of Reconstruction: Race, Leisure, and the Politics of Segregation at the New Jersey Shore, 1865–1920*.

David Prior, ed., *Reconstruction in a Globalizing World*.

Jewel L. Spangler and Frank Towers, eds., *Remaking North American Sovereignty: State Transformation in the 1860s*.

Adam H. Domby and Simon Lewis, eds., *Freedoms Gained and Lost: Reconstruction and Its Meanings 150 Years Later*.

David Prior, ed., *Reconstruction and Empire: The Legacies of Abolition and Union Victory for an Imperial Age*.

Sandra M. Gustafson and Robert S. Levine, eds., *Reimagining the Republic: Race, Citizenship, and Nation in the Literary Work of Albion W. Tourgée*. Foreword by Carolyn L. Karcher.

Brian Schoen, Jewel L. Spangler, and Frank Towers, eds., *Continent in Crisis: The U.S. Civil War in North America*.